Web Database Development for Windows Platforms

9 780130 139856

PRENTICE HALL SERIES ON MICROSOFT® TECHNOLOGIES

PRENTICE HALL SERIES ON MICROSOFT® TECHNOLOGIES

DAN D. GUTIERREZ

Web Database Development for Windows Platforms

Prentice Hall, Upper Saddle River, NJ 07458
www.phptr.com

Library of Congress Cataloging-in-Publication Data

Gutierrez, Dan D.
    Web database development for Windows platforms / Dan D.
    Gutierrez.
        p.   cm. -- (Prentice Hall series on Microsoft technologies)
        ISBN 0-13-013985-5 (paper : alk. paper)
        1. Database design.   2. World Wide Web (Information retrieval
    system)   3. Microsoft Windows (Computer files)   4. Intel
    microprocessors--Programming.   I. Title.   II. Series.
    QA76.9.D26G88   1999
    005.75'8--dc21
                                                                    99-23862
                                                                    CIP

Editorial/Production Supervision: Patti Guerrieri
Acquisitions Editor: Mike Meehan
Marketing Manager: Bryan Gambrel
Manufacturing Manager: Alexis R. Heydt
Cover Design: Talar Agasyan
Cover Design Direction: Jerry Votta
Series Design: Gail Cocker-Bogusz

Prentice Hall books are widely used by corporations and government agencies for training,
marketing, and resale.

The publisher offers discounts on this book when ordered in bulk quantities.
For more information, contact: Corporate Sales Department, Phone: 800-382-3419;
Fax: 201-236-7141; E-mail: corpsales@prenhall.com; or write: Prentice Hall PTR,
Corp. Sales Dept., One Lake Street, Upper Saddle River, NJ 07458.

Microsoft Windows, Windows NT, Microsoft SQL Server, Visual FoxPro, Access, Visual Basic, Visual InterDev,
ActiveX, Visual C++, Visual Studio, WebTV, Excel, PowerPoint, and BackOffice are trademarks of the
Microsoft Corporation. Java is a trademark of Sun Microsystems, Inc. Cold Fusion is a trademark of Allaire
Corp. Delphi and dBASE are trademarks of Inprise Corporation. Apple Macintosh is a trademark of Apple
Computer, Inc. AS-400 and DB2 are trademarks of International Business Machines, Inc. Sapphire/Web is a
trademark of Bluestone Software, Inc. WebSite is a trademark of O'Reilly & Associates, Inc. Purveyor is a
trademark of Process Software. pcANYWHERE is a trademark of Symantec Corporation. Zip and Jaz are
trademarks of Iomega Corporation. Clipper is a trademark of Computer Associates International. Oracle is a
trademark of Oracle Corporation. All other products or services mentioned in this book are the trademarks or
service marks of their respective companies or organizations.

Printed in the United States of America

10 9 8 7 6 5 4 3 2 1

ISBN 0-13-013985-5

Prentice-Hall International (UK) Limited, *London*
Prentice-Hall of Australia Pty. Limited, *Sydney*
Prentice-Hall Canada Inc., *Toronto*
Prentice-Hall Hispanoamericana, S.A., *Mexico*
Prentice-Hall of India Private Limited, *New Delhi*
Prentice-Hall of Japan, Inc., *Tokyo*
Prentice-Hall (Singapore) Pte. Ltd., *Singapore*
Editora Prentice-Hall do Brasil, Ltda., *Rio de Janeiro*

Dedication

Patrick Henry Junior High School (Granada Hills, California)
circa 1968 and the delightful experiment known as the TTT Math Lab,
for opening an important door in my life that started a
fascination with computers that persists to this day.

UCLA (Los Angeles, California) 1973-1978, for teaching me
how to think, and providing a glimpse of the birth of the Internet.

CONTENTS

PREFACE

As a database developer who grew up with the DOS Xbase environments (dBASE, FoxPro, and Clipper), and then moved to Microsoft Access upon its initial release, it made immediate sense to me that the marriage of the World Wide Web and database technology would one day occur. When I first witnessed the Web using the first Mosaic browser, I saw mostly static text content with some hypertext links using mile-long URLs. Hard as it was to imagine back then, I held out hope for the day when the Web would come alive with content emanating from databases. At the time, the tools just weren't there, and the pre-ODBC technology available at the time would only allow for custom approaches. Indeed, when I first began researching the prospect of publishing databases on the Web, in early 1994 there were only a handful of crude techniques for UNIX Web servers, but nothing widespread or refined enough to be considered a standard. Remember, at that time Microsoft hadn't awakened to the Internet, the Netscape browser was brand new, and HTML was still rapidly evolving.

I began collecting information on Internet database technology, much of which was publicly available on the Web, and in cutting-edge magazine articles and company white papers describing interesting new ways to connect a database to a Web site. I even wrote a couple of articles myself on the subject including "Developing Database Applications on the Internet" and "Link the Web with Your Relational Databases," both in the August 1995 issue of *Data Based Advisor* magazine (now known as *e-Business Advisor* from Advisor Publications, www.advisor.com).

There was one event that stood out in laying the course for Web databases running on the Microsoft Web platform. In 1995 I remember finding a startup company named Aspect Software Engineering operating out of a new technology park in Hawaii. The small group of young technophiles created a database enabling tool for the new Microsoft Web server IIS. The product, called dbWeb, was a first-of-breed technology enabling Web databases for the Windows NT platform. This product set the stage for a sustained period of innovation that continues today. Later, in 1996, I remember hearing that the company was acquired by Microsoft, presumably for riches beyond the imagination for the young principals (who had to move to rain soaked Redmond from the sun drenched beaches of Honolulu). I've been following the evolution of Web databases ever since.

Why This Book?

I wrote this book because I was continually asked by students, clients, and associates how to publish simple databases on the Web and how databases play a role in e-commerce. It is a natural question once one gets past the static nature of many Web sites. Since the people asking the question were not too Web savvy, their desire to publish a database on the Web was somewhat naive in terms of expectations. Why should it be any harder to view a Microsoft Access inventory table from a Web browser than from a PC desktop application? The answer, as we'll see in this book, centers around native HTML's inability to directly interface to a server database (although the emerging Dynamic HTML, known as DHTML, addresses this problem). Instead, some server-side development is required to implement database enabled Web sites. The technologies involved, however, are varied, and one of the purposes of this book is to provide an overview of the major ways to go about publishing a database on the Web for the Windows NT environment.

Still, we don't necessarily have to address these requirements from a highly technical perspective. Publishing a simple Access database takes some know-how, but not the level of technical awareness required to build a large complex e-commerce Web site. Thus, this book addresses the needs of the lower-end Web developer, possibly even a Web designer getting into dynamic content for the first time. There are plenty of other books on the market that cater to the higher-end developer. I wrote this book for the mass of developers who have standardized on the Windows Web platform, have all the necessary software on their servers, and are ready to experiment with Web databases.

Who Should Read This Book?

This book is directed towards corporate and independent developers who need to quickly get up to speed with contemporary ways to publish a database on a Web site for either the Internet or intranet using the Windows NT computing platform. The developer's company or client has already standardized on Microsoft Windows NT, Back Office, and Office and as a result already has most of the tools required to publish the database. Microsoft has made it much easier to facilitate Web databases by providing all the necessary technologies as part of existing mainstream product lines, e.g., the IIS Web server is part of Windows NT Server, SQL Server is part of Back Office, and Access is part of Office. All the tools are there, but the typical developer needs a place to start and a roadmap to outline the steps.

There are many such people in the target group for this book who just need to grasp the basics and who do not need to necessarily address the related though more advanced topics such a scalability, security and fire walls, transaction processing, application servers, etc. There are plenty of other books that focus on these areas. This book starts at the beginning.

How to Read This Book

The reader may approach the material found in this book in different ways depending on the specific Web database technologies she or he intends to use for future projects. Consequently, only certain chapters may be germane. If, for example, only Microsoft technologies are of interest, then the material describing JDBC in Chapter 6, which promotes cross platform Web database development, might be skipped. If the reader is not a programmer and wants to keep it that way, then some of the more automated HTML approaches would be appropriate (see the sections in Chapter 4 about the IIS Web Server's IDC feature and the SQL Server Web Assistant, or the section in Chapter 9 describing the Access Publish to the Web Wizard). If the reader is experienced with Microsoft Access VBA programming, then Chapter 9, which touches on custom HTML generation using VBA, has useful material. If the reader has a liking for the Java language and wants to build contemporary intranet applications, then Chapter 5 describing Visual J++ offers an important direction. Certainly, if the reader is an experienced programmer and wants to adopt favored technologies for the IIS Web server, Chapter 7 on Active Server and ADO and Chapter 8 on Visual InterDev will provide the most useful information.

Regardless of the reader's direction or goals, the CGI case study, based on Cold Fusion and found in Chapter 10, will be helpful in seeing the process of publishing a database on the Web from start to finish.

From frequent comments by my UCLA students, I've also found that the hardware issues discussed in Chapter 3 are often a complete mystery to the beginner, and this material should dispel many questions.

Lastly, for those readers using SQL Server as the back-end database for holding Web data, the SQL Server for NT section in Chapter 3 represents some real-life experience I obtained while doing a large e-commerce Web site.

How This Book Is Organized

This book starts at the very beginning, covering the basics with respect to setting up a database enabled Web site. I present an overview of available technologies, cover hardware and software issues, and demonstrate how to create a simple Web database. Many books do not take the time to present exactly how to get started, but rather assumes the reader has already taken the first steps, or has personnel to assist in getting started. I make no such assumptions. I then get into specific development platforms such as Microsoft Visual J++, cross platform JDBC, Active Server Pages and ADO. After this, we look at the Microsoft tool specifically designed for creating database Web sites, Visual InterDev, and show some automated approaches for publishing desktop databases such as Access. I wrap up the book by presenting a complete case study using the Cold Fusion CGI-based environment.

Chapter 1 – expands on this Preface by setting the stage for presenting your options for building a database-enabled Web site. This chapter represents "ground zero" for important establishing directions when building a Web database.

Chapter 2 – defines a number of technical areas upon which Web database technology is based, including discussions of CGI, server API platforms, server side includes, Java, and Microsoft Active Server technologies.

Chapter 3 – discusses special hardware considerations for implementing a Web site having database connections. This chapter is crucial for departmental staff having little or no IS support within their organization or independent developers who are new to the Web.

Chapter 4 – focuses on building simple database sites using tools integrated into Windows NT and SQL Server such as the Internet Database Connector and the SQL Server Web Assistant.

Chapter 5 – highlights the Microsoft Visual J++ development environment for creating Windows-based intranet applications using the Microsoft Windows Foundation Classes.

Chapter 6 – overviews the JDBC API from Sun as a technique for connecting databases to Web sites requiring cross platform capabilities.

Chapter 7- introduces the Microsoft Active Server platform including a description of the Active Server Pages programming environment that uses server-side VBScript programming.

Chapter 8 – provides a reference for the Microsoft Visual InterDev tool that is part of the Visual Studio suite. InterDev is the primary tool from Microsoft that enables the integration of ASP code and data connections.

Chapter 9 – shows how to publish desktop databases using a variety of techniques including Access Publish to the Web Wizard.

Chapter 10 – presents a case study that examines the design and implementation of an actual Web database using the Cold Fusion CGI-based tool.

A Goal for the Reader

As a writer, the surest indication that I've done my job of disseminating information is for my readers to use the material I've provided. Therefore, my goal for the reader is to actually publish a database on the Web using one or more of the technologies and techniques discussed in this book. Start small by creating a simple intranet application that prompts the user for some selection criteria, runs a query, and displays some results in HTML. Or try building a guest registration page for your current Web site and save the form contents in a database. The hardest part of embracing any new technology is getting your feet wet, but once you gain the experience, you'll wonder how you ever got along without database-enabled Web sites.

Internet Databases: A Natural Evolution

*T**he subject matter of this book is developing database software applications specifically designed for operation on the World Wide Web
(WWW) component of the Internet. Currently, this burgeoning segment
of the custom software development industry is a swiftly moving target,
as established database software vendors such as Microsoft, Inprise
Corp., Computer Associates, Oracle, Sybase, and many other big-name
players rush to posture themselves wisely by producing tools for this new
market as the Web matures. These industry dynamics have also created
an environment whereby new software vendors both large and small
have a chance to provide even more tools and development platforms,
filling in niches left open by the bigger companies. This situation is
already quite evident in industry, where many of the tool products that
initially popped up to satisfy the need for building interactive, data-
aware sites came from small start-up firms with innovative and timely
ideas. In the second stage the larger firms acquired many of these fledg-
ling firms and their technology for incorporation into broad-based
product lines. Now the third stage is well underway, with the major
industry players refining their Web database offerings to address even
more demanding requirements.*

One may view this flurry of activity as a natural evolutionary process
similar to a biological organism accepting favorable mutations to meet the
challenges of a changing environment. What we'll see, as the survivors
emerge, is a world better suited to providing exciting new active content,

involving interactive querying capabilities on the blossoming number of data-rich Web sites around the Net.

A research report commissioned by International Data Corp. (IDC) states that companies building commercial Web sites can expect hardware and system software to consume 20 percent of a Web site's overall budget; the remaining 80 percent goes to custom software development and integration. The report indicates further that companies participating in the survey have begun to go beyond static pages to facilitate linkages back to, for example, a billing system or an inventory database. From a user point of view, this change in priority is good news, as the rise of more data-centric sites means more information at their fingertips.

Another research study conducted by the Gartner Group, Inc., shows that companies building business applications for the Web are not meeting the demands of their customers. According to the study, 90 percent of enterprises conducting business via Web sites are not delivering the kind of services and information customers want. This deficiency is destined to change once the phase-over to interactive applications takes place, since users will then be able to tailor their experiences at a particular site to match their interests.

As the database and tool vendors adapt their desktop, file server, and client server database systems to a more contemporary *Webtop* topology, we're also seeing a tremendous interest in these tools by traditional database software developers, both independent and those in corporate IS (information systems) departments. Part of the reason for this interest stems from the growing realization that *static content* Web pages only serve to impress during an initial period but soon lose their appeal after the financial bottom-line fails to see a positive effect from their existence. After all, a pretty picture is still only a picture, and plain text is only text.

Current estimates through various surveys and studies indicate that nearly 80% of all Fortune 500 firms now have some sort of formal presence on the Web, but that 20% of those are reconsidering their commitment to expanding or even maintaining their Web sites in the future, because the financial results do not indicate a successful exploitation of all that the Web has to offer. This stance is unfortunate, because in the Web, we are truly faced with a global revolution unparalleled in recent technological history. Widely held confidence exists that the Web and its successors are here to stay. Only the content must change. *Active content*, allowing the user to interact with the site by posing queries against vast data stores just like a normal computer application, forms the destiny of the Web. By selecting this book, you have indirectly indicated that you acknowledge the need for Web sites that contain interactive, query-driven content capable of doing more than deliver a pretty picture, colorful video, or soothing sound.

In this chapter, I review the state of the Internet database industry, identifying how the needs have thus far manifested themselves, what classes of tools and techniques are available to address these needs, and several important directions the industry is taking.

From the Desktop to the Webtop

Let's begin with a discussion of how PC computing has historically expanded past physical boundaries, offering increasing flexibility and reach of services with each step forward. Remember the days when PC computing was only available on the desktop and all databases were stored along with programs on the local 20 MB hard drive? This was enough power at the time, because serious business applications were uncommon—the hardware and system software did not yet support anything more. As PC applications got more serious, along with more robust hardware, multi-user applications began to take hold. Here, the file server was king, providing for a central location for data and often programs to share across a local area network (LAN). A direct extension of this organization was the wide area network (WAN), where the same LAN services were distributed over a larger geographical area. Next, the client-server architecture evolved out of this organization to address the inherent problems with a network structure that spent most of its time pushing around large streams of data from the file server to the workstations for local processing of the data. Instead, with client-server, the processing is off-loaded to a back-end database capable of high-speed fulfillment of query requests. Only the information requested is transferred over the wire to the workstation.

The next and current stage in the evolution of computing architectures is the Web whose structure may be thought of as the ultimate in client-server computing. Here, the client Web browser presents the user interface for the collection of user-specified selection criteria. At the same time, a remote Web server operating a back-end database processes the requests for information. Instead of the client and the server components being in close proximity through a LAN or at greater distances over a WAN, the client component is any person running an authenticated Web browser connection from any point on the globe, and the server is a back-end database system running on a Web server, potentially at any other point on the globe.

From this description, you can easily recognize the logical progression taken during the move from the desktop to the Webtop. The effect of this transition is only now coming into focus, as software developers begin to plan for database-driven applications for many classes of organizations wishing to capitalize on the global nature of the Web. From electronic commerce to conducting online research, the new genre of Web sites shall provide international corporations, government agencies, non-profit organizations, and many others the unique ability to adapt their content to specific user requirements.

The Rise of the Wintel Platform on the Web

The Internet and its predecessor, the ARPANET (where on November 21, 1969, computer scientists at UCLA sent the very first message over an experimental computer network that would become the Internet), have historically been the realm of UNIX machines. This is due to the fact that the Net grew up in the computer rooms of universities, research institutions, and government agencies, all running some flavor of UNIX. Even today, the proportion of Web servers running various forms of UNIX versus those based on competing platforms, predominantly Windows NT, is quite high. Figure 1-1 contains the results of a survey of over 4 million Web sites, which shows the Web server market share from 1996 through 1999. The statistics were collected as the result of research conducted by Netcraft (www.netcraft.com/survey). The current numbers indicate a commanding lead by the non-Windows Apache platform; however, the tide is slowly but clearly changing. As Windows NT becomes more accepted as a robust and scaleable corporate network operating system, the Web OS percentages may one day favor the so-called *Wintel* (Microsoft Windows™ and Intel) platform.

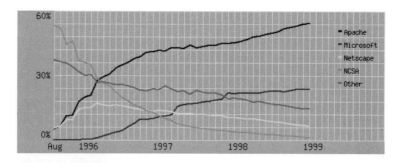

Figure 1-1   *Market Share for Top Servers across All Domains for 1996-1999*

This book embraces this market share trend in the Web server arena, given the financial and marketing strength of both Intel Corporation and Microsoft Corporation, as the one with a potentially greater future prospect. Specifically, we shall consider only Microsoft Windows NT™ Web server platforms, back-end database processing based on Microsoft SQL Server™ and Access™, and development tools designed expressly for Windows NT (predominantly supplied by Microsoft).

The one technology not originating from the Wintel camp that we will consider is Java™, the Web-centric object-oriented programming language. Both Microsoft and Intel, however, have enthusiastically embraced Java; consequently, that Java will play an important role in Web database connectivity is pretty clear.

Developmental Directions

Currently, an application developer can follow a number of possible directions to publish database content on the Web. As stated earlier, Web database technology is evolving at a rapid pace, and to attempt to declare a winning strategy is premature at this stage in the process. The purpose of this book is to explore the many options. In this section, I review many contemporary approaches, so that you may make appropriate preparations for these technologies. Which path you ultimately choose is a determination that may be based on various factors dictated by the intended goals of the application, economic and technological limitations, and future factors not even in play today.

Since the early days of widespread publishing of database content on the Web, around the 1994–1995 time frame (the first Web browser, Mosaic, was released in February 1993), a number of enabling technologies have existed. Beginning in 1997, however, a shake-out of sorts occurred, with a number of the larger software vendors aligning themselves under several predominant technology umbrellas. Currently, these include CGI, Microsoft Web database technologies, and Java. Evidently, based on these trends, the Web database of the future will be developed around these vehicles.

Static Content Prevails

We now see many Web sites having limited quantities of data, arranged in an orderly fashion for Web users to browse. Much of what is now published in this manner is, however, manually constructed and updated using an ordinary HTML editor or site management software. This direction is particularly true of the current breed of Web site developers who do not have programming and/ or software design experience. As an example, many regional Web sites are established by executive search firms who publish their employment openings for potential candidates to peruse. The jobs may be grouped by industry or location and placed in individual pages for users to access by following a hierarchical web page tree via hypertext links. If these lists require updates, the search firm must manually maintain the pages with an HTML editor. The process is arduous and not very efficient in terms of time and efficiency of presentation of information. Even more important, however, is the fact that only very rudimentary search facilities are possible for such a site. Users are bound to following a predefined hierarchical structure with no true searching capabilities. Such sites need true database functionality to adequately compete with more technically state-of-the-art implementations.

Other sites enlist the aid of their Internet Service Provider (ISP), which may be far-thinking enough to realize that static Web pages, currently the rage, are not going to address the needs of future sites. These providers have made available some rudimentary tools for providing site search capabilities, but most stop far short of true database queries. The major drawback to using

ISP facilities is that a database administrator, the person or persons responsible for database performance tuning, monitoring, and maintenance, requires intimate on-site or remote access to the Web server for the purpose of setting and experimenting with low-level operating system and database server parameters. Changes to these parameters may affect the operation of the Web server itself, and on an ISP's server shared by a number of customers, this level of access is generally not permitted. On the other hand, many ISPs now offer private co-located servers that can be administered remotely via remote access programs such as pcAnyWhere. The bottom line is that many ISPs are cognizant of the fact that Web sites requiring data connections are quickly becoming the norm, not the exception.

Technology Directions

With this said, let's now examine several methods of implementing a Web database. The following list represents the predominant Web database technologies currently available for the Wintel platform. The list is arranged according to a historical perspective, beginning with older technology still widely in use, and ending with approaches holding the most promise for the future in terms of widespread acceptance, server efficiency, and site scalability.

- In the early days of the Web, programming interactive services and databases involved writing C code, shell, or Perl scripts. These so-called CGI (Common Gateway Interface) applications were popular because several implementations of Perl could invoke SQL engines running on UNIX machines. Up until mid-1995, this approach accounted for a vast majority of database-aware Web sites. Today, one can still write a custom CGI program using C or even Visual Basic™. Comparatively, much labor is involved with this method, because an in-depth knowledge of Internet protocols and Web server operations is required. This situation detracts from the business at hand, producing database applications for Web deployment. As the tools outlined below mature, the native CGI approach will become extinct except for very special cases.

- One of the most attractive alternatives to writing a custom CGI application today is to use a development tool that is implemented either as a CGI-compliant gateway or as an application that communicates directly via an application programming interface (API) supported by the Web server software, which runs on the Web server and uses Open Database Connectivity (ODBC) to connect to a wide range of databases. A number of products are in this category, such as the Cold Fusion™ product from Allaire Corp. These Web/ODBC development tools provide a quick way to bring up a database on the Web. Although the first versions of these tools allowed for only relatively simple database applications, later versions such as Cold Fusion

Server 4.0 Professional and Enterprise provide a platform for the development of a wide range of Web applications from simple departmental intranet applications to major Internet applications.

- Also available is the scripting solution involving two popular scripting languages: *JavaScript* (developed by Netscape) and Microsoft's *Visual Basic Scripting Edition (VBScript)*, an adaptation of the popular Visual Basic language for use on the Internet. A scripting solution, however, does require an additional piece of software, often a CGI program, to provide the database connections. For example, Netscape's LiveWire Server Side JavaScript component of Netscape Enterprise Server 3.0 is well suited for JavaScript implementations, whereas Microsoft's Active Server Pages (ASP) serves as the host for VBScript.

- An easy-to-use automated approach is the special Web-aware features in the back-end database itself. Microsoft's SQL Server 6.5, for example, includes an ODBC gateway to the Microsoft Internet Information Server (IIS) called the *SQL Web Assistant*. The database includes bi-directional replication technology based on ODBC, permitting data transfer between SQL Server and third-party databases. Making the server aware of Internet links at the database level may provide a certain level of extra flexibility and performance.

- Yet another approach is to use database hooks in the Web server software itself, such as the integrated component in the Microsoft Internet Information Server (IIS) Web server software platform. The component designed for this purpose is called the *Internet Database Connector* (IDC). This feature uses the Internet Information Server API (ISAPI), allowing users to dynamically access SQL Server databases and other ODBC-compliant databases. The server integration approach may prove beneficial, since certain optimizations may be performed by the server to enhance database access.

- Another method entails an offline, non-interactive approach towards Internet database publishing. Here, the organization with less stringent needs in terms of immediately reflecting changes in a database on the Net may opt to replicate their database onto the Web server on a periodic basis, say each night. Any changes, additions, or deletions would be uploaded according to a set schedule. To facilitate the replication, a desktop database system could be used, such as Microsoft Visual FoxPro™, Access, Visual Basic, or Inprise Delphi™. In this scenario, queries could be queued asynchronously via e-mail transmission of HTML form entries and processed in a batch mode of sorts, with the results sent back to the user again via e-mail.

- The next, and potentially most exciting, alternative is to use a specific programming language designed expressly for Web development which produces interfaces to back-end databases. Of course, I am referring to the *Java* programming language pioneered by Sun Microsystems. Included with the Java Developer's Toolkit (JDK), version 1.1 and 1.2, are the *Java Database Connectivity* (JDBC) classes that make database connectivity part of the language. The major vendors appear to be quite serious about Java, and Microsoft has an "embrace and extend" tactical response to the language's initial success. Constructing database applications based on Java seems likely, as desktop developers make the transition to the Web and search for programming environments with which they are familiar.

- Rapid Application Development (RAD) tools have come on very strongly of late to address the rising complexity of building database-driven sites. Many being based on the Java language, these tools provide for "point-and-shoot" construction of interactive forms bound directly to a data source. Providing database connections, however, is a side benefit of using RAD environments, since they can be viewed as general-purpose application-generating tools for building forms, menus, animations, and other typical parts of an application.

- As a final technique, we see *Active Server Pages* (ASP), which is quickly becoming the preferred way to develop Web sites with data connections when using the Microsoft IIS 4.0 Web server software. Using ActiveX™ Data Objects (ADO) and server-side scripting using either VBScript or JScript (Microsoft's implementation of JavaScript), you can effectively attach ODBC-compliant databases to any Web page. The Microsoft Visual InterDev™ (part of the Visual Studio 6.0 suite) tool brings together HTML, ASP, and ADO under one integrated environment.

My opinion is that two of the above technologies hold the most promise for developing database-enabled Web sites on the Wintel platform in the future: Java and ASP. Java is important because of its cross-platform capabilities. An applet written in Java, containing a connection to a server database, may be successfully run on any computing platform with a *Java Virtual Machine* (JVM). At the same time, the tight integration of the operating system, Web server, database server, data connection API, and the developer tools is a strong force in Microsoft's favor. By focusing on Java-based database technologies and the Microsoft Active Server platform, you will be assured that an investment in these technologies will bear fruit for many years to come. I will direct considerable attention, therefore, towards these and supporting technologies in the chapters that follow.

Database Connectivity Standards

As the interest in Web databases rises, the subject of standards involving the connection of existing databases has received much attention. Currently several competing camps exist, all vying for a strong position in this market. One significant advantage of basing your Web server on Windows NT is the potential integration of the Microsoft *Open Database Connectivity* (ODBC) API between the server and external data sources. ODBC has become the de facto standard for communicating with heterogeneous databases and thus fits in naturally with the Web.

The JavaSoft unit of Sun Microsystems, the creator of the Java programming language for Web development, included the *Java Database Connectivity* (JDBC) API with the *Java Development Kit* (JDK) 1.1 and 1.2. JDBC is a class library designed to allow Java applets to directly access back-end databases. JDBC is similar to Microsoft's ODBC standard in that it provides a standard mechanism for Java applets to access a range of different data sources. Java developers may then write to the JDBC API to tie their applets to back-end database servers, but may continue to use existing ODBC interfaces to connect to databases. The difference is that JDBC is tuned to Java and taps into the language's built-in communication capabilities. The inclusion of the JDBC classes is a continued step towards Java's use as a full-fledged client/server development language.

Many Web databases are now implemented through a CGI application for each database query. By contrast, Java applets written to the JDBC specification will establish a session with a specific database rather than rely on the Web server to negotiate database queries with a particular application. Because the specification assigns a specific database to the Java applet, JDBC will not be suitable for dynamically locating data across several unspecified databases.

Java-Based Development

The Java *Object Oriented Programming* (OOP) language developed by Sun Microsystems, Inc., has been widely welcomed in the Web software development community. As mentioned before, it allows for active content to replace static pages in today's Web sites. One of the appeals of Java is its platform-independent nature. The same applet can execute in a Web browser running on an Apple Macintosh™, a Windows 95/98 PC, or a UNIX workstation, as long as the browser software incorporates a Java virtual machine. This level of compatibility is due to the fact that Java is currently an interpretive language (although so-called "just in time" or JIT compilers are now appearing, which translate the Java code into a form optimized for the client machine), where each Web browser supporting the Java language has a built-in Java language interpreter used to take the Java source code coming down the wire and execute it on the client machine.

Although runtime performance is often forsaken in favor of universal compatibility, Java technology remains a viable method of producing reusable Web "objects" that one can combine together in order to construct complete applications. This process has already begun even though Java is a relatively new phenomenon (as of the time of writing, Java is only about three years old), as programmers traverse the latest Java Web sites in search of new and exciting programming techniques. One inherent Java capability, relatively untapped thus far, is a tie to external data sources. As stated in the previous section, however, this is beginning to change, too. Once this feature is firmly in place, Java-based Web database development will have arrived. One may then equate this environment to the early days of the PC desktop database development market. Prior to programming-based environments, the old desktop systems were centered around rudimentary menu-driven systems. The flexibility of a special Web programming language, especially a truly object oriented one, will lead to unprecedented Webtop applications.

Scripting Language-Based Development

Much of Microsoft's Internet strategy hinges on how well industry embraces the Internet-specific version of Visual Basic. VBScript (VBS, or Visual Basic Scripting Edition) code, unlike Java but similar to JavaScript, is inserted directly into the Web page's HTML and is downloaded from the server each time a browser hits the page. Although not an entire implementation of Visual Basic, VBScript contains many important ingredients for adding logic to a page's design.

As with Java, VBScript code can be used only by a browser specifically designed to recognize it. Currently, the Internet Explorer 3.0, 4.0, and 5.0 browsers from Microsoft are the only browsers able to do so. Also, a Netscape plug-in available from Ncompass Labs allows Netscape browsers to recognize VBScript.

VBScript is also used as a server-side programming language, in that it is the basis of Active Server Pages. The code is run directly on the server, not the client browser, so compatibility is not an issue.

Back-end Relational Databases

Regardless of the path chosen towards implementing an Internet database, ultimately a back-end database solution must exist for processing user queries. All the methods mentioned in earlier sections of this chapter provide some mechanism for translating user entries in an HTML form into an equivalent SQL statement. Whether the statement is generated by a native CGI application, a CGI or server API database tool, the Web server software, a Java applet, an ASP page, or the back-end database system itself, the bottom line is that SQL becomes the final goal in the translation. The development techniques followed in this book all center around the SQL language providing the data conduit.

In addition to processing user queries, the back-end database may also prove useful for a related purpose, providing statistics regarding the types of queries users perform. Whether users consistently request particular types of queries over others or how they structure their queries can be extremely valuable pieces of information when trying to determine the ease of use of your query vehicle or even when tuning the back end for better performance. The way you can obtain this kind of information is by using *triggers* or *stored procedures* on the database itself. For example, you might embed a SELECT query inside a trigger to record the types of queries that users perform. Since both triggers and stored procedures represent optimized, server-side programming, they can yield high performance results.

After evaluating the benefits of using SQL databases on the Web, the question then becomes which back-end database to use and what criteria should be used for its selection. As one might expect, the answer often lies with ease of compatibility with existing systems, if any. Let's examine several scenarios that may govern the decision-making process.

The Standalone Web Database

Consider the scenario where a new enterprise, say a sales or distribution company, opens its doors and part of the business plan calls for an Internet database solution designed for promoting business development. This situation, where they have no existing systems and applications to consider, allows for the simple case solution where a single PC and associated hardware (a subject for Chapter 3) become the sole Internet connection. Here, the back-end database, say Microsoft SQL Server for NT, processes requests on the Web server hardware running Windows NT. In turn, a client application developed in Microsoft Access, for example, and running on an Ethernet-connected workstation provides database maintenance capabilities through SQL pass-through queries. In summary, this simple case involves no complex gateways to foreign systems or legacy data sources to consider. All hardware, software, and data are self-contained on the physical Web server. Although logically distinct, the physical nature of the implementation may be distributed over a number of servers.

Organization-Wide LAN/WAN

Now consider a logical progression up from the simple, single PC scenario, involving a hypothetical Internet Web server connected to an existing, potentially large, compliment of Local Area Networks (LANs) and/or Wide Area Networks (WANs). The design for the new Web-based database application calls for an interface with existing corporate systems based on Oracle, specifically the company-wide accounting system's product inventory table. For example, the Web application needs to select product data such as product ID, description, quantity-on-hand, retail and wholesale price, and supplier ID from the table and format the results in HTML for presentation in a Web browser.

This situation differs considerably from the previous case, because we must consider the existing corporate systems in our decision of which back-end database to consider. In this hypothetical example, we must build the application based on the Oracle database. Fortunately, through ODBC support by virtually all current database management systems, this interface is not a problem (although the selection of the specific ODBC driver used is crucial to the success of the application for performance and reliability reasons).

The security issue must also be considered in the design and implementation of the new application, since corporate systems must be protected from outside influence when data is published on a public network such as the Internet. Specifically, firewall hardware and/or software must be considered in the architecture of the application.

Interfacing to Legacy Hardware and Database Systems

Potentially the most delicate scenario involves the connection to legacy hardware and software systems outside the realm of the PC environment. Many companies continue to base their corporate systems on mainframe or mid-range mini-computer technology such as IBM mainframes, HP-3000 minicomputers, IBM AS-400s™, etc. Aside from the foreign hardware, these machines use operating system and application software optimized for their hardware environments. Corporate data may be locked up inside an IBM DB2™ relational database or an HP Image database, for example. A successful Internet database implementation then boils down to whether a specific ODBC driver exists for the foreign data source. Fortunately, many small driver vendors have sprung up to address these needs; the matter is simply one of locating required driver. As in the LAN/WAN scenario, the decision for a back-end database already was made prior to the implementation, and the question was more of connectivity to the legacy database system.

Back-end Focus for This Book

Due to the potentially enormous number of possible configurations for connecting corporate LANs, WANs, and legacy systems to an Internet or intranet database application, for your purposes in this book, I consider only the simple case of a single PC box Internet connection. This allows us to focus on the primary subject of this book, developing Web-based database applications. I assume that given sufficient research, the proper connections can generally be made for the more complex cases. Furthermore, for purposes of discussion, I consider the Microsoft SQL Server 6.5/7.0 enterprise database and the Microsoft Access desktop database as my primary ODBC data sources for the examples I have you examine in this book.

Revamped Back-end Licensing Fees

The use of contemporary back-end database software for supporting Web databases as well as online commerce servers, presents somewhat of a dilemma for the vendors who have historically based their licensing fees on complicated per-user or concurrent connection schemes. Instead, many vendors have re-thought this arrangement in favor of a more Web-centric plan, by basing their licensing fees on other measures such as server processing capacity. The plan enables companies to deploy Internet database and commerce applications without fear of incurring hidden costs. Such applications could feasibly expose corporate databases to thousands of Web surfers. The willingness of major vendors to re-think the business end of their back-end products is a good sign that they are serious about supporting Internet databases.

For example, Microsoft, Oracle, Sybase, and Computer Associates have all committed to new license options that allow an unlimited number of users to access a single copy of the database software. Microsoft's SQL Server *Internet Connector* is an add-on product (really just an expanded licensing agreement), now required for any deployment connecting a Web server to SQL Server. A Web server hosting organization would be in violation of the license if, say, 10-user LAN license on a Web server were used. The theory behind this new pricing model is that the Web server administrator cannot reasonably police incoming database requests if, for example, 100 concurrent requests arrived on a server equipped with only a 5-user license. Some vendors will base one-time fees on server size, and the agreements will most likely differentiate between Internet and "intranet" (internal corporate Webs) connections.

Object and Object/Relational Databases

The object database vendors view the rise of the Web as a windfall to their industry, because object databases possess the inherent ability to store a large number of complex data types prevalent on the Web, along with their relationships. This capability makes object databases ideal for storing an HTML page as a series of objects. A relational database, on the other hand, runs out of steam when the structure reaches tens or hundreds of layers deep of nested objects. Traditional table joins result in slow performance under such conditions.

Object databases hold much promise on the Web, and already, many object database vendors have publicly announced they would adopt Sun's JDBC specification to accommodate online applications.

Intranets and Extranets

Much of the subject matter in this book, although tailored to physical network topologies that include or are based on public Internet connections, you may find good reason to extrapolate further to include internal corporate Webs, now commonly referred to as *intranets*. Many vendors, such as Sun Microsystems with their Java language, view the intranet as their path towards future revenue and market share. This conclusion appears to be logical, since they are now looking to capitalize on the Internet's global infrastructure by building corporate systems based on it.

An intranet is a private, internal Web using a corporate network infrastructure or a secure portion of the public Internet to support such private applications as human resources procedure manuals, company-wide bulletin boards, project management, resource scheduling, travel schedule coordination, etc. This enterprise-level groupware has become quite popular in corporate IS circles. The rise of Lotus Notes is testimony to this observation, but even Notes is experiencing stiff competition from intranets by those excited to use common browser technology based on the global HTML standard to publish internal corporate data.

An extension to a corporate intranet that allows selective access from outside the firewall for certain client or associate companies is called an *extranet*. For example, a company may allow its vendors to access a secure portion of its corporate intranet to obtain order status information. Many firms who consider Internet applications too broad and intranets too restrictive have come to embrace the extranet as a middle ground.

Thus, when reading the balance of this book, consider applying the principles and techniques herein to intranet/extranet as well as Internet solutions.

Databases: Basis for Web Commerce

One of the obvious goals for publishing information on the Web is to make the data available to potential customers so that they may browse through product inventories, course offerings, property listings, flight schedules, etc. Just as a very long list of potential desktop client/server applications exists, the list is even longer for Webtop applications. To complete the economic circle, electronic commerce (e-commerce) capabilities are necessary to provide a means whereby a user can use sophisticated queries to find products and services, which also allows for monetary fund transfers in order to purchase these items.

We are still at the infancy of electronic commerce, as many vendors put forth attempts at secure transaction processing using data encryption techniques. Using a *Secure Sockets Layer* (SSL) enabled browser, for example, order information is encrypted while being transmitted between a user's browser and a Web server database application. Soon, however, as such transactions become a widespread reality, Internet databases will be the crux of these platforms.

A number of quality e-commerce application development environments are available for building database-enabled sites. The premiere technology from Microsoft is called Site Server 3.0 Commerce Edition. Using its "order pipeline" metaphor, Site Server makes the development process of such sites relatively simple. Site Server is already the basis of a number of high-end e-commerce Web sites, including www.barnesandnoble.com.

Extraordinary Opportunity for Software Developers

We are indeed witnessing an exciting time in the software development industry, and the technology is evolving at an extraordinary pace. Truly, the advent of software-based (as opposed to static HTML-based) Web development represents a tremendous opportunity for experienced database software developers coming from the desktop and LAN/WAN arenas. Many of the same techniques used in building traditional software systems, such as database design, object oriented analysis and design, OOP implementation, debugging, and software testing, are all still very necessary in building Web applications. Making the transition to the Webtop now means that the savvy developer will be well equipped to participate in a global media revolution.

As I stated earlier, active content is crucial to the success of the Web, because static HTML solutions can no longer do the job. The current crop of non-programming Web designers will have a very difficult time adapting to new demands that require a professional software development background. In addition to graphic design and artistic abilities, experience with traditional software development practices, including object oriented principles, is now an important prerequisite for contemporary Web developers. My own development firm has already found that Web-aware software development houses are recipients of growing outsourcing opportunities from Web design companies lacking in software development expertise.

Tools for Web Database Developers

Historically (in *Internet-time,* that is prior to mid-1995), Internet database applications were approached from an entirely custom perspective for the simple reason that no widely available commercial development tools existed at the time. This situation is changing rapidly, however, as enterprises around the world move towards a global presence in their markets. The development tool industry has reacted quickly and effectively to provide quality development environments with which to build interactive databases on the Web. We are now seeing many vendors, traditionally in the database software systems arena for desktop, LAN, and enterprise-level computing, entering into the Web development market. Every week, the trade press writes about yet another firm announcing a Web product to complement its existing product line. In addition, a whole new crop of small, innovative firms is working hard to compete in this emerging market. Among the larger players, much posturing is occurring for just the right way to enter the market, and for this reason this book is but a snapshot of an early segment of the path of a speeding bullet. What we see happening now is emerging standards for active Web content and alignments with new programming languages such as Java, JavaScript, and VBScript, not to mention new object models such as ActiveX, Component Object Model (COM and COM+), Distributed Component Object Model (DCOM), and CORBA.

These are exciting times indeed that have brought well known luminaries out to publicly express their enthusiasm. Apple co-founder Steve Jobs said in an interview for the February 1996 issue of *WIRED* magazine: "The Web reminds me of the early days of the PC industry. No one really knows anything. There are no experts." True, currently we may have no experts, but as experience builds, the developer community will remain long after the casual HTML designer exits the picture.

The Web database developer needs to keep up with all the new technologies and products available on the market, especially those that specifically address emerging technologies such as JavaBeans, the component technology for Java. The database technologies highlighted in this book are exhaustive as of the time of writing, at least for the Wintel hardware/software platforms this book addresses.

Fortunately, an exponentially increasing number of development resources are available on the Web for Internet database developers. Some general classes of resources are: white papers discussing general technology, online documentation for available products, complete and trial versions of commercial products, test applications, class libraries, Frequently Asked Questions (FAQs) documents, and much more. In fact, even though we've only begun our guided tour of the realm of Web databases, you can get a head start and begin visiting the major search engines to locate the various resource sites to see what each has to offer. These resources change all the time; however, the wonderful thing about the World Wide Web is that as the number of offerings grow, so do the hypertext links to new sites, showing off new and exciting products.

Sample Database-Enabled Web Sites

From the discussion thus far, you may have found creative energies beginning to flow about how your organization may benefit from an Internet database. At this stage, you may usefully pause and take a look at some typical applications. I enable this by presenting three actual commercial Web sites that have implemented a Web database by using one of several of the techniques and tools highlighted in this book. We've selected the companies from rather diverse industries to demonstrate the breadth of applications an Internet database may address. In each case, we have supplied the Uniform Resource Locator (URL), also known as the Web address, of the site so that you can visit it yourself to test out the features described herein. These are all public sites, requiring no authentication to gain access.

Infinite Humanity

Our first example is the *Infinite Humanity* e-commerce Web site found at www.123456789.net. This database-enabled site is a repository of human history as told by the individual. The user can enter various forms of information about his or her life, memorials of family and friends who have passed on, baby biographies, etc. The information is entered in free-form narratives, which are stored in a relational database. Once entered, anyone equipped with a Web browser may search through the data store using a form-based criteria mechanism.

The site was developed using Active Server Pages for server-side business logic and JavaScript for client-side user interface logic. It is hosted on a Windows NT 4.0 Web server running IIS 4.0 and SQL Server 7.0 as the back-end database.

Let's first take a look at how the database search feature was implemented in the Infinite Humanity site. Figure 1-2 shows the primary search form. It uses

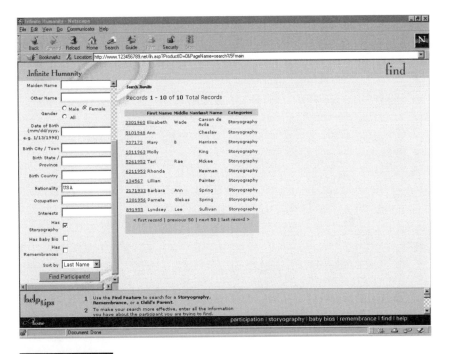

Figure 1–2   *Search Selection Criteria Form*

HTML frames, where the left-hand frame is used for entering the selection criteria, and the right-hand frame for the search results as well as other messages. In the example shown, we requested all participants (users of the site) who are female and have a USA nationality. We further asked to sort the resulting list by last name. In order to initiate a search of the database, the user must click on the Find Participants button on the form. At this point, a SQL string is dynamically created to match the specified criteria. This string is passed along to the database to obtain a result-set (rows of data returned by the database).

The search results are shown in the right-hand frame of the display. Several columns are selected from the database and formatted for the user to review. This Web site implements a commonly used search facility called "drill-down" queries. In this case, the first column of the search results frame contains a unique Participant ID, which is also a hypertext link (notice that the field values are underlined). When the user clicks on one of these link fields, a secondary query is initiated against the database, where additional information is retrieved. This process could feasibly continue to many query levels.

We see the results of the second-level query for the drill-down search in Figure 1-3, specifically, the software used the selected Participant ID in order to retrieve the detail information for that participant. Additional hypertext links are on this page, but in this case, they do not initiate another search

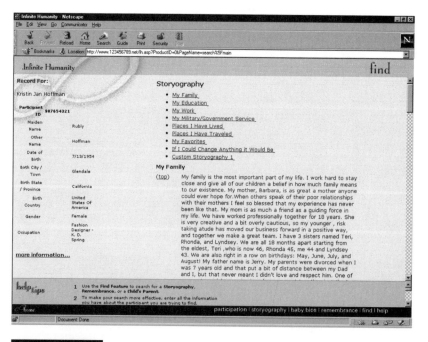

Figure 1–3   *Search Selection Criteria Form*

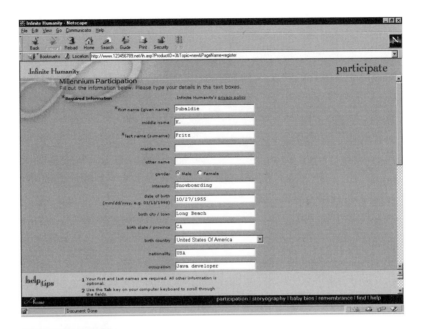

Figure 1–4   *Participant Information Form*

level (the difference is not immediately apparent). Instead, these links are simply anchors to specific places in the frame so that users may more easily navigate to them. An anchor is a common HTML technique for providing navigation control within a page containing a relatively large amount of text.

Another area of the site that depends on an underlying database is the e-commerce component. Figure 1-4 shows the Participant Information form where new users enter their information. The need to store customer information is common in sites where products or services are sold. Furthermore, Figure 1-5 shows a simple order form where information describing what the user is paying for is stored. One of the fields on this form lets the user select the name of a charity. The list of charities shown in the combo box may be based on values stored in a database table.

The Real Estate Book

Our next sample database-powered Web site is *The Real Estate Book* at www.treb.com. This site provides a residential property locator service for all of North America, and it's typical of many of the real estate sites around the Web. The real estate industry was one of the first to utilize the Internet to automate its business process by allowing users to specify various criteria for a home purchase and access listings in a desired area. Most contemporary real

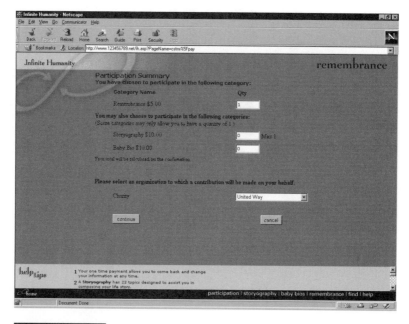

Figure 1–5   *E-Commerce Order Form*

estate Web sites go so far as to include actual graphic images of the properties for the prospective buyer to view.

The site was implemented using a product called Sapphire Web™ from Bluestone Software, running on Windows NT 4.0, IIS 3.0, and SQL Server 6.5. Sapphire Web is a development environment consisting of server-side and client-side components for the construction of Web client/server database applications. The site was developed for Network Communications, Inc.

Let's demonstrate The Real Estate Book's user interface for searching the company's property listing database. Figure 1-6 shows the first step in the query process, where you must specify the region of North America of interest. You have a choice here to use a map of the region where you can click on the desired location, or the pull-down lists, one for U.S. states and the other for Canadian provinces. We'll select the state of Maine. To proceed with the query, you clicks on the *Select* button. This selection is stored and combined with the selections in the next form.

Using a drill-down approach, the next step requires you to specify the desired city in the region previously selected. A list of city names, all hypertext linked, is presented to you. We'll select the city of Bangor by clicking on the name. In Figure 1-7, we see a more traditional form-based criteria page where you may enter the specific town, price range, and number of bedrooms and bathrooms on which to base the search. Many Web database implementations

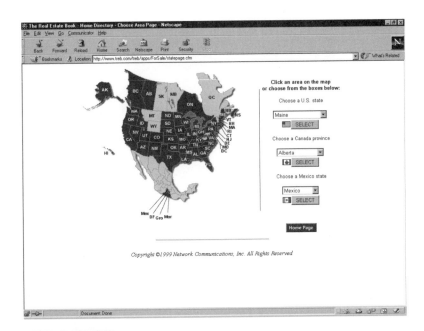

Figure 1–6   *Real Estate Page Map Criteria*

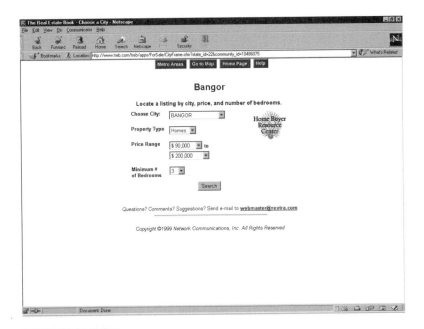

Figure 1–7   *Using a Form to Specify Property Criteria*

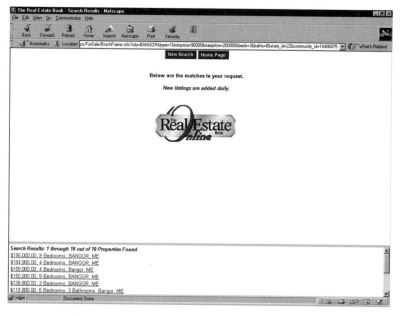

Figure 1–8 *Property Search Result-Set*

use this kind of combination of both drill-down and form-based querying. You click the *Search* button to submit the query to the database.

In Figure 1-8, we are presented with the result-set for the query. We see that there are 12 rows, appearing in a scrollable list, in the result-set corresponding to the number of property listings that match our criteria. The list is sorted descending by price. Each line in the list contains the price, number of bedrooms, number of bathrooms, and city.

Let's click on the first entry in the list to obtain detailed information describing the property. Figure 1-9 shows the additional information displayed for the selected property, including a graphic image of the home, some descriptive words, and a house ID number.

UCLA Store Bookseller E-Commerce Site

Our final example database-enabled Web site illustrates a high-end database application with an integrated electronic commerce component. The *UCLA Store* site was developed by a combination of internal IS department staff and several outside consulting companies for the Associated Students of UCLA (ASUCLA). Using Microsoft Site Server 3.0 Commerce Edition for the electronic commerce integration, this site provides for online purchases of student textbooks and specialty products, such as various clothing items with school logos. Another part of the site implements a general bookseller department in

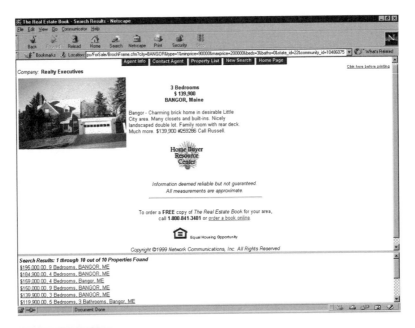

Figure 1-9   *Property Search Result-Set*

the campus bookstore called the *Book Zone*. Using a dynamic and flexible book search facility, students and the general public may look for and purchase books using a variety of criteria. The site's database connectivity components were implemented using Microsoft SQL Server 6.5. Site branching logic, and query execution was handled by Site Server as opposed to any kind of server-side scripting or Java code. The URL for the site is www.ucla-store.ucla.edu. My development firm was responsible for the database design, book search facilities, query optimization, and back office database population for the site.

The UCLA Store site should be considered a high-end database implementation because of the demands and expectations placed on the site. One of the primary goals for the site was to allow users to search through over 2 million book titles, using a flexible and easy-to-use interface, and retrieve results in under three seconds per query. The database must also maintain this performance when under a reasonably heavy concurrency load. A robust, enterprise-level relational back-end database such as SQL Server was the only possible choice to support these requirements.

The primary user interface component for the UCLA Store book site is the search page shown in Figure 1-10. This page allows users to search for books by a single keyword, title beginning with a specified character string, author last name (author beginning with a specified string), author last and first name (complete name search), subject, ISBN, and publication date. A

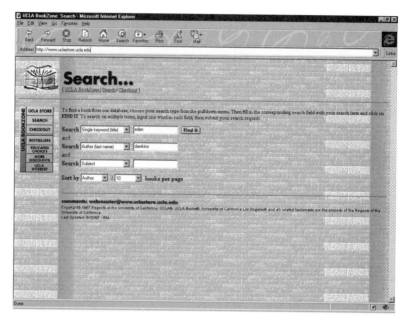

Figure 1–10   *UCLA Store Book Zone Search Page*

simple query might be based on only the author's last name, but the search mechanism also supports queries of up to three criteria at once. An implied logical "and" operation occurs between multiple criteria. The user can even specify the sort order of the result-set output of the query by title, author, or publication date. For example, if you wanted to see only the latest publications for a specific author, you'd select the publication date order.

To see how this site processes book search query requests, consider Figure 1-10, which shows the primary search form. Here, we've specified two criteria, a title keyword "eden" and an author's last name "Dawkins." The third criteria, since it is not used, remains blank. Clicking on the *Find It* button begins the search process.

The query results are shown in Figure 1-11. The result-set is limited to a maximum of 200 rows, with the ability to specify how many rows at a time to show on a single result page. The limit is placed on the query to prevent users from specifying overly loose criteria yielding an enormous result-set.

A good result page will always repeat the criteria specified by the user to produce the results being viewed. Here, the top line of the display shows the title and author criteria selected. This line also reports the number of rows returned from the query. In the book results lines, you see the title, binding information (i.e., paperback, hardback, etc.), author names, and retail price.

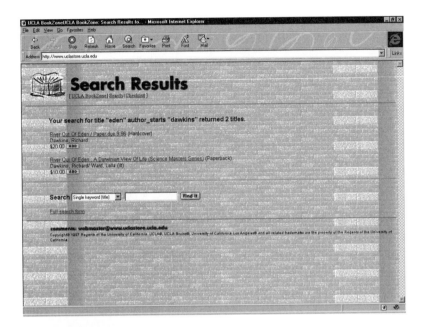

Figure 1–11   *Book Search Query Results*

Clicking on the *Add* button adds the book to the shopping cart. Notice, you can also pose a different, albeit more simple, query from the search results page.

If you need additional information about a book before adding it to your shopping cart, you can click on the book title, which is a hypertext link to the book detail page (see Figure 1-12). This page contains more specific book information, including any related subjects. In order to obtain books on related subjects, you can click on one of the subjects listed and another query is automatically generated and run. You can also click on one of the author's names to search for additional books by that author. This flexible "drill-down" approach to Web-based database queries directly coincides with the underlying nature of the Web, namely additional information becomes available at the click of the mouse.

As a Web application containing constantly changing data, the UCLA Store site has another very important facet, which is the back office processing and importation of external data. A number of commercially available sources of book title information exist, all in ASCII text format and each with a very unique format. Custom software had to be written to import this text data and write it to SQL Server tables. This software was written in Visual Basic 5.0 and runs during off-peak periods so as to not adversely affect response times.

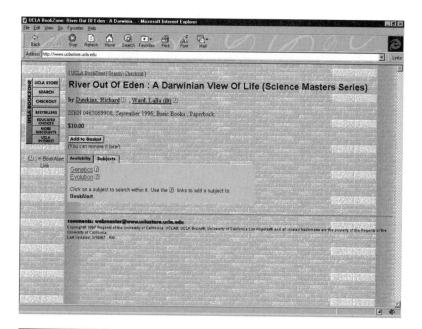

Figure 1-12   *Book Detail Information Page*

Summary

This initial chapter has set the stage for Web database development on the Wintel platform by reviewing the major areas of technology currently available. At this point, you should now have a grasp of the need for Internet databases and how several organizations have already taken advantage of this emerging new technology. I strongly recommend that you actually visit the database-enabled Web sites referenced in this chapter to get a true feel for how an Internet database operates compared to a familiar desktop database equivalent.

Web Database
Technical
Overview

· ·

An abundance of technical material surrounds the publishing of database information on the Web. In this chapter, I present an overview of a number of distinctive Web database technologies in order to provide a framework for understanding exactly what happens when a user issues a database query from a Web browser. You'll find many currently available technologies discussed here; however, this field is one of rapid innovation and we see new methodologies all the time. By the time you reach the later chapters in this book that discuss implementation and usage specifics for some of the more popular and contemporary technologies, you'll already possess a fundamental understanding of the underlying technology.

Historically, the process of providing hooks to back-end databases involved *Common Gateway Interface* (CGI) programming using languages such as *Practical Extraction and Report Language* (PERL) and C/C++. In the early days of the Web, writing custom CGI scripts (which are, in essence, server-side executable programs) to provide database functionality was an arduous task, as few generalized prototypes were available. For this reason, we did not see a lot of database-enabled Web sites until early 1995 due, in part, to the influx of new development tools. But still, many database development tools operate using CGI, even though they provide high-level tools to insulate the developer from the harshness of this level of Web access.

Some Internet database development platforms have opted for another approach away from CGI, due to its inherent inefficiencies. Some tools, for example, support special server Application Programming Interfaces (APIs) like the *Netscape Server API* (NSAPI) or the Microsoft *Internet Information Server API* (ISAPI), both of which offer database applications better performance than equivalent implementations using CGI scripts. Next, Server Side Includes (SSI) allow for database connections using extensions to the SSI specifications. Also, a whole genre of tools utilizes Java as the basis of database queries. Lastly, the Microsoft ActiveX control technology (the blueprint of which has been officially released to the public domain) and the Active Server provisions also have considerable database connection ramifications. Each approach is very different from the others, and each has its own strengths and weaknesses. Let's first take a closer look at the World Wide Web technology, *HyperText Transfer Protocol* (HTTP), upon which these methods depend.

HyperText Transfer Protocol (HTTP)

The World Wide Web began in 1989 as a research project of the European research laboratory for particle physics called CERN (Council for Nuclear Research). The goal of the project was to provide scientists with a way to share information electronically, but it rapidly evolved into a global information system based on the Internet. The primary foundation of the Web is HTTP, an application-level protocol that allows platform-independent communications among HTTP-aware clients and servers. An HTTP client refers to data sources residing on an HTTP server through a naming mechanism known as *Uniform Resource Locators* (URLs). For example, the URL http://www.amuletc.com refers to the home page of the structure of Web pages belonging to my company, which resides at the Internet domain name amuletc.com.

The URL is composed of several items:

- Retrieval protocol
- Internet node
- File system directory
- File name of the resource to be served to the HTTP client

The data files that form the network of hypertext links of the Web are ASCII text documents coded in *HyperText Markup Language* (HTML). HTML is a specialized subset of the *Standard General Markup Language* (SGML), a page layout language long used by publishers to describe the structure of electronic documents. SGML does not directly describe the formatting of documents, but rather specifies a grammar for creating document-type definitions (DTDs) that can be used to identify structural items for classes of documents. HTML is a DTD for hypermedia documents. A variety of HTML versions are in use on the Web, with the most popular being HTML version 4. A number of good sources of information regarding HTML are both in print and on the Web. A prerequisite for this book is a fundamental understanding of basic HTML.

Web clients are designed to interpret HTML-formatted documents retrieved from HTTP servers. Connections among Web resources are built by embedding URL links in HTML documents. When a URL link is selected by the client, a request goes to the appropriate HTTP server on the Internet to retrieve the referenced resource for display by the client. Thus, a single HTML document might reference other pages on the same server or it might reference pages scattered around the globe, largely transparent to the user. This ability to build flexible links among resources provides the Web's hypertext nature and has produced what is arguably the biggest assembly of "spaghetti code" ever to exist. This scenario, however, presents a tremendous opportunity to database applications, since, as a resource, a database or multiple databases can be distributed throughout the world to comprise a single application.

Still, were that the sum of the Web's capabilities, it would not have become the fastest-growing resource on the Internet today. The appeal of the Web comes from two additional capabilities of the HTTP protocol. The first is HTTP's capability to transfer complex data types as messages, using a format similar to Internet mail's Multipurpose Internet Mail Extensions (MIME). Therefore, the Web goes beyond hypertext to hypermedia, and Web servers are able to supply clients with text, graphics, sound, and video information integrated with HTML documents. Some HTTP clients can display various data types directly; often, however, the client software is configured to invoke other "helper" applications to display more complex data types such as sound and video images. The advent of graphical interface multimedia-aware HTTP clients, such as Microsoft's Internet Explorer or Netscape's Navigator/Communicator, has helped facilitate these features. The original Web browser program, *Mosaic*, from which contemporary browsers grew, was produced by the National Center for Supercomputing Applications (NCSA) at the University of Illinois at Urbana-Champaign (see www.ncsa.uiuc.edu). This program literally transformed the Web overnight into the Internet's most popular environment.

The second key factor is HTTP's ability to facilitate communications among HTTP clients and other protocols using different gateways. The URL naming scheme identifies not only the location but also the protocol needed to retrieve a resource. There, HTTP clients can be presented with an almost seamless environment that integrates HTTP servers with other popular Internet services such as SMTP mail, NNTP-based network news, FTP-based file transfer, Gopher information servers, and WAIS information servers. The browser (beginning with NCSA's Mosaic) has packaged together in a single client all the best protocols for end-users to take advantage of on the Internet. Users need learn only a single piece of software to access just about any information available on the Internet. See Figure 2-1 for a graphical description of this scenario.

The Web as described thus far is a relatively one-sided system. Information providers develop HTML documents containing links to other HTML or hypermedia files and publish this information on the Internet for browsing by

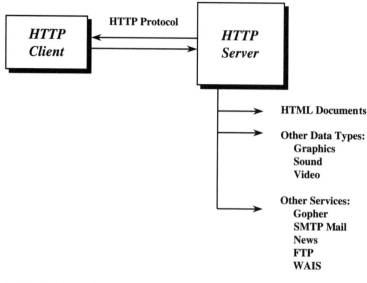

Figure 2–1   *HTTP Serves Various Data Types and Protocols*

HTTP clients. Although HTML's hypermedia nature allows for a complex and interesting presentation of information, the structure is nevertheless static unless changed by the information provider. The user's only control lies in choosing which hypermedia links to explore in the Web's expanse.

HTML 2.0 first offered the capability for *forms* to exist in HTML documents. Forms present the user with a traditional GUI display of input elements such as text fields, check boxes, and radio buttons. Thus with forms, developers can give clients the ability to provide complex input via an HTTP request. When the form's contents are submitted to the HTTP server, it passes the information on to a back-end "query server" for processing. HTML forms are very useful for certain types of database access (although two leading technologies, Java and ActiveX, use component technology instead).

Common Gateway Interface

The *Common Gateway Interface* (CGI) is an interface for running external programs, or gateways, under an information server, usually an HTTP server (although the CGI standard is designed for a cross-platform audience catering to all kinds of different hardware and software, the Windows CGI 1.3 Specification is platform-specific to Microsoft Windows 95/98 and Windows NT). We refer to gateways as programs that connect an information server (such as a Web server) to external applications. With CGI, your server can serve information that is not in a form readable by the client, such as data existing in a SQL database, and act as a gateway between the two to produce something that client browsers can use. Often, these gateway programs are called *scripts,* which in turn perform some sort of back-end processing.

This type of back-end processing requires communications among the HTTP server and other software. This process is accomplished through the CGI mechanism, which provides a means for the HTTP server to dynamically call a script. Each time a client requests the URL corresponding to your gateway, the server will execute your program. The output of your program will go more or less directly to the client. CGI scripts may be implemented in a variety of environments, including Visual Basic, C/C++ programs, PERL programs, or operating system shell scripts. In this setup, the HTTP server software becomes a type of middleware between the HTTP client and the CGI script, receiving the request from the HTTP client, passing it on to the CGI script, receiving back the results from the CGI script, and passing them in turn back to the HTTP client. The results must be in the form of an HTML document or some other document type that the client can process. However, since the resulting HTML document can be produced by the CGI script, it now becomes dynamic. Thus, the Web can facilitate true interactive client/server computing, with the client specifying a dynamic request that produces dynamic results from the server.

The CGI script, and whatever components lie behind it, functions as a black box to the HTTP server. The server merely receives the client request and then passes it along to the CGI script. The CGI script in turn passes its output back to the HTTP server. This data can be made up of the script's actual output or instructions for finding and retrieving the output that is stored in a file produced by the script. The HTTP server then passes the output back to the requesting client. Figure 2-2 illustrates how the HTTP server can communicate with other services via CGI.

With CGI, the Web can be extended to practically any back-end software service, including relational databases. The only requirement is that the database must have an API that allows it to communicate with the CGI script. Figure 2-3 shows how the CGI gateway serves as middleware between the HTTP server and the database API. The CGI script plays the role of translator between the HTTP server and the database API. Any program that can connect to the database and produce HTML-formatted output can act as the CGI script. So, for example, to communicate with a Microsoft SQL Server database, Allaire's Cold Fusion DBML.EXE program can be used as the CGI script to provide the interface between the HTTP server and SQL Server.

One common misconception about CGI is that you can send command-line parameters to the script program. CGI, however, uses the command line for other purposes. Instead, CGI uses environment variables to send parame-

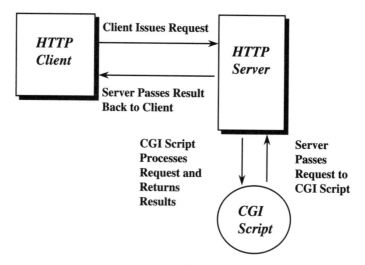

CGI Processing Model

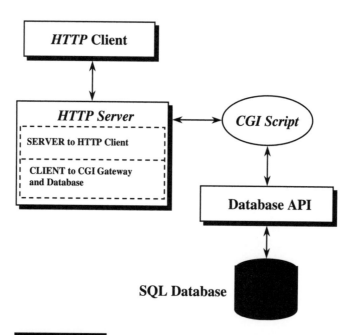

CGI Database Middleware

ters to the script program. The two primary environment variables used for this purpose are:

1. QUERY_STRING. This variable is defined as anything that follows the first question mark character (?) in the URL used to access your gateway.
2. PATH_INFO. CGI allows for extra information to be embedded in the URL for your gateway, which can be used to transmit context-specific information to the scripts. This information is usually placed after the path of your gateway in the URL. For example, let's say that you have an "Employee Update" CGI program in the /scripts directory called empupdate. When you access the script from a particular document, you wish to tell it to update the "west coast" region. So in this case, you could access your script in an HTML document as:

```
<A HREF="/scripts/empupdate/region=west"> empupdate</A>
```

Whenever the server executes empupdate, it will pass PATH_INFO of /region=west, and the script can decode this and proceed accordingly.

The major difficulty in interfacing Web clients to relational databases lies in the differing transaction models of the two environments. The Web, defined by HTTP, is a stateless system with a simple request/response transaction model. An HTTP transaction is defined by four steps:

1. Open a connection to the server
2. Issue the request
3. Receive the results from the server
4. Close the connection

Connections with the server are maintained only long enough to receive the results of a single request, and no information on state is maintained by the server. Every request between client and server requires the establishment of a new connection that is terminated upon completion of the request; typically, the time-out period on failed connection is short.

The database environment, in contrast, typically allows multiple transactions to occur in a single database session, with the state of the session being maintained between transactions. Thus, a client may perform several queries, issue several update transactions, and have several commit points within a single database session. Still, the single-transaction-per-session environment of the Web is quite useful in a great many applications, allowing the client to specify a request for information and allowing the database to return the results of that request within the constraints of the HTTP connection. Each additional request for information requires a new database connection, but for many applications, information on status need not be maintained between requests.

Several basic methods exist to facilitate more complex interactions among Web clients and the database. The first is to store and pass state information between the client and the server, so that each subsequent database session is provided with information about the preceding history. This approach is typically accomplished by appending state information to the results passed back to the client by the CGI script. Each subsequent client request includes these results, which are processed in turn by the CGI script in order to maintain state information.

The second method is to have the CGI script open a database session and keep it open while processing subsequent clients' requests. In this model, identifying information must be passed between the client and the CGI script in order to link subsequent requests with the proper database session. The CGI script must also be able to terminate database sessions after a specified time-out period of inactivity. In both methods, the burden of translating between the stateless environment of the Web and the richer environment of the database falls on the *middleware*, which is the CGI script.

Other methods of maintaining state include modifying/adding state information to the URL itself and using "cookies." We'll see in Chapter 7, "Active Server and ADO," that these last two techniques are quite widely used.

Generic Database Scenario

Before you see some specific CGI database implementations, I want to lay out a framework for such discussions by showing a completely generic scenario for using the CGI and gateway software method for talking to SQL databases. Consider the diagram shown in Figure 2-4.

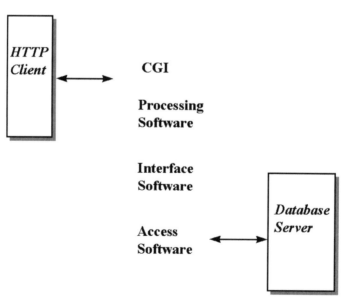

| Figure 2–4 | *Generic CGI/Database Interface* |

The *processing software* is the program called directly from an HTML document by the HTTP client. This software reads the input passed to it from standard input or gets information from environment variables set by the HTTP client. The CGI call determines the method of data passing. Once the data, or specifically an SQL string (or pieces of one), is read, the processing software uses the *interface software* to prepare the SQL for submission to the *access software*. The processing software uses the interface software to process the results passed back by the database.

The interface software is the database-specific interface necessary to translate queries into a format recognized by the type of database being used. The interface software also contains any data structures, variables, and function calls needed to communicate with the database.

The access software is usually software that is distributed with the database. The access software allows access to the database through a programming API, command-line interface, etc. Formatted queries are submitted to the access software, the database returns the result set or an error message, and the access software passes that back to the processing software via the interface software. Any additional software, such as an HTTP server, networking software, etc., adds additional links to the processing chain.

This construction is generic. Specific gateway software may use any number of variations on this theme, or bypass it entirely. This is, however, a valid database access scheme that does work.

Now let's consider two actual CGI environments, one a programmatic solution with Visual Basic and the other a custom scripted solution using Cold Fusion.

Visual Basic/CGI Interface

The Visual Basic language is the development platform of choice for a large segment of the general programming population. Coupled with the fact that its Visual Basic for Applications (VBA) derivative is found in Microsoft Office suite components such as Access, Excel, PowerPoint, and Word, the language is a natural choice for programming CGI scripts. As it turns out, VB is an excellent programming environment for building such gateways. In fact, one Web server vendor, O'Reilly & Associates, has built a CGI framework in VB for use with their WebSite™ server product.

WebSite ships with a VB module named CGI32.BAS, which provides all the interface code needed to get the CGI environment set up in VB global variables. Building a CGI-compliant VB program using WebSite's provisions goes like this: The CGI32.BAS module contains the `Sub Main` procedure. You include CGI32.BAS in your Visual Basic 6.0 project. You set the project options for "Sub Main" startup. Once the CGI environment has been established as mentioned above, the Main() calls your own main procedure, which must have the name CGI_Main(). The CGI32.BAS framework consists of the VB procedures in Table 2-1.

Table 2–1	WebSite's CGI32.BAS Procedure List
Procedure Name	**Description**
Declarations	Manifests constants, types, global constants, CGI global variables, and Windows API declarations.
ErrorHandler	Generates an HTTP/1.0 HTML-formatted error message into the output file, and then exits the program if a VB runtime error occurs during the execution of the CGI script program.
FieldPresent	Checks whether the form field is present.
FindExtraHeader	Gets the text form of an "extra" header.
GetAcceptTypes	Creates the array of accept type structs.
GetArgs	Parses the command line.
GetExtraHeaders	Creates the array of extra header structs.
GetFormTuples	Creates the array of POST form input key-value pairs.
GetProfile	Gets a value or enumerates keys in the GI_Profile file.
GetSmallField	Gets the value of a "small" form field, given the key.
InitializeCGI	Fills in all the CGI variables.
Main	CGI script back-end main procedure.
ParseFileValue	Parses the form file value strings.
Send	Shortcut for writing to the output file.
PlusToSpace	Removes plus-delimiters from an HTTP-encoded string.
SendNoOp	Tells the browser to do nothing.
Unescape	Converts an HTTP-escaped string to normal form.
WebDate	Returns an HTTP/1.0 compliant date/time string.
x2c	Converts a hex-escaped character to ASCII.

The WebSite manual does an excellent job of presenting CGI programming concepts by including a completed sample application for a database of students, classes, and a linking table describing which students are currently taking which class. Although the sample is rather simplistic, it does show the various techniques that make VB a great language to use for Web database development. The sample assumes the use of 32-bit Visual Basic 6.0 with an Access 8.0 (Access 97) database as the container for all table objects, relationships, and stored procedures (in Access terminology, *parameter query objects*) interfacing to the Microsoft JET 3.5 database engine.

DATABASE DESIGN

The simple database design involves three tables: Classes, Students, and StudentAndClasses. This type of relationship is called a *Many-to-Many* (M:M)

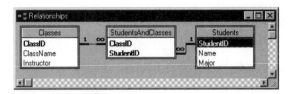

Figure 2–5   *VB CGI Sample Application Table Relationships*

relationship and has two orientations, Students-by-Classes and Classes-by-Students. Figure 2-5 shows the Access relationship window for this design. Each table has a primary key field that is an Auto-number data type, guaranteeing unique key values.

STORED PROCEDURES

The sample application uses the stored procedures (parameter queries) listed in Table 2-2. These are really QueryDef parameter query objects.

Table 2–2	Sample Application QueryDef Objects

QueryDef Name	**SQL Type**
ClassesForStudent	SELECT
DeleteClass	DELETE
DismissStudent	DELETE
DropClass	DELETE
StudentsInClass	SELECT (INNER JOINs)
TakeClass	INSERT (Append Query)

Here is the SQL statement for the StudentsInClass stored query. This is one orientation of the M:M relationship upon which this database is based. It is used to get a list of students in a class, by class name. The query contains a parameter pClass, which has the name of the class for the list.

```
PARAMETERS pClass Text;
SELECT DISTINCTROW Students.Name,
    Students.Major FROM Students
    INNER JOIN (Classes INNER JOIN
      StudentsAndClasses
    ON Classes.ClassID =
      StudentsAndClasses.ClassID)
      ON Students.StudentID =
      StudentsAndClasses.StudentID
      WHERE ((Classes.ClassName=[pClass]));
```

Figure 2-6 shows the query design windows for this query object.

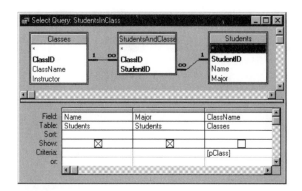

Figure 2–6   *Query Design for StudentsInClass Query*

HTML

The following is the HTML code required to start the sample application. This HTML is stored on a Web page on the server for satisfying requests by the Web browser. It initiates the CGI script written in VB that runs on the server:

```
<A HREF
http://www.amuletc.com/scripts/DBSAMPLE.EXE>
```

The first part of the Case statement in the DoGet() procedure shown in the code listing below generates HTML code that presents a list of options to the Web browser. The resulting HTML page is as follows:

```
<H2>Choices:</H2>
<A HREF="/cgi-win/DBSAMPLE32.EXE/students">
    List of students</A><BR>
<A HREF="/cgi-win/DBSAMPLE32.EXE/frm_Enroll">
    Enroll a student</A><BR>
    <A HREF="/cgi-win/DBSAMPLE32.EXE/frm_Dismiss">
    Dismiss a student</A><P>
<A HREF="/cgi-win/DBSAMPLE32.EXE/classes">
    List of classes</A><BR>
<A HREF="/cgi-win/DBSAMPLE32.EXE/frm_Add">
    Add a class</A><BR>
<A HREF="/cgi-win/DBSAMPLE32.EXE/frm_Del">
    Delete a class</A><P>
<A HREF="/cgi-win/DBSAMPLE32.EXE/frm_cl4st">
    Classes for student</A><BR>
<A HREF="/cgi-win/DBSAMPLE32.EXE/frm_st4cl">
    Students in class</A><BR>
<A HREF="/cgi-win/DBSAMPLE32.EXE/frm_Take">
    Take a class</A><BR>
<A HREF="/cgi-win/DBSAMPLE32.EXE/frm_Drop">
    Drop a class</A><BR>
```

VISUAL BASIC CGI APPLICATION CODE

Now I want to take a look at the Visual Basic 6.0 code that implements the CGI application that uses calls to procedures within CGI32.BAS, but I want to present a sample VB application that uses the procedures found in this Basic module. The code for the CGI implementation is too lengthy to provide here, but you can download it yourself at the O'Reilly & Associates Web site at http://www.oreilly.com. The CGI code as well as the sample application was developed by Robert B. Denny. At this site, you can also try a live demonstration of this Web database sample to get a feeling for response time and the interactive nature of a Web database application based on Visual Basic.

```vb
Option Explicit
Dim sSelector As String
Dim db As Database
Dim qd As QueryDef
Dim ds As Dynaset

Sub CGI_Main()

' Remove leading "/"
sSelector = UCase$(Mid$(CGI_LogicalPath, 2))

Set db = DBEngine.Workspaces(0). _
    OpenDatabase(App.Path & "\dbsample.mdb")
Send ("Content-type: text/html")
Send ("X-CGI-prog: WebSite Access Demo V1.2
    (VB4/32)")
Send ("")

Select Case UCase$(CGI_RequestMethod)
    Case "GET":
      DoGet
    Case "POST":
      DoPost
    Case Else:
      Send ("<H2>Cannot do """ & _
        CGI_RequestMethod_ &
        """ method</H2>")
End Select

db.Close
End Sub

Sub DoGet()

Dim LinkStart As String

LinkStart = "<A HREF=""" & CGI_ExecutablePath
```

```
Select Case sSelector
    Case ""      ' No "selector", list choices
        Send ("<H2>Choices:</H2>")
        Send (LinkStart &
          "/students"">List of
          students</A><BR>")
        Send (LinkStart &
          "/frm_Enroll"">
          Enroll a student</A><BR>")
        Send (LinkStart &
          "/frm_Dismiss"">
          Dismiss astudent</A><P>")
        Send (LinkStart & _
          "/classes"">
    `     List of classes</A><BR>")
        Send (LinkStart &
          "/frm_Add"">Add a class</A><BR>")
        Send (LinkStart &
          "/frm_Del"">
          Delete a class</A><P>")
    Send (LinkStart & _
          "/frm_cl4st"">
          Classes for student</A><BR>")
        Send (LinkStart &
          "/frm_st4cl"">
          Students in class</A><BR>")
        Send (LinkStart &
          "/frm_Take"">
          Take a class</A><BR>")
        Send (LinkStart &
          "/frm_Drop"">
          Drop a class</A><BR>")

    ' List all students
    Case "STUDENTS"
        Send ("<H2>Students:</H2>")
        Set ds =
        db!Students.OpenRecordset(dbOpenTable)
        Do Until ds.EOF
          Send (ds("Name") & " (" &
            ds("Major") & ")<BR>")
          ds.MoveNext
        Loop
        ds.Close

    ' Send Enroll Student form
    Case "FRM_ENROLL"
        Send ("<H2>Enroll a Student</H2>")
        Send ("<FORM METHOD=""POST""
          ACTION=""" & CGI_ExecutablePath &
```

```
      "/enroll"">")
   Send ("Name: <INPUT TYPE=TEXT
      NAME=""Name""><BR>")
   Send ("Major: <INPUT TYPE=TEXT
      NAME=""Major"">")
   Send ("<P><INPUT TYPE=SUBMIT
      VALUE=""Enroll"">")
   Send ("</FORM>")

' Send Dismiss Student form
Case "FRM_DISMISS"
   Send ("<H2>Dismiss a Student</H2>")
   Send ("<FORM METHOD=""POST""
      ACTION=""" & CGI_ExecutablePath &
      "/dismiss"">")
   OptionList "Student", "Students",
      "Name"
   Send ("<P><INPUT TYPE=SUBMIT " &
      "VALUE=""Dismiss"">")
   Send ("</FORM>")

' List of all classes
Case "CLASSES"
   Send ("<H2>Classes:</H2>")
   Set ds =
   db!Classes.OpenRecordset(dbOpenTable)
   Do Until ds.EOF
      Send (ds("ClassName") & " (" &
      ds("Instructor") & ")<BR>")
      ds.MoveNext
   Loop
   ds.Close

' Send Add Class
Case "FRM_ADD"
   Send ("<H2>Add a Class</H2>")
   Send ("<FORM METHOD=""POST""
      ACTION=""" & CGI_ExecutablePath &
      "/add"">")
   Send ("Class Name: <INPUT TYPE=TEXT " &
      "NAME=""ClassName""><P>")
   Send ("Instructor: <INPUT TYPE=TEXT " &
      "NAME=""Instructor"">")
   Send ("<P><INPUT TYPE=SUBMIT " &
      "VALUE=""Add Class"">")
   Send ("</FORM>")

' Send Delete Class form
Case "FRM_DEL"
   Send ("<H2>Delete a Class</H2>")
```

```
Send ("<FORM METHOD=""POST""
  ACTION=""" & CGI_ExecutablePath &
  "/del"">")
  OptionList "Class", "Classes",
    "ClassName"
Send ("<P><INPUT TYPE=SUBMIT " &
  "VALUE=""Delete Class"">")
Send ("</FORM>")

' Send Classes for Student form
Case "FRM_CL4ST"
  Send ("<FORM METHOD=""POST""
    ACTION=""" & CGI_ExecutablePath &
    "/cl4st"">")
      OptionList "Student", "Students",
      "Name"
  Send ("<P><INPUT TYPE=SUBMIT " &
    "VALUE=""List Classes"">")
  Send ("</FORM>")

' Send Students in Class form
  Case "FRM_ST4CL"
    Send ("<FORM METHOD=""POST""
      ACTION=""" & CGI_ExecutablePath &
      "/st4cl"">")
        OptionList "Class", "Classes",
        "ClassName"
    Send ("<P><INPUT TYPE=SUBMIT " &
      "VALUE=""List Students"">")
    Send ("</FORM>")

' Take a class
  Case "FRM_TAKE"
    Send ("<FORM METHOD=""POST""
      ACTION=""" & CGI_ExecutablePath &
      "/take"">")
      OptionList "Student", "Students",
      "Name"
    Send ("<P>")
      OptionList "Class", "Classes",
      "ClassName"
    Send ("<P><INPUT TYPE=SUBMIT " &
      "VALUE=""Take Class"">")
    Send ("</FORM>")

' Drop a class
  Case "FRM_DROP"
    Send ("<FORM METHOD=""POST""
      ACTION=""" & CGI_ExecutablePath &
      "/drop"">")
```

```
           OptionList "Student", "Students",
             "Name"
        Send ("<P>")
           OptionList "Class", "Classes",
             "ClassName"
        Send ("<P><INPUT TYPE=SUBMIT " &
           "VALUE=""Drop Class"">")
        Send ("</FORM>")

    Case Else:
        Send ("<H2>Bad GET selector """ &
           sSelector & """</H2>")
End Select

End Sub

Sub DoPost()

Dim buf As String
Dim buf2 As String

On Error GoTo OnPostError

Select Case sSelector

    ' Enroll a student
    Case "ENROLL"
       buf = GetSmallField("Name")
       Set ds =
       db!Students.OpenRecordset(dbOpenTable)
       ds.AddNew
       ds("Name") = buf
       ds("Major") = GetSmallField("Major")
       ds.Update
       ds.Close
       Send ("<H2>" & buf &
          " enrolled successfully</H2>")

    'Dismiss a student
    Case "DISMISS"
       buf = GetSmallField("Student")
       Set qd = db.QueryDefs!DismissStudent
       qd.Parameters!pName = buf
       qd.Execute
       qd.Close
       Send ("<H2>" & buf &
          " dismissed successfully</H2>")

    Case "ADD"
       buf = GetSmallField("ClassName")
```

```
                  Set ds =
                  db!Classes.OpenRecordset(dbOpenDynaset)
                  ds.AddNew
                  ds("ClassName") = buf
                  ds("Instructor") =
                    GetSmallField("Instructor")
                  ds.Update
                  ds.Close
                  Send ("<H2>" & buf &
                    " added successfully</H2>")

            Case "DEL"
                  buf = GetSmallField("Class")
                  Set qd = db.QueryDefs!DeleteClass
                  qd.Parameters!pClass = buf
                  qd.Execute
                  qd.Close
                  Send ("<H2>" & buf &
                    " deleted successfully</H2>")

            Case "CL4ST"
                  buf = GetSmallField("Student")
                  Send ("<H2>Classes for " & buf &
                    ":</H2>")
                  Set qd = db.QueryDefs!ClassesForStudent
                  qd.Parameters!pName = buf
                  Set ds =
                    qd.OpenRecordset(dbOpenDynaset)
                  Do Until ds.EOF
                    Send (ds("ClassName") & " (" &
                      ds("Instructor") & ")<BR>")
                    ds.MoveNext
                  Loop
                  ds.Close
                  qd.Close

            Case "ST4CL"
                  buf = GetSmallField("Class")
                  Send ("<H2>Students in " & buf &
                    ":</H2>")
                  Set qd = db.QueryDefs!StudentsInClass
                  qd.Parameters!pClass = buf
                  Set ds =
                    qd.OpenRecordset(dbOpenDynaset)
                  Do Until ds.EOF
                    Send (ds("Name") & " (" &
                      ds("Major") & ")<BR>")
                    ds.MoveNext
                  Loop
                  ds.Close
```

```
      qd.Close

   Case "TAKE"
     buf = GetSmallField("Student")
     buf2 = GetSmallField("Class")
     Set qd = db.QueryDefs!TakeClass
     qd.Parameters!pName = buf
     qd.Parameters!pClass = buf2
     qd.Execute
     qd.Close
     Send ("<H2>" & buf & " is now taking "
        & buf2 & "</H2>")

   Case "DROP"
     buf = GetSmallField("Student")
     buf2 = GetSmallField("Class")
     Set qd = db.QueryDefs!DropClass
     qd.Parameters!pName = buf
     qd.Parameters!pClass = buf2
     qd.Execute
     qd.Close
     Send ("<H2>" & buf & " has dropped " &
        buf2 & "</H2>")

   Case Else
     Send ("<H2>Unknown POST selector """ &
        sSelector & """</H2>")
End Select

DoPostFinish:        ' Can come here via error,
                     ' State of ds & qd unknown
   On Error Resume Next
   ds.Close          ' else db.Close will fail
   qd.Close
   Exit Sub


' =================
' Exception Handler
' =================
'
OnPostError:
   ' Resignal if a CGI.BAS error
   If Err >= CGI_ERR_START Then Error Err

   Send ("<H2>There was a problem:</H2>")
   Send ("VB reports: <CODE>" & Error$ &
     " (error #" & Err &
     ")</CODE><H3>Best Guess:")

   Select Case sSelector
```

```
      Case "ENROLL":
        Send ("Already enrolled")
      Case "DISMISS":
        Send ("?? This is ugly ??")
      Case "ADD":
        Send ("Class already exists")
      Case "DEL":
        Send ("?? This is ugly ??")
      Case "CL4ST":
        Send ("?? This is ugly ??")
      Case "ST4CL":
        Send ("?? This is ugly ??")
      Case "TAKE":
        Send ("Already taking " &
          "this class")
      Case "DROP":
        Send ("Not in this class")
      Case Else:
        Send ("Programmer error: " &
          "Unknown selector " & _
                  "in POST exception " &
          "handler.")
    End Select

    Send ("</H3>")
    Resume DoPostFinish
End Sub

Sub Inter_Main ()
    MsgBox "This is a Windows CGI program"
End Sub

Sub OptionList(FieldName As String,
    Tbl As String, Col As String)
    Send ("Select " & FieldName &
      ": <SELECT NAME=""" & FieldName &
      """>")
    Set ds =
      db.OpenRecordset(Tbl, dbOpenDynaset)
    Do Until ds.EOF
      Send ("<OPTION>" & ds(Col))
      ds.MoveNext
    Loop
    ds.Close
    Send ("</SELECT>")
End Sub
```

Let's discuss the CGI application above. The main procedure, CGI_Main(), opens the Access database containing the data table and Query-Def objects (in a sense, QueryDefs can be thought of as stored procedures) for the application. You'll notice the use of the Send procedure throughout the code. Send is found in CGI32.BAS and simply writes characters to an

ASCII text file whose file number is defined by a CGI global variable CGI_OutputFN. This output text file is the HTML file containing the results of the Web database query request.

The CGI_OutputFN variable, along with many others, is found in the declaration section of CGI32.BAS. The server passes data to the CGI program via a Windows private profile file, in key-value format (i.e., ordered pairs of key names and values). The CGI program may then use the standard Windows API services for enumerating and retrieving the key-value pairs in the data file. Each value is then made available to the CGI application through use of the CGI global variables declared in CGI32.BAS. Another variable is CGI_RequestMethod, which is a standard CGI variable containing either GET or POST, two commonly used CGI methods.

The DoGet() procedure takes the event from the HTML form and decides what the user selected. For example, if the user selected a list of all students, DoGet() opens a RecordSet object using the JET Engine *Data Access Objects* (DAO) method OpenRecordSet() and then sequentially walks the table using the MoveNext() method. For each record, the student name and major are output to the HTML text file. Several of the other options dynamically construct additional HTML forms used to retrieve required user input. Notice that each of these uses the POST method, which, as you'll see in the discussion of DoPost(), initiates a database process. For example, if the user selects the StudentsInClass query, the form shown in Figure 2-7 is generated.

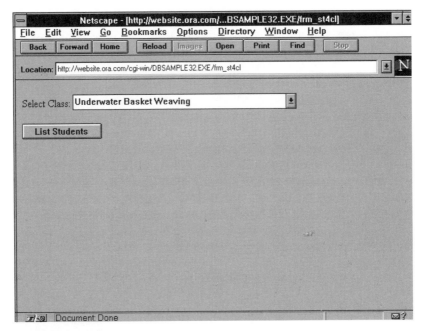

Figure 2-7   *HTML Form to Prompt for Class Name*

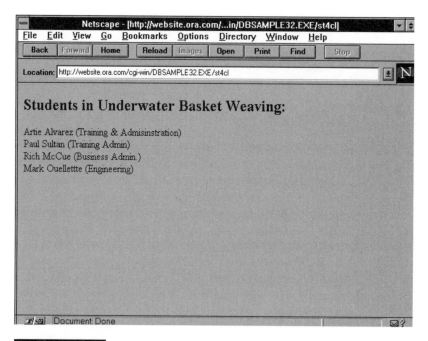

Figure 2–8   *Query Results for StudentsInClass*

Once the user selects a class name from the pick list and clicks on the List Students button, the QueryDef is executed and the result-set is translated into HMTL, as shown in Figure 2-8.

The DoPost() procedure decides what to do for each POST request. For example, in the case of an "ADD" request, we open a record set, issue the DAO AddNew() method, set the field values, and issue the Update() method. You can see that any kind of standard VB DAO code can be attached to POST method HTML code. This concept can produce some very flexible Web database possibilities.

One of the real challenges in developing a VB Web database is error handling. Only the simplest kind of error handling is done in the sample code above. The database design is built to prevent duplicate student and class names, and the database is designed to enforce referential integrity. All of this error handling is done at the JET database engine level and signals a POST error. See the OnPostError procedures that handles these errors.

CGI Database Scripting

Another very attractive solution for providing a Web database connection is to use one of several available CGI-based development products. These products are relatively easy to use, since they are basically scripting products that use standard HTML in conjunction with a proprietary database markup lan-

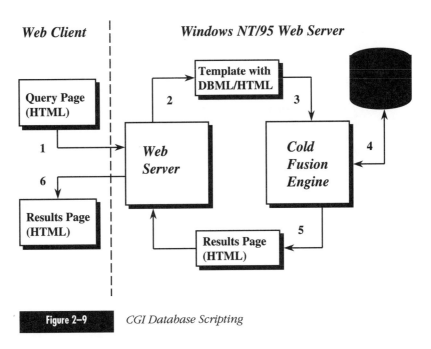

Figure 2–9   *CGI Database Scripting*

guage as the primary gateway to their CGI database interface. In most cases, ODBC is used to establish connections to SQL databases using SQL statements embedded in the special HTML files. Although I discuss this method of building Web databases more in depth in Chapter 4, for the purposes of this chapter, I define the technical basis of the CGI scripting solution now. The discussion will focus on the *Cold Fusion* product by Allaire Corp. Consider Figure 2-9 to get an idea of the information flow for this process.

As you can see, no programming is involved with this method, but rather a combination of standard HTML files with high-level, database markup tags. All database interactions are encapsulated in a single database processing engine. Let's detail the information flow shown in Figure 2-9 by looking at how a query request from a remote client is processed:

1. The user clicks on the "Submit" button on a form or a hypertext link on a page, and the client Web browser sends a request to the Web server.

2. The Web server opens a CGI database script process (in this case, the Cold Fusion process), passing to it the data submitted by the client and pointing it to the appropriate template file.

3. Cold Fusion reads the selection criteria data from the client and processes DBML (the name of the Cold Fusion CGI script) commands used in the template, including the type of request to send to the database and the format that should be used to present information to the results page.

4. Cold Fusion interacts with the database using ODBC.

5. Cold Fusion dynamically generates an HTML page containing the results of the form submission or query and returns it to the Web server.
6. The Web server returns the generated HTML page to the Web browser.

HTML FORMS

HTML supports a relatively complete set of user-interface controls that can be integrated into HTML pages. These controls include single- and multi-line text boxes, list boxes, radio buttons, and check boxes. These input forms are used extensively in CGI database scripting applications.

When an HTML form is submitted from a Web page, the Web server to which it is sent has two responsibilities: capture the data sent by the client browser, and generate a response to be sent back to the client browser. The server fulfills these responsibilities using the CGI script in collaboration with the gateway applications running on your system.

Each HTML form you create has an ACTION attribute that instructs the Web server which CGI script should be executed to process the form submission. This script is passed the contents of the form (data values entered by the user) as well as other relevant contextual information. In order to fulfill the request, the application must then either dynamically generate an HTML page to be returned to the client or route the client to another URL. Here is an example of calling a CGI script from an HTML form:

```
<FORM ACTION="/scripts/
dbml.exe?template=employee.dbm"METHOD=POST>
```

Developing CGI database scripting applications does not require any detailed knowledge of CGI. All client requests are processed using a CGI script included with the scripting product. For example, in Cold Fusion, the script's name is DBML.EXE. Although the term *script* is used here, this program is really a specially configured Win32 application program most likely written in the C language. This script handles interacting with the Web server and database as well as dynamically generating HTML to be sent back to the client browser.

SQL

Structured Query Language is an internationally standardized language used for interacting with relational databases. When developing CGI database scripting applications, you will use SQL to specify precisely what information you want to retrieve from the database, as well as how you want it grouped and sorted. The SQL statements are embedded in the database markup language files as in the following simple example:

```
<DBQUERY
    Name="Employees"
    DataSource="EmployeeData"
    SQL="SELECT * FROM dbEmployees
      WHERE EmpID = '#Form.EID#' ">
```

The special <DBQUERY> tag is recognized by the Cold Fusion CGI script, and the various attributes, specifically the SQL attribute, provide a mechanism for embedding a SQL statement for satisfying the query request.

ODBC

ODBC is a database access API standard proposed and developed by Microsoft. It provides a framework for disparate database systems so that a single application, such as a CGI database scripting application, can easily communicate with all of them.

ODBC works in a parallel fashion with databases. Database vendors provide drivers that implement the specifics of interacting with their database system. Users then use the ODBC Administrator Control Panel to provide logical names for data sources, called Data Source Names (DSNs). CGI database scripting applications can then do their work without knowing any of the particulars of the database system being used. This scheme allows all applications to be compatible with all databases.

DATABASE MARKUP LANGUAGE

A CGI database scripting application enables you to dynamically generate HTML pages based on user queries. These queries are submitted to the CGI script, which passes the data to the database engine. As mentioned earlier, the CGI script for Cold Fusion is called DBML.EXE. The engine processes the data according to a specified template file, runs necessary database queries, and then generates the HTML page, which is sent back to the user. The key to dynamic page generation is the set of database-oriented markup tags contained in the template file. These tags are collectively referred to as Database Markup Language (DBML). DBML tags are similar to HTML tags but are database-oriented. I take a much closer look at this kind of tag in Chapter 4.

Server API

Several Web server software vendors have responded to the renowned CGI performance problem by developing proprietary APIs. An API is native code residing on the Web server that, in a similar manner to CGI, extends the Web server's capabilities. Figure 2-10 shows how proprietary APIs provide tight integration to special features and processes of the Web server. Each API, however, is unique to a particular Web server. Server APIs allow Web database developers to achieve results identical to those with CGI, but allow further customization to meet specific Webtop application requirements.

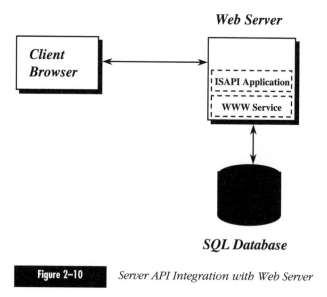

SQL Database

| Figure 2–10 | *Server API Integration with Web Server* |

Server API Overview

APIs are native and proprietary to the Web server software for which they were built. They are created from the ground up to provide the best performance for their native Web servers. ISAPI, for example, is able to improve performance fivefold over CGI on a Web server running Microsoft's IIS. Moreover, APIs use the fewest system resources of the various methods discussed in this chapter. The single most important caveat for developing with server APIs is that the process is considerably more difficult than developing CGI applications, especially if you are coding manually.

API development requires specialized programming techniques like multithreading, process synchronization, direct protocol programming, and error handling. Server API applications or scripts for Windows NT 4.0 Server can be written in almost any 32-bit programming language, such as C or C++ (or virtually any programming language that understands the call-level interface of Microsoft's API). Several flavors of API exist, including Microsoft's ISAPI, Netscape's NSAPI, and O'Reilly's WSAPI. Caution should be taken when using the server API approach, since a buggy ISAPI application could feasibly bring down a Web server.

ISAPI, the native API for Microsoft's IIS and Process Software's Purveyor™ server, allows developers to build interactive applications. ISAPI is able to provide better performance than CGI, since ISAPI applications are Dynamic Link Libraries (DLLs) that are loaded into the same address space as the Web server. Resources are therefore available to all HTTP server processes, and less overhead is available than when calling out to an external CGI script.

Like ISAPI, NSAPI provides Web developers with the ability to customize the base services of the Netscape Web server. NSAPI gives developers the ability to build interfaces with the Web server and external resources such as database servers.

WSAPI is native to O'Reilly's WebSite Web server, providing a set of tools for dynamic Web application development as well as interfaces with back-end resources. In addition to its own proprietary features, WSAPI is able to run ISAPI through an ISAPI-compatibility mode.

Although developing for APIs is potentially difficult, both Netscape's and Microsoft's Web server products include easy-to-use scripting capabilities that run on top of the API. Netscape Enterprise Server comes with LiveWire, and Netscape FastTrack Server offers LiveWire as an option. LiveWire includes a Database Connectivity Library for direct SQL connectivity to relational databases. Microsoft's IIS provides the Internet Database Connector (IDC), an application running on ISAPI. Many third-party tools are also available for linking Web servers to databases.

Another good example of a database development alternative using the server API method is the Microsoft *dbWeb* freeware product. dbWeb is finely suited for building simple database schemas. It runs as an NT service using ISAPI.

ISAPI

ISAPI was designed to provide a foundation for developing new Web server functionality and for operating in conjunction with other systems in the enterprise, such as Microsoft Back Office applications. ISAPI for Windows NT can be used to write applications that Web users can activate by filling out an HTML form or clicking on a link in an HTML page on a Web server. The remote application can then take the user-supplied information and do almost anything with it that can be programmed, and then return the results in an HTML page or post the information in a database. ISAPI also helps developers extend existing Win32 applications for use on the Internet. Documentation for ISAPI as well as the ISAPI Software Development Kit (SDK) is available from Microsoft via subscription to the Microsoft Developer Network (MSDN). ISAPI Internet Server Applications (ISAs), as they are called, are DLLs that are similar to CGI scripts. ISAs are loaded by the IIS (or any other ISAPI-compliant server) WWW service at startup in the same address space as the HTTP server, unlike CGI, which creates a separate process space for every request. Once an ISAPI ISA has been loaded, it remains loaded until the WWW service is stopped. This scenario creates a back-end scripting solution that is higher-performance than CGI and consumes far less RAM. We can examine some of the more important technical aspects of ISAPI now.

The ISAPI specification calls for two entry points into an ISAPI DLL. The first, named GetExtensionVersion(), allows you to return version information about your DLL, making backward compatibility easy in future versions of IIS. The second, named HttpExtensionProc(), is the entry point into your DLL that gets called for every client request. Inside this procedure, you must call either WriteClient() or ServerSupportFunction() to return a formatted response back to the client. Once that step is accomplished, the DLL's API is available to the server and can be executed via a Web browser.

As discussed briefly above, ISAPI competes with NSAPI. NSAPI has the appeal of being cross-platform, at least until you start using operating-system-dependent functionality such as making calls to the Win32 API. As long as you restrict yourself to the ANSI-standard "C" library, porting between different flavors of UNIX and Windows NT should proceed fairly easily. NSAPI appears to be a bit lower-level than ISAPI, and, although more flexible, is also more complicated.

The ISAPI architecture allows for a smaller footprint, since Windows NT does not have to create a separate process or thread for each call to ISAPI. IIS does not create a thread for each connection to it. Instead, Microsoft has opted to create separate threads for each processor in a symmetric multi-processor (SMP) machine. You must manage your data structures internally to avoid relying on writeable static data inside your ISAPI DLL.

Linking an HTML page to your ISAPI DLL is similar to the way CGI works. Using the <FORM> tag, you simply specify a reference to your ISAPI DLL, where the functional method maps to functions in the custom DLL, as in the following:

```
<FORM ACTION=
    "http://207.217.22.134/scripts/amulet.dll"
    METHOD=xxxx>
```

ISAPI also provides for a *filter* mechanism to trap all HTTP requests. Filters allow pre-processing of requests and post-processing of responses, permitting site-specific handling of HTTP requests and responses. You can use this mechanism for implementing custom compression, encryption, authentication (access control), or logging. You can install multiple filters. Once a filter has determined that it must monitor a request, it will receive that data regardless of whether the request is for a file, a CGI application, or an ISAPI application. Figure 2-11 shows how the filter applications operate between the network connection to the clients and the HTTP server. Depending on the options that the filter application chooses, it can act on several server actions, including reading raw data from the clients, processing the headers, conducting communications over a secure port, and other stages in the processing of the HTTP request.

ODBC has proven to be a useful method for transparently communicating with a database, allowing for developers to write to one common API that supports multiple database vendors. Certainly, you can also make ODBC calls from ISAPI-enabled Web servers. You can in fact create very complex data-

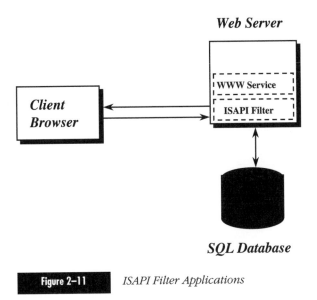

Figure 2-11   *ISAPI Filter Applications*

base-enabled sites by using both ISAPI filters and applications. ISAPI extensions can also be combined with the Internet Database Connector to create highly interactive sites (see Figure 2-12), which could include connections to Microsoft SQL Server databases, Microsoft Access using the desktop ODBC driver, or even other relational and non-relational data sources using one of the ODBC drivers available from various vendors.

Internet Database Connector

The Internet Database Connector is a component of IIS (beginning with version 2.0) that allows Web browsers ODBC database access for HTTP requests. Developers can use this feature to create Web pages with information from the database; to insert, update, and delete information in the database based on user input; and to perform other SQL commands. This concept is represented in Figure 2-13.

Web browsers submit requests to IIS by using HTTP. The server responds with a document formatted in HTML. Access to SQL databases is accomplished through IDC. The IDC, Httpodbc.dll, is an ISAPI DLL that uses ODBC to gain access to databases. Figure 2-14 illustrates the components for connecting to databases from IIS. Httpodbc.dll uses two types of files to control how the database is accessed and how the output Web page is constructed. These files are Internet Database Connector (.idc) files and HTML extension (.htx) files. The IDC files contain the necessary information to connect to the appropriate ODBC data source and execute the SQL statement. An IDC file also contains the name and location of the HTML extension file. The

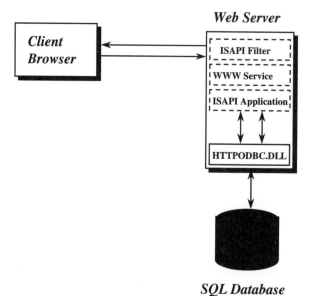

Web Server

Client Browser

ISAPI Filter

WWW Service

ISAPI Application

HTTPODBC.DLL

SQL Database

Figure 2–12 *Server with Filter, ISAPI Application, and IDC*

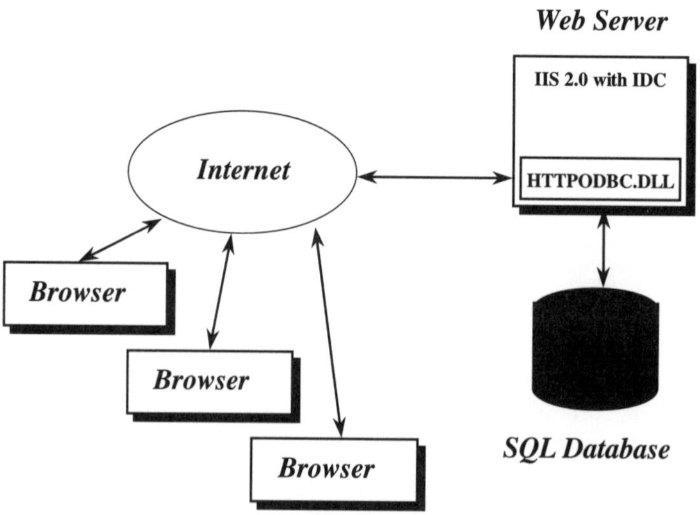

Web Server

IIS 2.0 with IDC

HTTPODBC.DLL

Internet

Browser

Browser

Browser

SQL Database

Figure 2–13 *IDC Database Connectivity Concept*

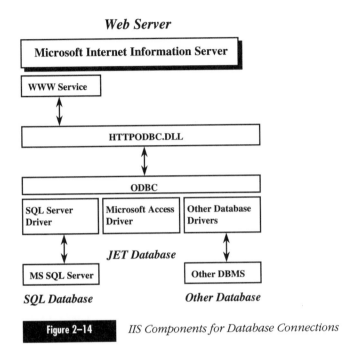

Web Server

Microsoft Internet Information Server

WWW Service

HTTPODBC.DLL

ODBC

| SQL Server Driver | Microsoft Access Driver | Other Database Drivers |

JET Database

MS SQL Server   **Other DBMS**

SQL Database   *Other Database*

Figure 2–14   *IIS Components for Database Connections*

HTML extension file is the template for the actual HTML document that will be returned to the Web browser after the database information has been merged into it by Httpodbc.dll. You see how to use the IDC technology to build an active content Web database in Chapter 4. Although IDC is also available in IIS 4.0, the newer Active Server Pages (ASP) technology has replaced IDC as the database development technology of choice, although ASP requires more programming expertise.

In order to develop a dynamic database Web site using IDC, one way is to use Microsoft Access 97 (part of the Microsoft Office Professional application suite). Access 97 has the ability to save tables, queries, forms, or reports in formats that allow database data to be updated dynamically in a Web page. For static updates of data into HTML tables, Access 97 also has the Internet Assistant for Access now integrated into the product with the *Publish to the Web Wizard*.

Server Side Includes (SSI)

The next technology area that provides the means for Web database connectivity is *Server Side Includes*. In general, SSI is an easy way to have the Web server insert small amounts of dynamic data directly into an HTML document. Figure 2-15 depicts an overview of SSI server organization. A simple example

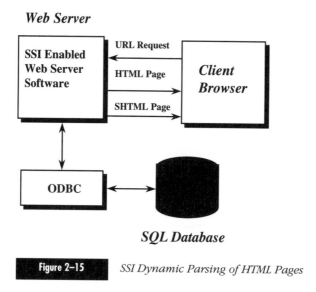

Figure 2–15   *SSI Dynamic Parsing of HTML Pages*

of SSI, which is understandable to anyone with experience surfing the Web, is a Web page counter (although counters are also implemented in various ways not involving SSI). SSI can echo back information such as the current date/ time, the host name of the browser or Web server, provide conditional executions based on logical comparisons, dynamically include one file within another, execute a program (such as a CGI script), send e-mail, and query or update a database. Often, SSI requires no programming.

SSI, however, is not as well suited as CGI or Server APIs are for sending and receiving database information to and from the browser, because SSI doesn't provide the rich programming capability or advanced API-level access to external resources such as database servers that the other techniques offer. Also, SSI requires a fair amount of system CPU and memory overhead, because the Web server has to scan through an entire HTML document to find SSI commands and take the appropriate action.

Not all Windows-NT-based Web servers support SSI. The SSI technology was born on the freeware National Center for Supercomputing Applications (NCSA) HTTPd Web server for the UNIX software platform and continues to be popular on that environment. The official NCSA specifications for SSI can be found at http://www.ncsa.uiuc.edu. Microsoft IIS 3.0 and 4.0 for Windows NT 4.0 supports SSI. The WebQuest NT Web server provides extensions to the NCSA SSI specifications called SSI+ 2.0.

Technical Components

The SSI concept employs special commands and tags included in HTML documents that are processed by the server as the document is served up to the requesting client. Before I address the database-specific issues, look at SSI's basic components. Table 2-3 contains a complete list of standard SSI commands. As the server sends the file, it detects commands of the form shown in the following sample, and processes them by replacing the commands with their results after executing them:

```
<!--#SSIcommand
     tag1="value1" tag2="value2" … -->
```

Notice that the SSI tags are surrounded by HTML comment markers. This technique ensures that the SSI commands are completely ignored by the browser; however, an SSI-enabled server knows to look for them.

Table 2–3	Standard SSI Commands
Command	**Tags**
Config	errmsg, timefmt, sizefmt
Include	virtual, file
Echo	Var
Fsize	virtual, file
Flastmod	virtual, file
Exec	cmd, cgi

HTML is normally rendered in the client browser. So if special SSI commands are present in the document as it is being delivered, the server must parse the document looking for these commands. For this reason, HTML containing SSI commands is non-standard HTML. Ultimately, however, the document arriving at the client PC has only standard tags, because the file containing SSI commands has been parsed by the server prior to delivery. As mentioned before, a performance penalty occurs if the server parses all documents while sending them, so a better method is to assign a special file name extension to files containing SSI commands, such as .SHTML, .SHTM, or .STM. This way, the server need examine only these files for SSI usage. Let's now take a quick look at some examples of each SSI command.

CONFIG COMMAND

The *config* command controls the way other commands are rendered by the browser as the file is parsed. The following example advises the server that all file sizes should be displayed in bytes:

```
<!--#config sizefmt="bytes"-->
```

As another example, the following command requests that the server display file sizes in KB or MB:

```
<!--#config sizefmt="abbrev"-->
```

You can also use config to tell the server which date format to use and what message to send back to the client if an error occurs while parsing the document.

INCLUDE COMMAND

The *include* command instructs the server to insert another file into the current file. For example, the following command tells the server to place the contents of orderform.htm at the location of the SSI command:

```
<!--#include file="orderform.htm"-->
```

ECHO COMMAND

The *echo* command tells the server to include the contents of an SSI environment variable. SSI supports all environment variables available to CGI scripts, plus those shown in Table 2-4.

Table 2–4	SSI Environment Variables
Variable Name	**Description**
DOCUMENT_NAME	The current file name.
DOCUMENT_URI	The virtual path to this document, such as /wwwroot/amuletc/default.htm.
QUERY_STRING_UNESCAPED	The unescaped version of any search query the client sent, with all shell special characters escaped with \.
DATE_LOCAL	The current date, local time zone, subject to the timefmt tag for the config command.
DATE_GMT	Same as DATE_LOCAL, except in Greenwich mean time.
LAST_MODIFIED	The last modification date of the current document. Subject to the timefmt tag for the config command.

For example, you can use the echo command and the *var* tag to render the document name by telling the browser to insert the name of the document in place of the command:

```
<!--#echo var="DOCUMENT_NAME"-->
```

FSIZE COMMAND

The *fsize* command inserts the size of the specified file or directory, as in the following example:

```
<!--#fsize="searchmode.htm"-->
```

FLASTMOD COMMAND

As an example of how you might use the *flastmod* command, suppose that you want to automate reporting the last date and time a page was updated instead of manually editing this information in static HTML. This goal can be achieved with the flastmod SSI command and the *file* tag, as in the following example where the HTML file name appears in quotes after the file tag:

```
<!--#flastmod file="default.htm"-->
```

EXEC COMMAND

The *exec* command executes the specified CGI script, ASP application, or ISAPI application. Caution is necessary when executing a CGI to make sure that it doesn't output a non-HTML file type, such as a graphic image. The following example runs a program named showstats on the Web server located in the standard CGI script directory on Windows NT 4.0 and IIS 4.0, \winnt\system32\inetsrv\scripts:

```
<!--#exec cmd="showstats"-->
```

Note that this command can be used only in HTML pages; it cannot be used in ASP pages.

Database SSI Extensions

Although the concepts illustrated in this section show that SSI is a step in the right direction, the components clearly do not go far enough in terms of providing a means of connecting to a database. True, a CGI script could connect to a database, but with the standard SSI commands, you have no way to control the process. One NT Web server product mentioned earlier, WebQuest, goes much further by offering two ways of extending the SSI specifications to include some new, database-specific methods. The first method involves new SSI commands designed for connecting to and manipulating databases. Table 2-5 contains a list of these new commands.

Here are a few examples of what you might do with these new commands in conjunction with the standard SSI commands. You could record in a database the host name and IP address of the browser coming into a particular page each time a given document is accessed from the Web. Going further, you could meter access to the page, limiting access to the page a certain number of times. You could also add HTML form contents directly to a database after the user submits the form. Let's take a closer look at two examples of the SSI database interface by considering issuing a simple SQL SELECT statement and a SQL INSERT statement.

Table 2–5	SSI Database Extensions for WebQuest Server
Command	**Tag/Description**
odbc	Provides for querying and updating ODBC databases without CGI. Four tags are available: *debug, connect, statement*, and *format*.
Email	Provides for sending an e-mail message without CGI programming and without the *mailto:* HTML component, whenever an HTML page is accessed or an HTML form is submitted. WebQuest includes an SMTP client that can use any SMTP server to send e-mail.
if	Provides for conditional execution of SSI operations and conditional printing of HTML text, based on logical comparisons.
goto	Provides for unconditional jumping to a label without executing any SSI code or printing any HTML text between the goto and label.
label	Provides a location to which a goto may jump.
break	Provides for termination of HTML documents at any point.

SQL SELECT

Probably the most likely operation initiated by a Web page with a database connection is to submit a SQL SELECT statement and display the result-set on the client browser as an HTML document. For example, say that we have an ODBC data source (in this case, a SQL Server database) called *Accounting*, which contains a table named *Customers*. We wish to display a complete list of all customers, contact names, and phone numbers (where the table field names are CompanyName, Contact, and Phone, respectively). To do so, we need some HTML that uses the SSI+ 2.0 ODBC commands to open the database connection, define the proper formatting using table tags, and define the SQL SELECT statement for retrieving the data.

```
<HTML>
<HEAD>
<TITLE>SQL SELECT QUERY EXAMPLE</TITLE>
</HEAD>
<H3>SQL Select Query Example</H3>
<BODY>
<HR>

Query processed on
<!--#echo var="DATE_LOCAL"-->
<BR>Result set follows:
<TABLE BORDER>
<TH>Customer</TH>
```

```
<TH>Contact</TH>
<TH>Phone</TH>

<!--#odbc connect=
     "Accounting,amuletuser,amuletpswd" -->
<!--#odbc format=
     "<TR ALIGN=CENTER>
     <TD>%s</TD> <TD>%s</TD>
     <TD>%s</TD></TR>" -->
<!--#odbc statement=
     "SELECT CompanyName, Contact, Phone
       FROM Customers;" -->

</TABLE>
<HR>
</BODY>
</HTML>
```

In the above HTML code, I specify the ODBC connect string so that a connection to the SQL back end can be made. This includes the ODBC DSN, the user name, and the password. Then I define how the output is to appear with the format tag. Notice how I use "%"s as placeholders for data coming from the database. Since I have three fields specified in the SQL SELECT statement, I have three occurrences of "%"s. I also use HTML <TR> and <TD> table tags to place the data in aligned columns. Finally, I embed a standard SQL SELECT:

```
SELECT CompanyName, Contact, Phone
FROM Customers;
```

Every record in the result set is returned as a line of HTML, as defined by the ODBC format tag. Figure 2-16 shows how the result-set of the query appears in the browser.

SQL INSERT

As a second example, take the point of view of a user who fills out an HTML form and wishes to post the data as a new row in a table in a SQL database. We'll use SSI+ 2.0 to open a database connection and issue a SQL INSERT statement so that the Web-based data entry can occur. Since this example uses an HTML form, we need two documents instead of the one required for the SELECT example. The first file, named *vendor.htm*, contains standard HTML that includes the <FORM> tags and associated tags. Figure 2-17 shows the appearance of this form in a browser. The second file is a parsed HTML document named *insert.sht* containing the SSI tags for the ODBC connection and the SQL Insert statement. Here is the vendor.htm file:

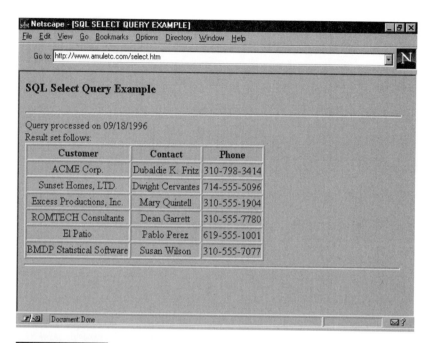

Figure 2–16   *SELECT Query Result-Set*

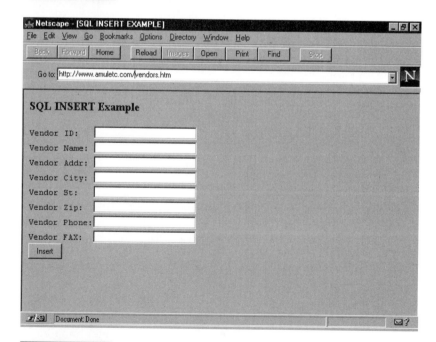

Figure 2–17   *SSI Data Entry Form*

```
<HTML>
<HEAD>
<TITLE>SQL INSERT EXAMPLE</TITLE>
</HEAD>
<H3>SQL INSERT Example</H3>
<BODY>
<FORM ACTION="insert.sht" METHOD="Post">
<PRE>
Vendor ID:    <INPUT NAME="VID" TYPE="Text">
Vendor Name:  <INPUT NAME="VName" TYPE="Text">
Vendor Addr:  <INPUT NAME="VAddr" TYPE="Text">
Vendor City:  <INPUT NAME="VCity" TYPE="Text">
Vendor St:    <INPUT NAME="VSt" TYPE="Text">
Vendor Zip:   <INPUT NAME="VZip" TYPE="Text">
Vendor Phone:<INPUT NAME="VPhone" TYPE="Text">
Vendor FAX:   <INPUT NAME="VFAX" TYPE="Text">
<INPUT VALUE="Insert" TYPE="submit">
</PRE>
</FORM>
</BODY>
</HTML>
```

Take note that the parsed SSI file is referenced by the ACTION attribute of the <FORM> tag. Notice further the VALUE attribute of the <INPUT> tag, which defines an Internet button on the form. Note that problems are inherent with checking user input in forms using Web database applications. For example, most desktop database development environments provide some level of field validation while a user enters data. On the Web (unless the form is actually a client-side scripted, Java, or ActiveX application), the form data cannot be verified until the user clicks on the *submit* button on the form.

Now, here is the insert.sht file:

```
<HTML>
<HEAD>
<TITLE>SQL INSERT EXAMPLE RESULTS</TITLE>
</HEAD>
<H3>SQL INSERT Example Results</H3>
<BODY>
<!--#odbc connect=
      "Accounting,amuletuser,amuletpswd" -->
<!--#odbc statement=
      "INSERT INTO Vendors (VendorID,
      VendorName, VendorAddr, VendorCity,
      VendorSt, VendorZip, VendorPhone,
      VendorFAX) VALUES
      ('&&VID&&', '&&VName&&', '&&VAddr&&',
      '&&VCity&&', '&&VSt&&', '&&VZip&&',
      '&&VPhone&&', '&&VFAX&&')" -->
<HR>New vendor record inserted into table<HR>
</BODY>
</HTML>
```

When the user clicks on the *Insert* button of vendors.htm, the server parses and processes insert.sht, using the values from the form in place of the items (e.g., &&VID&&) in the INSERT SQL statement. The successful completion of the INSERT statement adds a row to the table.

Java Database Connections

The Java language is also able to provide database connectivity, but it does so in a way quite different from CGI, Server API, or SSI. Although Java connectivity is the subject for Chapters 5 and 6, I provide an overview here. The primary vehicle for building Java database connections is the JDK 1.1 and 1.2 component called Java Database Connectivity (JDBC). Chapter 6 is devoted entirely to JDBC access. If you restrict your client users to accessing the database from Windows machines (a likely prospect in the case of an NT-based Intranet), you may also use standard Data Access Objects (DAO), which are part of the Microsoft JET database engine. A section of Chapter 5 discusses the use of DAO with the Microsoft Visual J++ environment. A number of vendors have also developed quality Java-based Rapid Application Development (RAD) tools that include database connections as an integrated application component. I highlight RAD tools for Java in Chapter 5. Also available is a method that is growing in popularity, to use the Common Object Request Broker Architecture (CORBA) with Java in order to communicate with databases by using the Internet Inter-ORB Protocol (IIOP).

I want to first discuss Java database connections in general terms. Instead of connecting to a process or an API from the Web server, users download compiled Java applets embedded in HTML documents for local execution inside a Java-enabled browser. Java's security model makes sure that the running applet is able to link back to a database found on the Web server from which the applet was downloaded. Furthermore, the database access is directly under the control of the Java application logic and does not rely on static HTML representations of the data, as assembled by slow CGI servers.

Using Java usually removes the Web server from the equation entirely. However, some Web servers, including Netscape's, come with an integrated Java interpreter. When an incoming request points to a Java application, the server passes the request to the Java interpreter, which executes the application on the server.

Java applets are able to connect to database servers using native database APIs from the database vendors, or by using JDBC, a common API layer for Java that's functionally equivalent to Microsoft's ODBC.

JDBC

JDBC is a SQL-level API that allows you to embed SQL statements as arguments to methods in JDBC interfaces. To allow you to do so in a database-independent fashion, JDBC requires database vendors to furnish a run-time implementation of its interfaces. The implementations route your SQL calls to the database in the proprietary fashion that it recognizes. As the programmer, however, you need not worry about how JDBC routes your SQL statements. The facade provided by JDBC gives you complete freedom from any issues related to particular database issues. You can run the same code regardless of what database is present.

JDBC accomplishes its goals through a set of Java interfaces, each implemented differently by individual database vendors. The set of classes that implement the JDBC interfaces for a particular database engine is called a *JDBC driver*. In developing a Web database application, you do not have to think about the implementation of these underlying classes in any way. The whole point of JDBC is to hide the specifics of each database and let you worry about only your application.

Without JDBC, only disparate, proprietary database access solutions exist. These proprietary solutions force the developer to build a layer of abstraction on top of them in order to create database-independent code. Only after that abstraction layer is complete can the developer move to actually writing the application.

Of course, the ODBC specification exists to provide this universal abstraction layer for languages like C/C++ and Visual Basic. Unfortunately, ODBC does not enjoy the platform independence of Java. Using the JDBC interface design, however, your server application can pick the database at runtime based on which client is connecting.

DAO

For many desktop and LAN database developers, the Microsoft Access JET database engine serves as the data store for a majority of applications. Certainly some tools, through use of the standard Access ODBC driver, allow for building WebTop applications using JET. However, if your environment of choice is Java, JET may seem to be a thing of the past. Fortunately, this is not the case.

Microsoft has bundled the JET engine with the Visual J++ Java development environment to allow you to easily manipulate Access database tables (stored in standard .MDB files). Instead of a GUI front end to this engine (such as Access), Microsoft has provided a programmatic interface to JET called Data Access Objects (DAO), which is a library of ActiveX components allowing you to instantiate and control JET from any ActiveX-capable programming language.

This scenario does have its limitations however. For example, DAO cannot be used in a cross-platform Java solution. As an ActiveX component, it is available only in the Windows environment. So if the users running your applet or application use anything but Windows machines, DAO is out. Instead, JDBC can run on any platform that supports Java. You see more of using Java with DAO in Chapter 5.

Active Server

With the inclusion of Active Server technology in Microsoft's Internet Information Server (IIS) 3.0 and 4.0 Web server software, database development for the Web took a significant step forward. This is primarily due to the fact that Active Server technology is based on the VBScript scripting language, a derivative of Visual Basic. As a result, the multitude of VB programmers can leverage their programming skills in connecting databases to Web pages.

The server-side scripting engine provides a facility for providing features like:

- Server-side ActiveX controls and ActiveX automation servers
- Pure HTML that is sent unchanged to client browsers
- Reduced dependence on CGI or Server API applications (such as ISAPI)
- Direct database connections using Active Server components
- Client-side ActiveX components
- Both VBScript and JScript (Microsoft's version of JavaScript)

IIS 4.0 adds a smart server framework and the feature set of a reliable scripting engine. The IIS scripting engine uses VBScript on the server and supports sending VBScript and JScript to the browser in the HTML stream. In addition to the scripting engine, IIS also supports its own object model, to help provide the functionality required by active-content Web pages. Active Server also includes a number of ActiveX components designed to execute on the server rather than the client machine. You can even develop custom server-side Active Server components yourself using Visual Basic.

Server-side scripting for IIS differs from the scripting model that you may have used in the past. Traditional scripting requires that the browser support the scripting language being used. When your browser loads a page containing VBScript code, the script code executes within the browser on the client workstation. Active Server scripting, on the other hand, executes entirely on the server. As it executes, it prepares an HTML stream to send to the browser. ActiveX controls used by the server script execute on the server and return information in the HTML stream to the browser.

In the server scripting process, when the browser calls for an Active Server Page (actually an ASCII text file with an .ASP extension), it is first read by the server. Any HTML found in the page is passed directly to the browser, as is any client-side scripting code in the ASP file. When the server encounters server-side script code, it runs the code on the server, instead of sending it to the browser. The script can generate output based on whatever conditions exist at the time.

This capability gives the page its dynamic quality. Depending on what the user has entered in a form or what data resides in a database on the server, the output of the server-side script is created each time the page runs. This output can then go to the browser. Dynamic output from a script can intermingle with static HTML meant for the browser. The browser doesn't know that the page was created dynamically; it simply sees HTML and displays it.

Such a server-generated display may resemble what you see from browser-generated script; however, the process in which it was generated is quite different.

ActiveX Data Objects

The data access component that accompanies Active Server technology is called ActiveX Data Objects (ADO). Microsoft created ADO as a general-purpose Component Object Model (COM) based object model for going against the new OLE DB specification for enterprise data. Although it can be used as a replacement for both Data Access Objects (DAO) and Remote Data Objects (RDO) when interacting with the JET database engine through Visual Basic and VBA, ADO was first released as part of the IIS Active Server technology for providing access to database from Web pages. The primary benefit of ADO over both DAO and RDO is that you can independently create objects. With RDO and DAO, you had to create a hierarchy for your objects. Also, ADO is faster and more efficient. ADO is now included with Visual Basic 6.0.

COM defines the basic protocol for object communication in programming the object model. A useful aspect of ADO is that it is independent of its implementation. What this means is that in the future, you could be using the ADO object model instead of DAO to manipulate the Microsoft Access JET Engine, or FoxPro for that matter. This change is possible because the object model remains constant and the corresponding implementation can be optimized as necessary.

The main principle behind OLE DB is to provide an object-based interface that makes remote objects appear as if they were local. You can see how this model would help you in your development. The goal is to give you helpful objects that provide seamless access to your database, which could reside on a remote server or locally on your machine. See Figure 2-18, which illustrates how ADO and OLE DB team up to provide database access for a SQL Server database. The concept here presents a configuration for a typical Webtop application built using Visual InterDev (the topic of Chapter 8). You can see that the ActiveX Data Object resides within an ASP file on the Web server. When the browser sends a request for database information, the ASP file is called and ADO submits the request via OLE DB to the database server. The topic of ADO is important enough to warrant a separate and focused treatment in Chapter 7.

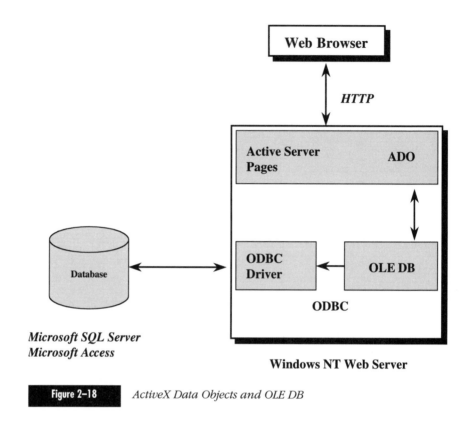

Figure 2–18 *ActiveX Data Objects and OLE DB*

Summary

This chapter has presented a case for using each mainstream methodology in publishing corporate data on the Web. Depending on many factors, such as software development expertise, hardware/software resources, and desired performance, just to name a few, you might prefer one method over the others. Some techniques are simply more contemporary—for example, Java and Active Server technologies have become quite popular as of late, whereas CGI and SSI, once the tools of choice, are now losing the popularity contest. For some of the database technologies examined, I provided some examples and will not discuss them further, whereas others will be studied more in depth in later chapters of this book. Specifically, I continue our focus for Web databases by examining the following technologies: the IIS Internet Database Connector (IDC), SQL Server Web Wizard, Visual J++, Java and JDBC, Active Server Pages and ADO, Access Publish to the Web Wizard, and Cold Fusion (CGI script).

Hardware/ Software Requirements

This chapter identifies all hardware and software components required for establishing a Web server capable of processing database queries. Many of these requirements are the same as those for a server that is not database-enabled; however, given that another major piece of software, namely a back-end SQL database, enters the equation, special considerations must be examined. Much of the planning behind a Web database installation must take into account and be able to accommodate not only expected HTML page hit counts, but also the query volume and the structure of the queries being submitted. A single user request from a query dialog form, for example, could result in a multi-join query that on average yields a sizable result-set.

I start by enumerating the various required PC system hardware components as well as special communication hardware. Then I discuss some options for obtaining sufficient bandwidth from an Internet connection, allowing for effective processing of database requests. Finally, I review the three major pieces of software running on a database-enabled Web server: the operating system (Windows NT), the Web server software (Microsoft IIS), and the back-end SQL database (Microsoft SQL Server). I assume the simple case, where all software components reside on a single Web server, whereas in a production environment these components are often distributed among multiple servers—for example, a dedicated Web server for the Web server software, and another dedicated NT server for running SQL Server.

The other software running on the server is the query application, the process under which the database is queried. In some environments, this software runs on the same server as the Web server software, yet in others, some of the applications may run on a server distinct from the Web server. Many strategies exist for implementing this software. These are covered in later chapters.

Choosing a Hosting Solution

The reason may not be entirely obvious why a developer cannot simply apply the same business model currently in effect for building static-content Web sites with active-content sites that include database connectivity. In this section, I discuss some tradeoffs regarding the hosting solution for a database-enabled Web site. Fundamentally, you have three choices: a hosted site, a co-located server, and an in-house Web server. Each solution has its own set of pros and cons for constructing Internet, Intranet, and Extranet database applications.

Hosted Web Site

Many static-content Web site designers rent space on a physical Web server belonging to an Internet Service Provider (ISP) on behalf of their clients. The designer creates an account in their client's name and obtains access to the secure directory assigned to the account. In this directory, HTML text files, graphic images, sound, video, and any other file type supported by software operating on the server is stored away and given appropriate names so that Web browsers may find this information. Typically the maximum amount of server space for a particular Web site is limited by the ISP (for example, 10 MB of combined space for all file types). Additional charges are levied for additional hard disk space. Any continued development of the Web site or later enhancements are first performed locally on the designer's PC or LAN and then transferred via File Transfer Protocol (FTP) to the Web server.

This division of responsibility is very clean because each professional involved in the process provides the customer with specialized service. The ISP is generally not in the business of developing Web sites (although ISPs do offer such services, and others refer Web design projects to partner firms) and makes its profit on re-selling bandwidth and server space while providing administrative functions such as account maintenance, billing, backup, maintaining constant connections, and providing new server-side facilities that the sites operating on their server may utilize (such as streaming audio and video server components, and e-commerce components such as shopping carts).

The Web site designer may ignore many of the details of the physical server, often times to the extent that they don't care whether the server is based on Windows NT, UNIX, or even MAC-OS. Designers operate at a higher level of abstraction, caring more about the content of the pages they place on the server. So for this reason, changing servers is frequently a simple task of substituting the IP address (e.g., 207.217.39.6) of the new site for the old IP address. ISPs typically "own" a block of IP addresses that they assign to individual clients.

Problems may arise, however, if the Web designer requires special software residing on the server used for development of the site. A different Web server owned and operated by a new ISP may not have this software available for its customers. In this situation, the Web site would not function properly. Examples of such specialized, server-side software are an audio server, an authorization server, electronic commerce software, and of specific concern for the readers of this book, database management software. The new server may have different software (possibly because the server runs a different OS) or may not even support the services provided by the current server. Certainly, sufficient research should precede the move of a Web site to another server.

For the above reasons, ISPs have been slow to introduce sophisticated database software for use by their clients' Web sites. As you'll see in later chapters, developing database applications requires both client- and server-side software: database access software for the server and application design software for the client (the remote Web designer). Such cooperation can be difficult, especially over great physical distances. Some of the more contemporary ISPs have begun offering simplistic database software capabilities on their servers (e.g., allowing sites to access Microsoft Access databases), but for reasons that will become clear by the end of this chapter, this solution is far from optimal.

One of the biggest drawbacks with the hosted solution is that the ISP typically offers very limited remote access to NT services, such as the NT performance monitor, IIS Service Manager, ODBC DSN creation, modifying NT Registry settings, SQL Server configuration, etc. This means that the Web designer is at the mercy of the ISP to provide him/her adequate access to the server.

Co-Located Web Servers

Another solution that can be quite attractive as a cost-effective step up from the hosted solution, yet quite at the level of flexibility of an in-house solution, is co-location. Co-location is now offered by many larger ISPs, many of which do not offer hosting at all. With co-location, the client must purchase the server PC themselves and physically place the server in the ISP's data center, typically in a large room full of other co-located servers. In essence, you're renting rack space and benefiting from the close proximity to the large "pipes" (bandwidth sources).

One of the benefits of co-location is that the ISP provides 24/7 (24 hour per day, 7 days per week) facility management to guard against power outages, brown-outs, theft, fire, etc. This avoids the need to hire such personnel yourself. In addition, the ISP staff is often available to reboot the server, insert tapes for backup, check system status, and perform other administrative tasks.

Since you "own" the server, you also have complete control over what happens inside your box. This means that you may use a remote control program such as pcAnyWhere™ to obtain remote NT console access and perform the same operations as you would if you were typing on the system console. Some ISPs will even allow you to install remote boot hardware devices in the event you need to issue a "hard" reboot of the server. The only time you'd need to actually pay a visit to your server is when you need to install new software and have to physically insert a CD-ROM or diskette.

Another important benefit is that with a co-located Web server, your site is the only site running on the server and thus will not be affected by any potential misdeeds of any one of a number of other sites all running on the same server with the hosting solution (some ISPs host upwards of 100 sites on a single server, each vying for server resources).

Generally speaking, the co-location approach is more costly than hosting, but much less than maintaining an in-house server.

In-House Web Servers

When building Web database applications, an in-house Web server is often the optimal choice. The bottom line is that you frequently need hands-on control over the Web server for performing various tasks relating to authoring sites with database content. For instance, each database publishing tool that I highlight in this book has a server-side component that must be installed and maintained on the Web server itself. This server-side software depends on the target hardware/software platform. For example, some of the new tools are designed for Windows NT only, so if your host server is UNIX-based, you have inherent incompatibility. In addition, the back-end database software requires tuning for specific applications and regular administrative maintenance. Replication is another distributed database requirement best handled with hands-on access.

As an example, consider the use of Microsoft's Visual InterDev 6.0 site development environment coupled with SQL Server as the back-end database. This configuration requires the Microsoft IIS 4.0 software and the Active Server Pages server-side extensions. It also requires the Visual InterDev client-side software. To manage this arrangement effectively, you'll need access to the IIS Service Manager from the NT server's console. If your site accesses SQL Server, you'll need to administer the database with either SQL Server Enterprise Manager or Visual InterDev. Both methods require a close connection to the Web server, i.e., console access, or from a workstation on the LAN to which the server is connected.

Another important area of flexibility is the ability to quickly address increased demands for the site. If user demand suddenly shoots upward, an in-house Web server means that you can easily add RAM, add an additional hard drive, or even add additional servers. With either the hosted or co-located solution, scaling the server architecture is not as easily performed.

Scalability

Regardless of the hosting solution you choose, a given Web database application may need a scaleable architecture to address rising demands for the service provided by the Web site. This situation is especially true of e-commerce Web sites (which are all based on database systems). One reliable approach towards scalability is the three-tier computing architecture. Here, the three main services of a software application are distributed across multiple servers.

The client-tier represents the user interface with which the user interacts. The so-called middle-tier is where you store the business logic of the application, namely rules that decide how the program should process data. Finally, the data-tier is program code embedded in the back-end database server, typically in the form of stored procedures and triggers.

By spreading the processing requirements across more than one server, you're better able to balance the processing load so that the application can handle more users and more data.

Web Server Hardware Platform

Now turn your attention to the specific hardware components involved with building a database-enabled Web server. I consider items such as the microprocessor, CPU cache, memory requirements, as well as optimal hard disk characteristics. Next, I look at several secondary, though important, hardware factors, such as CD-ROM, backup capabilities, and system power. Figure 3-1 shows an overall structure of a representative Web server hardware configuration.

Intel Processor Based

As one of the themes of this book, I consider only Web servers based on the Intel (or equivalent) family of microprocessors. Generally speaking, the server supporting database query processing should contain the latest and fastest processors available. At the time of writing (and this is sure to change even by the time this book hits the shelves), the fastest processors have a clock speed of 450MHz. Normally, however, the speed of the CPU around which a Web server is based is not the most crucial factor when predicting overall performance. If any bottlenecks do arise, the CPU will most likely not be the cause. Other facets such as the bandwidth of the Internet connection, amount of available RAM, or even hard disk average seek time, often dictate perfor-

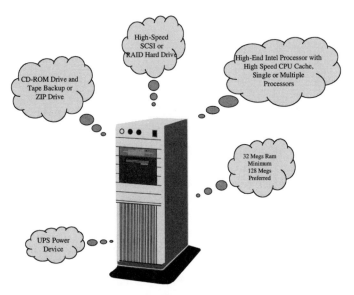

Windows NT Web Server "Ideal Configuration"

Figure 3-1	*General Web Server Hardware Configuration*

mance. Still, Web database applications running on the server will surely appreciate and use as many CPU clock cycles as are available. This use is a sign of the special nature of back-end database processing.

Scalability is another important consideration when planning a Web server environment. In many computing environments, a single processor can become taxed, given certain consistent workloads. Scalability is the trait of a hardware and operating system configuration that allows for adding multiple processors and using incrementally increased processing power for distributed computing tasks. Fortunately, multiple Intel processors, formally known as Symmetric Multi-Processors (SMP), are supported by Windows NT Server. In fact, both NT and SQL Servers can utilize the benefits of SMP if available.

High-Speed CPU Cache

Traditionally, a Web server is a member of the group of traditional file server architecture PC-based systems, in that most of what happens internally involves moving files around the network. To be specific, not much CPU-intensive processing occurs on a typical Web server. The basic HTTP protocol does not yield CPU-intensive processing. This fact, however, is rapidly changing due to the active content requirements, including database components, of today's Web sites. Simply stated, more is happening on the server side than ever before. The so-called emphasis on "thin clients" offloads more and more processing requirements on the server. For example, the back-end database optimizes queries and applies business rules in the form of stored procedures, server-side Java applets, ODBC layers, etc., and runs them all on the server.

Memory caches are now quite popular and tend to improve performance even when using the increasingly popular Extended Data Out (EDO) RAM. Make sure that the external cache is at least 512K and uses 15ns or less cache chips. A cache works because typical applications (such as a back-end database) and custom code (stored procedures) perform repetitive operations. A given program tends to run loops of code or data that fit in 4K or 64K. By keeping chunks of data of this size in very fast cache memory, you improve the chances that the requested data can be found in the cache instead of going out to the hard disk. Disk access is very expensive in terms of system performance. Some vendors offer machines with 1 MB of external cache, while some servers with less than the full 512K cache, namely 256K, are too small for a high-powered server CPU with a 64-bit data bus. In this section, I itemize the various popular CPU caching mechanisms. Performance-wise, the pipeline burst cache is considered the fastest.

INTERNAL CACHE

The internal cache or L1 cache is integrated into the processor chip itself. Since it is integrated on the chip and uses the CPU's internal rather than external clock for memory access, data in an L1 cache can be accessed more quickly than anywhere else except for data in the CPU's registers. Unfortunately, an L1 cache is typically small, as some chips have only 2K to 16K internal caches.

EXTERNAL CACHE

An external cache, or L2 cache, is cache memory that is not integrated onto the processor itself, but rather in an external chip on the motherboard (typically 64K to 512K of 12-15ns SRAM chips, where main memory is commonly 60-80ns DRAM chips). L2 is clocked using the external clock rather than the internal CPU clock. It serves to supplement the L1 cache and enlarges the total cache size (it does not disable the L1 cache). Several types of L2 caches exist, and they can vary considerably in size. In general, asynchronous L2 caches are the slowest; synchronous burst or pipeline burst L2 caches are somewhat faster. Typical systems have between 256K and 1 MB per processor of L2 cache.

PIPELINE BURST CACHE

This is a type of L2 cache that offers considerable advantages in performance with chip sets that can support it. A synchronous pipeline burst secondary cache can give as much as 20% boost in performance over standard asynchronous caches of the same size on motherboards that support it and can cut the time required for some 90% of RAM accesses by more than half, a considerable savings that can't be realized via faster CPU clock speeds. For some motherboards, this type of L2 cache is the most desirable to have.

WRITE-BACK L1 AND L2 CACHE

This type of cache can operate in two different modes: write-back and write-through. They differ in when a write to memory is seen as completed by the processor. Write-through cache waits to report completion of a write until both the cache and DRAM have been updated. Write-back cache reports that the write is complete when the transfer cycle memory has completed the write; the DRAM can then be updated when the memory bus is free from the content of the cache. Write-back cache is faster, but is more complex to implement, and is not supported by some older systems.

Conventional RAM Requirements

One potential bottleneck in a Web server configuration is the total amount of RAM available for system software tasks. Plain and simple, Windows NT Server is quite memory-hungry, that is, the operating system will gladly use all the memory you give it. Typically, the minimum advisable amount of RAM for an NT Server PC is 64 MB, although considering that a database-aware Web server also has two additional and demanding pieces of software, the Web server software and the back-end database, more memory is typically required for reasonable performance. 128 MB seems to be the consensus minimum amount, although more is even better. I show you in the SQL Server for NT section later in this chapter that the back-end database software component has its own agenda as far as memory goes. Many high-capacity sites that handle thousands of hits and consequent database queries per day, may require up to 512 MB for adequate performance. Some sites have even added an extreme amount of RAM, e.g. 1 GB, to ensure that much of the database remains in cache for speedy queries.

Hard Disk

In any server configuration, one of the most limiting factors when considering overall performance has to be hard disk speed. When determining the size and speed of the hard drive around which the server shall be based, you have two disk technologies to consider: IDE (Integrated Digital Electronics) and SCSI (Small Computer Systems Interface). Performance-wise, SCSI is the winner, no question, but when price enters into the equation, the IDE solution becomes more attractive. Most PC servers use a form of the SCSI interface. SCSI is designed with performance in mind. Many desktop systems, however, automatically come with an IDE drive and controller installed. The reason is that desktop PCs do not typically require extremely fast disk access, but servers, on the other hand, have the task of providing data to requesting applications as quickly as possible. Given that your Web server has a reasonably fast Internet connection, the success of your active content Web site may depend on the disk component of your system.

An age-old computing scenario still applies to Web server technology, namely, how much data you can siphon from a disk is at least indirectly related to the speed of the drive's spindle. A RAID (Redundant Array of Inexpensive Disks) increases the number of spindles. If a Web server has an array of five 8 GB drives that each have a spin rate of, say, 7200 RPM and your data is distributed across the five drives, then when a data request occurs, all five spindles may participate; therefore, the information is pulled at an effective rate of 5 times the speed of an individual drive. Dual controllers may further improve throughput.

Here is a typical scenario using a RAID: use one drive for the operating system and system paging file, one or more pairs of mirrored drives for logs, as many spindles as possible in a RAID 5 set for the data including indexes; and use non-RAIDed or striped disks for dumps and/or input files. You can use hardware mirroring and hardware RAID also.

CD-ROM

Server software and database software have both evolved to the point where the distribution media of choice is now exclusively CD-ROM. The mere size of most software packages warrants CD distribution due to the size of the components, often including Windows help documentation, drivers, server-side and client-side components, sample files, etc. An efficient Web server should have a CD-ROM drive for loading new pieces of software as they are required. Currently, a variety of CD-ROM drive speeds are available, although this factor is not important, because server-side software needs to be loaded on an infrequent basis and once loaded, the CD is typically not needed again.

Backup Methods

The importance of some form of fast, high-capacity backup facility cannot be overemphasized. On a Web server hosting a Web site(s) containing database connectivity (or even simple static content sites), you have many important files such as databases, indexes, not to mention standard HTML, graphics, multimedia, CGI programs, configuration files, and many others that contribute to the overall picture. Often, more than one site is hosted on a single server; thus you must provide regular and frequent backup of all important site files. On a less frequent basis, system and application software should also become part of the backup process.

One popular form of backup is a high-capacity tape drive, which may be your best choice. You should note that SQL databases are generally quite compressible. For extremely large databases, you may consider using a tape changer to further automate the process. Another approach is to backup the SQL database to disk and then backup to tape, but this is feasible only if you have the spare disk space.

Another method of backing up data components is through a workstation that has a backup device. Zip™ and Jazz™ drive technology from Iomega (another competing technology comes from Syquest) has become quite popular of late and offers inexpensive and flexible means for backing up crucial portions of the Web server. You can also use writable CDs and DVD devices as other possible choices for backup.

Power Considerations

As with any PC server, your Web server's power should be regulated in a quality manner. Three types of power protection devices are available to protect your server from power problems. First, an *Uninterruptible Power Supply* (UPS) is mandatory to insure that your Web server remains operating during a power failure or low power situation. If you lose primary AC power in the wall from the commercial source, the UPS kicks in to keep the server running. The cost of a UPS is partially tied to the length of time the server continues to run after the power goes away. The lower-cost units provide several minutes (all the way up to 30 minutes for the more costly devices) of up time while informing the operating system that it must clean up and shut down. Software accompanies most UPS devices, with the more robust versions actually able to interface to a public paging system so as to send out a page for the responsible person. Today's Webmasters can now be summoned in real time by their Web servers as they lose power.

Next is the *power filter*, a device that senses very sharp and short duration spikes of power that last only for a few millionths of a second, but are in the range of 10K volts or more. Such spikes could be caused by lightning. A filter takes this excess voltage and runs it off to an electrical ground. A filter, however, does nothing for a voltage sag or surge, as those power conditions occur relatively slowly with respect to a power spike. The filter is designed to respond to rapid changes in power situations.

Finally, a *power conditioner* is a device that senses the power changes generated by power anomalies such as those generated by large appliances such as an air conditioner, elevator, or refrigerator. A conditioner senses relatively slow changes in power and compensates by adjusting the output power to the device to a constant 120 VAC. A conditioner does not filter voltage, but rather maintains a steady 120 volts.

Internet Connection and Communication Hardware

The most obvious and potentially critical ingredient in the database-enabled Web server equation is the type of Internet connection you select to supply the bandwidth required for the target application(s). Often, when initially launching a site, the reaction of its intended audience and therefore its bandwidth requirements may be a complete surprise or at least difficult to estimate. For example, a product distributor going global for the first time may be pleasantly surprised to learn that publishing its inventory files on the Web resulted in increased sales, and over a span of a few months, the bandwidth the site designers thought would be enough turned out to be insufficient. For this reason and the additional costs of changing your type of Internet connection, every attempt should be made to project bandwidth requirements upward based on the expected type, style, and result-set size of the queries your database-enabled Web server must support. In this section, I review the bandwidth options currently available from Internet Service Providers (ISPs) and your telephone company (*telco* for short). As with all the connection alternatives discussed in this section, the charges levied by ISPs and local phone companies vary widely. You must do your homework to get the best deal.

I focus on two common scenarios: the case where you intend to operate a standalone Web server, not attached to a LAN, and the case in which in addition to your Internet connection, your Web server will be a part of (or even the center of) at least a small-scale LAN with workstations running Windows 95/98 or Windows NT 4.0 Workstation. The small LAN approach allows you to more easily do Web database development and administration, since these tasks can be performed remotely from a workstation instead of the server console. While I'm at it, I also outline the additional communication hardware components required.

Suffice it to say, an organization running an Intranet application may not need an Internet connection at all, since the users of the database application are limited to users of the corporate TCP/IP LAN.

Point-to-Point

A point-to-point (PTP) Internet connection is the optimal choice in terms of performance and bandwidth, but it also carries the highest price tag. The most common examples of such lines are called T1 (and higher-speed variants such as T2 and T3). The T1 class of connection involves a direct connection between your Web server and the ISP through use of a leased data line from the phone company. One characteristic of a point-to-point connection is that the phone company will charge a per-mile fee for the distance between the Web server and the ISP. Depending on the distance, this cost could be prohibitive.

Frame Relay

Frame Relay is a popular alternative to the high-speed connections described above. Unlike the direct connections between the ISP and the Web server for PTP, Frame Relay makes use of the *Frame Relay Cloud* supported by your local telephone company, although some ISPs advertise private Frame Relay clouds that guarantee certain bandwidth availability. This indirect connection passes data packets between your server and the ISP. You have no mileage charges from the phone company for Frame Relay, as long as you are within the phone company's rather large Frame Relay service area.

You'll find a variety of bandwidth capacities with Frame Relay technology, beginning with a 56 KB digital circuit. From here is 128 KB and 384 KB Fractional T1 Frame Relay and then a full T1 Frame Relay. A good initial choice of speed for Frame Relay is 128 KB. Even though you may not expect to use all this bandwidth initially, going with the slower and less expensive 56 KB option will cost you a premium when you do decide to upgrade the connection. The reason is that a different type of connection is needed to move to 128 KB and thus requires additional set-up fees and hardware components. Considering this factor, to go with 128 KB up front is best.

ISDN

The *Integrated Services Digital Network* (ISDN) offers yet another connection option for your Web server. You may face the same mileage-sensitive costs associated with the Point-to-Point technique, however. The additional hardware required is an ISDN router needed for LAN-to-Internet communication over inexpensive ISDN lines.

The main differentiating characteristic of ISDN versus other types of bandwidth connections is that it can accommodate three types of data: voice/phone, fax, and pure data. All three types of data share the bandwidth of a single line and get separated out on the receiving side. ISDN links are available in several styles and speeds: 32 KB, 56 KB, 64 KB, 128 KB. For a database-enabled Web server, the 128 KB speed provides the widest bandwidth for pure data. At 128 KB, you'd actually be using two 64 KB data channels multiplexed together on one virtual circuit. When you connect to your ISP, a single 64 KB data channel is started and the second channel is started only after the first one fills up.

Dedicated SLIP/PPP

Another type of low-bandwidth alternative is a dedicated SLIP/PPP connection. Unlike a dial-up SLIP/PPP connection, the dedicated type is available 24 hours per day and typically requires a modem capable of supporting up to 56.6K baud. This type of connection may prove useful during the testing phase for a newly developed Web-database-enabled site.

DSL

A very cost-effective alternative to costly T1 lines is the *Digital Subscriber Line* (DSL) technology now available. Using existing copper wiring, DSL provides data access speeds that compare to T1 access at a fraction of the cost. DSL is relatively new, and some telephone companies are still not up to speed with this technology. DSL, however, does have the most attractive cost of the connection types mentioned thus far. An additional piece of hardware, a DSL router, is required for DSL operation.

Router

Regardless of whether your server is part of a LAN, if a high-speed type of Internet connection makes sense for your database application, you're going to need a piece of hardware called a *router*. The function of a router is to act the role of data traffic director on a very congested highway. It is the hardware component responsible for directing data packets to their intended recipient through use of IP addresses.

Router devices come in varying degrees of design and power. Generally, routers are classified in terms of the number of connections they can handle. A router designed to handle only a few connections costs much less than one that can handle 1000 users. Many vendors are available for routers, and the specific type of router you need largely depends on the type of Internet connection you decide to obtain.

CSU/DSU

A bit of mystery seems to be surrounding this required piece of hardware when connecting up to a Web server; even the definition of the acronym varies. A Customer Service Unit/Data Service Unit (aka Channel Service Unit, Digital Service Unit), or *CSU/DSU* for short, is a communications device, similar in function to a modem. Originally, this piece of equipment was two pieces, the DSU being owned by the phone company and the CSU by the customer. However, when the ruling came to pass that the telephone companies had to allow customers to connect their own equipment directly to the phone lines, these boxes merged and are now found as a single CSU/DSU unit.

The CSU/DSU, as stated above, is similar in function to a modem, only it performs its functions over leased lines. The CSU/DSU translates standard computer protocols such as RS-232 or V.35 to the four-wire setup used by the phone company. Just like a modem, a CSU/DSU of similar functionality has to be on the opposite end of the line. In most cases, this is your ISP. The CSU/DSU also connects into a router, which is in turn connected via Ethernet to your LAN. A CSU/DSU also provides and generates status about its operational state and the state of the communication line. This enables your provider to test your CSU/DSU and line condition from inside their office. Many bandwidth providers will either offer to sell you a router and CSU/DSU package, or tell you what kind you need. Although you can go out and purchase a different brand and possibly achieve a working connection with your ISP, this is not a certainty. However, you may decide that some of the CSU/DSU special features of a certain brand, such as data compression, network management, encryption, and more, are worth the investigative effort required to ensure compatibility.

As with routers, many quality products are available from a variety of vendors. In fact, many contemporary routers now include CSU/DSU functionality all in a single unit.

Hub

A *hub* is a piece of hardware needed to connect network devices in a LAN environment. With respect to your Web server, the hub is responsible for connecting all the hardware components together: the Web server, the workstations, print server, and the router (which is in turn connected to the Internet connection). Consider the simple Web server communication configuration shown in Figure 3-2. This network topology can be expanded using multiple hubs. A hub can act as the central device in a small network or it can be a part (subnet) of a large network. Attaching two or more hubs together requires a configuration called *cascading* and involves connecting one hub to another hub using a special crossover port.

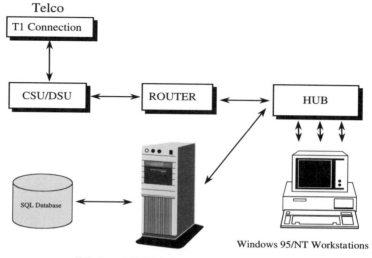

Figure 3–2   *Web Server Communication Configuration*

The physical connections between the hub and individual components are commonly made via 10BASE-T cable (or the higher-capacity 100BASE-T), an Ethernet cable system that uses unshielded twisted-pair wiring with RJ-45 eight-conductor plugs at each end. Although some companies still use the thin Ethernet cable consisting of quarter-inch black coaxial cable, most LANs now use 10BASE-T cabling. Length limitations exist with both types of cabling. 10BASE-T cable segments must not exceed 100 meters (around 328 feet) in length, while thin Ethernet cable segments should not exceed 185 meters (around 600 feet) in length. The minimum distance between nodes must be .5 meters (approximately 1.5 feet).

Bandwidth Requirements Analysis

Estimating precisely how much bandwidth is necessary for a particular Web site is not always an exact science. Such factors as the number of expected concurrent connections, type of information transferred (e.g., graphics, audio, video, etc.), electronic commerce transactions, and many others all play a role in making this important determination. Database-enabled sites present yet another twist. You must add query complexity (in terms of join types and WHERE complexity), table sizes, and result-set size to the standard list of factors.

One thing that is certain is that you should always put a limit on the result-set size being delivered by the SQL back end. You can easily imagine a user, or even more damaging, a group of users submitting a virtually unbounded query (such as the query that selects all rows from a table: `SELECT * FROM Inventory`) and the burden that would be placed on the Web server, as well as the connection to transfer all the data back to the browser. Fortunately, in Microsoft SQL Server, for example, the SET ROW-COUNT Transact-SQL statement limits the size of the result-set for a query.

Regardless of how precisely you can determine the bandwidth requirements formula ahead of time, you need to be able to monitor the bandwidth utilization of a database-enabled Web site. Fortunately, many contemporary ISPs provide bandwidth analysis facilities for their clients' hosted and co-located Web sites. Through use of a browser-based application, clients may determine how much bandwidth was used during a fixed time interval, e.g., a certain 24-hour period.

TCP/IP Intranet Test Case

Before going live with your new server, a prudent and cost-effective step (considering the costs going to your telco and ISP) would be to configure and tune all the system software components, as well as develop the Internet database offline using a simple TCP/IP network in your development office. This type of LAN can be viewed as a test case *intranet*, which is nothing more than an Ethernet LAN using the TCP/IP protocol and running Internet software (i.e., a Web server and client browsers). Since you're not actually live on the Net yet, you can have your choice of IP addresses or just use DHCP for dynamic assignment of IP addresses. For example, you could set up a trivial case (1 node) test network using a Windows NT 4.0 Server configured for TCP/IP along with a Network Interface Card (NIC) to connect to a single Windows NT 4.0 Workstation PC or Windows 95/98 PC, also configured appropriately for TCP/IP. Both Windows NT and 95/98 support multiple communications protocols. You'll need both TCP/IP and NETBUI protocols installed for the architecture we're discussing. The workstation must also have a NIC installed and you must string a physical cable from the server. The cabling scheme you decide to use may require an additional hardware component. If you use thin coax, the familiar chained approach with standard BNC connectors works fine. If you would rather go with the popular 10BASE-T cabling with RJ-45 connectors, then a hub device is necessary. A hub promotes the star network topology, because all network machines are attached directly into its own port in the hub.

After building your Web application and installing the server-side software components, you could then bring up a Web browser on the workstation to point to your new Web page on the server for the purpose of testing out all the potential queries. Working offline first allows you to concentrate on the software development in an isolated environment, necessary for efficient debugging; plus your database performance during development will be vastly superior to the live Web.

Windows NT 4.0 Server

In this section, I look at using Microsoft Windows NT Server as the operating system upon which your database Web server runs. I consider only the 4.0 version of the operating system, because most NT installations have now upgraded from the older 3.51 release. The issues discussed here will be OS-specific. In the next section, I explore tuning issues dealing with SQL Server.

When attempting to install the Microsoft IIS 4.0 (for NT 4.0) Web server software, you should note that the latest NT Service Pack may be required. To obtain the latest NT release information as well as technical support relating to many of the topics in this chapter, I recommend the Microsoft Web site's technical support area and knowledge base, the CompuServe Windows NT forum (GO WINNT), or the Beverly Hills Software Web site's Windows NT Resource Center (see Figure 3-3 for this home page) at www.bhs.com.

Let's now take a look at some NT tuning topics that you should be aware of during system testing and production operations. I present this detailed information as a roadmap of sorts for the technical Webmaster in administering database Web sites.

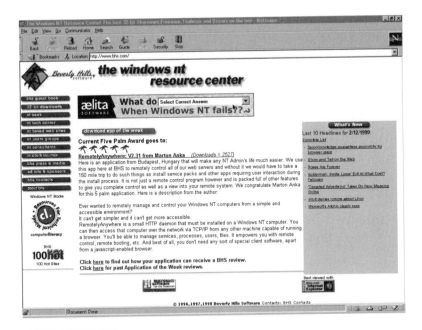

Figure 3–3   *The Windows NT Resource Center Web Site*

CPU Performance

Windows NT comes with an excellent system monitoring utility called Performance Monitor (Perfmon). With Perfmon, you can add various *Counters* to the utility's charting component to see a real-time graph of these statistics. See Figure 3-4 for the Add to Chart dialog box. To determine whether your server's CPU is becoming overtaxed, you should bring up Perfmon and watch the *Processor* object with the *Processor Time* counter activated. This counter shows processor time as a percentage of the elapsed time that a processor is busy executing a non-idle thread. See Figure 3-5 for an example of this administration tool. When monitoring an NT Server, you are really monitoring the behavior of its objects. If your CPU is being utilized 90% or more on a regular basis, then you're a candidate for a processor upgrade (even if it's just a clock doubler). When you select your server hardware, seriously consider those that have sockets for extra processors. Adding an additional processor chip later is a much more economical way to buy more power than having to build a whole new server.

Often apparent CPU bottlenecks are actually subtle hardware problems. To find out whether this case applies, take a look at the *Interrupts/second* counter in the Processor object. On a moderately busy Web server (several dozen concurrent connections), an average of 100 interrupts per second may

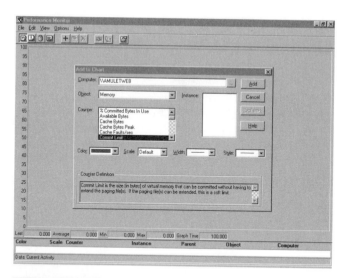

Figure 3–4 *Adding Counters to Chart with Perfmon*

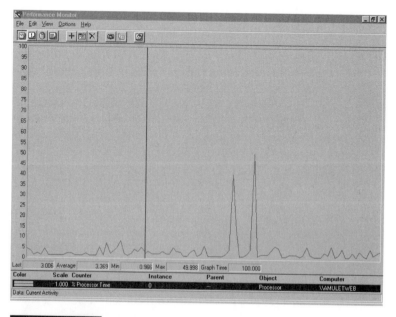

Figure 3–5 *Perfmon with Processor Time Counter Active*

occur. Even an NT server doing very little will idle around that number. This indicates that if the interrupts per second approach 600 or more, you probably have a failing board that is producing a flood of interrupts or a badly written device driver. You can flush out badly designed device drivers. Monitor that the *Context Switches* counter in the *System* object stays less than 500. If it becomes greater, then some device driver has built-in critical sections that are too long. If the Context Switches are smaller, additional diagnostic software may be required to point out the offending hardware.

Here's another cause of poor server performance that may not be at all obvious. Use Perfmon to check the CPU utilization of your screen saver program. Some screen savers have extremely CPU-intensive interfaces and could steal more than 90% of the CPU's power. Switching to another screen saver could actually improve server performance to a considerable degree.

Memory Tuning

In addition to CPU bottlenecks, memory utilization can also become a problem area in terms of NT server performance. For example, NT uses a high percentage of available memory, as much as half, as a disk cache. To review memory status using Perfmon, check the *Memory* object, *Committed Bytes*. Its value should be less than your server's actual physical memory. Then check to make sure that Available Bytes is at least 1 MB.

Another counter, *Pages/second*, also found in the Memory object, should be 5 or less. If it's greater than this limit, the server is paging in and out of virtual memory to a higher degree than desired. To solve the problem, you need to speed up the disk so that virtual memory will respond more quickly, add more RAM, or remove services to lower memory consumption. The TCP/IP services, Dynamic Host Configuration Protocol (DHCP), and Windows Internet Name System (WINS), all use large amounts of RAM but do not carry much CPU utilization. For this reason, you should not be tempted to add an extra DHCP server on your database Web server.

NT is also known for its memory-grabbing *services* (a service is a special type of program running under Windows NT). By default, NT starts up numerous services that you may not need. For example, if your server does not have a printer, then the Spooler service is unnecessary. If all your hard disk storage devices are SCSI, you can deactivate the ATDISK, IDE interface. Also eliminate any protocols not currently in use.

You can always check the amount of free memory by bringing up the WinMSD utility and finding *Memory Index*. Clicking on the *Memory* button loads a memory usage meter indicating how heavily your server's memory is loaded.

Virtual Memory

NT was designed around a virtual-memory memory model. The OS requires at least some virtual memory, no matter how much RAM is available, because

NT often allocates half the system's RAM to a disk cache. You can adjust your Web server's memory by opening up the Control Panel and the Network applet. Double-click on Server, and you'll see a dialog box controlling how NT uses RAM. Click on the radio button labeled *Maximize throughput for network application.*

One frustrating part of the paging process in terms of time is finding a place to put the data on the disk. Consequently, NT pre-allocates a large block of disk in an area called *pagefile.sys*. NT uses this contiguous area of disk to bypass the file system and perform direct hardware disk reads and writes. To optimize speed, these are done in a higher-privilege level called *Ring 0*. NT can exceed the pre-allocated space if it needs more virtual memory, but having to stop and look around for free space slows down the process as well as the Web server. You can control the amount of pre-allocated space on disk by using the *System/Virtual Memory* component in the Control Panel.

Now I turn your attention to some examples of fine tuning NT's virtual memory system. Say that you have a 16 MB machine (admittedly the low-end range); NT expects that it can get up to 27 MB of disk space with direct hardware reads and writes. When it needs memory, it can also use RAM. The question is how much RAM is left after you load the operating system? NT can run in about 5.5 MB, specifically the part that cannot be paged out to disk. On a 16 MB machine, that leaves 10.5 MB of free RAM for NT. If you add the remaining 10.5 MB to the 27 MB of pagefile.sys space, NT has 37.5 MB of working space. Perfmon refers to this amount of memory as the *Commit Limit*. The sum of the program regions that NT is running at a particular point in time is called the *working set*. If the working set remains at 37.5 MB or less, then NT does not need to enlarge the paging file. If, on the other hand, NT needs more memory, it can expand the paging file, but this process can be time-consuming. The paging file can grow up to 77 MB on our hypothetical system, so NT can execute up to 77 MB plus 10.5 MB, or 87.5 MB of programs on a 16 MB system before it runs out of memory.

A problem situation can arise if NT does not enlarge the paging file enough. This can lead to an irregular size for the paging file, as NT continues to allocate more space until it finally runs out. You can avoid this situation by monitoring the server's Commit Limit. Add the Commit Limit counter and the Committed Bytes counter to Perfmon and watch the difference between them. When Committed Bytes exceeds Commit Limit, NT has to increase the paging file size. If you want to see the size of the data structures and processes that won't be paged, add the *Pool Nonpaged Bytes* counter. One further suggestion is to keep a running log of Committed Bytes over a few weeks with Perfmon, and then note the maximum value recorded. Increase that value by a small amount, say 10–20%, and make your system's minimum paging file that size.

Hard Disk Fragmentation

The Windows NT 4.0 NTFS file system is notorious for becoming fragmented over time. For technical reasons, to defragment an NTSF partition is not a simple task. This is why NT does not come with a defragmentation utility like the one that ships with Windows 95/98. A third-party utility is highly recommended for periodic runs on your Web server. Several third-party utility software companies produce an NT defrag program. The program that receives the most praise is Disk Keeper.

Monitoring Site Connections

When your Web database application goes live for the first time, you should immediately begin monitoring the number of concurrent users that arrive at the site. The Windows NT Performance Monitor has a server diagnostic component that shows the activity on the server. Fundamentally, the tools show how much of the site is in use and by whom. Specifically, it displays how many users are connected, what they are doing, and for how long (on a site whose primary application is a database process, most users will be seen accessing the SQL back end). As the site administrator, you can monitor how much of the server's resources are being used, how much of these resources are free for the system to use, and the average loading factor on the physical server. Over time, all these statistics will provide insight into potential and real bottlenecks on the server and determine future upgrades for various hardware components.

Furthermore, you can define monitoring parameters, which allow you to review average CPU time, interrupts per second, and other related information. In general, you should save all generated statistics for later analysis. As a matter of administrative policy, you should gather these log statistics once per week and scrutinize them to gain a better understanding of your server's performance under different conditions.

Web Server Software

As Windows NT expands its market penetration, the number of available Web server software packages also continues to increase. You have quality choices for Web servers. The top three, in terms of overall features and installations, are Microsoft's *Internet Information Server* (IIS), Netscape's *Enterprise Server*, and O'Reilly's *WebSite Professional*. My focus for this book is IIS 4.0, which accompanies Windows NT 4.0 at no additional charge (you can also download the software for free at the Microsoft Web site). Because it's pretty hard to beat in price, many new Web servers running NT have chosen to adopt IIS. You have other good reasons to use IIS, however; for instance, *Active Server*

Pages (ASP) is an integral component that allows for very easy database connectivity, specifically with SQL Server.

When selecting Web server software, your selection criteria should include most of the following areas: performance, cost, support, market share (future viability), content management, application development features, administration, integration with the NT operating system (e.g., access control, Performance Monitor, and Event Viewer), support for Secure Sockets Layer (SSL) 2.0, and integration with the back-end database.

Web servers are actually quite simple in their operation. As mentioned in detail in Chapter 2, Web browsers communicate with Web servers using HTTP, a simple request/response protocol for information transfer using TCP/IP. The Web server receives the request, retrieves the file, sends it to the browser, and then tears down the connection. The graphics in the page are serviced in the same manner. Database result-sets are just formatted text. Browsers then display the downloaded HTML document.

Although Web servers typically store HTML pages and graphics, a Web server can store and serve up any file type including word processing documents, video streams, or sound files. Much of today's Web traffic is one-way; browsers read files and databases on the Web server, but this condition will change as wider adoption of the HTTP 1.1 draft becomes more common. With this draft, we have the *put* method, which provides a way to write files to a Web server.

A Web server also runs applications, including database connectivity processes. Standards like the CGI and scripting languages such as JavaScript and VBScript, as well as full programming languages such as Java and Visual Basic, are being used for developing Web applications.

In the future, however, standalone Web server software may evolve out of existence as it merges with operating systems and other server applications.

Microsoft Internet Information Server (IIS)

Although I consider only IIS version 4.0, actually four versions are now in common use: the 1.0 release (as an add-on package downloadable from the Microsoft Web site) with NT 3.51, the 2.0 release (as mentioned before, included on the initial shipping CD) for NT 4.0, the 3.0 release for NT 4.0 that first included ASP, and IIS 4.0, which is included in the NT Option Pack. I have built database-enabled sites running on all four versions and found the software to be increasingly stable and capable of supporting heavy connection loads.

IIS runs only on Windows NT, unlike many of the competing Web servers that have versions for a variety of platforms. Installing IIS with the Install Wizard is quite simple and creates a generic user account on the NT server. This account has read-only rights to the files in the IIS server directory. In addition to an HTTP (WWW) server, IIS also includes an FTP server. By default, the installation wizard sets up both servers, which run as NT *Services*. For Web database applications, the IIS service of primary importance is the WWW server, although FTP is often necessary as well, for providing a conduit for accepting new and/or updated data for publication on the Web.

The *Internet Service Manager* (based on the Microsoft Management Console interface) is a simple Control Panel type (alternately browser-based) application included with IIS that lets you start, stop, and configure both the WWW and FTP services. Figure 3-6 shows the IIS Internet Service Manager tool that assists you in administrating your server. Double-clicking on the WWW Server icon brings up the property dialog. The Internet Service Manager allows you to control access, specify server directories, and set logging options. The application has four tabs labeled Service, Directories, Logging, and Advanced. Figure 3-7 contains a view of the tabbed property dialog box for the WWW Service. The Directories tab provides you with options for selecting the location of the scripts and HTML pages, including the default home page that users see when they first browse over to your site. You should normally accept the directory defaults suggested by IIS and at the same time become familiar with these defaults. The reason is that many of the database development tools (especially the CGI based tools) you'll be using to build custom applications need to install themselves here, although most tools also have their own directory structures apart from IIS.

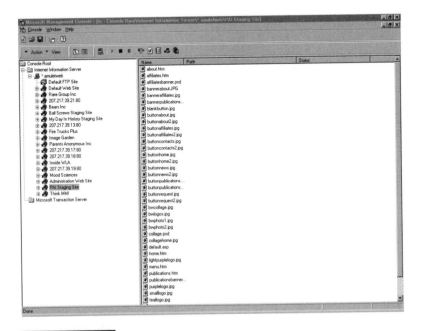

Figure 3–6   *IIS Internet Service Manager*

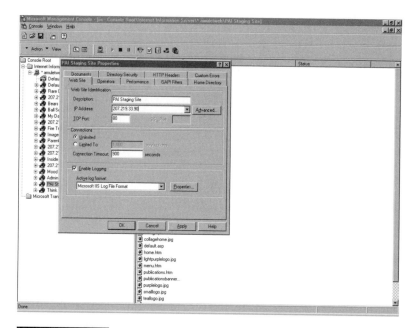

Figure 3–7   *IIS WWW Service Properties Dialog*

IIS produces a user log that you can save as a text file or write directly to an ODBC database, such as SQL Server. This is a particularly nice feature, because you can offer better insight into your Web database usage statistics if you can analyze the log data more easily. Click on the Logging tab to specify options pertaining to the configuration of the logging function. For example, you can have IIS automatically log server activities for a specified amount of time. So if you choose the weekly reports option, the next report will automatically be created at the start of the next week, while the old data is retained.

IIS provides good security that is well integrated with Windows NT. You can set up IIS to require a user name and password for accessing the Web server or any pages or directories on the server. You can also allow or deny access based on IP address range or specific IP addresses. IIS uses the Windows NT user database, which means that you can manage your Web user list with the same tools you use for your NT server users. This eliminates the need to keep a separate database of Web server users. For users with more advanced security needs, IIS supports SSL 2.0 security, which is a private and public key encryption mechanism to move data across the server to the clients in a secure format. This may be crucial if your database application contains financial or privileged data. You can have a mix of SSL and non-encrypted pages on the same server. Microsoft provides an SSL key generator program to simplify the process of obtaining an authentication certificate.

With Internet Services Manager, you can give different IP addresses to specific directories on the NT server. This feature allows you to set up several *virtual servers* on a single physical server. The virtual Web sites appear to users to be running on separate computers, and each of the Web servers can have a unique host and/or domain name. This feature should appeal to ISPs or Web database development firms that intend to host multiple sites on a single machine. My firm, in fact, does exactly this with much success. Hosting our client's Web database sites allows us to provide them better application features, support, and security, since we provide Webmaster services in addition to site development services.

You start with an IP address assigned to the Web server's network card itself and assigned to an alias directory. For example, let's say that the Web server's NIC is configured for 207.217.125.2. Furthermore, you wish to assign an address of 207.217.125.10 to the virtual server pointing to the \\AMU-LETWEB\apps\webserver virtual directory using Universal Naming Convention (UNC), and give this directory the alias of http://www.amuletclient.com. The browser will end up at the specified virtual directory instead of going to the Web root specified in the IIS setup.

IIS also supports a variety of programming interfaces. It supports not only CGI and Perl scripts for simple database application development, but also the Internet Database Connector (IDC) and Internet Server API (ISAPI), a heavy-duty API developed by Microsoft and Process Software that lets programmers create complex Web applications. In addition, IIS supports server-side scripting through ASP using the VBScript and JScript (Microsoft's implementation of JavaScript) languages. Support for the Java language is missing in IIS, opting rather for Visual Basic for writing Web applets.

As mentioned above, Microsoft includes IDC, an ISAPI-based application that offers hooks into Microsoft Access, Microsoft SQL Server, Oracle, Sybase, Informix, DB2, and other ODBC-compliant databases.

SQL Server for NT

Probably the most crucial ingredient of a database-enabled Web server is its back-end database on which queries originating from a Web browser will be processed. In Chapter 9, I discuss using common desktop databases for publishing data on the Web, but for most business applications, often mission-critical in nature, more power is needed. An industrial-grade, SQL-based, relational database engine is absolutely necessary to provide the flexibility and robustness needed to process concurrent database requests from a Web browser. Although you have many choices for a back-end solution, such as Oracle, Sybase SQL Server, Informix, DB2, etc., I examine the Microsoft offering, SQL Server 6.5 and 7.0. Many, if not most, of the characteristics described here also apply to competing products. In this section, I discuss database capacity and performance considerations as well as tuning tips.

Database Capacity

Assume at the outset that back-end databases in this class are capable of handling considerable quantities of data efficiently and quickly. For example, database sizes ranging anywhere from 500 MB to hundreds of gigabytes are within the realm of possibilities. The set limits for the SQL Server environment place the maximum database size at 1 terabyte, spread over a maximum of 256 devices, each with a maximum of 32 GB per device. These limits constitute a foundation for a considerably sized data store. For example, the Microsoft Terra Server test site demonstrates the use of SQL Server 7.0 against a multi-terabyte database.

If your data is expansive, however, you should consider backup and recovery time, which is performed on a per-database basis. You may probably want to partition the data into separate databases on a single server.

Performance Tuning

Pay close attention to several areas when optimizing SQL Server for handling Web database requests. Properly configuring and tuning the back-end DBMS of a Web server constitutes one of the most important tasks a Web database administrator can perform in obtaining an efficient query-processing environment. This does place an important responsibility on the administrator, as he/she must constantly monitor and measure performance results in the background as production query processing occurs. In this section, I provide a short checklist that identifies several important areas of concern. Over time, as your familiarity grows with the server's various parameters and tuning mechanisms, you have room for growth and experimentation using your creativity, in order to obtain even better performance. SQL Server is a robust and complex piece of software, requiring intimate knowledge of its internal operation as well as the front-end application in order to obtain optimal performance.

SQL Server's tight integration with NT's Perfmon has been a big selling point since SQL Server's initial release. Versions 6.5 and 7.0 improve performance monitoring by adding a variety of new counters in key areas. SQL Server also allows user-defined counters so that you can measure what you consider important. You can add custom counters by creating special stored procedures that return one integer value. The Probe login account runs these procedures to get the appropriate statistic, and Perfmon reports the appropriate integer value.

The *New Procedure Cache* object also has 10 new counters used to monitor the procedure cache, as well as a counter that measures the maximum tempdb space used, so that you can more easily and accurately monitor these resources. These features stem from the frustration that results from trying to properly size the procedure cache and tempdb, which are both crucial in maintaining an efficient server.

RAM CONSIDERATIONS

One of the best ways to improve SQL Server performance is to increase the amount of available RAM. NT requires that a portion of RAM be available to SQL Server. The more memory available, the better SQL Server is able to cache data and therefore reduce the amount of physical disk I/O required. Your goal in tuning SQL Server queries is always to reduce physical I/O requests. Regardless of the speed of your hard drive, physical input and output devices are the slowest components of the server, and their use should be minimized. Allowing the system to cache data is the most direct approach towards this reality. As stated earlier in this chapter, a recommended amount of RAM is 128 MB for an NT Server running SQL Server, although the database can effectively function with as little as 32 MB. As the server's Web query requirements increase, especially if more than one database-enabled Web site is running on the server, RAM requirements may increase for such things as additional threads, page tables, etc. Table 3-1 contains a guideline to determine how much memory to allocate to SQL Server in relation to the amount of total RAM in the system.

Adding RAM indiscriminately is not as expensive a prospect as it used to be. Every attempt should be made to analyze database requirements by performing user and data volume simulations, often called a Database Sizing Study. The results of these benchmarks will determine how much RAM is needed for SQL Server to optimize both the application speed and the server hardware costs. Still, specific PC server hardware may limit the maximum amount of RAM. Consider the motherboard with four memory expansion slots, each allowing at most a 16 MB SIMM. The maximum amount of RAM in this example is 64 MB. When drawing up the blueprints of a new Web server, such considerations should be taken into account.

Table 3–1	SQL Server RAM Requirements
Total RAM (in MB)	**SQL Server RAM Allocation**
16	4
24	8
32	16
64	40
128	100
256	216
512	464

CACHE MEMORY

SQL Server maintains two types of software cache memory (distinct from the hardware caches described earlier in this chapter), the data cache and the procedure cache. The data cache contains pages, 2 KB blocks of data, from the most recently accessed database objects, normally tables and indexes. The procedure cache holds the optimized query *plans* (the result access method as determined by SQL Server's intelligent cost-based query optimizer) for the most recently executed stored procedures (triggers and system stored procedures).

As the size of the data cache increases, the speed of data retrieval also increases. The speed of subsequent retrievals is increased accordingly. On one project my firm completed, the response time for an important query was reduced from over 1 minute to just 3 seconds by increasing the amount of memory allocated to SQL Server (from 16 MB to 100 MB). Cache memory is allocated to data and procedures, depending on the application. An application using triggers (which are treated as stored procedures for cache purposes) needs more procedure cache. The default configuration for SQL Server is 30% of cache for procedures and 70% for data; however, this may not be sufficient for a given application.

One way to estimate the size of the procedure cache is to run the system command *dbcc memusage*. This command displays information about how SQL Server uses memory, providing snapshot information about both the data cache and the procedure cache. In particular, it shows how much memory is used by the largest objects in the procedure cache, i.e., stored procedures, triggers, views, rules, and defaults. You can get the size of the largest plan from this display. Take this size and multiply it by the maximum number of concurrent users configured and then add 25% to determine the optimal size for your procedure cache. As an example, if the largest plan uses 400 KB and the application has a maximum of 20 concurrent users, then the procedures cache should be 10 MB in size: 20 times 400 KB times 1.25 (adding 25%) = 10 MB.

To illustrate the advantages of caching, consider the following example. A Web-based community business directory application can potentially retrieve tens or hundreds of rows of business names using a complex SQL statement with multiple table joins. Say that the initial query takes 15 seconds. Subsequent retrievals for other businesses can take less than 3 seconds each, since the application data is already in the cache. The key is that the business directory data is basically fixed, even though multiple Web browsers are being served.

The default installation size for SQL Server memory, including all cache plus kernel and server data structures, is 8 MB for a system with 32 MB of RAM or less. The cache is 16 MB for systems with more than 32 MB of RAM. If 64 MB is available, consider increasing the cache to at least 40 MB. Larger is better in this case, because after the cache fills up, it is recycled on a first-in-first-out (FIFO) basis. Generally, the desire is to have enough cache to handle multiple SQL statements and if the cache is too small, the server has to empty every time a new SQL statement executes. In this case, the benefit of a cache is lost. The memory situation for a Web database is often uncertain, because the number of concurrent user connections is difficult to predict at a given point in time.

SQL SERVER PERFORMANCE MONITOR

SQL Server contains a *Performance Monitor* program that measures the performance and behavior of objects such as processors, memory cache, threads, and processes. Each of these objects has an associated set of *counters* that provide information on such things as device usage, queue lengths, and delays, as well as information used for throughput and internal congestion measurements.

For example, you should begin with testing a fully populated database by using the ISQL/w utility that comes with the product. While manually issuing a SELECT statement, you can check performance by using the SQL Server Performance Monitor program to monitor various counters for determining the percentage of time that a request was found in the data cache instead of being read from disk, the number of physical pages read per second (an indication of excessive paging), and others. Many additional SQL Server statistics can be obtained from the counters in six Performance Monitor objects.

You should also check to see how much NT memory is allocated to SQL Server. To find out, use the Enterprise Manager, select the server, then select the Server menu, select the Configurations dialog box, and scroll down to the memory. The memory reported is in 2 K pages, so 8192 (the default) represents 16 MB. In the case of a Web server that does not use file or print services, you can safely allocate up to 40 MB on a 64 MB server. You should also set your NT server options to "Minimize Memory," which will reduce the caching and general footprint that NT uses. Note that the NT cache is not the same as the SQL Server cache. You might also consider setting the priority boost option to a value of 1, which raises the priority of the SQL Server threads. Further, check the read-ahead settings, nr threads, etc.

Another item to check for better performance is the database indexes. Look in the *Manage Indexes* window, where you can see the distribution. If the size of the index is higher than the maximum recommended, then performance could suffer. An index rebuild operation may cure this situation.

Later, when running the server under a typical load, use the Performance Monitor to check the SQL Server cache-hit ratio. If it is over 90%, adding more memory will not help. Additional memory is used mainly for SQL Server data cache to increase the hit ratio. If the hit ratio is already high, then the maximum improvement possible is quite small. If the hit ratio is less than 90%, adding more memory may improve overall performance.

One additional item to check when trying to eliminate bottlenecks is the SQL Server *I/O Lazy Writes* per second. This counter measures how often the

Lazywriter process flushes out dirty, aged buffers and makes them available to user processes by placing them in the free buffer pool, thus making room in the cache. The process ensures that the number of free data buffers stays higher than a predefined threshold. More memory may improve performance by reducing unnecessary stress on your I/O subsystem.

The kernel and server data structures consist of configurable options: user connections (37 KB per user connection), open databases (1 KB per open database), open objects (70 bytes per object), and locks (32 bytes per lock). As these options increase in number, the caches suffer. For example, if 20 user connections are added at 37 KB each, the memory available for the caches is reduced by 740 KB.

SQL TRACE

SQL Server 6.5/7.0 has a SQL Trace graphical utility for monitoring and recording database activity at the connection level. SQL Trace can display all server activity in real time or use filters to focus on the actions of particular users, applications, hosts, or SQL commands.

Web server administrators can monitor connections in three ways: connections shown on-screen, connections written to an activity log, or connections reproduced in Transact SQL scripts to be rerun later so that you can use the Trace utility to script complex activities that you run with a GUI tool. Administrators can also write custom trace utilities with the xp_sqltrace extended stored procedure, which simplifies the use of this tool.

STORED PROCEDURES

When developing client/server architecture applications, especially Web-based, many advantages abound to using *Stored Procedures* for frequently used SQL queries. Fortunately, most Web database application development tools possess a mechanism for using stored procedures. A query inside a stored procedure is saved in a pre-compiled form and does not need to be checked for syntax as an interactive SQL statement would. This translates into better runtime performance, since the overhead of compiling the query each time has been eliminated.

Stored procedures are reusable but not re-entrant. So although the same stored procedure can be used for multiple queries (making it reusable), multiple copies are still necessary because a single copy cannot handle more than one session. For example, if two Web browsers enter queries that execute the same stored procedure simultaneously, two copies of the plan are loaded into memory. Since procedure query plans are constructed and optimized the first time they are read from disk, you have no guarantee that the plan is optimal every time the procedure is invoked. If the stored procedures accept parameter lists that may require different forms of optimization, consider using the Transact SQL statement `EXEC WITH RECOMPILE`.

One of the primary reasons for using stored procedures is that they reside on the server and using them reduces network traffic. Only the requests must be sent across the Internet. Consider an example. If a Web browser needs to retrieve and examine 100 rows to modify only 5 of them without a stored procedure, the following sequence of events must occur:

1. A SQL SELECT must be executed to retrieve the 100 rows.
2. The result-set must be sent from the Web server to the client browser.
3. The rows must be examined by the user.
4. Five SQL UPDATE statements must be sent to the server, and the result of the updates must be returned to the client.

With a stored procedure, all this activity takes place on the server side, and only the result is sent over the wire to the client.

Stored procedures can also guarantee *Referential Integrity* using triggers, by ensuring that no child rows (primary key) are added without a parent row (foreign key) and that no parent row is deleted without first deleting all its child rows. With stored procedures, you do not need additional coding on the client side to ensure database integrity.

The impact of triggers on performance is low, because the time involved to run a trigger is spent mostly to reference other tables, either in memory or on the database device. Tables that the user is issuing SQL INSERT or DELETE operations against are always in memory and, therefore, do not significantly add to processing time. The location of any other tables referenced in the trigger determine how long the operation takes.

Stored procedures can also help to maintain code modularity. For example, several places in an application may update a customer list. If a stored procedure performs the SQL UPDATE, it simply executes each time the list needs updating. You do not need to code separate but equivalent queries in various locations.

TEMPORARY DATABASE SIZE

SQL Server uses a temporary database, tempdb, to store temporary tables and provide working storage (SQL Server refers to tempdb as a work table in its output). The default size of tempdb is 2 MB (it is not located in RAM). Chances are that's not enough for your application.

The most significant factors in determining the space required for tempdb are the size of the temporary tables, the activity on them (which fills up the tempdb log), the size of any sorts, subqueries, and aggregates that use the GROUP BY clause, and the number of open cursors. In addition, any query that uses the DISTINCT clause automatically uses tempdb. tempdb is created by default on the master device.

You can add more space on the master device or on any other properly initialized device. You can also use the SHOWPLAN function to determine whether a query uses tempdb. But the easiest way to determine its proper size is to observe its usage during normal system operations.

Putting tempdb in RAM can significantly affect overall server performance. Queries that require frequent sorts benefit because that eliminates a lot of physical disk accesses. Don't consider this option, however, unless you have at least 64 MB of RAM. If you have less than this, SQL Server can probably manage the data cache better than you can.

QUERY OPTIMIZATION ANALYSIS

Many times, the SQL you devise for a given Web database application is not always the most optimal for use with the SQL Server query optimizer. This means that the optimizer may develop an execution plan different from the one you had intended. On the other hand, you may not fully realize how the optimizer is interpreting your SQL. In either case, you may require more insight. You can use a number of different techniques to look beneath the scene with the optimizer in order to gain insight as to how your query is actually being executed. Say that we have the following left outer join SQL statement that we wish to analyze:

```
SELECT authors.au_lname, titleauthor.title_id
FROM authors, titleauthor
WHERE titleauthor.au_id =* authors.au_id
```

To begin, execute the SQL statement using the SQL tool in Enterprise Manager but only after setting the following query optimizer options:

```
set showplan on
set statistics io on
set statistics time on
dbcc traceon (330)
dbcc traceon (3604)
```

Review all the above settings and see what kind of insight they deliver. Turning on the showplan generates a description of the processing plan for the query. Turning on the IO statistics displays the number of scans, the number of logical reads, and the number of physical reads for each table referenced in the statement. Turning on the time statistics displays the time, in milliseconds, required to parse and compile each command, as well as the time required to execute each step of the command. The 330 trace flag enables full output when using the SET SHOWPLAN option, which gives detailed information about joins. The 3604 trace flag sends trace output to the client.

The following output is what displays in the Results tab of the SQL tool. The first part of the display is the showplan output, followed by the result-set for the query. At the very end of the display are the logical and physical reads. Notice how in our example, 23 logical reads occur (the number of actual records in the table) but only 1 physical does. This result is good, since your goal in designing SQL queries is to minimize physical reads. Apparently, this query should perform optimally as it stands.

```
STEP 1
The type of query is SELECT
FROM TABLE
authors
Row estimate:  23
Cost estimate: 16
Nested iteration
Table Scan
LEFT OUTER JOIN : nested iteration
FROM TABLE
  titleauthor
  JOINS WITH
  authors
  Row estimate:  25
    Cost estimate: 60
    Nested iteration
    Table Scan
SQL Server Parse and Compile Time:
  cpu time = 10 ms.
```

au_lname	title_id
White	PS3333
Green	BU1032
Green	BU2075
Carson	PC1035
O'Leary	BU1111
O'Leary	TC7777
Straight	BU7832
Smith	(null)
Bennet	BU1032
Dull	PC8888
Gringlesby	TC7777
Locksley	PC9999
Locksley	PS7777
Greene	(null)
Blotchet-Halls	TC4203
Yokomoto	TC7777
Del Castillo	MC2222
DeFrance	MC3021
Stringer	(null)
MacFeather	BU1111
MacFeather	PS1372
Karsen	PS1372
Panteley	TC3218
Hunter	PC8888
McBadden	(null)
Ringer	MC3021

```
Ringer                              PS2091
Ringer                              PS2091
Ringer                              PS2106

(29 row(s) affected)

Table: authors scan count 1, logical reads: 1,
   physical reads: 1,  read ahead reads: 0
Table: titleauthor scan count 23,
    logical reads: 23,  physical reads: 1,
    read ahead reads: 0


SQL Server Execution Times:
    cpu time = 0 ms.  elapsed time = 30 ms.
```

WEB APPLICATION ANALYSIS

Often, the most important aspect of back-end database tuning is an in-depth analysis of the front-end Web application(s). Two general classes of applications exist: *query-intensive* applications and *update-intensive* applications. An application that supports a high proportion of users updating (adding, editing, and deleting records) a database may be considered a transaction-oriented application and should be tuned in a manner different from one where users only issue queries against the database. A query-intensive application does not require frequent backups, since the data is not continuously changing. An update-intensive application, however, requires frequent backups to avoid the possibility of losing large quantities of data.

When implementing and tuning a Web application, always keep the size of the database to a minimum. One factor that affects the size of a database is the number of indexes it uses. Update-intensive applications typically do not need many indexes, because data is modified more often than it is read. One useful technique is to create a *Clustered Index* for those update-intensive application tables subject to a high volume of SQL INSERT and UPDATE activity. If no clustered index exists, new rows are inserted on the last page of the table, because an UPDATE is actually just a DELETE followed by an INSERT. Concurrency contention for the last page can evoke serious server performance problems. Using a clustered index forces SQL Server to insert all data in index-key order, eliminating the last page contention problem. Distributing INSERTs across the whole table has a positive impact on the transaction volume that your Web application can support. Query-intensive applications, on the other hand, can require many indexes per table due to intensive database queries. Without the proper indexes in play, a user can spend a lot of time waiting for the browser to display the result-set.

Another difference between query-intensive and update-intensive applications is in how the data is stored on an index page. In update-intensive applications, a good idea is to set the *Fill Factor* (with values from 0 to 100, default is 0) to 50 to keep half of each index page of data empty. Using values less than 100 reduces the number of rows per page on data pages and leaf index pages. This allows for better performance during INSERT operations. For query-intensive application access to read-only databases, set the fill factor to 100 so that SQL Server uses all of the 2 KB index page, enabling it to process fewer data pages for retrieval. Since the fill factor takes effect when the index is built, the Web database administrator should rebuild indexes frequently for an update-intensive application.

One final area that serves to improve an update-intensive application's performance is to regularly update its *statistics*. Every attempt should be made to run the Update Statistics SQL statement on all user tables at least once a week. A higher frequency may be warranted on tables that regularly receive a lot of activity. For example, tables with mass INSERT, UPDATE, DELETE, and bulk-copy activity using the bcp utility, are prime candidates. If, as a result of monitoring the style of queries being posed, a certain class of Web-based query suddenly begins to run slowly, updating the statistics is the first step to take. A stored procedure could run Update Statistics on all user-defined tables, updating the statistics on the distribution of key values in the indexes. This would give the SQL Server optimizer better information about which indexes to use when it processes a query, and it would make queries on frequently modified tables run more efficiently.

Summary

This chapter has put forth a definition for placing together a hardware and system software foundation requisite for developing Web database applications. The focus was entirely on the so-called "Wintel" platform, Windows NT and 95/98 system software with Intel-based hardware, as well as the Microsoft SQL Server relational database. With all the physical components now in place and finely tuned, you may begin to experiment with building some initial applications and perform your own benchmarks to gain a more complete understanding as to how your new Webtop applications will succeed.

Building Webtop Databases

*T*he goal of this chapter is to introduce the process of implementing a simple database-enabled Web site. In doing so, I focus on the three main functional development areas that must be addressed to fully create such a site. These areas are the same general areas required to build desktop, LAN, or client/server database applications as well—an indication that a Webtop application is really just a generalization of these previous forms of software.

First, I look at the database design for the application. Here, I explore how to put together tables, indexes, relationships, stored procedures, and other primary components that will become the data repository of the Webtop application. Next, you see how to define interactive queries, where the user supplies selection criteria and the back-end database processes the query. In the above two areas, I use a popular Windows database management system, Microsoft Access, to see how to generate the query SQL strings needed by the Web application. Finally, I examine the various ways query result-sets may be rendered into a usable form of display on a client Web browser. Using the HTML link feature ubiquitous on Web pages, the number of ways to interactively represent query results, using drill-down approaches, increases many-fold.

For our purposes in this introductory chapter, I shall focus on an environment commonly available on Windows NT-based Web servers, the *Internet Database Connector* (IDC) component of the IIS 3.0 and 4.0 Web server software. IDC leverages ODBC to create Web pages with information contained in a database. IDC is a component of ISAPI (Internet Server API) and is included in the Microsoft Internet Information Server (IIS). IIS also supports Windows CGI, the Windows-specific implementation of CGI. As noted before,

CGI was once considered the traditional approach to creating server-based programs that interact with a Web server to create dynamic HTML documents; however, more contemporary tools like IDC offer much more favorable and easy-to-develop results.

I chose the IDC tool here because it is commonly available, is integrated with the Web server, is free of charge, and demonstrates the basic elements of a Web site containing database connectivity. Note that you have many other ways to integrate a data connection, including Active Server Pages (the topic of Chapter 7), which Microsoft itself favors over IDC. The benefit that IDC has over ASP with respect to our introduction is that IDC requires no programming.

Internet Database Connector (IDC)

I begin with a complete description of the IDC environment with which we'll create a database-enabled Webtop application. With the WWW service and ODBC drivers that come with IIS 3.0/4.0, you can do the following:

- Create dynamic Web pages containing information from a database.
- Insert, update, and delete information in a database based on user criteria from a Web page.
- Perform additional SQL commands.

The diagram shown in Figure 4-1 depicts conceptually how database access is performed by IIS.

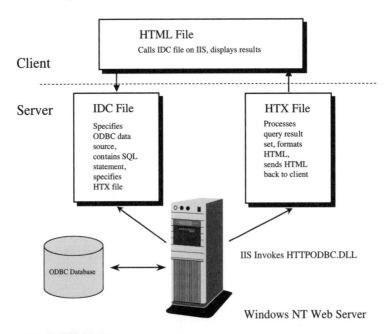

HTML File	
Calls IDC file on IIS, displays results	

Client

Server

IDC File	**HTX File**
Specifies ODBC data source, contains SQL statement, specifies HTX file	Processes query result set, formats HTML, sends HTML back to client

ODBC Database

IIS Invokes HTTPODBC.DLL

Windows NT Web Server

Figure 4–1   *Conceptual Database Access in IIS*

Here, Web browsers submit requests to IIS using HTTP. The Web server responds with a document formatted in HTML. Access to databases is accomplished through IDC, which allows you to access any ODBC-compliant server-based database from a Web browser. IDC is actually contained within an ISAPI DLL (dynamic link library) program called HTTPODBC.DLL, which uses ODBC to gain access to databases. The DLL is installed on your Web server when you install IIS. IDC applications are fairly straightforward to build; the only challenging part is constructing a SQL statement to send to your database. You see later in this chapter how you can automatically generate these SQL strings.

IDC Architecture

Figure 4-2 shows the overall IDC architecture having components for connecting to databases from IIS. HTTPODBC.DLL uses two types of files to control how the database is accessed and how the generated Web pages containing the results are constructed. These files are the *Internet Database Connector* (with the .idc file extension) files and *HTML Extension* (with the .htx exten-

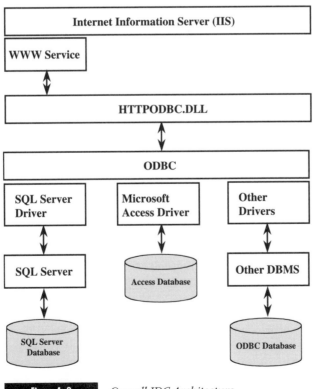

Figure 4-2   *Overall IDC Architecture*

sion) files. In addition, a standard HTML file (.htm) is needed to reference and invoke the other two file types.

The IDC file contains the necessary information to connect to the appropriate ODBC data source and execute an SQL statement that is embedded in this file. The IDC file is a specially formatted text file located on an IIS Web server containing three required segments of information: an ODBC data source, a reference to a template file (the HTX file) that will format and process the results of the query, and an SQL statement that contains the query sent to the database.

The HTML extension file is the template, pointed to by the IDC file, for the actual HTML document that will be returned to the Web browser after the database information has been merged into it by HTTPODBC.DLL. The job of the HTX file is two-fold: to process results returned by a database query or stored procedure, and to format those results, combining them with static HTML if necessary, before they are sent back to the Web browser. The reason this file is called an HTML extension file is that it has extended standard HTML syntax to do such things as loop through result-sets, handle conditional logic, and work with variables. Do not worry that these extensions will make your site incompatible with non-Microsoft browsers because all extensions are processed on the server by the IDC. By the time the results are sent back to the client, all the client sees is the final rendered HTML code. In order to provide access to a SQL database from your Web page, you will need to create .idc, .htx, and .htm files. You'll see examples of these files later in this chapter (see sections: Internet Database Connector (.idc) Files, and HTML Extension (.htx) Files).

IDC processing begins at the Web browser by sending a URL, possibly with some HTML form fields, to IIS. The URL designates an IDC file. As mentioned above, this file consists of several fields, three of which are required (I discuss a complete list of these fields later in this chapter). The data source field identifies an ODBC resource to process. The SQL statement field is an SQL command string, the syntax of which depends on the SQL conventions of the database type in the data source field. The template field references an HTX file, a text file that includes standard HTML tags along with other special tags for formatting the result-set.

As indicated in Figure 4-2, the browser issues a URL. The URL references a server-based IDC file. When the IIS receives the input, it passes control to the Internet Database Connector that interprets the IDC file along with any HTML form field contents passed by the browser. IDC passes SQL commands to the ODBC driver for processing. When the ODBC driver completes execution of its SQL command string, the IDC uses the HTX file to format the result set so that IIS can pass an HTML page back to the browser.

Developers manage three key points in the process. First, they write code to pass the URL and form fields to the server. Client-side JavaScript or VBScript can help at this point, and we look at some combined client-side scripting and

IDC solutions in a later section of this chapter. Second, they write an IDC file to specify the processing for a data source. The key SQL Statement field requires some knowledge of SQL, but you see in a later section of this chapter that several commonly available development tools can assist you in creating SQL. Third, they prepare an HTX file to format the result-set for client Web browsers. Client-side scripting can enhance this effort as well.

Creating ODBC DSNs

An important task the developer must also attend to before completing an IDC database Web page is to set up the ODBC data source for the target database. You must specify a new System Data Source Name (DSN) or File DSN using the Windows NT 32-bit ODBC Data Source Administrator program. In addition, you must make sure that all ODBC drivers you require are also installed on the Web server hosting the database you intend to attach to your IDC files. For example, you should see all your installed drivers listed in the ODBC Administrator; if you do not, you'll have to install them separately. For example, you should see the drivers for Microsoft SQL Server, Microsoft Access 97, etc. Unfortunately, the Access 2.0 ODBC driver does not work with IIS, so you'll have to use the conversion process of a later version of Access to ready your Access 2.0 data for publication on the Web.

IDC Processing Walk-Through

Let's now take a quick walk-through of how IDC processes a database request by looking at a specific example. Consider a simple Web page named Title-View.htm. The page contains simple HTML tags along with a single hypertext link that executes a query using the SQL Server ODBC driver, with the result-set returned on another page. The following are the contents of this Web page file:

```
<HTML>
<HEAD>
<TITLE>Title View Query</TITLE>
</HEAD>

<BODY>

<H2>IDC Query Walk-Through</H2>

<H3>In order to submit the query:
<A HREF=
"http://amuletweb/book/
     titleview.idc?sales=4000">
Click here</A>
</H3>

</BODY>
</HTML>
```

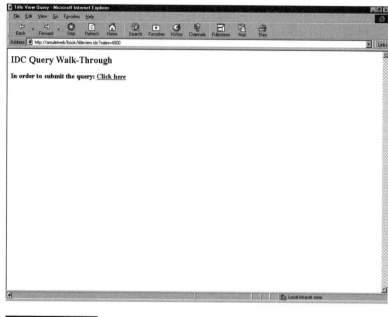

Figure 4–3 *TitleView.htm Web Page*

Figure 4-3 contains TitleView.htm as rendered by the Internet Explorer 4.0 Web browser.

When the user clicks on the link shown as "Click here," another URL is sent to the server that refers to an IDC file. The IDC file for HTTPODBC.DLL to use is named TitleView.idc and is referenced in the URL. Extension file mapping precludes the need to reference the DLL in the URL. Here are the contents of the TitleView.idc file:

```
Datasource: PubsDSN
Username: sa
Template: titleview.htx
SQLStatement:
+SELECT au_lname, ytd_sales
+ FROM pubs.dbo.titleview
+ WHERE ytd_sales>%sales%
```

In our example, the IDC file first references the ODBC system data source name (DSN) previously set up on the Web server, PubsDSN. This particular DSN uses the SQL Server ODBC driver to point to the Pubs sample database (distributed with SQL Server). Next, the "sa" user for the system administrator is used to log into the database. You may also need a password for this database if one has been specified during installation of SQL Server. Since these are server-side files that never travel out to a user's browser, you do not need to worry about embedding security information. I also specify the name of the HTX file that will be used by IDC to format the results returned by the query. Finally, I have the SQL string for the query. In this case, I'm executing a SQL Server view that is part of the Pubs database. Notice in the WHERE clause of the SELECT statement that the logical expression depends on a comparison to %sales%, an IDC parameter. You have the option of specifying this parameter in the link tag in TitleView.htm. The SQL view is called TitleView and its definition is the following:

```
CREATE VIEW titleview
AS
SELECT title, au_ord, au_lname,
    price, ytd_sales, pub_id
FROM authors, titles, titleauthor
WHERE authors.au_id = titleauthor.au_id
    AND titles.title_id = titleauthor.title_id
```

The HTX file, named TitleView.htx, for the walk-through sample query is as shown here:

```
<HTML>
<BODY>
<HEAD>
<TITLE>Title View Query Results</TITLE>
</HEAD>

<%if idc.sales EQ ""%>
    <H2>Selection criteria not specified</H2>
<%else%>
    <H2>Authors with sales greater than
        <I><%idc.sales%></I></H2>
<%endif%>

<P>
<H3>Query results:</H3>
<table border>
    <tr>
      <th>Author</th>
      <th>YTD Sales</th>
    </tr>
    <%begindetail%>
      <tr align=right>
        <td><%au_lname%></td>
        <td><%ytd_sales%><BR></td>
      </tr>
```

```
    <%enddetail%>
    </table>

<P>

<%if CurrentRecord EQ 0 %>
    <I><B>Sorry, no authors had YTD sales
      greater than </I><%idc.sales%>.</B>
    <P>
<%else%>
    <HR>
    <I>The query was successfully run against
      SQL Server using IDC</I>
<%endif%>

</BODY>
</HTML>
```

Given the scenario as described above, now review the entire process of using IDC with IIS by examining several steps.

1. The Web browser sends the URL to IIS via standard HTTP protocol.
2. IIS loads HTTPODBC.DLL and provides it with the remaining information in the URL. Files with .idc extensions are mapped to HTTPODBC.DLL, and the DLL loads and obtains the name of the IDC file from the URL passed to IIS.
3. HTTPODBC.DLL reads the IDC file. The IDC file contains several entries of the form: field:value. I completely define this file in a later section of this chapter (see section Internet Database Connector (.idc) Files). In the TitleView.idc file shown above, I define the ODBC data source, the valid SQL Server logon user name, the HTML extension file to use to merge the results, and the SQL statement to execute.
4. HTTPODBC.DLL connects to the ODBC data source using the ODBC driver for SQL Server. Once the connection is made, the SQL statements found in the IDC file are sent to the SQL Server ODBC driver, which in turn sends it to SQL Server for execution.
5. HTTPODBC.DLL fetches the data from the database and merges it into the HTML extension file. After the SQL statement has been executed, the DLL reads the .htx file (TitleView.htx) specified in TitleView.idc. You see in a later section that .htx files contain special HTML tags that the DLL uses to control where and how the data returned from the SQL statement is merged.
6. HTTPODBC.DLL sends the merged document back to IIS, which then sends the results back to the client browser. Figure 4-4 shows the resulting Web page.

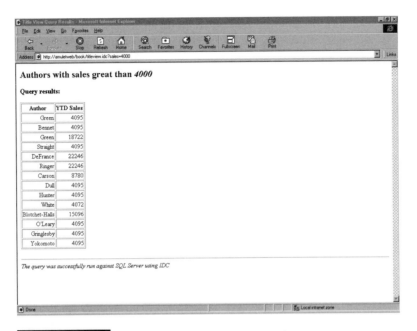

Authors with sales great than *4000*

Query results:

Author	YTD Sales
Green	4095
Bennet	4095
Green	18722
Straight	4095
DeFrance	22246
Ringer	22246
Carson	8780
Dull	4095
Hunter	4095
White	4072
Blotchet-Halls	15096
O'Leary	4095
Gringlesby	4095
Yokomoto	4095

The query was successfully run against SQL Server using IDC

Figure 4–4   *Results-Set Output for TitleView.htx*

Database Design

In this section, I explore how to develop the database design: table and index structures, relationships, queries/views, and stored procedures necessary to support a database-enabled Web site. In the walk-through above, the database design for the SQL Server Pubs database was already complete prior to the creation of the IDC-based Web query page. This case is rare, however, so we must investigate some commonly available tools that facilitate the design process.

Choosing a Design Tool

The precise tool you end up choosing for designing a Web database, in part depends on the underlying database engine. If, for example, the Webtop application is to be centered around a desktop database engine such as Access, then to use the Access table and query designer views is quite natural, as well as the relationships window, to fully develop the database design. On the other hand, if your database is based on SQL Server, then you'd need a tool compatible with that environment.

Many times, the design tool you pick is the one bundled with the engine itself. For example, going with the Oracle 8 database would suggest using the

Oracle Enterprise Manager database tool. Sometimes, however, the design tool included with the database is not sufficient for building Web databases. A good instance of this situation is Microsoft SQL Server 6.5, whose SQL Server Enterprise Manager (version 7.0 is better with managing the design process) is only a maintenance tool with no visual design provisions. In this case, a more general-purpose tool such as Microsoft Visual InterDev (the subject of Chapter 8) proves more useful. The reason is that Visual InterDev has the ability to make low-level changes to table design such as changing the data type of a field in a table or the identity flag. Unfortunately, Visual InterDev offers these flexible design features only for SQL Server.

For our purposes in this section, I use the Microsoft Access 97 design tools along with the Northwind Traders sample database (bundled with Access), to illustrate various concepts. A good database design tool is certainly the first step in arriving at a solid structure for building a Web database. This is not to minimize the importance of following tried and proven design principles that are outside the scope of this book. Many good sources for such information are available.

Building Database Schemas

Building a database design for a Webtop application generally proceeds in the same manner as the design for a traditional desktop, file server, or client/server environment. However, you must adhere to some special considerations.

One consideration involves the way table lookup values are presented on the Web, often using the standard HTML form <OPTION> tags. Typically this process works by obtaining a result-set from a SQL SELECT statement and then using the values from the returned rows as values for multiple <OPTION> tags. Dynamically populating a combo box using HTML can be a slow process, if the lookup table is somewhat large because the resulting HTML is correspondingly large. For this reason, care should be taken to minimize the size of such tables. In the Northwind database, a good example of this kind of table is the Shipper table (related to the Orders table with the Shipvia field). If the lookup table is large, you should use a more direct approach by prompting for a string or partial string value and then searching for the value in the table.

Another consideration is validation rules. If you specify table- and field-level validation rules and validation text strings in the Access database, no vehicle exists for enforcing these rules and presenting the messages over the Web. Remember, the Web is now your client front-end, not native Access form objects. You should consequently implement validations using the Web development environment you choose to use, such as Java, Active Server Pages, or a CGI approach as with Cold Fusion. If you plan to build an Access front-end to run against the same database as the Webtop application, then you also have to implement the validations at the Access form level.

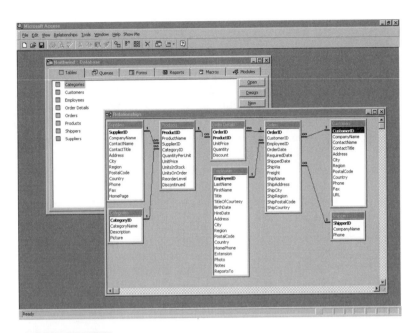

Figure 4–5   *Database Design Using Microsoft Access*

The use of indexes for expected database searches is still the rule when using Access on the Web. When the Webtop application submits an SQL statement containing an ORDER BY clause to the JET database engine, it is still optimizable with JET's embedded Rushmore query optimization technology.

Referential integrity and cascading operations (updates and deletes) may also be included in the database design as you would in any routine Access application.

Creating an ODBC Data Source

Once you finalize the database design for your Web application, the next step is to enable the Web server to find and attach to the database. Windows NT-based Web database development environments, including IDC, require an ODBC data source name associated with the database. The process of creating and ODBC DSN is covered in-depth in Chapter 9, "Publishing Desktop Databases."

Converting Access Objects

With Access 97, you can use the *Publish to the Web Wizard* to convert various application objects for use with IDC. The wizard offers the ability to convert tables in datasheet view, queries, forms, and reports to a pseudo dynamic presentation on the Web. The wizard will convert to both IDC and Active Server Pages (ASP) dynamic forms. Chapter 9 focuses on the static and ASP dynamic output, but for our purposes here, I show what the HTX/IDC dynamic output yields.

From Access 97, you can choose the *Save As HTML* item from the File menu to invoke the Publish to the Web Wizard. From here, you can select any number of database objects for conversion: tables, queries, forms, or reports. Converting tables, queries, and forms yields a tabular presentation of the data using standard HTML tables. The wizard creates both the IDC and HTX files, but you need to create a simple HTML file to test the pages. If you choose to convert a table object, the wizard generates a SELECT * statement to retrieve all fields. Here is a sample Web page used to invoke the generated IDC and HTX files:

```
<HTML>
<HEAD>
<TITLE>Northwind Products Table Query</TITLE>
</HEAD>

<BODY>

<H2>Access to IDC Conversion</H2>

<H3>In order to submit the query:
<A HREF=
    "http://amuletweb/book/products.idc?">
    Click here</A></H3>

</BODY>
</HTML>
```

Now, look at the IDC file contents. In the following file, the ODBC data source name is dbnwind, which was previously defined on the Web server processing the query request. Notice also that the generated SELECT statement retrieves all fields from the Products table.

```
Datasource:dbnwind
Template:Products.htx
SQLStatement:SELECT * FROM [Products]
Password:
Username:
```

Finally, here are the contents of the HTX file as generated by the wizard. The detail lines of the page are handled by the special <%BeginDetail%> and <%EndDetail%> tags that IDC recognizes, which will be discussed in a later section of this chapter (see section HTML Extension (.htx) Files).

```
<HTML>
<HEAD>
```

```
<META HTTP-EQUIV="Content-Type"
    CONTENT="text/html;charset=windows-1252">
<TITLE>Products</TITLE>
</HEAD>
<BODY>
<TABLE BORDER=1 BGCOLOR=#ffffff CELLSPACING=0>
<FONT FACE="Arial" COLOR=#000000>
<CAPTION><B>Products</B></CAPTION>

<THEAD>
<TR>
<TH BGCOLOR=#c0c0c0 BORDERCOLOR=#000000 >
<FONT SIZE=2 FACE="Arial" COLOR=#000000>
Product ID</FONT></TH>
<TH BGCOLOR=#c0c0c0 BORDERCOLOR=#000000 >
<FONT SIZE=2 FACE="Arial" COLOR=#000000>
Product Name</FONT></TH>
<TH BGCOLOR=#c0c0c0 BORDERCOLOR=#000000 >
<FONT SIZE=2 FACE="Arial" COLOR=#000000>
Supplier</FONT></TH>
<TH BGCOLOR=#c0c0c0 BORDERCOLOR=#000000 >
<FONT SIZE=2 FACE="Arial" COLOR=#000000>
Category</FONT></TH>
<TH BGCOLOR=#c0c0c0 BORDERCOLOR=#000000 >
<FONT SIZE=2 FACE="Arial" COLOR=#000000>
Quantity Per Unit</FONT></TH>
<TH BGCOLOR=#c0c0c0 BORDERCOLOR=#000000 >
<FONT SIZE=2 FACE="Arial" COLOR=#000000>
Unit Price</FONT></TH>
<TH BGCOLOR=#c0c0c0 BORDERCOLOR=#000000 >
<FONT SIZE=2 FACE="Arial" COLOR=#000000>
Units In Stock</FONT></TH>
<TH BGCOLOR=#c0c0c0 BORDERCOLOR=#000000 >
<FONT SIZE=2 FACE="Arial" COLOR=#000000>
Units On Order</FONT></TH>
<TH BGCOLOR=#c0c0c0 BORDERCOLOR=#000000 >
<FONT SIZE=2 FACE="Arial" COLOR=#000000>
Reorder Level</FONT></TH>
<TH BGCOLOR=#c0c0c0 BORDERCOLOR=#000000 >
<FONT SIZE=2 FACE="Arial"
    COLOR=#000000>Discontinued</FONT>
</TH>

</TR>
</THEAD>

<TBODY>
<%BeginDetail%>
    <TR VALIGN=TOP>
    <TD BORDERCOLOR=#c0c0c0  ALIGN=RIGHT>
```

```
<FONT SIZE=2 FACE="Arial" COLOR=#000000>
<%ProductID%><BR></FONT></TD>
<TD BORDERCOLOR=#c0c0c0 >
<FONT SIZE=2 FACE="Arial" COLOR=#000000>
<%ProductName%><BR></FONT></TD>
<TD BORDERCOLOR=#c0c0c0 >
<FONT SIZE=2 FACE="Arial" COLOR=#000000>
<%SupplierID%><BR></FONT></TD>
<TD BORDERCOLOR=#c0c0c0 >
<FONT SIZE=2 FACE="Arial" COLOR=#000000>
<%CategoryID%><BR></FONT></TD>
<TD BORDERCOLOR=#c0c0c0 >
<FONT SIZE=2 FACE="Arial" COLOR=#000000>
<%QuantityPerUnit%><BR></FONT></TD>
<TD BORDERCOLOR=#c0c0c0  ALIGN=RIGHT>
<FONT SIZE=2 FACE="Arial" COLOR=#000000>
<%UnitPrice%><BR></FONT></TD>
<TD BORDERCOLOR=#c0c0c0  ALIGN=RIGHT>
<FONT SIZE=2 FACE="Arial" COLOR=#000000>
<%UnitsInStock%><BR></FONT></TD>
<TD BORDERCOLOR=#c0c0c0  ALIGN=RIGHT>
<FONT SIZE=2 FACE="Arial" COLOR=#000000>
<%UnitsOnOrder%><BR></FONT></TD>
<TD BORDERCOLOR=#c0c0c0  ALIGN=RIGHT>
<FONT SIZE=2 FACE="Arial" COLOR=#000000>
<%ReorderLevel%><BR></FONT></TD>
<TD BORDERCOLOR=#c0c0c0  ALIGN=RIGHT>
<FONT SIZE=2 FACE="Arial" COLOR=#000000>
<%Discontinued%><BR></FONT></TD>

    </TR>
<%EndDetail%>
</TBODY>
<TFOOT></TFOOT>
</TABLE>
</BODY>
</HTML>
```

The Web page containing the rendered result-set appears in Figure 4-6.

If you choose an Access query object to convert to an HTX/IDC dynamic page, the SELECT statement you'll find in the generated IDC file matches the one in the query object's SQL view. Form objects are converted in a simplistic manner, yielding only a tabular representation regardless of the layout of the form. Form controls are not translated to a Web equivalent. Report objects are handled in a non-dynamic manner from the perspective of generating the output, i.e., no IDC or HTX files are generated. Instead, a series of linked HTML pages is created, having a set of navigation links on the bottom of each page. Figure 4-7 show the style of output generated for the

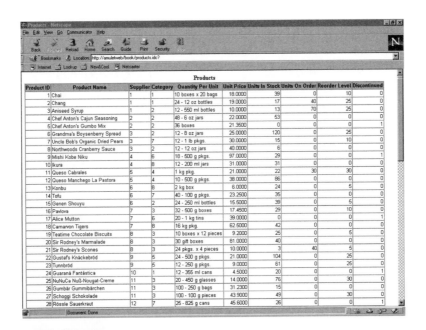

Figure 4–6   *IDC Output for Access Table Object*

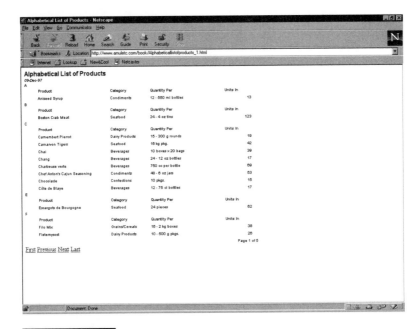

Figure 4–7   *HTML Output for Access Report Object*

Access report object named *Alphabetical List of Products,* as found in the Northwind database.

Getting the Most from Stored Procedures

Although not a feature of desktop databases like Access, stored procedures offer a particularly attractive optimization mechanism for Web applications based around relational back ends such as Microsoft SQL Server, Oracle, or Sybase SQL Server. The reason is that stored procedures are optimized queries that may include procedural code using a proprietary language (for Microsoft and Sybase SQL Server, the language is Transact SQL). Since the stored procedure code resides on the database server, it can be optimized. Many Web applications can take advantage of this optimization by embedding critical business logic inside a stored procedure. This way, the Web application need only call the stored procedure and pass along parameters coming in from the client browser.

Query Design

Once you have properly completed the design of the underlying relational database for your Webtop application, the next step in the process is to determine what queries are necessary to support the desired functionality. This process generally takes both a design and implementation phase, just like database design. First, you might use a visual query design tool using standard query-by-example (QBE) or other techniques. Second, you would translate the visual query design to a SQL syntax compatible with the target database of the Webtop application. In this section, I explore the process of obtaining working, debugged SQL strings for the purpose of including them in IDC files.

Designing Queries

You have many good choices for a visual query design tool. If your target database is Microsoft SQL Server, unfortunately, no good solution comes bundled with the product. The SQL Server Enterprise Manager software does not have such a design tool. However, two other development products such as Microsoft Access 97 and Visual InterDev do include query tools that generate SQL strings. Visual InterDev is an excellent choice for designing queries for SQL Server; however, if you use this tool, you'll probably opt for an ASP implementation instead of IDC.

For our purposes of discussion here, I use the Microsoft Access query designer to build a typical query that could be used to produce a result set for publication on the Web. As in the last section, I use the standard Northwind Traders sample database.

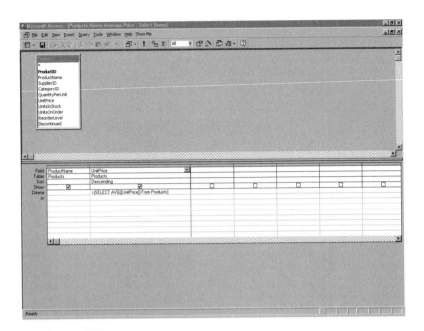

Figure 4–8 *Design View of Products Above Average Price Query*

Let's take one of the sample queries in the Northwind database. The query object, *Products Above Average Price*, could be a query that is useful in a Webtop application. Figure 4-8 illustrates the query in design view. Notice that the query involves a sub-query in order to calculate the average product price. The Access QBE is nice to have available in order to experiment with different results. Once the results (in this case, only the product name and price fields) have been verified, you can then review the SQL corresponding to the design view using SQL view. Figure 4-9 shows this SQL.

Now, using an HTML editor of your choice (such as the Windows Notepad program), you can copy the SQL text from the SQL View window to the clipboard and then paste it (while adding bit of special formatting) into a new IDC file as follows:

```
Datasource:dbnwind
Template:ProductsAboveAverage.htx
SQLStatement:
+ SELECT DISTINCTROW Products.ProductName,
+ Products.UnitPrice
+ FROM Products
+ WHERE (((Products.UnitPrice)>
+ (SELECT AVG([UnitPrice]) From Products)))
+ ORDER BY Products.UnitPrice DESC
```

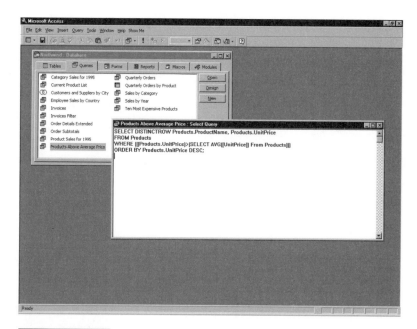

Figure 4–9   *SQL View of Query*

You can then create an appropriate HTX file that utilizes the query to render the desired results. You see much more about both IDC and HTX files in the next several sections of this chapter.

Internet Database Connector (.idc) Files

Internet Database Connector files contain the information used to establish a connection to the database and access information. This section defines the features of these files. Table 4-1 contains a description of each required field for an IDC file. Table 4-2 contains all the optional fields.

Table 4-1	IDC File Required Fields
Field	**Description**
Datasource	The name of the ODBC System Data Source Name (DSN) created earlier by using the ODBC Administrator program.
Template	The name of the HTX (HTML extension file) that formats the data returned from the query.

Table 4–1	IDC File Required Fields (Continued)
Field	**Description**
SQLStatement	The SQL statement to execute. The SQL statement can contain parameter values from the client. The parameters must be enclosed with percent characters (%). The SQL statement can occupy multiple lines in the IDC file. Following the SQLStatement field, each subsequent line beginning with a plus sign (+) is considered part of the field. Multiple SQLStatements can appear in the same file.

Table 4–2	IDC File Optional Fields
Field	**Description**
Content-Type	Specifies a valid MIME type describing the returned result set.
Default-Parameters	The optional parameter values that will be used in the IDC file if a parameter is not specified by the client.
Expires	The number of seconds to wait before refreshing a cached output page. IDC caches pages only when the Expires field is used. If a subsequent request is identical, the cached page will be returned without ever accessing the database. With the Expires field, you can force a requery of the database after a certain time interval.
MaxFieldSize	The maximum buffer space allocated by IDC per field (default value is 8192 bytes). Any characters found beyond this limit will be truncated.
MaxRecords	The maximum number of records IDC is able to return from a query. You can set this value to limit the records returned.
ODBCConnection	Specifying the value *"pool"* for this field adds the connection to the connection pool, which keeps the connection to the database open for future requests. Keeping the connection open improves performance of IDC. IDC then sends data through a pooled connection for subsequent execution of an .idc file that contains the same values for Datasource, Username, and Password. The value *"nopool"* specifies that the connection for the .idc file in which this option is set should not be taken from the connection pool.
Password	Specifies the password that corresponds to the user name to access an ODBC database.
Required-Parameters	Contains an optional comma-separated list of parameter names that HTTPODBC.DLL will require the client to pass.
TranslationFile	Specifies the path to the file that maps non-English characters so that browsers can display them properly in HTML format.
UserName	Specifies a valid username needed to access the ODBC database.

Retrieving Result-Sets

In the previous sections, I designed the database against which the database-enabled Web site is to process queries and described how you can define the actual SQL queries themselves using the Internet Database Connector component of IIS. Now you need the means by which you can format and display the query results in a manner compatible with contemporary Web browsers. For this discussion, I also focus on IDC methods using standard HTML as well as special tags recognized only by IDC.

First, I explore the use of a new file type that serves as a companion to the IDC files described in the previous section, "Query Design." These so-called *HTML Extension Files* provide the means to iterate through a query result-set and apply special formatting to the data. Then I show a simple example Web database query that utilizes all the concepts I've developed thus far. At the end of this chapter, you see more extensive example uses of IDC for processing database queries.

HTML Extension (.htx) Files

HTML extension files work in conjunction with IDC files by defining how the query results are to be displayed on the client browser. These files have a file extension of .htx. HTX files contain a number of keywords that control how the output HTML document is constructed. This section details each of these keywords.

DETAIL SECTIONS

The <%begindetail%> and <%enddetail%> keywords surround a section of the HTML extension file in which the data output from the database will be merged. Within this section, the column (query fields) names delimited with <% and %> are used to mark the position of the data returned from the SQL query. Consider, for example, the following HTX code snippet:

```
<%begindetail%>
    <%au_lname%>: <%ytd_sales%>
<%enddetail%>
```

This code lists the columns au_lname and ytd_sales. You can refer to any column in this manner. You can also refer to column names elsewhere in the HTX file. If the query returns no records, the <%begindetail%> section is skipped.

CONDITIONAL LOGIC

HTX files may contain conditional logic with the <%if%>, <%else%>, <%endif%> statement to control how the Web page is constructed. The general syntax of this statement is as follows:

```
<%if condition%>
    Place HTML text here
[<%else%>
    Place HTML text here]
<%endif%>
```

The *condition* expression is of the form: value1 operator value2 (*operator* can be one of the operators listed in Table 4-3). Note that the <%else%> portion of the statement is optional. The operands *value1* and *value2* can be column names, an HTTP variable name, one of the built-in variables (e.g., CurrentRecord), or a constant. For example, to check for a specific value for the author last name field, you could use the condition:

```
<%begindetail%>
    <%if au_lnames EQ "Gibson"%>
       Possibly William Gibson.
    <%endif%>
<%enddetail%>
```

The <%if%> statement can also be used to do special processing based on information from HTTP variables. For example, to format a page differently based on the type of client Web browser, you could include the following in the HTX file.

```
<%if HTTP_USER_AGENT contains "Mozilla"%>
    Contemporary browser
<%else%>
    client is <%HTTP_USER_AGENT%>
<%endif%>
```

Table 4–3	IDC Conditional Operators
Operator	**Description**
EQ	If value 1 equals value 2
LT	If value 1 is less than value 2
GT	If value 1 is greater than value 2
CONTAINS	If any part of value 1 contains the string value 2

BUILT-IN VARIABLES

Two built-in variables, *MaxRecords* and *CurrentRecord,* can be used only in <%if%> statements. The CurrentRecord built-in variable contains the number of times the <%begindetail%> section has been processed. The first time through the <%begindetail%> section, the value is zero. The value of CurrentRecord is incremented every time another record is retrieved from the database.

The MaxRecords built-in variable contains the value of the MaxRecords field in the IDC file.

PARAMETERS FROM IDC FILES

You can access parameters from IDC files in the HTX file by prefixing the name of the parameter with the string "idc." For example, to refer to the values of the parameter %ytdsalary%, the following syntax is required:

```
YTD Salary parameter value
  is: <%idc.ytdsalary%>
```

HTTP VARIABLES

HTTP variables specified in HTX files can provide considerable information about the operating environment and the Web client connected to the server. All headers sent by the client are also available. To access the variables with IDC, you must convert them to an IDC-compatible form. First, you must add the prefix "HTTP_", convert all hyphens to underscores, and convert all letters to uppercase. Table 4-4 contains a list of default variables that are environment variables for CGI applications and HTTP variables for IDC applications.

Table 4–4	IIS Variables
Variable	**Description**
ALL_HTTP	Variables of the form HTTP_<*header field name*>, for all HTTP headers that were not already parsed into one of the variables listed below.
AUTH_TYPE	The type of authorization in use. The authentication type is determined by examining the Authorization header that the Web server might receive with an HTTP request. If the server has authenticated a user, the authentication type used to validate the user is stored in this variable.
CONTENT_LENGTH	The number of bytes that the script can expect to receive from the client browser.
CONTENT_TYPE	The type of information supplied in the body of an HTML POST request. The MIME content types are used to label various types of objects (e.g., HTML files, graphic image files, Microsoft Word files, etc.).
GATEWAY_INTERFACE	The revision of the CGI specification with which this server complies.
HTTP_ACCEPT	Special case HTTP header indicating the different MIME types handled by the Web client. Values of the Accept fields are concatenated, and separated by commas.

Table 4–4	IIS Variables (Continued)
Variable	**Description**
HTTP_USER_AGENT	This value indicates which Web browser the client is using. The general format of this variable is software/version library/version. For example, the value returned when using Microsoft IE 4.0 is *Mozilla/4.0 (compatible; MSIE 4.0; Windows NT)*.
LOGON_USER	The user's Windows NT account.
PATH_INFO	Additional path information, as given by the client. This comprises the trailing part of the URL after the script name but before the query string (if any).
PATH_TRANSLATED	The value of PATH_INFO, but with any virtual path name expanded into a directory specification.
QUERY_STRING	The information that follows the question mark (?) in the URL that referenced this script.
REMOTE_ADDR	Client's IP address.
REMOTE_HOST	Client's host name.
REMOTE_USER	The user name supplied by the client and authenticated by the server.
REQUEST_METHOD	The HTTP request method. Values like HEAD, POST, GET, or PUT are typical.
SCRIPT_NAME	The name of the script program being executed.
SERVER_NAME	The DNS hostname alias or IP address of the Web server as it should appear in self-referencing URLs.
SERVER_PORT	The TCP/IP port on which the request was received. Typically, a Web server listens to HTTP requests on port 80.
SERVER_PORT_SECURE	The value of 0 or 1. The value 1 indicates that the request is on the encrypted port.
SERVER_PROTOCOL	The name and version of the information-retrieval protocol relating to this request, usually HTTP/1.0. The format of this variable is protocol/revision.
SERVER_SOFTWARE	The name and version of the Web server under which the Internet Server Extension is running. The format of this variable is name/version.
URL	URL of the request.

IDC Development Techniques

This section presents several commonly used techniques in building Webtop applications with the IDC component of IIS. The examples use an ODBC data source pointing at the Microsoft Access Northwind Traders sample database that comes with the Access product. You can easily test out each technique yourself in order to get the feel for the various ways to integrate database connection into a Web site. As you work through the techniques, try to think about how you may use each one in your Web site projects.

In the following examples, I assume that the application is being developed for a corporate intranet where the IS department has standardized on the use of the Microsoft IE browser. This being the case, I use the VBScript scripting language to implement some simple client-side logic. If the application were to run on the public Internet instead, then we'd have to use JavaScript for broader browser compatibility. Netscape browser, for example, does not by default recognize VBScript.

Multiple Select List Box

A common HTML form technique used to dynamically modify the query's SQL involves the use of the <SELECT MULTIPLE ... tag. This tag allows the user to select multiple items from the displayed list. IDC converts the items selected into a comma-separated list. The list can be referenced in the IDC file just like other parameters. Since the "value" of the parameter is actually a list, it is typically used only for SQL SELECT statements with an IN clause. The IN clause allows you to compare a field's value against several elements of a set of values. Consider some examples.

If the multi-select parameter name in the IDC file is enclosed in single quotation marks, an equivalent string value consisting of each element of the list will be generated where each element is also enclosed in single quotation marks. In general, you should enclose a multi-select parameter name in single quotation marks whenever the column in the IN clause is a character column or is another type in which literals are quoted, such as dates and times. If no single quotation marks are around the parameter name, no quotation marks will be placed around each element of the list (appropriate for numeric list values). You should not enclose the parameter name in single quotation marks when the column in the IN clause is a numeric type or any other type in which literals are not enclosed in single quotation marks—for example, if an HTML form contained the multiple select list box shown here:

```
<SELECT MULTIPLE NAME="region">
<OPTION VALUE="Western">
<OPTION VALUE="Eastern">
<OPTION VALUE="Northern">
<OPTION VALUE="Southern">
</SELECT>
```

Now, here's an IDC file with a SQL statement that refers to the list value.

```
SQLStatement: SELECT name, region
+ FROM Customer
+ WHERE region  IN ('%region%')
```

If the user selected "Western" and "Eastern" from the HTML form, the resulting SQL statement would be:

```
SQLStatement: SELECT name, region
+ FROM Customer
+ WHERE region IN ('Western', 'Eastern')
```

Precisely which elements appear in the IN clause list depends on which elements were selected by the user.

Another example of an HTML form is shown here, but this time I use numeric data, and therefore I do not enclose the parameter in the IDC file inside of quotation marks.

```
<SELECT MULTIPLE NAME="year">
<OPTION VALUE="1995">
<OPTION VALUE="1996">
<OPTION VALUE="1997">
<OPTION VALUE="1998">
</SELECT>
```

The IDC file and SQL statement I use this time is as follows:

```
SQLStatement: SELECT product, sales_year
+ FROM Sales
+ WHERE sales_year IN (%year%)
```

If the user selected "1996" and "1997" from the HTML form, the SQL statement would be converted to:

```
SQLStatement: SELECT product, sales_year
+ FROM Sales
+ WHERE sales_year IN (1994, 1995)
```

Parameter Passing

This technique demonstrates passing parameters to IDC with HTML forms. Using the Northwind database, the Web application is dynamic, because it changes as orders are added or deleted. This factor provides a clear advantage over static Web pages, since the user has control over the results presented on the page. The page is based on a group-by query defined in the IDC file. The SQL defined there includes references to two parameters from the HTML form, a month, and a year numeric value. The following HTML page provides two text boxes where the user can specify the month and year over which to count orders. You can see this page rendered in Figure 4-10.

```
<HTML>
<SCRIPT LANGUAGE="VBScript">
<!--
Sub Calculate_OnClick()

'Validity check routine for the Month textbox
If IsNumeric(frmMoYr.Month.Value) Then
    frmMoYr.Submit
Else
    Msgbox "Value must be numeric, try again."
End If

End Sub
-->
</SCRIPT>

<BODY>
<H2>
Calculate total number of orders as of
date specified.
</H2><HR>
Enter month and year.
<HR>

<Form NAME=frmMoYr ACTION=
    "/book/ParmPassing.idc" METHOD=Post>
<UL>
<LI>Enter the month (1-12):
<INPUT TYPE=Text NAME=Month SIZE=3 VALUE="1">
<LI>Year:
<INPUT TYPE=Text NAME=Year SIZE=4
    VALUE="1998">
<P><P><P>
<HR>
Click on the Calculate button to count orders.
<HR>
<LI>
<INPUT TYPE=Submit NAME=Calculate
    VALUE="Calculate">
</UL>
</FORM>

</BODY>
</HTML>
```

You can verify the validity of the form's data with VBScript code to avoid unnecessary error messages. In this case, I check whether the month value is numeric. When using an HTML form to launch an IDC query, you must specify the IDC file's URL in the form's ACTION attribute. Use either the Post or Get method to have IDC process the query. Use the Post method for IDC files that change the data source on the server.

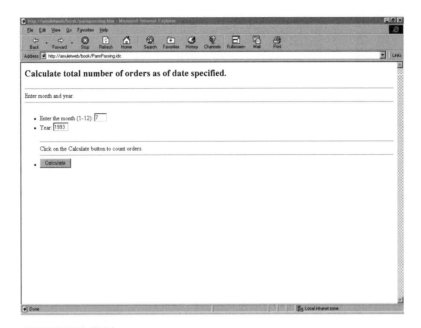

Figure 4–10 *Criteria Form to Collect Parameters*

After verifying that the fields contain valid data, invoke the form's Submit method. This requires a general-purpose button on the form rather than a Submit button.

In the IDC file that follows, you bind passed parameters in percent signs (%). Notice the Month and Year in the following IDC file. The parameter's names must match their NAME attribute in the form on the HTML page launching the request.

```
Datasource: dbnwind
Template: ParmPassing.htx
SQLStatement:
+ SELECT Count(Orders.OrderId)
+ AS TotalNumberOfOrders,
+ Month([OrderDate]) AS RetMonth,
+    Year([OrderDate]) AS RetYear
+ FROM Orders
+ WHERE (((Month([OrderDate]))=%Month%)
+ AND ((Year([OrderDate]))=%Year%))
+ GROUP BY
+ Month([OrderDate]), Year([OrderDate]);
```

Recall that the Web is stateless, since it has no direct way to remember the passed parameters. Nevertheless, you often need to show these parameters along with your return set. You can work around this difficulty by including passed parameters in the return set (see the RetMonth and RetYear alias names in the preceding SQL Statement).

The HTX file referenced in the preceding IDC file, as shown here, simply displays the values returned by the SQL statement. The HTX file includes a line showing the month and year for which it reports a count of orders. Figure 4-11 shows the results of this query.

```
<HTML>
<HEAD>
<TITLE>Northwind Order Count Information
</TITLE>
</HEAD>
<BODY>
<H2>Northwind order count as of month =
    <%RetMonth%>, and year = <%RetYear%></H2>
<B>Total Number of Orders = </B>
<%TotalNumberOfOrders%>
<P>Date of this query:
<SCRIPT LANGUAGE="VBS">
RightNow = Now
Document.Write RightNow
</SCRIPT>
</BODY>
</HTML>
```

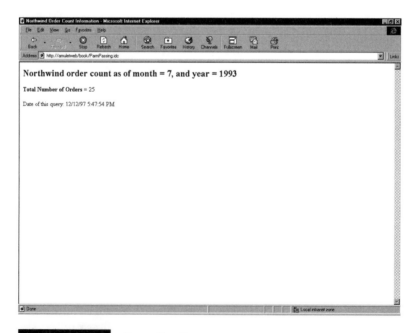

Figure 4-11 *Query Results*

Counting

The following technique represents a Web page for counting the number of orders in the Northwind database. The user can initiate the process by clicking a hypertext link or a button. The VBScript code below illustrates how to construct and pass a URL to the server. Notice that the <INPUT> tag appears outside a pair of <FORM>, </FORM> tags. You might wonder what value such buttons provide—little or none, unless you supply the onClick event, along with a piece of VBScript code to execute when the user clicks the button. Thus empowered, regular buttons can be used to validate form contents, update fields, manipulate the document, and initiate all sorts of client-side activity. In this case, the way you transition to the IDC file is using the button's onClick event. This is legal in the HTML standard; however, I found that the newer browsers, IE 5.0 and Communicator 4.5 (or Navigator 3.0) do not recognize the button (no HTML errors occur) as specified in this manner. See Figure 4-12, which shows this form rendered with the IE 3.0 browser.

```
<HTML>
<SCRIPT LANGUAGE="VBScript">
<!--
Sub Calculate_OnClick()
    Dim strAnchor
    StrAnchor = "/book/Counting.idc"
    Location.Href = strAnchor
End Sub
-->
</SCRIPT>

<BODY>
<H2>Compute total number of orders as of
    current date/time</H2>
<A HREF=
    "/book/Counting.idc">Total Number of
    Orders</A>
<BR>
<BR>
<INPUT TYPE=Button NAME="Calculate"
    VALUE="Calculate">
Click for total number of orders

</BODY>
</HTML>
```

The IDC file shown here is referenced by the URL in the VBScript code Location.HRef and the <A HREF> HTML tag.

```
Datasource: dbnwind
Template: Counting.htx
SQLStatement:
+ SELECT Count(Orders.OrderID)
+      AS TotalNumberOfOrders
+ FROM Orders;
```

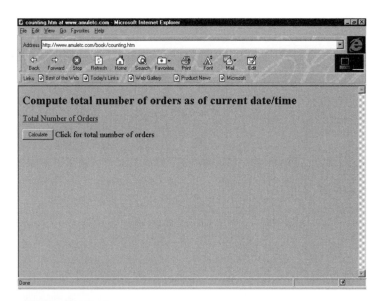

Figure 4–12   *Calculate Form*

The following code shows the Counting.htx HTX file, with a couple lines of VBScript code to time-stamp the count page. Now a built-in VBScript function returns the current date and time. This value is in turn assigned to a variable. The code uses the Document object's Write method to stamp the HTML page. The field bound to the column returned in the IDC file result-set has the alias name, TotalNumberOfOrders, in between the percent sign (%) delimiter character. The results of this query appear in Figure 4-13.

```
<HTML>
<HEAD>
<TITLE>Northwind Order Count Information
</TITLE>
</HEAD>
<BODY>
<H2>Northwind Count Example</H2>
<B>Total Number of Orders = </B>
<%TotalNumberOfOrders%>
<P>Date of this query:
<SCRIPT LANGUAGE="VBS">
   CurDateTime = Now
   Document.Write CurDateTime
</SCRIPT>
</BODY>
</HTML>
```

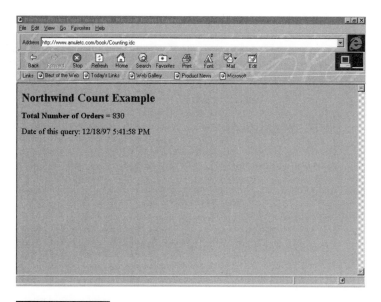

| Figure 4–13 | *Query Results* |

Adding Records

Now turn your attention to the action of adding new records to an Access table. In general, you may perform operations involving appending, updating, and deleting records for an existing table, creating a new table, etc. As discussed earlier in this chapter, you can use the Access query designer to write the SQL command string to be used in the IDC file.

In this example, I add new shippers to the Northwind Shippers table. This table includes just three fields, one of which is an AutoNumber field named ShipperID. The other two fields are CompanyName and Phone.

The following code presents the first page of the application that appends new records to the Shippers table. It includes two text boxes for CompanyName and phone, respectively, and a button used to execute the SQL INSERT statement in the reference IDC file. The VBScript onClick event procedure for the button performs a simple validity check, preventing empty shipper company names, and submits the form to the server. The process also invokes the AddShipper.idc file:

```
<HTML>
<SCRIPT LANGUAGE="VBScript">
<!--
Sub AddShipper_OnClick()

Dim strAnchor
```

```
'A simple validity check routine
If Document.Forms(0).CompanyName.Value <>
      "" Then
   frmAddShipper.Submit
Else
MsgBox "Must enter a company name, try again."
End If
End Sub
-->
</SCRIPT>

<BODY>
<H2>Enter new shipper company name and phone.
</H2>
<HR>
<FORM NAME=frmAddShipper ACTION=
    "/book/Adding.idc" METHOD=Post>
Company Name:
<INPUT TYPE=Text NAME=CompanyName SIZE=40><BR>
Telephone:
<INPUT TYPE=Text NAME=Telephone SIZE=24><BR>
<HR>
<INPUT TYPE=Button NAME=AddShipper
    VALUE="Add">
</FORM>
</BODY>
</HTML>
```

The IDC file shown below is very simple. It uses the SQL INSERT INTO statement to add a new record containing the CompanyName and Telephone fields from the browser input form. You do not need to add the ShipperID field, because the Access JET database engine automatically adds an appropriate AutoNumber field value.

```
Datasource: dbnwind
Template: Adding.htx
SQLStatement:
+ INSERT INTO Shippers
+ (CompanyName, Phone)
+ VALUES('%CompanyName%' , '%Telephone%');
```

Since the query only adds a record to a table, nothing is displayed after the query successfully executes. However, to display a confirming message after the addition has been completed would be informative. Recall that the IDC invokes the HTX file only after the SQL statement field in the IDC file runs. The HTX file shown below issues a confirmation that the new record was added successfully. Notice that the CompanyName field for the confirmation message is pulled directly from the IDC file with the reference <%idc.CompanyName%>.

```
<HTML>
<HEAD>
<TITLE>Confirm Add Shipper</TITLE>
</HEAD>
<BODY>
The addition of a new shipper is confirmed:
    <%idc.CompanyName%>.
</BODY>
</HTML>
```

Drill Down

Drill-down Web database applications are very important in that they allow the user to obtain an increasing level of detail that matches their information requirements. Drill-down techniques involve at least two linked result-set pages. Users begin by viewing a data page containing links to additional pages with greater detail information. They *drill down* into the database by clicking on any of these links.

Consider the HTML page here (shown in Figure 4-14) as a means to illustrate this technique. The user specifies a month and year and then clicks the form's Query button to launch the first of two IDC files. The ACTION attribute of the form tag specifies the DrillDown.idc IDC file. Clicking the form's button creates a result-set listing orders for the specified date.

```
<HTML>
<TITLE>IDC Drill Down Technique</TITLE>
<BODY>
<H2>
List orders for date specified.
</H2><HR>
Enter month and year.
<HR>

<FORM NAME=frmMoYr
    ACTION="/book/DrillDown.idc" METHOD=Post>
<UL>
<LI>Enter the month (1-12):
<INPUT TYPE=Text NAME=Month SIZE=3 VALUE="1">
<LI>Year:
<INPUT TYPE=Text NAME=Year SIZE=4
    VALUE="1998">
<P><P><P>
<HR>
Click on the Query button to submit query.
<HR>
<LI>
<INPUT TYPE=Submit NAME=Query
    VALUE="Query">
</UL>
</FORM>

</BODY>
</HTML>
```

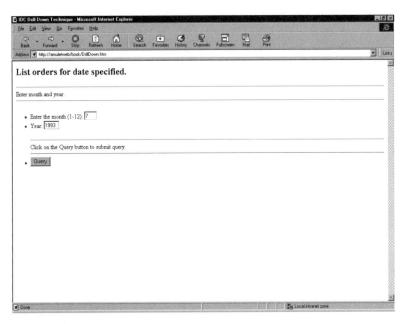

Figure 4-14   *Drill-Down Query Criteria Form*

Here's the IDC file, DrillDown.idc, that generates the list:

```
Datasource: dbnwind
Template: DrillDown.htx
SQLStatement:
+ SELECT orders.OrderID,
+    Orders.OrderDate as OrderDate,
+    Orders.CustomerID AS Customer,
+ Sum([Quantity] * [UnitPrice])*100/100
+ AS Amount
+ FROM Orders INNER JOIN [Order Details]
+ ON Orders.OrderID = [Order Details].OrderID
+ WHERE ((Month([OrderDate])=%Month%)
+ AND (Year([OrderDate])=%Year%))
+ GROUP BY Orders.OrderID, Orders.OrderDate,
+    Orders.CustomerID
```

The IDC file generates a result set having four columns: OrderID, Order-Date, CustomerID, and the sum of Extended Price across all the line items in an order. I multiply and divide the extended price total by 100 to convert the value so that it has just two spaces after the decimal point. This process compensates for the lack of a built-in currency formatting function in VBScript.

The result-set is then passed along to the DrillDetail.htx HTX file that contains the <%BeginDetail%> and <%EndDetail%> tags. This HTX file illustrates how to use these tags for the first of two drill-down screens. The tags surround the portion of a table that lists the result-set from a query. The first-level result-set page appears in Figure 4-15.

```
<HTML>
<TITLE>IDC Drill Down Level 1</TITLE>
<BODY>
<H2>
List of orders for month/period specified.
</H2><HR>

<TABLE BORDER>
<TR>
<TH>Order Date</TH><TH>Order ID</TH>
<TH>Customer</TH><TH>Amount</TH>
</TR>
<%BeginDetail%>
<TR>
<TD><%OrderDate%></TD>
<TD>
<A HREF=
    "/book/DrillDown2.idc?OrderID=
    <%OrderID%>">
<%OrderID%></A></TD>
<TD><%Customer%></TD>
<TD>$<%Amount%></TD>
</TR>
<%EndDetail%>
</TABLE>

</BODY>
</HTML>
```

An important ingredient of the HTX file is that it includes an anchor to the second-level drill-down screen. This anchor is the drill-down hypertext link. Clicking on the anchor opens a view of the individual line items of the selected order.

The anchor has two parts. First, it includes a reference to the second-level IDC file. Second, it includes a parameter reference to the OrderID field returned by the first-level IDC file. OrderID appears inside <% and %> delimiters, and the whole anchor reference appears in quotes. Notice that the reference to the OrderID field is repeated so that it displays in the table. This indicates the link that a user clicks to view the detail line items in an order.

When a user clicks on an OrderID number, he or she invokes the DrillDown2.idc file and passes the order number as a parameter. The IDC file uses the order number to extract the detail line item records that make up the order. The DrillDown2.idc file is as follows:

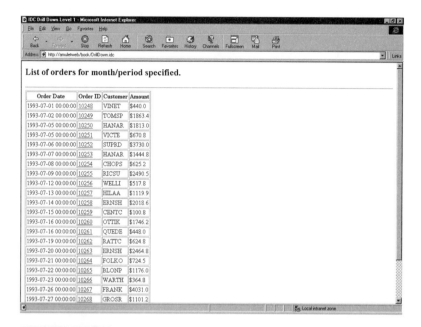

Figure 4–15   *First-Level Result-Set Page with Hyperlinks*

```
Datasource: dbnwind
Template: DrillDetail2.htx
SQLStatement:
+SELECT Products.ProductID,
+ Products.ProductName,
+ [Order Details].OrderID, Quantity,
+ [Order Details].UnitPrice,
+ Quantity * [Order Details].Unitprice
+ AS Subtotal
+ FROM Products, [Order Details]
+ WHERE Products.ProductID =
+ [Order Details].ProductID
+ AND OrderID=%OrderID%
```

The following HTX file formats the second-level result-set output from
DrillDown2.idc. First, the OrderID is displayed at the top of the page. Next, a
separate line in a table is created for each record in the result-set. Once again,
the <%BeginDetail%> and <%EndDetail%> tags indicate where to insert the
detail records in the HTML page. The second-level result-set page is appears
in Figure 4-16. Here is DrillDetail2.htx:

```
<HTML>
<TITLE>IDC Drill Down Level 2</TITLE>
<BODY>
```

```
<H2>
List of detail line items for selected order.

</H2><HR>Details on Order #<%OrderID%>
<TABLE BORDER>
<TR>
<TH>Product Name</TH>
<TH>Unit Price</TH>
<TH>Quantity</TH>
<TH>Subtotal</TH>
</TR>
<%BeginDetail%>
<TR>
<TD><%ProductName%></TD>
<TD align="right">$<%Unitprice%></TD>
<TD align="right"><%Quantity%></TD>
<TD align="right">$<%Subtotal%></TD></TR>
<%EndDetail%>
</TABLE>

</BODY>
</HTML>
```

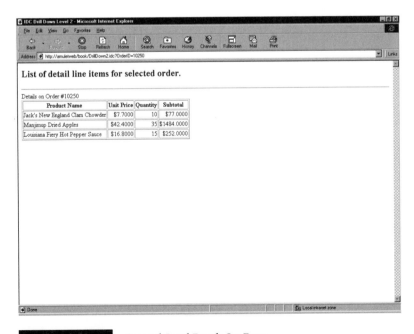

Figure 4–16   *Second-Level Result-Set Page*

Batch and Multiple Queries

You are able to group SQL queries in IDC files in two ways, as batch queries or as multiple queries. If you are querying a database that can simultaneously process several queries in a SQL statement (such as SQL Server database), you should format your statements in batch query syntax to optimize performance. For example:

```
SQLStatement:
+INSERT INTO perf(testtime, tag)
+ VALUES (getdate(), %tag%')
+SELECT au_lname, ytd_sales
+ FROM pubs.dbo.titleview
+ WHERE ytd_sales>5000
+SELECT count(*) AS nrecs
+ FROM pubs.dbo.titleview
+ WHERE ytd_sales>5000
```

If you are querying databases that cannot process a series of SQL queries simultaneously, the alternative is to specify your queries as multiple queries. For example:

```
SQLStatement:
+INSERT INTO perf(testtime, tag)
+VALUES (getdate(), '%tag%')
SQLStatement:
+SELECT au_lname, ytd_sales
+ FROM pubs.dbo.titleview
+ WHERE ytd_sales>5000
SQLStatement:
+SELECT count(*) AS nrecs
+ FROM pubs.dbo.titleview
+ WHERE ytd_sales>5000
```

Batch queries are processed together at once, whereas multiple queries are processed one at a time. Therefore, you will get better performance by formatting your queries as a batch, if your database can handle batch queries.

IDC-to-ASP Converter

Using the IDC component of IIS to publish database content on the Web can be an easy task, similar to building HTML-only pages. As you can see from the previous sections in this chapter, IDC is tightly integrated with IIS, because you do not have to obtain and install any additional software. The flexibility of IDC, however, is limited to the extent that the query and display logic can be represented in the IDC and HTX files, respectively. Although IDC has its place in the development of database-enabled sites, the newer and more powerful Active Server Pages, or ASP for short (an environment feature of IIS 3.0 and 4.0), offers more advanced and programmatic features (using server-side VBScript coding with ActiveX Data Objects) for implementing more complex and custom business logic.

If at some point you wish to migrate from an IDC-based implementation to ASP, a freeware tool called IDC2ASP can ease this transition. Developed by IntraActive Software Corporation, the converter is available at the Microsoft Web site. IDC2ASP ships as a command-line utility, IDC2ASP.EXE and an ActiveX Server Component, IDC2ASP.DLL. The IDC2ASP ActiveX Server Component can be used in any language that supports ActiveX, including Visual Basic, Visual J++, and Visual C++.

SQL Server Web Assistant

In this chapter thus far, I've concentrated on building database-enabled Web sites through use of the Internet Database Connector component of IIS. If you're using Microsoft SQL Server as your database back end, you have another alternative, the *SQL Server Web Assistant*. The main difference between IDC and the Web Assistant is that the latter is not designed to interact with the user. The Web Assistant is designed to publish pseudo-static content from a database. So the resulting Web pages can be automatically refreshed when a new record is inserted into the database or an existing record is changed or deleted. Although it doesn't afford you the flexibility of prompting for user criteria using HTML forms, it does provide a way of displaying changing content.

Figure 4-17 shows that the first step in using the Web Assistant is to log into SQL Server on the target NT Web server. In the next step in the process, you have three options selected by the option group buttons labeled: *Build a Query from the Database Hierarchy, Enter a Query as Free-Form Text*, or *Use a Query in a Stored Procedure*. Now take some time to examine each choice in-depth.

Build a Query from the Database Hierarchy

You choose this option to interactively build a query from an existing database/table hierarchy. To begin, select a database from the list displayed. You can expand the selected database to see all table and view objects by clicking on the plus-sign icon found next to each database name. Clicking on a table or view name will make the table icon next to each table or view object turn green. This has the effect of adding the SQL syntax *SELECT * FROM publishers* to the resulting query. If you wish, you can select multiple tables. The default * SQL syntax will select all fields in the table. If desired, you can click on the plus-sign icon next to each table name. This expands to display all fields

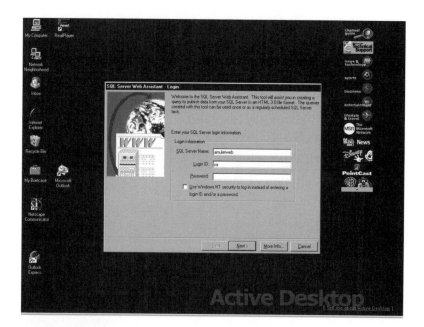

Figure 4-17   *Starting the SQL Server Web Assistant*

names in the table. From here, you can select one or more fields from each table. In the example shown in Figure 4-18, I've selected the publishers table and the fields pub_name, city, and state.

In the text box located at the bottom of the dialog box, you can also enter WHERE, ORDER BY, and GROUP BY SQL syntax to complement the query. In the example shown in Figure 4-18, I've requested the query to be ordered by the state field using the *ORDER BY state* SQL syntax.

Enter a Query as Free-Form Text

With this option selected, the dialog box appearing in Figure 4-19 prompts for the name of the database for which the query is to be built, as well as the actual SQL string. In the example shown, I've selected the pubs database and specified the SQL string equivalent to the one generated in the previous section, namely:

```
SELECT pub_name, city, state FROM publishers
ORDER BY state
```

Use a Query in a Stored Procedure

The third option allows you to identify an existing stored procedure for the basis of the new query. Figure 4-20 shows the dialog box for this option. The

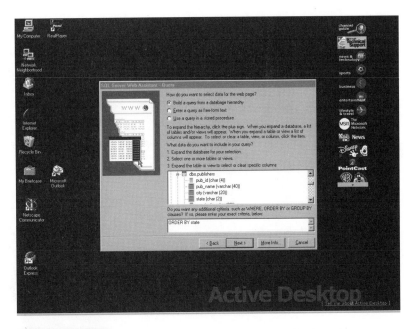

Figure 4–18   *Constructing a Query from the Database Hierarchy*

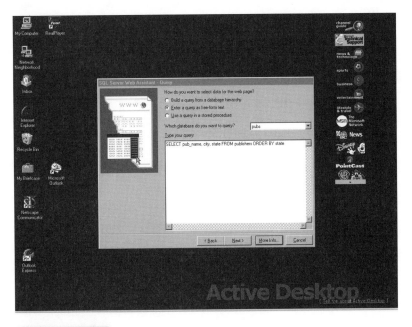

Figure 4–19   *Specifying a SQL String for the Web Assistant*

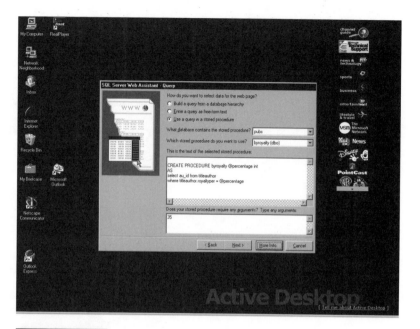

| **Figure 4–20** | *Specifying a Stored Procedure for the Web Assistant* |

dialog box prompts for the name of the database, *pubs,* and the name of the existing stored procedure, *byroyalty.* Once these are specified, the dialog box retrieves the Transact SQL text for the stored procedure and displays it. If the stored procedure requires any parameters, you can enter their values in the text box found on the bottom of the dialog box.

Scheduling Options

The next step in the Web Assistant process involves specifying a scheduling option, i.e., when the Web page is to be created. Figure 4-21 shows this dialog box. You may specify one of the following scheduling options:

- *Now.* The Web page will be created immediately.
- *Later.* The Web page will be created once, at a user-specified date and time. You'll be prompted for the date and time.
- *When Data Changes.* The Web page will be re-created automatically whenever the database changes. You'll be prompted for the tables/ views and optional fields that the Web Assistant will monitor for changes.
- *On Certain Days of the Week.* The Web page will be re-created on specific days at specific times. You'll be prompted for multiple days of the week and corresponding times.

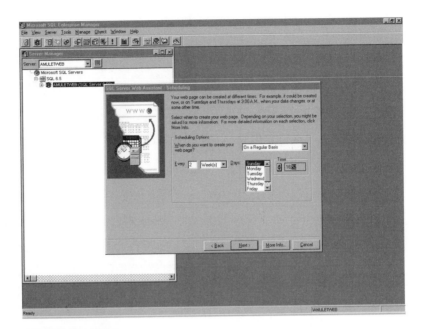

Figure 4–21   *Web Assistant Scheduling Options*

- *On a Regular Basis.* The Web page will be re-created at scheduled time intervals. You'll be prompted for the frequency, namely the number of times per: hour, day, week, or minute. In the example shown, the frequency is every 2 weeks, on Sunday afternoon.

File Options

The next dialog box of the Web Assistant requests various file options in preparation for generating the Web pages corresponding to the desired query. Figure 4-22 shows these options. First you must enter the path and file name of the Web page to be generated. If you have an HTML template file upon which the page is to be based, enter it in the text box provided. You can also provide a title of the generated Web page as well as a title for the results page. Finally, you can include a single link or multiple links on the Web page to another site or collection of sites.

Formatting Options

The final dialog box of the Web Assistant provides a simple mechanism for specifying formatting options for the resulting Web page. Figure 4-23 shows these options. First you can specify how the results title (as defined in the previous dialog box) is to look. Since I'm using HTML to define the formatting,

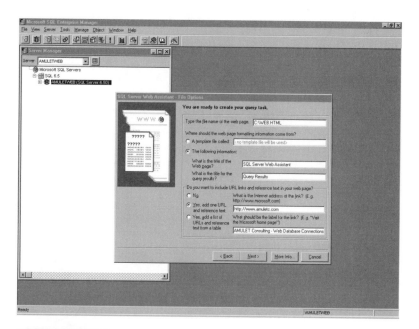

Figure 4–22   *Web Assistant File Options*

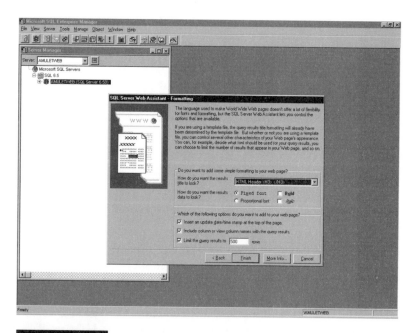

Figure 4–23   *Web Assistant Formatting Options*

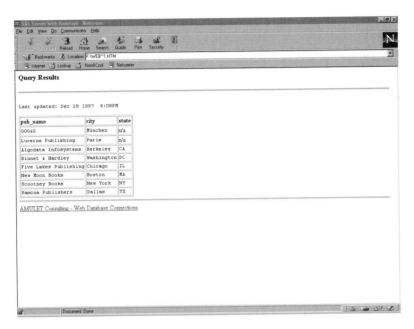

Figure 4–24 *Web Assistant Query Results*

you can use the <H2> and </H2> tag combination with values from H1 to H6. These values appear in the combo box appearing in this dialog form. Next, you specify how you want the results data to look: fixed font, bold, proportional font, or italic. Finally, you can specify if you wish an update date/time stamp to appear at the top of the page, to include column names with the query results, and to limit the query results to a specific number of rows. Since this is the last dialog box of the SQL Server Web Assistant, you must click on the Finish button to complete the process. After the pages are generated, you can see the results in a browser, as shown in Figure 4-24.

Summary

This chapter has introduced the process of building a database-enabled Web site using a commonly available development tool, the Internet Database Connector component of IIS 3.0/4.0. We successfully created several dynamic database pages using standard features of IDC and illustrated several special techniques for providing custom content. With this insight, you can now investigate more powerful techniques, including Java and Active Server environments, for providing more flexible and custom functionality. You also saw how the SQL Server Web Assistant can be used to publish pseudo-dynamic database content.

Database
Connections
with Visual J++

***T**he rise in popularity of the Java programming language is truly remarkable, considering its relatively short life span. Although the initial realm of Java applets consisted primarily of novelty animations and graphic manipulations, the problem domain space for this well conceived language has expanded considerably. Java is now being used as a serious contender for building enterprise applications containing database connections for the Internet and corporate intranets.*

Many quality rapid application development (RAD) environments are available for Java, from a wide variety of industry players, both large and small. Most of the vendors providing these tools tout the 100% pure Java party line. Java purity, however, requires the developer to avoid optimizations for a specific operating system. This independence is wise for use on a heterogeneous network environment such as the Internet; however, for private intranets, the story is quite different.

The Java development environment from Microsoft, Visual J++ 6.0, represents an excellent choice for building Java-based software for Windows-based intranet environments. Version 6.0 is a complete reworking of the prior version 1.1. Visual J++ is part of the Visual Studio™ developer suite of tools that includes Visual InterDev (the subject of Chapter 8) and Visual Basic.

In this chapter, I focus on building Java database applets and applications using Visual J++.

Visual J++ Overview

Version 6.0 of Visual J++ represents a rather late response to a burgeoning tools marketplace surrounding the Java language. It is based around the *Java Virtual Machine* (JVM) found in the Microsoft Software Development Kit (SDK 2.0) for Java. This JVM is compatible with Sun's Java Development Kit (JDK) 1.1, which sets the standard for the Java language. JDK 1.1 made many far-reaching and fundamental changes to Java over the prior JDK 1.0 release, and the newer JDK 1.2 extends Java technology even further.

WFC

Visual J++ includes the *Windows Foundation Classes* (WFC), which are a client-side and server-side superset of the Application Foundation Classes (AFC) found in previous Visual J++ versions. AFC were supersets of Java's core Abstract Window Toolkit (AWT). WFC enables developers to create Java applications that access the Win32 API. Developers who wish to create cross-platform Java applications can do so with Visual J++, but many of the development features in the product support only WFC. Unfortunately, J++ does not directly support the Java Foundation Classes (JFC), JavaBeans, or Enterprise JavaBeans. Doing JavaBean development within WFC applications is supported only when the JavaBean is hosted in an ActiveX container.

When building applications containing WFC, developers can obtain the same functionality, performance, and integration with the operating system needed to build commercially viable applications, as applications can that are written in Visual Basic, or Visual C++.

DHTML

Visual J++ also addresses the rising interest in Dynamic HTML (DHTML) by allowing developers to create DHTML components without having to manually code, or even learn, the markup language. For instance, you can create a button control in WFC that can be converted to DHTML requiring only minor code changes. Since the two leading browsers, namely Microsoft Internet Explorer 4.0 and Netscape Communicator 4.0, have different levels of DHTML support, developers have to write code to make sure that the application runs the same on both browsers. Of course, older or non-standard browsers do not contain any DHTML support.

The WFC DHTML generation offers developers the ability to write applications that are targeted for deployment either as Dynamic HTML Web applications or as Windows applications, all from precisely the same programming model. This unification of Web and Windows technologies allows programmers to switch between the two platforms more easily.

RAD Components

The Visual J++ interface is similar to other Microsoft Visual Studio tools, such as Visual Basic. The Visual Component Manager allows shared access to components. Development teams can quickly locate and reuse a variety of components, including ActiveX and HTML, using either Microsoft Access or SQL Server as the repository to store shared components. The Project Explorer allows you to navigate and sort your project files in a variety of ways, such as by type. Visual J++ also includes an integrated visual HTML editor (the same one found in Visual InterDev).

Using the same technology found in Visual Basic and Access, Visual J++ uses coding aids called *IntelliSense* that flag coding errors and provide information to correct them on the fly. In addition, when you type in a statement, IntelliSense pops up a window that displays the available methods for a given object. In the case of Java, where overloaded methods may have multiple argument (number and type) signatures, IntelliSense presents a spin-button style of picklist that lets you select from the parameter set you need. IntelliSense is not limited to WFC classes, but rather the entire Java class library. You may also use IntelliSense with imported Java class libraries.

Visual J++ includes several wizards, such as the Class Builder and the J/ Direct Call Builder. The former helps developers create new classes, and the latter is used to add a Windows method to a Java class.

After completing your application, you can use the integrated packaging feature to create your executables. The product also supports CAB and Zip distribution formats. The deployment tools also make implementation a relatively easy process.

Target Audience

The target audience for Visual J++ is corporate developers, most notably those building Windows-based intranets. Most intranet projects these days have some degree of database connectivity requirements, a need which is addressed by J++. For those developers wanting to build Win32 client applications using the Java language, J++ gives them the entire breadth of the Win32 API with which to develop applications. For those developers who desire a broader reach for multiple platforms and browsers, the Dynamic HTML integration in WFC will help them build both client- and server-side HTML applications using Java.

You could, of course, build these same systems with languages traditionally used for this purpose, namely Visual C++ and Visual Basic. C++ is, however, just C with object oriented extensions and the awkwardness associated with this afterthought. Moreover, Visual Basic although object-based, is not an OOP. Java, on the other hand, was built from the ground up as an OOP, taking the best ingredients from the leading object oriented languages. From a language purist point of view, Java is the best choice for long-term development.

A strong case can be made to approach Windows development, with the aid of J++, and cross-platform development using the same language.

Lastly, if you choose not to use WFC and disable the Microsoft language extensions (a switch is available under Compiler options in Project Properties), J++ can be used to build cross-platform applets and applications. For Internet development, you can import any Java library, including JFC, and still take advantage of IntelliSense, Statement Complete, the Task List, and Class Outline IDE features.

Windows Foundation Classes (WFC)

The Windows Foundation Classes (WFC) simplify and enhance Java development by integrating the Windows platform with the Java language. WFC is necessary when developing for Windows using Java for a number of reasons. First, relying on AWT for Windows applications is not efficient. The Windows API is richer than AWT, simply because Windows has been around longer and is more evolved. Performance is another big reason to use WFC. Since you're talking to a native API, the sluggishness normally encountered with AWT is gone. In fact, you cannot tell that a WFC application is written in Java. WFC applications run at the same speed and perform the same as an MFC (C++) or VB application. With WFC, you also have a data binding model, whereas in AWT, you don't. Data binding is important when creating sophisticated user interfaces that are bound to tables in a database. WFC supports ActiveX Data Objects (ADO) as a data binding model. This support allows you to mix data-bound components with ActiveX controls on a Web page. Of course, if you prefer to remain consistent with the cross-platform capabilities of pure Java, then you don't have to use WFC at all.

WFC is implemented as a Java class layer, or application framework, for Windows based on the Microsoft J/Direct API technology. WFC provides an object oriented set of classes for basic and advanced user interface routines as well as for several Windows system-level routines. WFC also enables developers to rapidly build applications and components for the Windows platform by encapsulating the Win32 API and Dynamic HTML programming model with a series of object oriented classes and methods. With WFC, Web server applications can respond to HTTP URL requests that in turn contain database connectivity. These applications return HTML compatible with Web browsers on a wide range of platforms, including but not limited to: Windows CE handheld devices, WebTV™, Windows 3.1, and the Macintosh.

Although WFC is a framework for application development, it is also a component model. Components built with WFC can be used in the visual design of GUIs. Whereas Windows-based programming constructs of the past were either one or the other, WFC is both, giving developers flexibility when developing applications for the Windows platform.

WFC is built using the J/Direct technology that Microsoft first supplied with its SDK for Java 2.0. J/Direct allows developers to import and use any method contained within a Windows DLL. Whereas in the past, developers were forced to use Java middleware APIs, J/Direct circumvents those APIs and gives programmers direct access to the Windows platform. Using J/Direct, WFC accesses the core Win32 API directly, and does so in an object oriented, Java-friendly manner. With WFC, developers have the ease and coherence of the Java language along with the Windows platform to assist them in developing commercial quality applications. WFC applications clearly will not run on non-Windows platforms. Using Visual J++ with WFC truly offers an alternative to both Visual Basic and C++ for developing Windows-based client/server applications.

WFC and COM

Because the Component Object Model (COM) is an integral part of developing Windows-specific intranet applications, you may need to meld the Java environment with COM. Fortunately, J++ provides this framework. In J++, all Java objects can become COM objects, allowing them to be used with common Windows applications, including Word, Excel, and Visual Basic. COM components created from J++ are indistinguishable from components built with other Windows development tools, such as C++.

Creating COM objects from Java classes is relatively easy. Simply select the COM Classes tab in the project properties and select which classes in the project are to be exported as COM objects. Java classes selected in this manner will obtain a class ID and be registered when the project is built. The necessary Type Library information will also be generated.

WFC accomplishes its goals by providing a common component model that emphasizes a relatively small set of consistent, simple rules about how a component is created, how you interface to it, how you can extend it, and how to reuse it. The key elements of the API include a uniform programming model that includes:

- UI based on either Win32 or DHTML
- Data binding to local or remote SQL Server, Access, XML, Oracle, or other tabular data
- Operations performed on the server or client with high-/low-speed connections or in a disconnected mode
- DOS command-line operation.

WFC Classes

WFC is comprised of a number of class groups, as illustrated in Figure 5-1.

The packages shown in Table 5-1 are those available in the Windows Foundation Classes for Java.

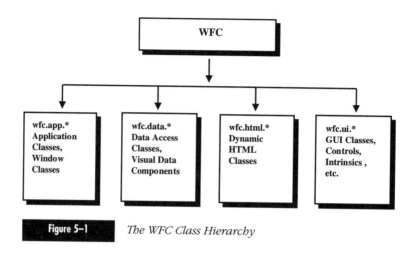

Figure 5-1   *The WFC Class Hierarchy*

Table 5-1	WFC Packages

Package	Description
Wfc.app	Contains classes encapsulating Windows application operations, i.e. threads, messaging, and access to the clipboard and registry.
Wfc.ax	Contains classes representing the ActiveX interfaces used internally by WFC components.
Wfc.core	Contains core component model classes.
Wfc.data.ui	Contains classes used to implement data bound controls.
Wfc.html	Contains classes for accessing DHTML.
Wfc.io	Contains classes and interfaces for creating and working with data streams.
Wfc.ole32	Contains Java wrapper classes and interfaces for OLE services used internally by WFC components.
Wfc.ui	Contains user interface component classes.
Wfc.util	Contains miscellaneous utility classes.
Wfc.win32	Contains Java wrapper classes for the Win32 API used internally by WFC components.

GUI Classes

WFC provides a series of objects that wrap the main Windows-based intrinsic controls—the list boxes, buttons, tabbed panels, and other GUI elements that comprise the look and feel of the Windows platform area available for developers to use within Visual J++. Additional controls, including date/time pickers, animation controls, and image display objects, help developers give their applications a more polished and consistent appearance. Application interfaces can be designed by simply dragging and dropping the GUI controls from the Toolbox onto the WFC Designer.

System Classes

WFC includes support for the direct manipulation of the underlying operating system. The objects that make up the system classes give developers the ability to create applications that harness the power of the Windows platform through encapsulation of file and memory management objects. In addition, developers who require more control over how their applications interact with the underlying platform can use J/Direct, upon which WFC is based, to get to low-level Windows functionality on their own.

Data Classes

WFC encapsulates the ActiveX Data Objects (ADO) framework in Java. ADO gives developers a high-performance, scalable solution for data access. In addition, visual data components and visual data tools make development of data-aware applications fast and easy with Java.

In a more general sense, the basis of data binding in WFC is the Universal Data Access architecture. At the programming level, WFC encapsulates the complexity of the UDA architecture while retaining all the functionality of the underlying data store. For example, a single HTML page may have both a WFC DataGrid control and an HTML form with different data sources, or you could even bind both objects to the same data source so that records navigated in the grid are reflected in the HTML. For client PCs that have not standardized on Internet Explorer or do not have WFC installed, the same application can be deployed and run from a server.

WFC achieves this independence by abstracting the data binding model for client and server UIs and efficiently handling client-side data binding versus server-side data binding.

DHTML Classes

Visual J++ includes a rich set of classes (found in the wfc.html package) that enables developers to generate Dynamic HTML (DHTML) code without having to learn a new language. Developers are more productive if they can learn one set of coding standards and practices and apply them while targeting different platforms. For example, consider the following block of Java code that creates a user interface built with the Win32 API:

```
import wfc.ui.*;

{
    Form queryForm = new Form();
    Button submit = new Button();
    submit.setText("Submit");
    submit.setPosition(20,50);
    queryForm.add(submit);
}
```

Now consider another block of Java code that generates standard HTML:

```
import wfc.html.*;

{
    DhPanel queryForm = new DhPanel();
    DhButton submit = new DhButton();
    submit.setText("Submit");
    submit.setPosition(20,50);
    queryForm.add(submit);
}
```

In both examples, the programming model is the same. In the first case, the code can run only on the client, but in the second case, the code can run on both the server and the client. If run on the server, the code can send the results of the generated HTML to a client machine.

DHTML is a reliable way to create cross-platform code. DHTML is a World Wide Web Consortium (W3C) standard, targeted for the development of applications across browser, operating system, and hardware configurations. It provides for user interaction and data presentation in an easy-to-understand combination of HTML, script code, and a document object model. Note that Microsoft has also embraced the Extensible Markup Language (XML) in the Office 2000 suite, and in all likelihood, J++ will also provide XML support.

The DHTML class library gives developers control over the Web page hosting the application. They can also change the Web container at runtime. Written in Java, DHTML applications are instantly able to run across a broad number of platforms, giving developers a reliable means of constructing applications that must perform in environments other than Win32.

Using the DHTML class library, developers can author DHTML pages using only the Java language. The resulting Java application can directly render DHTML on the fly, without any burdensome middle layer to administer. With the DHTML library, developers have the ability to design and deploy truly integrated Web- and Windows-based applications that can be executed on multiple platforms.

Here is an example of how you can build a simple DHTML page using Java. You first need to extend the DhModule class. This action ensures that the Java object can connect to the HTML document container. The container refers to the documentLoad method as the entry point into the Java object. Once the documentLoad method is called by the HTML container, the DhDocument class will enable the developer to manipulate the page. In the example, a new HTML text element is added to the document.

```
Public class NewDHTMLClass extends DhModule
{
    public void documentLoad(Object sender,
      DhEvent e)
    {
      DhDocument dhdoc = getDocument();
        Dhdoc.add(new
      DhText("Text to see in Web page"));
    }
}
```

In order to take advantage of Internet Explorer 4.0, you can use WFC to mix COM, Win32, and HTML components all in a single user interface. You can put WFC-based Win32/COM controls directly into the HTML page. For example, you could have a Win32 dialog box pop up over the browser and have it communicate with the HTML on the page. Consider the following example of this technique:

```
import wfc.ui.*;
import wfc.html.*;

{
    DhText textbox =
      getDocument().findElement("username");
    textbox.addOnClick(
    new DhEventHandler(this.onUserNameClick) );
}

public void onUserNameClick(Object sender,
    DhEvent e)
{
    Form loginForm = new Form();
    loginForm.showDialog();
}
```

In the above example, the DHTML page has a SPAN object defined (in DHTML, a text span is text found between the <SPAN> and </SPAN> tags) with the ID attribute set to "username." DhText is a class found in the wfc.html package that serves to represent static text in an HTML document. An instance of DhText is stored in textbox, and is then assigned a reference to the text span named username.

The method signature that you use as your event handler must have a void return type and two arguments, of type Object and DhEvent. The Object parameter is the object sending the event; in the example above, it would be the DhText. The DhEvent parameter is an object that can be queried for further information about the event.

Another important area in which WFC capitalizes on Internet Explorer is event handling. WFC unifies the programming model for firing and handling events, so that you can use the same code for both a Win32-based user interface as well as one that is based on HTML. Event handlers can be intermingled, including pointing events coming from Win32 and DHTML at the same listener, or having multiple listeners to a single event source embedded anywhere in the user interface. So code in any class becomes a listener simply by implementing a method with the proper argument signature and informing the source that someone wants to listen. Consider the following code that watches for the WM_LBUTTONDOWN event (the default is the left mouse button):

```
import wfc.ui.*;
{
    submit.addOnClick(new
      EventHandler(this.onClick));
}
public void onClick(Object s, event e)
{
}
```

And now look at the equivalent code that watches for the <INPUT ONCLICK=event. The only difference is in the method called to assign the event handler. DhEventHandler represents an event callback object. You create this when you need to link an event off an HTML element.

```
import wfc.html.*;
{
    submit.addOnClick(new
      DhEventHandler(this.onClick));
}
public void onClick(Object s, event e)
{
}
```

Security

WFC applications are developed with the same permissions-based security supported by the Windows operating system platform. WFC applications intended to be distributed via the Web should be digitally signed and housed inside a cabinet (CAB) file for optimal performance. J++ guides you through this process. In this way, you can be guaranteed that WFC applications downloaded to a local client machine will not have any more access to the system than explicitly defined by the end user. WFC applications are true Windows applications; thus they require considerable support from the underlying operating system. The WFC security restrictions prevent users from unknowingly downloading and executing potentially hazardous local code.

WFC Designer

The WFC Designer, included with Visual J++, is the fastest way to build Windows GUIs with the Java language. A developer can drag and drop objects onto a visual form and design the layout for an application's user interface. Additionally, the drag-and-drop components allow you to bind data sources to any visual control. By dragging the ADO Binding Component to the Visual Form Designer, developers can customize the component's access to any available data source. Other visual controls can then be attached to the visual ADO component, giving developers an easy way to build data-driven applications.

Applications built with the WFC Designer are true Windows-based applications, with the same functionality, performance, and integration to which developers using the Win32 API have grown accustomed and that users demand. In fact, an interesting note is that the WFC Designer itself is all written in WFC and Java, and so is the property inspector and the two-way code parser and code generator that underlies the Designer. A large amount of code is written using WFC and Java in the property editors, customizers, and property pages.

In this chapter, I explore the Designer from the perspective of building data-aware forms.

Data Access

To access data on a form, you can perform the following general steps in the WFC Designer:

- Make sure that the data controls are added to the Toolbox.
- Retrieve a set of records.
- Display the data on a form.
- Navigate the records.

Making the above recipe a bit more concrete, to display data on a form, you first use the DataSource control to retrieve the data. Next, you bind the data using either the DataBinder control or the DataGrid control. The DataBinder control binds the fields from a recordset to the properties of WFC controls. The DataGrid control directly displays the data from the fields that it binds in a grid format. I discuss these controls further in the sections that follow.

In order to use the data controls in the Designer, you must make sure that the controls are in the Toolbox. First display the Toolbox by clicking on

Toolbox on the View menu, and then on the Tools menu, click on Customize Toolbox. In the Customize Toolbox dialog, click on the WFC Controls tab. Select the following controls: DataBinder, DataSource, DataNavigator, and DataGrid. Click on OK, and the controls should now appear in the Toolbox.

DataSource Control

The *DataSource* control provides for data access in the Visual J++ Designer. This control allows you to connect to and query a database in order to retrieve a resultset. DataSource combines the functionality of the JADO (ADO for Java will be discussed later in this chapter) Connection, Command, and Recordset objects. The control is available from the J++ Toolbox, whereas the Connection, Command, and Recordset objects can be used only in code. When you place the control on a form, the component is visible and you have access to its properties in the Properties window. Since the DataSource control only retrieves data and does not display it, the control is not visible when you run the form. To begin using the DataSource control, you must add it to a form.

To connect to the database, you must set the *connectionString* property of the DataSource control. If you need to access an ODBC data source, the syntax of the connectionString is:

```
DSN=dataSourceName; UID=userID; PWD=password;
```

If you wish, you can use the newer OLEDB keywords, as in:

```
Data Source=dataSourceName; User ID=userID;
Password=password;
```

If you need to access a Microsoft Access database (an .MDB file) directly, without using ODBC, then the syntax of the connectionString is:

```
Provider=Microsoft.Jet.OLEDB.3.51;
Data Source=fileName;
User ID=userID; Password=password;
```

After completing the connectionString, you must then set the *commandText* property of the DataSource control to a SQL string. For example, to retrieve all rows from a table named Customers, you would enter Select * from Customers.

As mentioned earlier, if you wish to define and retrieve a recordset from code, you can also use the ADO for Java components—Connections, Command, and Recordset. The J++ Designer, however, supports only the DataSource component.

Now that you have retrieved a set of records, you must bind the data to display it on the form. Figure 5-2 shows how you configure a DataSource control.

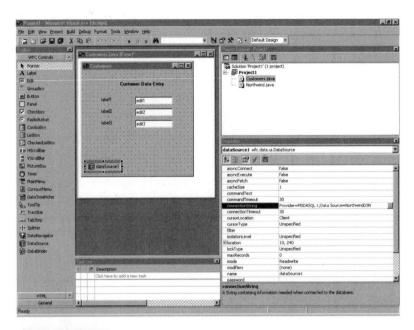

Figure 5–2   *Configuring a DataSource Control*

DataBinder Control

The *DataBinder* control binds a field from a recordset or DataSource component to the bindable properties of WFC controls. This action is called simple data binding. When a property is bound, data is automatically transferred between the field in the current record and the property. So if the value of the field changes, the new value is propagated to the property. If you navigate to a new row in the recordset, the current field value is propagated to the property. Furthermore, if the value of the property changes and the component supports a *property change notification*, the new value is propagated to the field in the recordset. The recordset is immediately updated when the property changes.

If an attempt is made to update a read-only recordset, the recordset will generate an ADO exception. You can catch this exception and set the bound property back to its previous value. If you don't, the value of the property and the value of the field will be inconsistent.

A single DataBinder component can manage multiple bindings; however, it is associated only with a single recordset. To bind the fields of a second recordset, you must use another DataBinder component. In addition, a DataBinder control can bind only to components that exist on the same WFC design surface as itself. So a DataBinder control cannot bind to a component from another form.

If the component of a bound property supports a change notification for that property, the field in the recordset is updated when the property changes. Note that the DataBinder component provides no mechanism for validating the change made to the property's value.

The DataBinder component can bind any property that is accessible, through methods matching the following syntax:

```
public <PropertyType> get<PropertyName>()
public void set<PropertyName>(<PropertyType>)
```

If a property is marked with the NotBindable attribute, then it is not enumerated in the DataBinder component's design page and cannot be bound within the Designer. You can, however, still bind the property programmatically. The NotBindable attribute is specified in the component's ClassInfo (meta-information describing the component's properties, methods, and events). The name property is a good example of a property that is marked as NotBindable.

The component of a bound property can provide events that signal when a property is about to be changed (a request) and when the property has been changed (a notification).

To support a property change request, the component provides a <PropertyName>Changing event. This event is triggered before the property is actually changed, and can be canceled to prevent the change. To support a property change notification, the component provides a <PropertyName>Changed event. This event is triggered after the property has been changed, and causes the associated field in the recordset to be updated with the new value.

Let's consider a programming example of the DataBinder component with JADO. The DataBinder component uses an array of DataBinder objects to manage the bindings. Here, we are setting the DataBinder's component's binding property to an array of DataBinding objects. This array defines the bindings between the text property of each Edit box control and the fields in the recordset.

```
import wfc.data.*;
import wfc.data.ui.*;
import wfc.ui.*;

// Connect to the SQL Server pubs database
Connection con = new Connection();
con.setConnectionString(
    "dsn=PubsDSN;uid=sa;pwd=");
con.open();
```

```
// Retrieve resultset consisting of authors
// table rows
Recordset rs = new Recordset();
rs.setActiveConnection(con);
rs.setSource("select * from authors");
rs.open();

// Create a DataBinder object
DataBinder dbind = new DataBinder();
// Set the DataSource property to associate
// the DataBinder with the recordset.
dbind.setDataSource(rs);

// Create some Edit box controls
Edit firstName = new Edit();
Edit lastName = new Edit();
Edit homePhone = new Edit();

dbind.setBindings(new DataBinding[] {
new DataBinding(firstName, "text",
    "au_fname"),
new DataBinding(lastName,"text","au_lname"),
new DataBinding(homePhone,"text","phone")});
}
```

Now I want to step through the procedure for using the DataBinder control through the WFC Designer. First, make sure that you have a DataSource control on the form to retrieve the data. Next, add one or more Edit controls to match the fields from the table you wish to represent on the form. Now add a DataBinder control to the form. Like the DataSource control, the DataBinder control is not displayed when the form is run, since it only manages the binding and does not actually display data. In order to associate the recordset from the DataSource control with the DataBinder control, set the DataBinder control's DataSource property to the name of the DataSource control.

To complete the process of binding data, you need to set the bindings property of the DataBinder control. This property identifies the bindings that are currently defined. To set this property, click on the Properties button in the Properties window or right-click on the DataBinder control and click on the Properties item on the shortcut menu. Figure 5-3 shows the Bindings Properties dialog box. In this dialog box, you select the *Data Field* from the picklist. This selection is the name of the data field to be bound. Next, you select the name of the Edit control from the *Control* picklist. From the *Property* picklist, choose the Text property. Finally, click on the Add button to add the binding to the list of bindings currently defined. At this point, you can add a DataNavigator control to the form to navigate through the records of data.

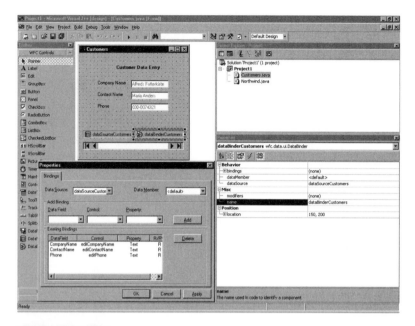

Figure 5–3 *Configuring a DataBinder Control*

DataNavigator Control

The *DataNavigator* control allows you to alter which record is considered the "current record" in a recordset. Only one current record can be in a given recordset. Any other component that is bound to the same recordset is then updated to reflect the new current row. You can use the DataNavigator control in conjunction with another data-bound control, such as the DataBinder control. The DataBinder control binds a property of another control to a field in a recordset. This property obtains data from the current record of the recordset, which is initially the first record. To move to another record, use a DataNavigator control that is bound to the same recordset.

The procedure for using the DataNavigator control in the WFC Designer is simple, requiring a few steps to follow. Begin by adding a DataSource control to the form to display the data. Next, use a DataBinder control to bind data from the recordset associated with the DataSource control. Then add a DataNavigator control to the form. Finally, in order to associate the recordset from the DataSource control with the DataNavigator control, set the Data-Source property of the DataNavigator control by selecting the name of the DataSource control from the picklist for this property. Figure 5-4 illustrates a configured DataNavigator control.

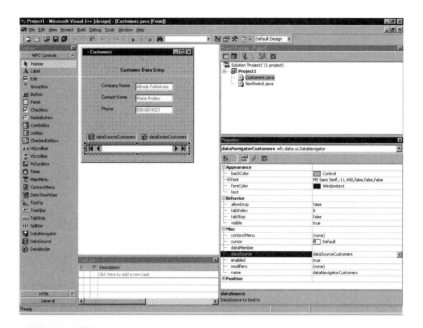

Figure 5–4 *Configuring a DataNavigator Control*

DataGrid Control

The *DataGrid* control binds multiple fields from a recordset and displays the data in a grid format (a series of rows and columns). The control is populated when you set its data source property to the name of your DataSource control.

In the WFC Designer, you can easily populate the DataGrid control. First, add a DataSource control to the form to retrieve the data. Next, add a DataGrid control to the form. Lastly, you need to set the DataGrid's Data-Source property in order to associate it with the recordset from the Data-Source control.

When the data from the recordset is displayed in the grid, the current record is identified by a marker in the corresponding row's header. To navigate through the rows in the grid, you can add a DataNavigator control to the form.

The data displayed in the DataGrid control may be updateable, depending on the cursor and lock types of the recordset (which also determines whether its data dynamically reflects the data in the data source). If the recordset allows data to be changed, you can set properties of the DataGrid control to specify that the user can change the data using the grid. The data in the recordset is always synchronized with the data displayed in the DataGrid; the converse is also true.

Universal Data Access

Universal Data Access is Microsoft's strategy for providing high-performance access to all types of information (including relational and non-relational data) across organizations, from the desktop to the enterprise. UDA enables access to any data source on any platform and provides a programming interface that is tool- and language-independent. The same API used with Active Server Pages, for example, can also be used from within Java.

The Microsoft data access components that make Universal Data Access possible are: ActiveX Data Objects (ADO), Remote Data Service (RDS, and formerly known as Advanced Data Connector or ADC), OLE DB, and ODBC. Universal Data Access extends these familiar data access technologies to allow for greater connectivity potential with diverse data sources in today's corporate computing environments. Figure 5-5 depicts the general architecture for Universal Data Access.

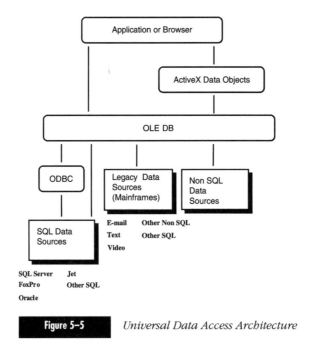

| **Figure 5–5** | *Universal Data Access Architecture* |

ADO for Java

As indicated in the previous section "DataSource Control," ADO plays a central role in providing data access to Java applications in Visual J++. JADO builds on the ADO event model and presents a simplified API. JADO is also the data access programming model for WFC applications. In Chapter 7, you see how ADO provides the same data integration with the Microsoft Active Server platform and Active Server Pages. For our purposes now, however, I limit our focus to the Java implementation of ADO. You are now able to access data using the ADO API with the Java programming language. ADO for Java, or *JADO* for short, supports all the standard ADO methods, properties, objects, and events. Operations that require a Variant data type as a parameter show good performance in a language like Visual Basic, but display not as favorable performance in Visual J++. For that reason, JADO also provides accessory functions on the Field object that take native Java data types instead of the Variant data type.

The core JADO components include the Connection, Command, and Recordset objects. The Connection object allows you to connect to a database. Once a connection is established, you can query the database to retrieve a recordset. The Recordset object represents the records returned from a query. You can use either a SQL string or a Command object to specify the query.

The goal of JADO (and ADO in general) is to provide access to, to edit, and to update data sources. The underlying programming model contains the facilities to accomplish this goal. JADO has classes and objects to perform the following activities:

- Establish a connection to a data source and optionally start a transaction using the *Connection* object.
- Create an object representing a SQL statement using the *Command* object.
- Parameterize the SQL statement's component parts, i.e., field names, table names, and WHERE clause values, with variable parameters using the *Parameter* object.
- Execute the above defined command with the *Connection, Command*, or *Recordset* object.
- Edit the data by adding, editing, or deleting rows and/or columns using the *Recordset* object.
- Cache the returned rows using a *Recordset* object if the command is row-returning.
- When desired, update the data source with changes from the cache using the *Recordset* object.
- Create a view of the cached results so that you can sort, filter, and navigate the rows using a *Recordset* object.
- Commit or roll back changes made during a transaction, and then end the transaction using the *Connection* object.

Once you retrieve a recordset, either through a Recordset object or a DataSource component, you can bind the recordset to a WFC component. JADO supports *simple data binding* through the DataBinder component, which was discussed earlier in this chapter. This type of binding refers to the relationship between a field in a recordset and the property of a WFC component. The binding is called simple because the component does not need to have explicit knowledge about the data protocol or data provider.

Visual J++ also provides *complex data binding*, through use of the Data-Grid and DataNavigator controls that interact directly with a recordset. This type of data binding refers to the direct relationship between a recordset and a WFC component.

This section defines the syntax for the JADO Connection object. Note in the following sections discussing JADO object usage that some objects have overloaded constructors and methods with a number of different argument signatures. This situation is common in Java. The default method and parameter list is denoted in boldface. In the following sections describing the JADO classes, I use the standard Java syntax definition format.

Connection Object

A Connection object represents an open connection to a data source. Your application can gain access to a data source directly, which is called a *two-tiered* system, or indirectly through a layer like IIS, which is called a *three-tier* system. JADO accesses data and services from OLE DB providers. The Connection object is used to specify a particular provider and any parameters. One use of a Connection object is to execute a query without a Command object. In this case, you would pass a query string to the *Execute* method of the Connection object. If, however, you wish to persist the command text and execute it again or use query parameters, then you must use a Command object.

Using the *Open* method of a Connection object establishes a physical connection to a data source. After this method successfully completes, the connection is live and you can issue commands against it and process results. You can use the *Close* method to close either a Connection object or a Recordset object to free any associated system resources. Closing an object does not remove it from memory, however. You can change its property settings and open it again later.

A transaction delimits the beginning and end of a series of data access operations that exist across a connection. JADO ensures that changes to a data source resulting from operations within a transaction boundary successfully complete in their entirety, or not at all. If any step of the transaction is unsuccessful, then the other completed steps are rolled back to their initial state. The data source will be as it was before the transaction began. The object model does not explicitly implement the concept of a transaction; however, transactions are represented with a set of Connection object methods.

```
Constructor
public Connection()
public Connection( String text )
```

```
Methods
public int beginTrans()
public void commitTrans()
public void rollbackTrans()
public void cancel()
public void close()
public com.ms.ado.Recordset
    execute( String commandText )
public com.ms.ado.Recordset
    execute( String commandText, int options )
public int executeUpdate( String commandText )
public int executeUpdate( String commandText,
    int options )
public void open()
public void open(String connectionString)
public void open(String connectionString,
    String userID)
public void open(String connectionString,
    String userID, String password)
public void open(String connectionString,
    String userID, String password, int options)
public Recordset openSchema( int schema,
    Object[] restrictions, String schemaID )


Properties
public int getAttributes()
public void setAttributes( int attr )
public int getCommandTimeout()
public void setCommandTimeout( int timeout )
public String getConnectionString()
public void setConnectionString( String con )
public int getConnectionTimeout()
public void setConnectionTimeout(
    int timeout )
public int getCursorLocation()
public void setCursorLocation(int cursorLoc)
public String getDefaultDatabase()
public void setDefaultDatabase( String db )
public int getIsolationLevel()
public void setIsolationLevel( int level )
public int getMode()
public void setMode( int mode )
public String getProvider()
public void setProvider( String provider )
public int getState()
public String getVersion()
public AdoProperties getProperties()
public com.ms.ado.Errors getErrors()


Events
```

```
public void addBeginTransCompleteHandler(
    ConnectionEventHandler handler)
public void removeBeginTransCompleteHandler(
    ConnectionEventHandler handler)
public void addCommitTransCompleteHandler(
    ConnectionEventHandler handler)
Public void
    removeCommitTransCompleteHandler(
    ConnectionEventHandler handler)
public void addConnectCompleteHandler(
    ConnectionEventHandler handler)
public void removeConnectCompleteHandler(
    ConnectionEventHandler handler)
public void addDisconnectHandler(
    ConnectionEventHandler handler)
public void removeDisconnectHandler(
    ConnectionEventHandler handler)
public void addExecuteCompleteHandler(
    ConnectionEventHandler handler)
public void removeExecuteCompleteHandler(
    ConnectionEventHandler handler)
public void addInfoMessageHandler(
    ConnectionEventHandler handler)
public void removeInfoMessageHandler(
    ConnectionEventHandler handler)
public void addRollbackTransCompleteHandler(
ConnectionEventHandler handler)
public void
   removeRollbackTransCompleteHandler(
    ConnectionEventHandler handler)
public void addWillConnectHandler(
    ConnectionEventHandler handler)
public void removeWillConnectHandler(
    ConnectionEventHandler handler)
public void addWillExecuteHandler(
ConnectionEventHandler handler)
public void removeWillExecuteHandler(
ConnectionEventHandler handler)
```

Command Object

A Command object is a definition of a specific command you intend to run against a data source. Typically, a Command adds, deletes, or updates data in the data source, or retrieves data in the form or rows in a table. You might use a Command object to query a database and return records in a Recordset object. You could also use Command to execute an update process or alter the structure of a database using SQL Data Definition Language (DDL). The existence of a Command object gives JADO the opportunity to optimize the execution of the command.

In order to execute a Command object, simply refer to its *Name* property on the associated Connection object. The Command object's *ActiveConnection* property must be set to the Connection object. Alternately, to create a Command object independent of a previously defined Connection object, set its ActiveConnection property to a valid connection string. In this case, JADO temporarily creates a Connection object, but does not assign its reference to an object variable.

Another feature of the Command object is the ability to associate multiple Commands with a single connection. If you choose to do this, you must explicitly create and open a Connection object and assign it to an object variable. Note that if you fail to assign the Command object's ActiveConnection property to this object variable, then JADO creates a new Connection object for each Command object, even if you use the connection string.

Another way to use the Command object is with the *Execute* method, which executes the query specified in the *CommandText* property of the object. If the CommandText property specifies a row-returning query, any results the execution generates are stored in a new Recordset object.

```
Constructor
Public Command()
public Command( String text )


Methods
public void cancel()
public com.ms.ado.Parameter createParameter(
    String Name, int Type, int Direction,
    int Size, Object Value)
public Recordset execute(Object[] parameters)
public Recordset execute( Object[] parameters,
    int options )
public Recordset execute()
public int executeUpdate(Object[] parameters)
public int executeUpdate( Object[] parameters,
    int options )
public int executeUpdate()


Properties
public com.ms.ado.Connection
    getActiveConnection()
public void setActiveConnection(
    com.ms.ado.Connection con )
public void setActiveConnection(
    String conString )
public String getCommandText()
public void setCommandText( String command )
public int getCommandTimeout()
public void setCommandTimeout(int timeout)
public int getCommandType()
```

```
public void setCommandType( int type )
public String getName()
public void setName( String name )
public boolean getPrepared()
public void setPrepared(boolean prepared)
public int getState()
public com.ms.ado.Parameter getParameter(
    int n )
public com.ms.ado.Parameter getParameter(
    String n )
public com.ms.ado.Parameters getParameters()
public AdoProperties getProperties()
```

Parameter Object

Often, commands require variable parts, or parameters, that can be altered before you issue the command. For example, you could repeatedly issue the same data retrieval command but each time vary your criteria. In general, parameters are useful for executing commands that behave like functions. Specifically, you may view the command as a black box, not necessarily knowing how it works. Instead, you would know its interface and how to pass parameters to it in order to obtain customized results.

A Parameter object represents a parameter or argument associated with a Command object based on a parameterized query or stored procedure. A Command having associated parameters is one where the desired action is defined once and where parameters are used to customize particular details of the command. Many OLE DB providers support parameterized commands. As a simple example of a parameterized command, consider a SELECT statement where a parameter is used to define the matching criteria of a WHERE clause and another defines the sort sequence of an ORDER BY clause.

A parameter object represents parameters associated with a parameterized query. It is also used to represent the IN and OUT arguments and the return values of a stored procedure.

You may use the *CreateParameter* method to create Parameter objects with the correct property settings and use the *Append* method to add them to the Parameters collection (if you know the names and properties of the parameters associated with the parameterized query or stored procedure you need to call). As a consequence, you can get and set return parameter values without having to call the Refresh method of the Parameters collection to obtain parameter information from the data provider.

```
Constructor
Public Parameter()
public Parameter( String name )
public Parameter( String name, int type )
```

```
public Parameter( String name, int type,
    int dir )
public Parameter( String name, int type,
    int dir, int size )
public Parameter( String name, int type,
    int dir, int size, Object value )


Methods
public void appendChunk( byte[] bytes )
public void appendChunk( char[] chars )
public void appendChunk( String chars )


Properties
public int getAttributes()
public void setAttributes( int attr )
public boolean getBoolean()
public void setBoolean( boolean v )
public byte getByte()
public void setByte( byte v )
public int getDirection()
public void setDirection( int dir )
public double getDouble()
public void setDouble( double v )
public float getFloat()
public void setFloat( float v )
public int getInt()
public void setInt( int v )
public long getLong()
public void setLong( long v )
public String getName()
public void setName( String name )
public int getNumericScale()
public void setNumericScale(int scale)
public int getPrecision()
public void setPrecision( int prec )
public short getShort()
public void setShort( short v )
public int getSize()
public void setSize( int size )
public String getString()
public void setString( String v )
public int getType()
public void setType( int type )
public com.ms.com.Variant getValue()
public void setValue( Object v )
public boolean isNull()
public void setNull()
public AdoProperties getProperties()
```

Recordset Object

If your command is a query that returns data as rows of information in a table—in other words, it is a row-returning query—then those rows are cached in local storage. A Recordset object is employed to represent these rows. More specifically, a Recordset object represents the set of records from a table or the results of an executed command. At any time, a Recordset object refers to only a single record within the set as the current record. A Recordset object is the primary means of examining and updating data in the rows in the following ways:

- Manage the state of the Recordset
- Add, update, or delete rows
- Traverse the rows
- Specify which rows are available
- Specify the order of the rows
- Update the data source with changes in the rows

You use a Recordset object to manipulate data from a provider. All Recordset objects are constructed using records (rows) and fields (columns). You can create as many Recordset objects as required. Four cursor types are defined in JADO: *Dynamic* cursor (may view additions, updates, deletions by other users, and allows all types of movements through the Recordset), *Keyset* cursor (prevents access to records that other users add or delete), *Static* cursor (provides a static copy of the set of records, used for client-side Recordset objects), and *Forward-only* cursor (allows you to scroll only forward through records).

Set the CursorType property prior to opening the Recordset to choose the cursor type. Alternately, you can pass a CursorType argument with the Open method. The default cursor type is Forward-only. Not all cursor types are supported by all providers.

When you open a Recordset, the current record is positioned to the first record and the EOF and BOF properties are set to False. In the case where the Recordset has no records, the EOF and BOF properties are set to True. The getEOF and getBOF methods are used to interrogate these properties.

Navigation within a Recordset object is done with the MoveFirst, MoveLast, MovePrevious, and MoveNext methods. Forward-only Recordset objects support only the MoveNext method.

```
Constructor
Public Recordset( Object r )
public Recordset()


Methods
public void addNew( Object[] fieldList,
    Object[] valueList )
public void addNew( Object[] valueList )
```

```
public void addNew()
public void cancel()
public void cancelBatch( int affectRecords )
public void cancelBatch()
public void cancelUpdate()
public Object clone()
public Object clone(int lockType)
public void close()
public void delete( int affectRecords )
public void delete()
public void find( String criteria )
public void find( String criteria,
    int SkipRecords )
public void find( String criteria,
    int SkipRecords, int searchDirection,
    Object bmkStart)
public void find( String criteria,
    int SkipRecords, int searchDirection )
public Object[][] getRows( int Rows,
    Object bmkStart, Object[] fieldList )
public void MoveFirst()
public void MoveLast()
public void MoveNext()
public void MovePrevious()
public Recordset nextRecordset(
    int[] recordsAffected )
public Recordset nextRecordset()
public void open()
public void open( Object source )
public void open( Object source,
    Object activeConnection )
public void open( Object source,
    Object activeConnection, int cursorType )
public void open( Object source,
    Object activeConnection,  int cursorType,
    int lockType)
public void open( Object source,
    Object activeConnection,  int cursorType,
    int lockType, int options )
public void release()
public void requery()
public void requery( int options )
public void resync()
public void resync( int affectRecords )
public void save(String fileName,
    int saveOption)
public boolean supports( int cursorOptions )
public void update()
public void update( Object[] valueList )
public void update( Object[] fieldList,
```

```
         Object[] valueList )
public void updateBatch()
public void updateBatch( int affectRecords )

Properties
public int getAbsolutePage()
public void setAbsolutePage( int page )
public int getAbsolutePosition()
public void setAbsolutePosition( int pos )
public Command getActiveCommand()
public void setActiveConnection( String conn )
public void setActiveConnection(
    com.ms.ado.Connection c )
public boolean getBOF()
public boolean getEOF()
public Object getBookmark()
public void setBookmark( Object bmk )
public int getCacheSize()
public void setCacheSize( int size )
public void setCursorLocation( int cursorLoc )
public int getCursorType()
public void setCursorType( int cursorType )
public Iunknown getDataMember(String bstrDM,
    com.ms.com._Guid riid)
public Iunknown getDataSource()
public void setDataSource(IUnknown dataSource)
public int getEditMode()
public Object getFilter()
public void setFilter( Object filter )
public int getLockType()
public void setLockType( int lockType )
public int getMarshalOptions()
public void setMarshalOptions( int options )
public int getMaxRecords()
public void setMaxRecords( int maxRecords )
public int getPageCount()
public int getPageSize()
public void setPageSize( int pageSize )
public int getRecordCount()
public String getSort()
public void setSort( String criteria )
public String getSource()
public void setSource( String query )
public void setSource(
    com.ms.ado.Command command )
public int getState()
public int getStatus()
public com.ms.ado.Field getField( int n )
public com.ms.ado.Field getField( String n )
public com.ms.ado.Fields getFields()
```

```
public AdoProperties getProperties()

Miscellaneous
public int getDataMemberCount()
public String getDataMemberName(int lIndex)


Events
public void addDataSourceListener(
    com.ms.ado.DataSourceListener pDSL)
public void removeDataSourceListener(
    com.ms.ado.DataSourceListener pDSL)
public void addEndOfRecordsetHandler(
RecordsetEventHandler handler)
public void emoveEndOfRecordsetHandler(
    RecordsetEventHandler handler)
public void addFieldChangeCompleteHandler(
    RecordsetEventHandler handler)
public void removeFieldChangeCompleteHandler(
    RecordsetEventHandler handler)
public void addMoveCompleteHandler(
    RecordsetEventHandler handler)
public void removeMoveCompleteHandler(
    RecordsetEventHandler handler)
public void addRecordChangeCompleteHandler(
    RecordsetEventHandler handler)
public void removeRecordChangeCompleteHandler(
    RecordsetEventHandler handler)
public void addRecordsetChangeCompleteHandler(
    RecordsetEventHandler handler)
public void
    removeRecordsetChangeCompleteHandler(
    RecordsetEventHandler handler)
public void addWillChangeFieldHandler(
    RecordsetEventHandler handler)
public void removeWillChangeFieldHandler(
    RecordsetEventHandler handler)
public void addWillChangeRecordHandler(
    RecordsetEventHandler handler)
public void removeWillChangeRecordHandler(
    RecordsetEventHandler handler)
public void addWillChangeRecordsetHandler(
    RecordsetEventHandler handler)
public void removeWillChangeRecordsetHandler(
    RecordsetEventHandler handler)
public void addWillMoveHandler(
    RecordsetEventHandler handler)
public void removeWillMoveHandler(
    RecordsetEventHandler handler)
```

Field Object

A row of a Recordset object consists of one or more *fields*. Fields are analogous to columns in a strictly relational view of a resultset. Each field has attributes, including a name, data type, and value. In order to update data in the data source, you modify the value of Field objects in the rows of a Recordset. Changes to a Recordset are ultimately sent to the data source. As mentioned before, the transaction management methods on the Connection object decide whether the changes succeed or fail.

Using the collections, methods, and properties of a Field object, you can perform the following operations:

- Get or set the data in the Field with the *Value* property.
- Get the name of a field with the Field object's *Name* property.
- Get the attributes of a field with the *Type*, *Precision*, and *Numeric-Scale* properties.
- Get the declared size of a field with the *DefinedSize* property, and the actual size of a field with the *ActualSize* property.
- Manipulate long binary or long character data fields with the *Append-Chunk* and *GetChunk* methods.
- Determine supported functionality for a given field using the *Attributes* property.

The *Value* property of a Field object is used to get or set the content of that object. The content is represented as a Variant type. A Variant is a type of object that can be assigned a value having any one of several data types. ADO for Java accesses the Value property with the getValue method (returns a Variant object) and the setValue method (takes a Variant object as an argument). The Variant data type is common in Microsoft Visual Basic and VBA; however, you can get better performance in Visual J++ by using native ADO data types.

In addition to the Value property, ADO for Java provides *field accessor* methods that use ADO data types to get and set the content of Field objects. Most of these methods have names of the form get*DataType* or set*DataType*. For example, you can use getBoolean and setDouble, as follows:

```
Constructors
public void appendChunk( byte[] bytes )
public void appendChunk( char[] chars )
public void appendChunk( String chars )
public byte[] getByteChunk( int len )
public char[] getCharChunk( int len )
public String getStringChunk( int len )


Properties
public int getActualSize()
public int getAttributes()
public int getDefinedSize()
public com.ms.com.IUnknown getDataFormat()
```

```
public void setDataFormat(
    com.ms.com.IUnknown format)
public String getName()
public int getPrecision()
public int getNumericScale()
public Variant getOriginalValue()
public int getType()
public Variant getUnderlyingValue()
public Variant getValue()
public void setValue( Variant value )
public AdoProperties getProperties()

Field Accessors
public native boolean getBoolean();
public void setBoolean( boolean v )
public native byte getByte();
public void setByte( byte v )
public native byte[] getBytes();
public void setBytes( byte[] v )
public native double getDouble();
public void setDouble( double v )
public native float getFloat();
public void setFloat( float v )
public native int getInt();
public void setInt( int v )
public native long getLong();
public void setLong( long v )
public native short getShort();
public void setShort( short v )
public native String getString();
public void setString( String v )
public native boolean isNull();
public void setNull()
public Object getObject()
public Object getObject( Class c )
public void setObject( Object value )
```

Error Object

An error can occur at any time in your Java application. Many potential causes exist for runtime errors. In general, however, several common reasons relate to the use of JADO, such as not being able to establish a connection, execute a command, or perform an operation on an object in a suitable state. For example, an error would occur if you attempted to navigate a Recordset object that had not been initialized. An error may actually produce one or more Error objects. As each error occurs, one or more Error objects are placed in the Errors collection of the Connection object. Any future errors cause the previous set of errors to be discarded. Specifically, the Errors collection is cleared, and the new set of Error objects is placed in the Errors collection.

The error represented by each Error object is a specific provider error, rather than a JADO error. You can read an Error object's properties to obtain details about each error, including: the *Description* property containing the error message, the *Number* property containing the error number (a Long integer value), the *Source* property that identifies the object that raised the error, the *HelpFile* and *HelpContext* properties indicating the Windows Help file and topic, and for SQL data sources, the *SQLState* and *NativeError* properties:

```
Properties
public String getDescription()
public int getHelpContext()
public String getHelpFile()
public int getNativeError()
public int getNumber()
public String getSource()
public String getSQLState()
```

Collections

Collections exist for Parameter objects, Field objects, and Error objects. A Collection is a type of object that contains other objects of a particular type. The objects in the collection can be retrieved with a collection method either by name, as a text string, or by an integer number referencing its position in the collection. JADO has four distinct types of collections:

- The Connection object has the *Errors* collection, which contains Error objects.

- The Command object has the *Parameters* collection, which contains Parameter objects.
- The Recordset object has the *Fields* collection, which contains Field objects. Each Field object defines a column of the Recordset object.
- The Connection, Command, Recordset, and Field objects have the *Properties* collection, which contains Property objects.

The following sections for each type of collection describe the methods and properties defined for the particular collection.

PARAMETERS

A Command object has a Parameters collection composed of Parameter objects. The *Refresh* method of the Command object's Parameters collection gets parameter information from the provider for the stored procedure or parameterized query (if they are supported), as specified in the Command object:

```
Methods
public void append(
    com.ms.ado.Parameter param )
public void delete( int n )
public void delete( String s )
```

```
public void refresh()
public Parameter getItem( int n )
public Parameter getItem( String s )

Properties
public int getCount()
```

FIELDS

A Recordset object has a Fields collection composed of Field objects. Each Field object corresponds to a column in the Recordset. Calling the *Refresh* method of the collection before opening the Recordset will serve to populate the Field collection:

```
Methods
public void append( String name, int type,
    int definedSize, int attrib )
public void delete( int n )
public void delete( String s )
public void refresh()
public com.ms.ado.Field getItem( int n )
public com.ms.ado.Field getItem( String s )

Properties
public int getCount()
```

ERRORS

The Errors collection contains all the Error objects created as a result of a JADO operation. Such an operation can generate one or more provider errors. As each error occurs, one or more Error objects can be added to the Errors collection or the Connection object. The set of Error objects in the Errors collection fully describes all errors that occurred in response to a JADO operation. You can enumerate the objects in the collection in your error handler to more precisely determine the cause of the error and appropriate steps for recovery.

```
Methods
public void clear()
public void refresh()
public com.ms.ado.Error getItem( int n )
public com.ms.ado.Error getItem( String s )

Properties
public int getCount()
```

Remoteable Recordsets

Developers can arrange for their data to be available offline. Using connectionless computing, you can build applications for mobile users and remote offices where data can be taken offline, analyzed, updated, and synchronized upon request. In other words, you can build data-driven applications that are aware of their presence on a network.

As an example, consider a traveling salesperson who uses a program on a laptop computer to keep track of customers, orders, and inventory. The program functions only while connected to the office LAN; the program works well because the computer is connected to the remote database. Most client/server-based applications work this way today. ADO, on the other hand, allows programmers to build an application that still works when not connected to the enterprise database.

ADO solves this problem by giving programmers the ability to download a subset of the data, a feature known as *Remoteable Recordsets*, from the database to the laptop computer. In addition, ADO gives programmers the ability to browse and modify the local data, known as a *Disconnected Recordset*, as if it were still being read from the remote database. When the laptop is reconnected to the remote database, the program can easily resynchronize with the master database.

JADO Event Handling

In order to handle events in JADO, you must understand that JADO intercepts ADO events, consolidates the event parameters into a single event class, and then calls your event handler. Let's describe a process for using ADO events in JADO:

- Prepare your event handler method to process an event. As an example, you might wish to process the EndOfRecordset event in the RecordsetEvent group using the following code:

```
public void onEndOfRecordset(Object sender,
  RecordsetEvent e)
{
  // process event
}
```

- Prepare a handler object to implement your event handler method. This object should have a data type of RecordsetEventHandler for an event of type RecordsetEvent, or ConnectionEventHandler for an event of type ConnectionEvent. To continue the example, here is the code for your EndOfRecordset event handler:

```
RecordsetEventHandler handler =
  new RecordsetEventHandler(this,
  "onEndOfRecordset");
```

- You'll find a number of methods having names of the form add*EventName*Handler(handler), which adds your event handler to a list of handlers defined to process a particular type of event. For the example, the method is addEndOfRecordsetHandler.

- The next step is handled automatically by JADO. An event fired by a Connection or Recordset operation is intercepted by a JADO event handler, since JADO implements all the ADO event handlers internally. JADO event handlers pass ADO RecordsetEvent parameters in an instance of the JADO RecordsetEvent class, or ADO Connection Event parameters in an instance of the JADO ConnectionEvent class. What's happening here is that these JADO classes serve to consolidate the ADO event parameters. Each JADO class contains one data member for each unique parameter in all the ADO RecordsetEvent or ConnectionEvent methods.
- JADO calls your event handler with the JADO event object. In the example, the onEndOfRecordset handler has an argument signature like the following:

```
public void onEndOfRecordset(Object sender,
    RecordsetEvent e)
```

The first argument has the type of object that sent the event, either Recordset or Connection, and the second argument is the JADO event object, either RecordsetEvent or ConnectionEvent.

- The next-to-last step is to simply return from your event handler to the JADO handler for the ADO event. JADO automatically copies selected JADO event data back to the ADO event parameters, and then the ADO event handler returns.
- To complete the process, remove your handler from the list of JADO event handlers. You can find a number of methods with names of the form removeEventNameHandler(handler). In the example, you'd use removeEndOfRecordsetHandler.

Data Form Wizard

One exciting feature of Visual J++ that should delight the Web database developer is the *Data Form Wizard*. The Data Form Wizard can generate a form bound to the fields in a database. You can add additional bindings with the *DataBinder* control. The Data Form Wizard supports Microsoft Access databases (.MDB files) and any database accessible from ODBC. You can bind data from a single table or query using the wizard. Boolean values are bound to CheckBox controls, whereas all other data types are bound to Edit controls. You cannot bind OLE Object data type fields.

You have two ways to start the Data Form Wizard. First, you may select the New Project item from the File menu. The resulting dialog presents various options, depending on what type of object you need to build. The list of

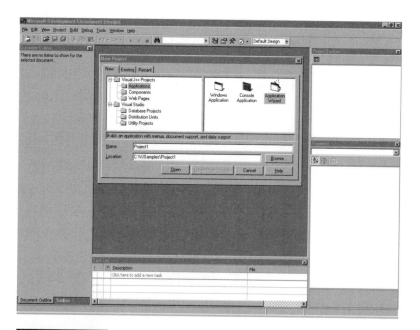

Starting the Application Wizard

Visual J++ projects includes applications, components, and Web pages. If you click on the Application selection, you see that you may choose from three types of applications: Windows application, Console application, and the Application Wizard. Choose the Application Wizard. Figure 5-6 shows the New Project dialog box.

The second way to start the Data Form Wizard is from the Project Explorer (the Project Explorer displays the hierarchy of all files in a given project). Right-click on the name of the project to which you wish to add a data form, and then from the shortcut menu, choose Add. Here, you see Add Class, Add Form, Add Web Page, and Add COM Wrapper. Choose Add Form to see the Add Item dialog box, as shown in Figure 5-7. Click on the Data Form Wizard icon and supply a name for the new class. Clicking on the Open button initiates the Data Form Wizard.

The first step in the Data Form Wizard process is specifying the name of an optional profile file that you previously saved. A profile contains the selections you made during a previous Data Form Wizard session. Figure 5-8 shows this dialog box.

If you start the Data Form Wizard through the Application Wizard, Figure 5-9 shows the next step in the wizard process. You have a choice between a *Form Based Application* or a *Form Based Application with Data*. The latter choice proceeds with building a form containing data bound con-

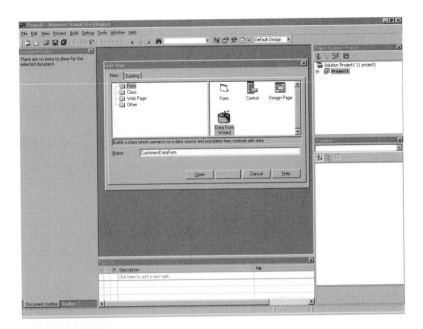

Figure 5-7   *The Add Item Dialog Box*

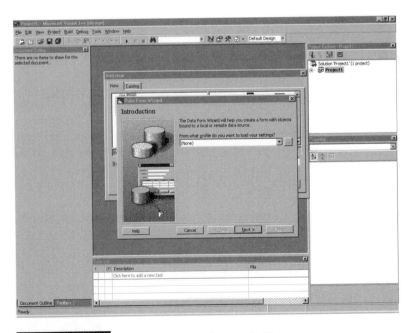

Figure 5-8   *Loading Settings from a Profile*

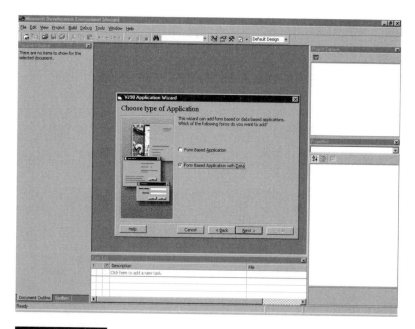

Figure 5–9   *Choosing the Type of Application*

trols. You can also build forms not bound to data (this choice results in an entirely different dialog box sequence from this point forward).

Now you need to choose the type of database to which your form will be bound. Figure 5-10 shows the next step in the wizard, where you must select the database format. You can select Microsoft Access or the ODBC option to access a database through ODBC. From ODBC, you can access an ISAM database, such as FoxPro, dBASE™, or Paradox, or a remote data source, such as SQL Server or Oracle. You can use the Access ODBC driver to connect to an .MDB file, but selecting the Access option in this dialog box yields better performance. If you choose ODBC here, the next dialog box will prompt you for the ODBC connection information: DSN, ODBC driver, user ID, password, server name, etc. For our purposes here, choose the Access option.

Figure 5-11 shows the next dialog box, where you must point to the Access database (.MDB file) on which you'll base your new form. Notice that you need to supply a complete path name as well as check off whether you wish to base the form on a record source from the database's table objects, query objects, or both.

The next step, as shown in Figure 5-12, has a dialog box that allows you to specify a name for the new form (the default name is the name of your database). You can also select a layout for the form. The choices here are Single record, Grid, and Master/Detail. A single record form displays one record at a time.

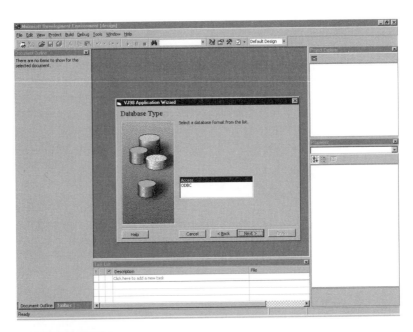

Figure 5–10   *Selecting a Database Format*

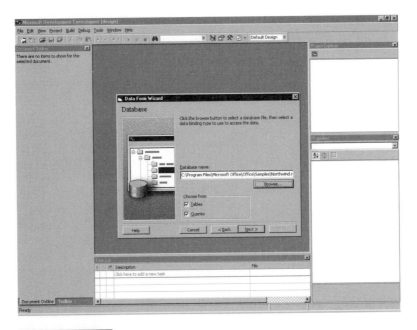

Figure 5–11   *Selecting a Database and Objects*

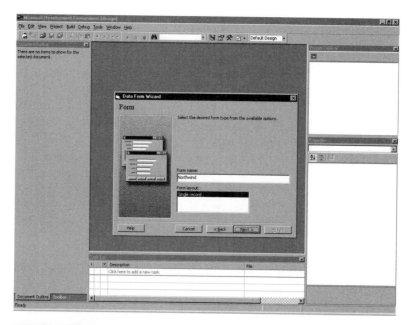

| **Figure 5–12** | *Naming the Form* |

The next step of the Data Form Wizard lets you choose the fields from the record source to bind to the controls on the form. Figure 5-13 shows the Record Source dialog box. You begin by selecting the table or query that contains the field you want to bind. Then you may choose the specific fields from the available field list. The fields will be bound to the form in the order selected. You can reorder the fields in the Selected Fields list by selecting a field and then clicking on the Up Arrow or Down Arrow buttons.

Figure 5-14 shows the next step in the wizard, where you're able to check off the particular controls you want on your form. The controls you can choose from are: Add button, Delete button, Refresh button, Update button, Close button, and Data navigator. The wizard automatically adds any Java code necessary to implement the functionality for a particular button.

The Data Form Wizard is nearly done constructing the form, but now needs to know how you wish to package the results. Figure 5-15 shows the dialog box that allows you to choose the type of package to create for the application the wizard has created. You can distribute the programs as a Java class, EXE file, or CAB file.

Choosing the *Class file* option causes the wizard not to package the project into a package file of any type. Use this option if you intend to use some other method for distribution. Choosing the *EXE file* option causes an executable (.EXE) file to be created when your project is compiled and built. This file can then be used by a user to run your new form.

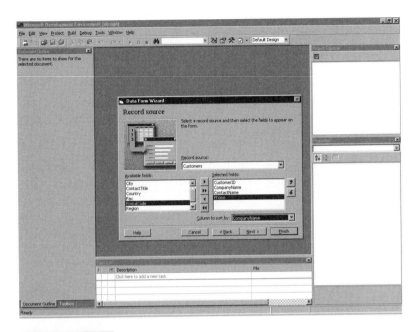

Figure 5-13   *Defining the Record Source*

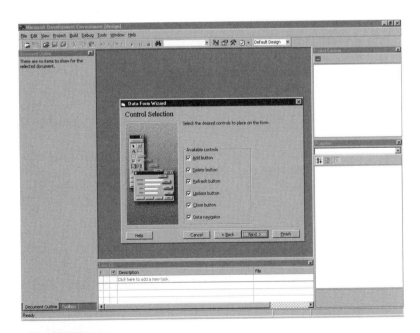

Figure 5-14   *Selecting the Form Controls*

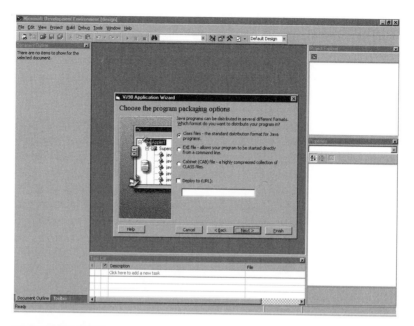

Figure 5–15 *Selecting the Packaging Option*

The CAB (cabinet) file approach towards Java application distribution has become quite popular for the Windows environment. A CAB file is a compressed file that contains all pertinent information about your project. Choosing the *CAB file* option causes the wizard to create a CAB file when your project is compiled and built. This option is appropriate if you plan to distribute your project via the Internet.

You also have the option to deploy the application to a specific URL. In the text box located next to the Deploy to URL option, you can specify the desired URL.

The final step for the Data Form Wizard, as shown in Figure 5-16, lets you store the various selections you made during the long process as a *profile* file. You can also view a summary report that contains all the selections you made during the wizard process.

Now that the wizard has completed its job, you can view the new form in design view, as shown in Figure 5-17. You can get to design view by expanding the project in the Project Explorer and then right-clicking on the Northwind.java class file. The property list shown in Figure 5-17 is for the form. You can explore the property lists for the other controls by clicking on each control. One area of the form that does not appear to be a control at all is actually the DataNavigator control, running across the bottom of the form.

The entire left-hand side of the Visual J++ screen has the Toolbox containing all the available WFC controls.

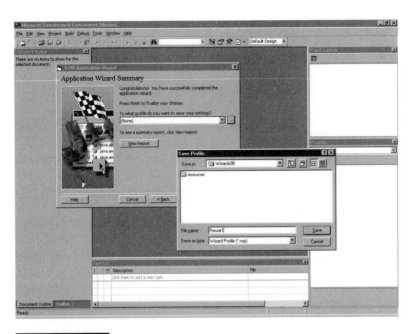

Figure 5-16 *Application Wizard Summary*

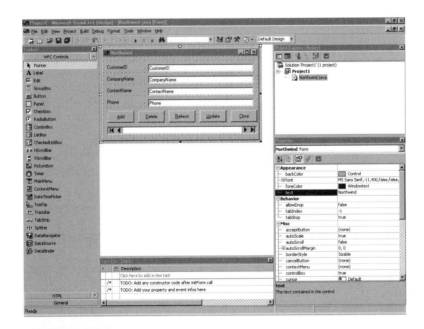

Figure 5-17 *New Form in Design View*

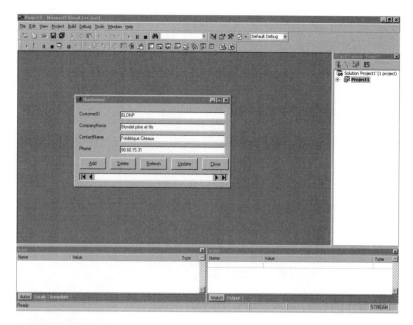

Figure 5–18 *New Form During Execution*

Figure 5-18 depicts how the new form looks when it is running. The look and feel of the form are very much like a normal Windows application.

Data Form Wizard-Generated Code

In addition to viewing the design of the data form, you also have access to the Java code generated by the wizard. In the Project Explorer, right-click on the Northwind.java file and select View Code. Also take a look at the Java code generated by the Data Form Wizard:

```java
//Northwind.java

import wfc.app.*;
import wfc.core.*;
import wfc.ui.*;
import wfc.data.*;
import wfc.data.ui.*;

public class Northwind extends Form
{
    public void btnAdd_Click(Object sender,
    Event evt)
    {
      try
```

```
      {
        m_rs.addNew();
        m_bAddNew = true;
        btnDelete.setText ("Cancel" );
        btnRefresh.setEnabled( false );
        btnAdd.setEnabled( false );
      }
      catch (Exception e)
      {
      handleADOException(e);
      }
    }
    public void btnDelete_Click(Object sender,
    Event evt)
    {
      try
      {
        if( m_bAddNew )
        {
          m_rs.cancelUpdate();
          m_bAddNew = false;
          btnDelete.setText (
            "Delete" );
          btnRefresh.setEnabled(
            true );
          btnAdd.setEnabled( true );
        }
        else
        {
          m_rs.delete(
          AdoEnums.Affect.CURRENT);
          m_rs.moveNext();
          if( m_rs.getEOF() )
            m_rs.moveLast();
        }
      }
      catch (Exception e)
      {
        handleADOException(e);
      }
    }
    public void btnRefresh_Click(Object sender,
    Event evt)
    {
      try
      {
        m_rs.cancelBatch();
        m_rs.requery();
      }
      catch (Exception e)
```

```
      {
        handleADOException(e);
      }
  }
  public void btnUpdate_Click(Object sender,
  Event evt)
  {
      try
      {
        m_rs.update();
      }
      catch (Exception e)
      {
        handleADOException(e);
      }

      m_bAddNew = false;
      btnDelete.setText ("Delete" );
      btnRefresh.setEnabled( true );
      btnAdd.setEnabled( true );
  }
  public void btnClose_Click(Object sender,
  Event evt)
  {
      Application.exit();
  }

  Recordset m_rs;
  Connection m_con;
  DataBinder m_dataBinder;
  boolean     m_bAddNew;

  protected void finalize()
  {
      try
      {
        m_rs.close();
        m_con.close();
      }
      catch (Exception e)
      {
        handleADOException( e );
      }
  }

  public Northwind()
  {
      //Required for Visual J++ Form Designer
      //support
      initForm();
```

```
    //TODO: Add any constructor code after
    //initForm call

    try
    {
      openDataConnection();
      initializeBindings();
    }
    catch (Exception e)
    {
      handleADOException( e );
    }
}

public void formClose(Event e)
{
  Application.exit();
}

public static void main(String args[])
{
  Application.run( new Northwind() );
}

void openDataConnection()
{
  m_con = new Connection();
  m_rs = new Recordset();
  // The Jet provider connection was not
  // used because your database contains
  // one or more memo/ boolean fields.
  // The Beta2 release does not support
  // binding to a memo/ boolean field
  // using the Jet provider. Here is the
  // Jet connection string:
  m_con.setConnectionString (
  "PROVIDER=Microsoft.Jet.OLEDB.3.51;
  Data Source=C:\\Program Files\\
  Microsoft Office\\Office\\Samples\\
  Northwind.mdb");

  m_con.setConnectionString (
  "Provider=MSDASQL;UID=admin;
  Driver=
  {Microsoft Access Driver(*.mdb)};
  DBQ=C:\\Program Files\\Microsoft
  Office\\Office\\Samples\\
  Northwind.mdb");
```

```
    m_con.setCursorLocation (
      AdoEnums.CursorLocation.CLIENT);
    m_con.open();
    m_rs.setActiveConnection(m_con);
    m_rs.setSource(
      "select * from Customers");
    m_rs.setCursorType(
      AdoEnums.CursorType.STATIC);
    m_rs.setCursorLocation(
      AdoEnums.CursorLocation.CLIENT);
    m_rs.setLockType(
      AdoEnums.LockType.OPTIMISTIC);
    m_rs.open();
    dataNavigator.setDataSource(m_rs);
}

void initializeBindings()
{
  try
  {
    m_dataBinder =
      new DataBinder(m_rs);
    m_dataBinder.addBinding(
      this.editCustomerID,"Text",
      "CustomerID");
    m_dataBinder.addBinding(
      this.editCompanyName,"Text",
      "CompanyName");
    m_dataBinder.addBinding(
      this.editContactName,"Text",
      "ContactName");
    m_dataBinder.addBinding(
      this.editPhone,"Text",
      "Phone");
    m_rs.moveFirst();
  }
  catch (Exception e)
  {
    handleADOException( e );
  }
}

void handleADOException(Exception e)
{
  e.printStackTrace();
  MessageBox.show( e.toString(),
    "Northwind" );
}

/**
```

```
 * NOTE: The following code is required by
 * the Visual J++ form designer.  It can be
 * modified using the form
 * editor.  Do not modify it using the code
 * editor.
 */

Container components = new Container();
Label labelCustomerID = new Label();
Edit editCustomerID = new Edit();
Label labelCompanyName = new Label();
Edit editCompanyName = new Edit();
Label labelContactName = new Label();
Edit editContactName = new Edit();
Label labelPhone = new Label();
Edit editPhone = new Edit();
Button btnAdd = new Button();
Button btnDelete = new Button();
Button btnRefresh = new Button();
Button btnUpdate = new Button();
Button btnClose = new Button();
DataNavigator dataNavigator =
  new DataNavigator();

private void initForm()
{
  labelCustomerID.setName (
    "labelCustomerID" );
  labelCustomerID.setBackColor (
    wfc.ui.Color.CONTROL);
  labelCustomerID.setTabIndex ( 0 );
  labelCustomerID.setText (
    "CustomerID" );
  labelCustomerID.setLocation (new
    Point ( 10, 20 ) );
  labelCustomerID.setSize (new
    Point ( 100, 20 ) );
  editCustomerID.setName (
    "editCustomerID" );
  editCustomerID.setBackColor (
    wfc.ui.Color.WINDOW);
  editCustomerID.setTabIndex ( 1 );
  editCustomerID.setText ("CustomerID" );
  editCustomerID.setLocation (new
    Point ( 120, 20 ) );
  editCustomerID.setCursor (
    wfc.ui.Cursor.IBEAM);
  editCustomerID.setAnchor(
    ControlAnchor.TOPLEFTRIGHT);
  editCustomerID.setSize (new
```

```
            Point ( 280, 20 )  );
        labelCompanyName.setName (
          "labelCompanyName" );
        labelCompanyName.setBackColor (
          wfc.ui.Color.CONTROL);
        labelCompanyName.setTabIndex ( 2 );
        labelCompanyName.setText (
          "CompanyName" );
        labelCompanyName.setLocation (new
          Point ( 10, 50 )  );
        labelCompanyName.setSize (new
          Point ( 100, 20 )  );
        editCompanyName.setName (
          "editCompanyName" );
        editCompanyName.setBackColor (
          wfc.ui.Color.WINDOW);
        editCompanyName.setTabIndex ( 3 );
        editCompanyName.setText (
          "CompanyName" );
        editCompanyName.setLocation (new
          Point ( 120, 50 )  );
        editCompanyName.setCursor (
          wfc.ui.Cursor.IBEAM);
         editCompanyName.setAnchor(
    ControlAnchor.TOPLEFTRIGHT);
       editCompanyName.setSize (new
          Point ( 280, 20 )  );
        labelContactName.setName (
          "labelContactName" );
        labelContactName.setBackColor (
          wfc.ui.Color.CONTROL);
        labelContactName.setTabIndex ( 4 );
        labelContactName.setText (
          "ContactName" );
        labelContactName.setLocation (new
          Point ( 10, 80 )  );
        labelContactName.setSize (new
          Point ( 100, 20 )  );
        editContactName.setName (
          "editContactName" );
        editContactName.setBackColor (
          wfc.ui.Color.WINDOW);
        editContactName.setTabIndex ( 5 );
        editContactName.setText (
          "ContactName" );
        editContactName.setLocation (new
          Point ( 120, 80 )  );
        editContactName.setCursor (
          wfc.ui.Cursor.IBEAM);
        editContactName.setAnchor(
```

```
        ControlAnchor.TOPLEFTRIGHT);
      editContactName.setSize (new
        Point ( 280, 20 )  );
      labelPhone.setName ("labelPhone" );
      labelPhone.setBackColor (
        wfc.ui.Color.CONTROL);
      labelPhone.setTabIndex ( 6 );
      labelPhone.setText ("Phone" );
      labelPhone.setLocation (new
        Point ( 10, 110 )  );
      labelPhone.setSize (new
        Point ( 100, 20 )  );
      editPhone.setName ("editPhone" );
      editPhone.setBackColor (
        wfc.ui.Color.WINDOW);
      editPhone.setTabIndex ( 7 );
      editPhone.setText ("Phone" );
      editPhone.setLocation (new
        Point ( 120, 110 )  );
      editPhone.setCursor (
        wfc.ui.Cursor.IBEAM);
editPhone.setAnchor(
    ControlAnchor.TOPLEFTRIGHT);
      editPhone.setSize (new
        Point ( 280, 20 )  );
btnAdd.setAnchor(
    ControlAnchor.BOTTOMLEFT);
      btnAdd.setName ("btnAdd" );
      btnAdd.setLocation (new
        Point ( 12, 140 )  );
      btnAdd.setSize (new
        Point ( 70, 30 )  );
      btnAdd.setTabIndex ( 8 );
      btnAdd.setText ("&Add" );
      btnAdd.addOnClick (new
      EventHandler ( this.btnAdd_Click )  );

      btnDelete.setAnchor(
        ControlAnchor.BOTTOMLEFT);
      btnDelete.setName ("btnDelete" );
      btnDelete.setLocation (new
        Point ( 94, 140 )  );
      btnDelete.setSize (new
        Point ( 70, 30 )  );
      btnDelete.setTabIndex ( 8 );
      btnDelete.setText ("&Delete" );
      btnDelete.addOnClick (new
        EventHandler (
        this.btnDelete_Click )  );
```

```
btnRefresh.setAnchor(
  ControlAnchor.BOTTOMLEFT);
btnRefresh.setName ("btnRefresh" );
btnRefresh.setLocation (new
  Point ( 176, 140 )  );
btnRefresh.setSize (new
  Point ( 70, 30 )  );
btnRefresh.setTabIndex ( 8 );
btnRefresh.setText ("&Refresh" );
btnRefresh.addOnClick (new
  EventHandler (
  this.btnRefresh_Click )  );

btnUpdate.setAnchor(
  ControlAnchor.BOTTOMLEFT);
btnUpdate.setName ("btnUpdate" );
btnUpdate.setLocation (new
  Point ( 258, 140 )  );
btnUpdate.setSize (new
  Point ( 70, 30 )  );
btnUpdate.setTabIndex ( 8 );
btnUpdate.setText ("&Update" );
btnUpdate.addOnClick (new
  EventHandler (
  this.btnUpdate_Click )  );

btnClose.setAnchor(
  ControlAnchor.BOTTOMLEFT);
btnClose.setName ("btnClose" );
btnClose.setLocation (new
  Point ( 340, 140 )  );
btnClose.setSize (new
  Point ( 70, 30 )  );
btnClose.setTabIndex ( 8 );
btnClose.setText ("&Close" );
btnClose.addOnClick (new
  EventHandler (
  this.btnClose_Click )  );
dataNavigator.setName (
  "dataNavigator" );
dataNavigator.setTabIndex ( 8 );
dataNavigator.setText ("" );
dataNavigator.setDataMember (null );
dataNavigator.setAnchor(
  ControlAnchor.BOTTOMLEFTRIGHT);
dataNavigator.setLocation (new
  Point ( 10, 180 )  );
dataNavigator.setSize (new
  Point ( 400, 20 )  );
this.setBackColor (
```

```
        wfc.ui.Color.CONTROL );
    this.setLocation (new
      Point ( 7, 7 ) );
    this.setSize (new Point ( 420, 240) );
    this.setText ("Northwind" );
    this.setNewControls (new Control[] {
      dataNavigator,
      btnAdd,
      btnDelete,
      btnRefresh,
      btnUpdate,
      btnClose,
      labelCustomerID,
      editCustomerID,
    labelCompanyName,
      editCompanyName,
      labelContactName,
      editContactName,
      labelPhone,
      editPhone}  );
    }

    //NOTE: End of form designer support
    // code.

    public static class ClassInfo extends
      Form.ClassInfo
  {
    //TODO: Add your property and event
    //infos here
  }
}
```

As you can see, the code is nicely organized, depending on the selections you made during the wizard process. Notice that the code imports all the pertinent WFC packages with:

```
import wfc.app.*;
import wfc.core.*;
import wfc.ui.*;
import wfc.data.*;
import wfc.data.ui.*;
```

The new class that implements the form is actually a subclass of the Form class as in:

```
public class Northwind extends Form
```

Starting and Stopping an Application

The wfc.app Java package includes the static Application class. This class performs all the window's registration, instantiation, message looping, etc. The Application.run() method creates a window by passing it the Form object that makes up the visual components of the window. This call appears in the main() method in the Form class.

```
public static void main(String args[])
    {
       Application.run( new Northwind() );
    }
```

The application is closed using the Click event of the window's Close button. The Application.exit() method is called for this purpose. You can, however, exit the application anywhere in the code by calling this method:

```
public void btnClose_Click(Object sender,
    Event evt)
    {
       Application.exit();
    }
```

Basic Application Structure

A basic WFC form is a public class extending the Form class with a default constructor, a main() method, and an initForm() method. When the Form class is instantiated, the class constructor calls the initForm() method. This is where the Designer puts all the code used to initialize the form and control properties. Other constructor code specific to your application follows this method. The constructor for our test application above is called Northwind(). This method calls initForm(), opens the data connection, and initializes the data bindings with the openDataConnection and initializeBindings respectively. In openDataConnection, you obtain object references that remain useful for the duration of the application, namely m_con and m_rs, which are ADO Connection and Recordset objects:

```
public Northwind()
    {
       //Required for Visual J++ Form Designer
       //support
       initForm();

       //TODO:Add any constructor code after
       //initForm call

       try
       {
          openDataConnection();
```

```
      initializeBindings ();
    }
    catch (Exception e)
    {
      handleADOException ( e );
    }
  }
```

The Designer adds declarations for any added controls in the main body of the class just before the initForm() method. In the case we're considering, I define various Label, Edit, and Button controls.

```
Container components = new Container ();
Label labelCustomerID = new Label ();
Edit editCustomerID = new Edit ();
Label labelCompanyName = new Label ();
Edit editCompanyName = new Edit ();
Label labelContactName = new Label ();
Edit editContactName = new Edit ();
Label labelPhone = new Label ();
Edit editPhone = new Edit ();
Button btnAdd = new Button ();
Button btnDelete = new Button ();
Button btnRefresh = new Button ();
Button btnUpdate = new Button ();
Button btnClose = new Button ();
DataNavigator dataNavigator = new
   DataNavigator ();
```

The Designer also generates the code in the initForm() method that sets properties of the form and the controls placed on the form. Event handling is also tightly integrated with the Designer, which can generate event-handler mappings in the initForm() method. The code in the initForm() method demonstrates how the Designer sets properties of an object and establishes an event handler for the object using the object's addOnClick() method.

```
btnClose.setText ("&Close" );
btnClose.addOnClick (new
   EventHandler ( this.btnClose_Click )  );
```

Handling Events

The Designer allows you to create easily skeleton event handlers for events and hook these up to the controls. For instance, each of the button controls you requested the wizard to create also has its own method. For example, the method btnAdd_Click implements the add record functionality. The Click event handler for each of the control buttons is appropriately enclosed in a *try* block. This way, you can implement any kind of special exception handling by filling in your own code in the *catch* block that is also provided.

```
public void btnAdd_Click(Object sender,
    Event evt)
{
  try
  {
    m_rs.addNew();
    m_bAddNew = true;
    btnDelete.setText ("Cancel" );
    btnRefresh.setEnabled( false );
    btnAdd.setEnabled( false );
  }
  catch (Exception e)
  {
    handleADOException(e);
  }
}
```

The initForm() method calls the addOnClick method of the Button control, which takes an EventHandler object. The EventHandler object is created with a reference to the method to call when that button is clicked. Basically, the EventHandler object monitors mouse clicks on the Button object and calls the appropriate handler when they occur. This model applies for all event handling in WFC and is based on a new object called a *Delegate*. The Delegate keyword is used as part of a class declaration to create method pointers. This keyword is an extension to the Java language, provided by Microsoft. All EventHandler objects are Delegates (bound method references). Java developers using WFC do not typically need to know about Delegates, since event handlers already exist in the WFC packages for the events they monitor.

Visual Database Tools

The Visual Database Tools are an important ingredient in the Visual J++ IDE. They allow for direct access to Microsoft SQL Server data stores, as well as ODBC-compliant data sources. These are the same tools described in Chapter 8, "Visual InterDev." Actually, the Database Tools are integrated into all members of the Visual Studio suite. For our purposes here, I summarize the individual components of the Database Tools:

- *Data View* is used to connect to any ODBC or OLE DB database. Once connected, you can explore the components of the database.
- *Database Designer* is used to create and modify SQL Server databases, including table structures and other schema components. With the Database Designer, you can alter field attributes such as name, data type, or size. For each such modification, the designer creates a Transact-SQL (T-SQL) script that can be run and/or saved. You can also create database diagrams that graphically represent the tables

and relationships in the database. These diagrams can be used to create, modify, or delete foreign-key relationships between tables, as well as any indexes and constraints attached to them.

- *Query Designer* provides a facility to design, execute, and save SQL queries. After establishing a connection to a database, you can use the Query Designer to design, view, and execute a SQL query. You can see the SQL automatically generated as you drag and drop tables to the design pane. The designer recognizes any relationships and generates the appropriate joins. The Query Designer has four panes—diagram, query grid, SQL, and results.
- *Stored Procedure Editor* lets you create, edit, and test SQL Server stored procedures written in T-SQL and Oracle PL/SQL subprograms, all within the J++ development environment.
- *Stored Procedure Debugger* enables you to remotely debug stored procedures for SQL Server databases, all within the J++ development environment.

Summary

This chapter has presented a very contemporary path towards building database-enabled Internet and intranet applications, and in a more general case, Windows applications, using the Java programming language. The Microsoft Visual J++ development tool provides a well conceived environment whereby developers may capitalize on their knowledge of Windows, while at the same time program these applications in Java.

The Windows Foundation Classes (WFC) are shown to be a useful encapsulation of the Win32 API for use with Java. Coupled with the WFC Designer, Data Controls, and DHTML support, Visual J++ represents a quality development environment for building Windows applications, Internet Explorer-specific intranet applications, and general Internet applications having database connections.

JDBC

*I*n this chapter, I explore the Java Database Connectivity (JDBC) specification as defined by JavaSoft (a division of Sun Microsystems). To
date, this is the only official, Sun-sponsored effort to bring database
connectivity to the Java language. Many view the Web as a global cli-
ent/server architecture and Java as the development language for this
environment; therefore, access to heterogeneous data sources is a primary ingredient in this equation. The JDBC specification can make this
a reality if many database vendors and connectivity solution vendors
decide to follow suit (something that at this point in history looks very
likely). In addition, several enterprise database vendors have even
expressed interest in using Java for writing stored procedures.

Although you can develop database-aware applets and applications with
prior JDK versions, namely version 1.x, JDBC first became part of the standard
JDK with version 1.1.x. JDBC is a java *package*, named java.sql.*, much like
other Java packages such as java.awt. The JDBC package contains the JDBC
base API classes. In this chapter, I use the latest JDK components to demonstrate the power of JDBC. You can travel to the Sun Web site to download the
latest JDK and other APIs (all for no charge).

A Web database developer using the Wintel platform may choose to
adopt the 100% Java pure JDBC approach in order to make the site cross-plat-
form-compatible for the public Internet. A database-enabled Web site based
on JDBC can certainly be hosted on a Windows NT IIS server using a
Microsoft database back end (or even a non-Microsoft database).

Some of the topics I consider here are some of the general design goals behind JDBC, the key classes that make up JDBC, including DriverManager, Connection, ResultSet and many others.

JDBC Fundamentals

JDBC is a recent development in the Java industry, making the prospect of a common database interface an even more tangible reality. In November 1995, Sun, having recognized the impact that database connectivity could have on the success of the Java language, began a public domain database specification called Java Database Connectivity (JDBC). Posted on the company's Web site for public review, scrutiny, and comment, the specification went through several revisions, some major, in terms of content changes, culminating in June 1996 with the 1.0 version. Thus far, numerous database vendors and database connectivity firms have proclaimed support for the directions put forth in the document and have committed to bringing out JDBC drivers.

JDBC was conceived as filling a void for a *call-level* SQL API for establishing database connections from within Java. Thus the focus is on executing raw SQL statements and retrieving their results. The general assumption was that third-party vendors would take the ball with this new technology and build high-level tools that developers could use to interface to the new API. For example, high-level interfaces could take the form of direct transparent mapping of tables to Java classes, semantic tree representations of more general queries, and an embedded SQL syntax for Java. As of this writing, a few actual tools and databases support JDBC, and many projects are in the works and additional products will soon surface.

When speaking of back-end databases, always the question comes up of precisely what style of SQL is acceptable. Databases typically support a wide variety of SQL syntax, and at the more advanced level, for outer joins and stored procedures (to name two areas), they tend to diverge. JDBC does not pass judgment on the query statements passed through to the driver, so an application may use any degree of SQL functionality supported by the database. Furthermore, a query may even pass something other than SQL strings or a special derivative of SQL tailored for textual search situations, for example. The least common denominator is that in order to pass the JDBC compliance test of approval, the driver must at least support ANSI SQL 92 Entry Level.

The JDBC API consists of a series of abstract Java interfaces (in Java, an interface is like a class but with only declarations of its methods, i.e., no implementations are given for the methods) to address standard database query requirements: connecting to particular databases, executing SQL statements, and processing the results of the queries. Figure 6-1 shows the basic relationship of these classes.

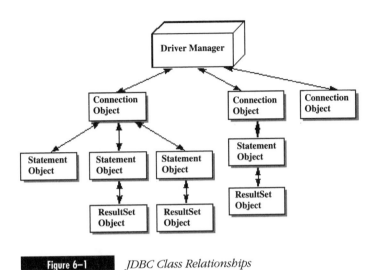

Figure 6-1	*JDBC Class Relationships*

One JDBC driver, part of the JDK, co-developed by JavaSoft and Inter-solv, is a bridge from JDBC to ODBC. The JDBC-ODBC bridge driver is found at sun.jdbc.odbc.JdbcOdbcDriver. The bridge was an effort to get the JDBC movement started by writing a *reference* driver against which other drivers can be compared, and it was partly an effort to allow developers to start using a JDBC driver. However, the expectation is that most JDBC drivers will be obtained from third parties using their expertise to connect to particular data-bases. Figure 6-2 depicts some possible implementations with JDBC in mind.

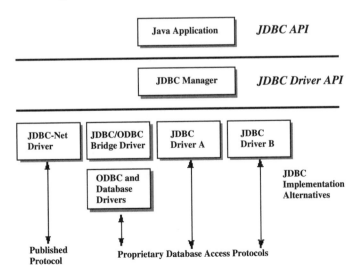

Figure 6-2	*Overall JDBC Structure and Implementation Alternatives*

In the figure, notice the aforementioned JDBC-ODBC bridge and another useful driver that goes directly to a DBMS-independent network protocol. In addition, notice third-party drivers that play the role of interfacing to proprietary database access protocols.

Keep in mind that most current Web browsers suppose Java version 1.0.2. So you'll have to run your applets using the AppletViewer, or rename and recompile the java.sql.* package, reflecting this change in the JDBC driver you're using. If you're using Java 1.1.x, then you can develop JDBC programs immediately. You will have to keep in mind that applets you create with this version will not work properly unless the Web browser is running a JVM that supports this new version of Java. You can always use the HotJava browser from JavaSoft to test applets based on the new Java specification while you wait for the other browsers to catch up to the new standard.

General Design Goals

The next section provides you with some valuable insight into the general and technical design decisions behind the JDBC specification. I believe that an understanding of how and why JDBC came into existence may prove useful when using the API for building database-enabled sites on the Web. If, however, you wish to get right down to seeing what the API is all about, please jump ahead to the Main JDBC Classes section later in this chapter.

In an ideal world, JDBC could have been provided as a library of pure Java code capable of connecting to any random database. Sun went out to the industry to ask two basic questions. The first was: Should we devise a standard Java API for SQL access? They received an overwhelming affirmative response to this question. The second question was: Should we try to standardize on a network protocol? Unfortunately, each of the database and database connectivity vendors has its own network protocols, so their interest in this project was limited to the use of their own protocols as the standard. Certainly, this was far from optimal, since no clear winner emerges. Each of the database connectivity vendors has done optimizations to its network protocol with the goal of providing higher performance, higher throughput, and richer semantics. Therefore, JDBC needed to provide a framework that would allow developers to provide modules that would talk to these specific database access protocols, but to bundle all of the protocols as part of the standard Java Developer Tool Kit (JDK) would not make sense. The resulting package would have been far too large. JDBC also needed to allow evolution to occur and allow these protocols to change over time. Different vendors have a variety of ideas determining the best way of providing them efficiently. JDBC had to have a model whereby database vendors and connectivity vendors could provide JDBC drivers. JavaSoft provides a standard API and DriverManager framework into which these drivers can be plugged and one sample driver will be provided as part of the JDK. This driver is a bridge from JDBC to ODBC. It is an effort by JavaSoft to get the JDBC movement started by writing a *reference driver* against which other drivers can be compared, and it is partly an effort to allow application writers to start using a JDBC driver. The expectation is, however, that most JDBC drivers will be obtained from third parties using their expertise to connect to particular databases.

Distributed Models

Two models describe the sort of distributed computing environment in which you may be using JDBC. The first case is where you have a large database and wish to have applets connect directly to that database. This is a *two-tiered* model, where you have a downloaded applet that's connecting directly back to a database, processing queries, and presenting results back to the user. This model tends to be appropriate when operating in a secure environment, such as an in-house Intranet, where applets are allowed to talk directly to the database. This model is also appropriate when the database is read-only.

Alternately, the *three-tiered* scenario has an application server written in Java that mediates access to the database. In this case, you download a Java applet that talks to the Java application server, which in turn talks to the relational database. This model becomes more appropriate when you want extra constraints, extra semantics, and database access that cannot easily be expressed directly to the database.

One of the primary goals of JDBC is to support both the two-tiered and three-tiered models.

The JDBC Vision

JavaSoft acquired a number of different perspectives of what the JDBC API should be. Coming from JavaSoft, the creators of the Java language, some of the priorities were to carry forward the Java message of simplicity and ease of programming. So the desire was to build an API that was easy for developers to use, that would support a good Java programming style, and that would fit in a coherent way with the other Java classes being developed. Other requirements came in from the database tool builders, who tend to have a more dynamic style of programming. These developers tend to use APIs that perhaps humans would not be comfortable using. Nevertheless, the JDBC team felt that to provide the kind of APIs needed to support these tools was important.

Another consideration was for the API to be easily implemented. In several places, the JDBC team designed a useful feature from the developer's point of view that turned out to be difficult for the JDBC driver development firms to implement. They made an attempt to balance these diverse needs. If the feature was just a trifle difficult to implement but produced a better API, the better API won.

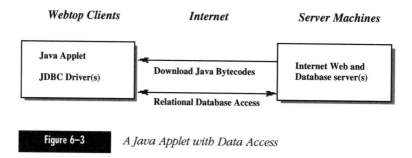

Webtop Clients   **Internet**   **Server Machines**

Java Applet

JDBC Driver(s)   Download Java Bytecodes   Internet Web and
                                                          Database server(s)

                        Relational Database Access

Figure 6–3   *A Java Applet with Data Access*

JDBC is very explicitly a SQL-level API; however, some database vendors are taking the JDBC concepts and building subsets of the API. As a result, their drivers will be used to connect to more limited databases and will not support some of features found in the specification. You may eventually see "JDBC-like" APIs for some of the legacy databases.

JDBC is envisioned to be used in a wide range of scenarios. Sometimes it can be used for small *applets* that are downloaded over the net as parts of Web documents. Some of these will be data access applets that will use JDBC to get to the databases. Take, for instance, an applet that displays historical results for a mutual fund's performance. The applet accesses a SQL database over the Web to obtain the historical data. Figure 6-3 illustrates the applet data access scenario.

Another consideration was the expectation for JDBC to be used in normal and potentially very large *applications*. In this case the Java code is *trusted* and is allowed to read and write local files and open network connections, similar to any other application code. One of the biggest growth area involving Java applications and JDBC is for use with corporate *Intranets*. For instance, a company could base all of its IS applications on Java using RAD development tools that generate Java code for forms based on corporate databases. These applications would then access database servers on local area or wide area networks as well as through the Internet. Figure 6-4 depicts the application scenario.

Another area of potential use of JDBC is in application servers, so efficiency of the API is also a very important concern. One particular area of efficiency was in terms of the number of interactions between the driver and the database. JavaSoft made a sincere attempt to make sure that JDBC did not add an extra load on the databases through a mis-designed API. This underlying philosophy has driven some of the details of the API design in several areas.

Lastly, JavaSoft has been trying to keep an eye on the standards in this area to make sure that, when appropriate, JDBC stays close to the X/Open SQL Call Level Interface (CLI), which is also the basis of ODBC, to ensure that the specification is not progressing in directions too different from the prevailing industry practice.

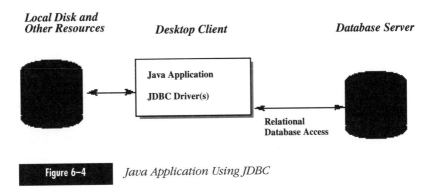

Figure 6–4   *Java Application Using JDBC*

The ODBC Influence

One the important APIs examined during the design of JDBC was the ODBC API. The JDBC team had a lot of experience with ODBC and routinely programmed with it. The result from this examination was both a positive and negative message from ODBC, and every attempt was made to apply these lessons in the JDBC API design. One good message from ODBC is that it works and has been widely accepted, but this was not always the case. When the ODBC API first came out, considerable concern existed about the idea of a standard C API working with a wide range of databases. In particular, people were quite concerned about whether it could be implemented efficiently. In fact, some performance problems indeed arose with some of the early ODBC drivers. As time passed, however, database companies and the database connectivity vendors figured out the kind of caching techniques and other optimizations that were needed in order to obtain good performance with ODBC. In certain cases, some vendors believe that their drivers are as efficient as some native database drivers. The lasting message is that developers have a general-purpose C API that can work efficiently with a range of databases.

Some unfavorable messages came from ODBC, however. First, ODBC is really an API for very experienced developers, with a lot of database experience. Details surrounding the API are quite complicated; a significant learning curve occurs prior to issuing your first SELECT query. Consequently, JavaSoft designed JDBC to make sure that the API was more approachable to the average developer. Again, aligning the API with the standard Java language model, developers could start off doing simple things, and as they progressed in the learning process by learning more sophisticated parts of the API, they could add more complexity to their applications.

Another problem with ODBC is the frequent use of VOID*. In the context for which ODBC was deigned, that was very appropriate, but it is a very non-Java thing to do. Java is a strongly typed language and is a key part of the API style. JDBC avoids using VOID * or anything like it in the API. Using the

Java *Object* type as an equivalent to VOID *, JDBC could play the same kind of games as ODBC, but that approach is not the Java language design style. At one point, JavaSoft actually looked into mapping ODBC directly into Java. Unfortunately, the heavy use of pointers in ODBC would have made that process difficult. In addition, the frequent use of multiple result types is very hard to express in Java. The JDBC designers tried writing some experimental code against these direct mapping APIs. Not only were they hard to understand, but they were also very hard to use. A lot of mental calisthenics were required. The programmer had to manipulate special place holder objects that simulated pointers, by loading them before calling the function and then checking them after calling the function to see whether they were updated. That style of programming resulted in an overabundance of source code and was very hard to read—an unfavorable combination.

Another Java programming style is the tendency to use lots of smaller methods. The ODBC style, on the other hand, is to use a smaller number of procedures with a richer set of flags. A single ODBC procedure may do a range of activities, depending on the flags and context. JDBC was designed to favor the Java model of using lots of simple methods rather than having large catch-all methods.

JDBC Technical Goals

One of the primary technical goals behind JDBC was to reuse concepts with which developers were already familiar. No one needed to reinvent concepts such as connection, statement, and result set, so you'll find that those same concepts were reused in the JDBC API. Following the ODBC model in that regard would allow application developers and database connectivity vendors to more quickly and easily learn JDBC. Although the primary focus was to deliver a low-level SQL API, JavaSoft consciously designed it for the future expectation of adding higher-level, more developer-friendly APIs, such as object relational mappings. Hence, they made an effort to simplify the interface by making a goal of having a much smaller interface than ODBC. Over time, however, as the developer community and the tools community added their input to the specification process, the JDBC interface has widened up somewhat. Now JDBC has most of the same functionality of ODBC, but with a smaller number of options and arguments. One particular force behind this end result was to provide one way of doing common operations. This philosophy did prove to simplify the API.

At one point, JavaSoft sat down and wrote a suite of test programs to study how they read. They wanted to allow for an API that was good for a human developer to write against that was also very readable. This goes back to JDBC's underpinnings to the Java language philosophy. With JDBC, as with

Java itself, the easy-to-read, easy-to-write message is a very clear part of why Java is so successful and widely adopted thus far. The JDBC design team didn't want to lose these successes in the database APIs.

Primary JDBC Classes

The JDBC specification contains about a dozen key class definitions and several associated classes (see Table 6-1) in the core java.sql interfaces and classes. The DriverManager class is a portable interface and is the entry point to all the different drivers. A given JDBC driver implements the other classes. The current class definitions can easily be extended. For example, if a given database vendor or connectivity vendor comes up with a cool API idea not found within JDBC, that vendor may implement these extensions as subclasses of the standard JDBC classes. For example, to see one day a Visigenic statement that subclasses the standard Statement class and adds a few extra methods is entirely plausible. So if you've decided to bind yourself tightly to one particular database from one particular connectivity vendor, you may be able to use value-added extensions that they add; however, those extensions will be non-portable. The benefits may be that they allow better performance or extended features against a particular database. JavaSoft has said, however, that over time, if they witness particular extensions being widely used, they hold the option to introduce them into a future revision of JDBC.

JDBC consists of an object hierarchy, starting with the DriverManager class. From the DriverManager class, you get Connection objects that point to the particular databases. Then from the Connection class, you get Statement objects that act as containers for a particular SQL statement execution. Then as part of executing a statement, you may get a ResultSet object that describes the result set you got back from a particular SQL SELECT.

A given Java applet can have a collection of these objects open, and moreover, a single applet can have multiple threads operating on these different objects. JDBC requires that each of these objects must be safe in a multi-threaded environment, so that the object (and the drivers that implement them) must behave rationally when several threads call into it concurrently. If you are multi-threading with things like Statement and ResultSet objects, to do some concurrency control at the application level becomes advisable.

Using multi-threading, an applet may, for example, handle multiple result sets. The program can run two statements simultaneously in two different threads on the same connection. Multiple result sets for a single statement can be handled by using the execute() method. Then after the execute is issued, the program can test whether a result set was returned, obtain that result set, then test to see whether another result set exists, get that result set,

Table 6-1	JDBC Classes
Class Name	
java.sql.Date	Java JDBC Classes
java.sql.DriverManager	
java.sql.DriverPropertyInfo	
java.sql.Time	
java.sql.Timestamp	
java.sql.Types	
java.sql.CallableStatement	Java JDBC Interfaces
java.sql.Connection	
java.sql.DatabaseMetaData	
java.sql.Driver	
java.sql.PreparedStatement	
java.sql.ResultSet	
java.sql.ResultSetMetaData	
java.sql.Statement	
java.sql.DataTruncation	Java JDBC Exceptions
java.sql.SQLException	
java.sql.SQLWarning	

iterate over the result sets, find out how many result sets were returned, and then process them.

One additional JDBC class requires a brief comment at this point. The *SQLException* class provides several kinds of information regarding a database access error. First is a string describing the error. This is used as the Java Exception message and is available via the getMessage() method. Next, you have a *SQLstate* string that follows the XOPEN SQLstate conventions. The values of SQLstate follow the XOPEN SQLstate conventions. Also, an integer error code is database vendor-specific and is normally the actual error code returned by the underlying database. Last is a chain to a next exception that can be used to provide additional error information. Along these same lines, JDBC has the *SQLWarning* class, which provides information on database access warnings. Warnings are chained to the object whose method caused the warning to be reported. Warnings are accessed via methods available from various classes.

DriverManager Class

Java database connections start with the *DriverManager* class. This is the class that keeps a record of all the loaded JDBC drivers (Table 6-2 has a list of all methods for the class). When a driver is loaded, it must first register itself with the DriverManager class. DriverManager understands database URLs, where a given URL is mapped to a particular JDBC driver. When an applet or application needs to connect to a database, DriverManager is passed a database URL and some properties. It then negotiates with the loaded drivers, finds an appropriate driver, and uses that driver to connect to the target database. In this sense, one difference between ODBC and JDBC is that once an applet opens a connection and begins talking to a database, the DriverManager is removed from the loop. At this point, all calls go directly through to the specific driver classes, so statements and result sets talk directly to code implemented by the driver. This minimized path eliminates overhead, but does put parameter-checking requirements on the driver, which must completely implement such things as Statement and ResultSet classes with all the error checking.

Here is an example of how you can load the JDBC-ODBC Bridge driver:

```
Class.forName("sun.jdbc.odbc.JdbcOdbcDriver");
```

You do not need to create an instance of a driver and register it with the DriverManager, because calling Class.forName will automatically create it for you. Once you have loaded a driver, it is available for making a connection with a database. Here is an example of how you can connect the driver to the database:

```
String url = "jdbc.odbc:amuletDSN";
Connection con = DriverManager.getConnection(
      url, "username", "password");
```

The string variable url contains the JDBC URL, which is discussed next in "Database URLs." In the above example, amuletDSN is the name of an ODBC data source. Of course, you'd have to supply the actual database user name and password in the getConnection method. The Connection class is described in greater detail in "Connection Class," later in this chapter.

Table 6–2	DriverManager Class Methods
Method	**Description**
deregisterDriver()	Remove a JDBC driver from the DriverManager set of registered drivers.
getConnection()	Establish a connection to the specified database URL by selecting an appropriate driver from the set of registered JDBC drivers.
getDriver()	Find a driver that understands the specified database URL from among the set of registered drivers.
getDrivers()	Retrieve an Enumeration of all currently loaded JDBC drivers to which the current caller has access.
getLoginTimeout()	Return the maximum time (in seconds) that drivers can wait when attempting to log in to a database.
getLogStream()	Return the logging/tracing PrintStream used by DriverManager and all drivers.
println()	Print a message to the current JDBC log stream.
registerDriver()	Register a newly loaded JDBC driver class with the DriverManager.
setLoginTimeout()	Set timeout period in seconds for a login attempt by the driver.
setLogStream()	Set the logging/tracing PrintStream used by DriverManager and all drivers.

Database URLs

If a Java applet wishes to connect to a database, it has to have some way of naming that database. JDBC naming is loosely based on the industry's experience and familiarity with the ODBC style of data source names with a more general-purpose mechanism for using the Internet. Specifically, JDBC allows for references like ODBC data source names (DSNs) as a sort of "pre-binding" of a target database, where a developer may assign the name "Inventory," referring to a remote SQL Server database.

The intent is to allow that kind of pre-configuration of databases. The desire is also to let developers use network name servers, where a company may have a convention that has a given set of name servers that map from database names to particular target database servers. In addition, a JDBC goal is to allow complete targets and database specifications, like target machines, target ports, and connection attributes, to be specified as part of the name—so that when the applet comes over the wire, it carries its full target database name with it and it just works. In the Internet context, the answer to this seems to be fairly obvious. In general, JDBC uses the URL-style naming convention. The syntax is as follows:

```
<protocolname>:<subprotocol>:<subname>
```

The protocol name is always "jdbc" and the subprotocol names a particular kind of database connectivity mechanism that may be supported by one or more drivers. One possible subprotocol is "odbc." The subname contents and syntax depend on the subprotocol. Also, other arguments may be specific to that subprotocol.

In a sense, JDBC acts like a registry for the different subprotocol names, in order to avoid accidental collisions, but really the individual database and driver vendors are responsible for deciding on the naming syntax most appropriate to them. So as JDBC rises in popularity, a range of different database URL syntax may develop, just like the current range of different general URL syntax. The difference is that they are all unified inside this one framework.

Here is an example of a JDBC database URL:

```
jdbc:odbc:inventory
```

This URL uses a JDBC-ODBC bridge, where the subprotocol name is ODBC and the ODBC style DSN is Inventory.

During the design of JDBC, the focus was to encode as much information as possible in the database URLs. Certain properties of a database URL are really end-user or end-user environment-specific, so JDBC allows these properties to be specified as a property set passed into the open connection. If a vendor or developer wishes to write generic tools that can work with heterogeneous databases, communication needs to take place between the user front-end GUI application and the database driver, so that the database driver can inform the application what properties the user had to supply in order to make the connection. Consequently, the GUI application can negotiate with the DriverManager to find what properties are required by the current database URL, get those properties specified by the user, then return to the DriverManager, and then open the connection.

Connection Class

The connection class is a high-level class used to interact with a database. The object is established from the DriverManager.getConnection method, which returns a Connection object. This class obtains information about the specific database connection via the instantiated JDBC driver. Primarily, it performs queries via the createStatement, prepareCall, and prepareStatement methods, which return Statement, PreparedCall, and PreparedStatement objects, respectively.

A connection represents a session with a specific database, and within this context, SQL statements are executed and results are returned. The object returned from the DriverManager is a *Connection*, representing access to a particular database (Table 6-3 contains a list of all methods for the Connection class). The connection is a source of statement objects, so you can use the Statement objects to execute particular SQL statements without parameters against the database. If the same SQL statement is executed many times, using a PreparedStatement is more efficient.

The connection, however, has another important role as a transaction session. JDBC treats transactions in two ways: *auto-commit mode* and *normal commit mode*. When in auto-commit mode, every SQL statement is executed as a separate transaction against the database. In normal commit mode, as SQL statements execute, they implicitly become part of a transaction. Then when commits and rollbacks are applied to the connection, the process applies to that whole set of statements.

An additional requirement is to have several connections open to the same database but in different transaction sessions. Fortunately, JDBC allows an applet to have more than a single connection to the database.

Some other items occur at the connection level. One is that at this level, you can specify that the connection will be read-only with the setReadOnly() method. This offers a hint to the driver that allows for some optimizations that will provide better performance. Next is the behavior of what happens to all the objects open in the database when a database commit or database rollback is issued. The unfortunate reality is that some databases insist on closing the prepared statements and result sets when performing a commit or a rollback, while other databases let the objects remain open. These diverse characteristics among databases caused some indecision during the JDBC API design. For example, one unappealing way to solve this problem is to require the developer to ask the database vendor whether the objects are closed or not after a commit or rollback. This requirement seemed unreasonable for the API; consequently, a firm direction had to be taken. As prescribed in the current specification, when doing a commit or rollback, all objects—PreparedStatements, CallableStatements, and ResultSets—are closed automatically. This behavior is called *auto close mode*, which is the default for a connection. Clearly, to keep the objects open is more efficient, so JDBC provides ways to find out what the target database supports. If it supports the ability to keep objects open across commits, you can choose to disable the auto-close mode in order to yield better efficiency.

A SQL stored procedure call is handled by creating a CallableStatement using the prepareCall() method. The CallableStatement provides methods for setting up its IN and OUT parameters and methods for execution. PrepareCall() is optimized for handling stored procedure call statements. Some drivers may send the call statement to the database when the prepareCall() is complete, whereas others may wait until the CallableStatement is executed.

The Connection class also has a very useful advanced usage method, getMetaData(). From information obtained with this method, you can get descriptions of a database's tables, its supported SQL grammar, its stored procedures, etc.

Table 6–3	Connection Class Methods
Method	**Description**
close()	Release the current connection's database and JDBC resources.
commit()	Commit all changes made since the last commit or rollback and release database locks.
createStatement()	Return a new Statement object that can be used to perform actual queries.
getAutoCommit()	Return the current auto-commit state.
isClosed()	Return the closed status of connection.
nativeSQL()	Return the native form of the SQL statement sent by the driver. A JDBC driver may convert the JDBC SQL grammar into the target database SQL grammar.
prepareCall()	Return a new CallableStatement object containing the pre-compiled SQL statement.
prepareStatement()	Return a new PreparedStatement object containing a pre-compiled statement (with or without IN parameters).
rollback()	Drop all changes made since the last commit or rollback.
setAutoCommit()	Turn on/off auto commit mode for the connection.
Advanced Features	
clearWarnings()	Cause getWarnings() to return null until a new warning is reported for connection.
getAutoClose()	Return current auto-close mode.
getCatalog()	Return connection's catalog name.
getMetaData()	Return a DatabaseMetaData object for this connection.
getTransactionIsolation()	Return connection's transaction isolation level.
getWarnings()	Return first SQL warning reported by calls on this connection.
isReadOnly()	Return read-only status of connection.
setAutoClose()	Enable (default)/disable auto-close mode.
setCatalog()	Set the catalog name if supported by the driver.
setReadOnly()	Enable/disable read-only mode of the connection.
setTransactionIsolation()	Set the transaction isolation level for the newly opened connection.

Statement Class

The *Statement* class is the fundamental way of executing a static SQL statement and obtaining the results produced by it. The class is used to execute an SQL query against the database via the Connection object. The Connection.createStatement returns a Statement object. Methods in the Statement class produce ResultSet objects that are used to fetch the result of a query executed in this class. Only one ResultSet per Statement can be open at any point in time. Therefore, if the reading of one ResultSet is interdependent with the reading of another, each must have been generated by different Statements. In addition to Statement are two related classes, *PreparedStatement* and *CallableStatement,* which shall be examined in the next two sections of this chapter. Statement lets you send a SQL string to the database, execute it, and get something back, namely a resultset (Table 6-4 lists all available methods for the class). Depending on the flavor of SQL you're executing (SELECT, UPDATE, DDL, etc.), several different kinds of things may come back. You may get a resultset back, containing the contents of a SELECT query, or you may get an update back.

Here is an example of using a Connection object con to create the Statement object stmt:

```
Statement stmt = con.createStatement();
```

In some cases, you execute a SQL statement and don't necessarily know what will come back. Consequently, support methods are available to find out exactly what the SQL returned. This situation arises in the database tools environment or during the execution of a stored procedure. In order to adequately handle all cases, JDBC provides three different methods of executing a Statement. You can issue the executeQuery() method of the Statement class when executing a SELECT and get a simple result-set back. You can issue the executeUpdate() method of the Statement class when executing any kind of database update, including a SQL UPDATE, INSERT, and CREATE TABLE. Finally, a generic execute() method of the Statement class simply executes the SQL and then lets you figure out what happened later. So when you do an execute(), you can subsequently call other support methods to find out exactly what this SQL returned.

Here is a code fragment that assigns a SQL string to a string variable and then uses it with the Statement object stmt to execute the update query:

```
String createInventory =
    "CREATE TABLE Inventory " +
    "(Inv_ID INTEGER, Item_Name " +
    "VARCHAR(50), Price FLOAT, "+
    "Cost FLOAT, Sup_ID INTEGER)";
Statement stmt = con.createStatement();

stmt.executeUpdate(createInventory);
```

You could then dynamically insert data into the new inventory table by executing one or more INSERT INTO SQL statements using the same Statement object:

```
Stmt.executeUpdate("INSERT INTO Inventory " +
    "VALUES (202, 'Widget A', 19.95, " +
    "16.50, 111)");
```

In general, JDBC has features for the typical developer, as well as advanced features for those requiring special capabilities. In each of the class definitions of JDBC, a comment section describes advanced features. The execute() method is found in the advanced feature section of Statement.

The execute() method lets you perform a SQL statement that may return multiple results. Under somewhat uncommon conditions, a single SQL statement may return multiple resultsets and/or update counts. In most situations, you can ignore these, unless you're executing a stored procedure that you know may return multiple results, or unless you're dynamically executing an unknown SQL string. The execute(), getMoreResults(), getResultSet(), and getUpdateCount() methods provide navigation through multiple results. First, execute() performs a SQL statement and indicates the form of the first result. You can then use getResultSet() or getUpdateCount() to retrieve the result, and then use getMoreResults() to move to any subsequent result.

The setCursorname() method of the Statement class defines the SQL cursor name to be used by subsequent Statement execute() methods. This name can then be used in SQL positioned UPDATE/DELETE statements to identify the current row in the ResultSet generated by this statement. If the database does not support positioned UPDATE/DELETE, this method is ignored. By definition, positioned UPDATE/DELETE execution must be done by a Statement different from the one that generated the ResultSet being used for positioning. Also, cursor names must be unique within a Connection.

Table 6—4	Statement Class Methods
Method	**Description**
cancel()	Cancel a statement executing in one thread by another thread.
clearWarnings()	Cause getWarnings() to return null until a new warning is reported for the statement.
close()	Release the statement's database and JDBC resources.
execute()	Execute a SQL statement that may return multiple resultsets.
executeQuery()	Execute a SQL SELECT statement that returns a single resultset.
executeUpdate()	Execute a SQL DELETE, INSERT, or UPDATE statement.
getMaxFieldSize()	Return the maximum amount of data for any column value.

Table 6–4	Statement Class Methods (Continued)
Method	**Description**
getMaxRows()	Return the maximum number of rows a resultset may contain.
getMoreResults()	Move to a statement's next result.
getQueryTimeout()	Return the number of seconds the driver will wait for a statement to execute.
getResultSet()	Return the current results as a ResultSet object.
getUpdateCount()	Return the current result update count. Must first check whether the result is a ResultSet or integer value.
getWarnings()	Return the first warning reported by calls on this statement.
setCursorName()	Set the SQL cursor name to be used by subsequent Statement object execute() methods.
setEscapeProcessing()	Enable (default) or disable escape scanning, allowing the driver to perform escape substitution before sending the SQL to the database.
setEscapeProcessing()	Enable (default) or disable escape scanning, allowing the driver to perform escape substitution before sending the SQL to the database.
setMaxFieldSize()	Set the maximum amount of data that can be returned for a column of type BINARY, VARBINARY, LONGVARBINARY, CHAR, VARCHAR, and LONGVARCHAR.
setMaxRows()	Set the maximum number of rows that can be retrieved in a ResultSet.
setQueryTimeout()	Set the number of seconds a driver will wait for a statement to execute.

PreparedStatement Class

This object extends Statement and is used to optimize and perform queries that will be executed repeatedly. The PreparedStatement class provides a means to pre-compile SQL statements with or without IN parameters in a PreparedStatement object. This object can then be used to more efficiently execute this statement multiple times. Table 6-5 contains a list of all methods for the PreparedStatement class.

Before each PreparedStatement execution, you can supply parameters to modify the pre-compiled statement. To do so, the SQL statement has question marks to act as parameter markers. You pass these parameters to modify the statement. Before each statement execution, you can issue JDBC setXXX() methods such as setString(), setInt(), setBigDecimal(), etc., to convert the Java value into its SQL equivalent in order to provide a parameter value. For instance, if the IN parameter has SQL type String, then setString() should be used. If arbitrary parameter type conversions are required, then the setObject() method should be used with a target SQL type.

Here is an example of creating a PreparedStatement object that takes two input parameters. The first parameter is used as a price increment factor like 1.05, and the other is used as a wild card character to select inventory item names.

```
PreparedStatement updateInventory =
 con.prepareStatement(
    "UPDATE Inventory SET Price = Price * ? " +
    "WHERE Item_Name LIKE ?");
```

You will also need to supply values to be used in place of the question mark place holders, before you can execute a PreparedStatement object. You do so by calling one of the setXXX methods defined in the class PreparedStatement. For example, if the value you want to substitute for a question market is a Java String data type, you call the method setString, etc. Using the PreparedStatement object updateInventory from the previous example, the following lines of code set the question mark place holders to a Java Float and String with a value of 1.05 and "Wid," and then the SQL UPDATE statement is executed.

```
updateInventory.setFloat(1, 1.05);
updateInventory.setString(2, "Wid");
updateInventory.executeUpdate();
```

Table 6–5	PreparedStatement Class Methods
Method	**Description**
clearParameters()	Release resources used by current parameter values; otherwise, the parameter values remain available for repeated use of a statement.
executeQuery()	Execute a prepared SQL query and return its ResultSet.
executeUpdate()	Execute a SQL DELETE, INSERT, or UPDATE statement.
setAsciiStream()	Send a large ASCII value to the LONGVARCHAR parameter via java.io.InputStream.
setBigDecimal()	Set a parameter to a Java long decimal value.
setBinaryStream()	Send a large binary value to the LONGVARBINARY parameter via java.io.InputStream.
setBoolean()	Set a parameter to a Java boolean value.
setByte()	Set a parameter to a Java byte value.
setBytes()	Set a parameter to a Java array of bytes.

Table 6–5	PreparedStatement Class Methods (Continued)
Method	**Description**
setDate()	Set a parameter to a Java date value.
setDouble()	Set a parameter to a Java double value.
setFloat()	Set a parameter to a Java float value.
setInt()	Set a parameter to a Java int value.
setLong()	Set a parameter to a Java long value.
setNull()	Set a parameter to SQL NULL.
setShort()	Set a parameter to a Java short value.
setString()	Set a parameter to a Java string value.
setTime()	Set a parameter to a Java time value.
setTimestamp()	Set a parameter to a Java timestamp value.
setUnicodeStream()	Send a large Unicode value to the LONGVARCHAR parameter via java.io.InputStream.
Advanced Features	
execute()	Handle multiple results returned by complex prepared statements.
setObject()	Set the value of a parameter using a Java object.

CallableStatement Class

The CallableStatement class allows for the execution of stored procedures (Table 6-6 contains a list of all methods for the CallableStatement class). A callable statement may return a ResultSet or multiple ResultSets. Multiple ResultSets are handled using operations inherited from Statement. The stored procedure can take both input parameters that you fill in using PreparedStatement syntax or by providing OUT parameters. IN parameter values are set using the set methods inherited from PreparedStatement. Before executing a stored procedure having OUT parameters, you must explicitly call registerOutParameter() to register the Java types, java.sql.Type, of each parameter.

Initially, during the JDBC specification review process, you had the requirement of issuing setInt(), setString(), etc., before statement execution to prepare the input state. This was followed by the execution of the statement, and then by getInt(), getString(), etc., to get the results. This sequence seemed like a good programming model, but performance/correctness problems arose over existing drivers. For a number of existing databases and drivers, the JBDC driver wanted to know the types of the OUT parameters at statement execution time. For some existing databases, this became a key requirement. So the effort was to come up with different ways of getting this information to the JDBC driver at statement execute time. The final solution was to require that before you execute a stored procedure having OUT parameters, you must register the types of the OUT parameters with the statement, using the registerOutParameter() method, and give the parameter number and parameter type.

Although this requirement was taken out of the JDBC specification on more than one occasion, it remains, due to strong feedback from several driver vendors who claimed it was necessary. The alternative was to implement this requirement by using database schema information. For example, the driver would have to interrogate the database in order to come up with the type of a stored procedure and the type of the OUT parameters. This action would have resulted in unacceptable performance overhead, and performance was not something to overlook for the developers who are executing stored procedures with OUT parameters, a reasonably sophisticated group of programmers who are most likely motivated by performance. The tradeoff decision was that having an interface that was perhaps a slight bit more unwieldy but allowed a high-performance implementation was better than opting for a simpler interface that added extra burden to the driver and would slow down statement execution.

The first step in utilizing this class is to create a CallableStatement object. As with Statement and PreparedStatement objects, this is done with an open Connection object. Remember that a CallableStatement object contains a call to a stored procedure, not the actual code of the stored procedure. Here is an example of a CallableStatement object calling a stored procedure named DISPLAY_INVENTORY:

```
CallableStatement cs = con.prepareCall(
    "{call DISPLAY_INVENTORY}");
ResultSet rs = cs.executeQuery();
```

The first line of code creates a call to the stored procedure using the connection con. The syntax enclosed in curly brackets is the escape syntax for stored procedures. When the driver sees "{call DISPLAY_INVENTORY}," it translates this escape syntax into the native SQL used by the back-end database to call the stored procedure.

You could also have created the stored procedure if it did not previously exist. For example, you could define the stored procedure used in the above example:

```
create procedure DISPLAY_INVENTORY as
    select * from INVENTORY order by inv_ID
```

The precise syntax for defining a stored procedure depends on the specific database in use. Now the following Java code puts the SQL statement into a string and assigns it to the variable newProcedure. The code then uses the connection object con to create a Statement object, which is then used to send the SQL statement creating the stored procedure to the database:

```
String newProcedure =
"create procedure DISPLAY_INVENTORY as " +
"select * from INVENTORY order by inv_ID";
Statement stmt = con.createStatement();
stmt.executeUpdate(newProcedure);
```

The procedure DISPLAY_INVENTORY is compiled and then stored in the database as a database object that can be called at any time.

Consider that the executeQuery method is used to execute cs, because cs calls a stored procedure that contains one query and therefore generates a single resultset. Sometimes, however, a stored procedure contains more than one SQL statement, in which case it will generate multiple resultsets, multiple update counts, or some combination of resultsets and update counts. In the case where multiple resultsets exist, the execute method should be used to execute the CallableStatement.

CallableStatement also has the getObject() method as a feature for the more advanced JDBC users. This method returns a Java object whose type corresponds to the SQL type that was registered for a specified OUT parameter using registerOutParameter(). It may also be used to read database-specific abstract data types.

Table 6–6	CallableStatement Class Methods
Method	**Description**
getBoolean()	Return the value of the BIT parameter as a Java boolean.
getByte()	Return the value of the TINYINT parameter as a Java byte.
getBytes()	Return the value of the BINARY or VARBINARY parameter as a Java byte array.
getDate()	Return the value of the DATE parameter as a Java Date object.
getDouble()	Return the value of the DOUBLE parameter as a Java double.
getFloat()	Return the value of the FLOAT parameter as a Java float.
getInt()	Return the value of the INTEGER parameter as a Java int.
getLong()	Return the value of the BIGINT parameter as a Java long.
getBigDecimal()	Return the value of the NUMERIC parameter as a Java Numeric object.
getShort()	Return the value of the SMALLINT parameter as a Java short.

Table 6–6	CallableStatement Class Methods (Continued)
Method	**Description**
getString()	Return the value of the CHAR, VARCHAR, or LONGVARCHAR parameter as a Java string.
getTime()	Return the value of the TIME parameter as a Java Time object.
getTimestamp()	Return the value of the TIMESTAMP parameter as a Java Timestamp object.
registerOutParameter()	Register the type of each OUT parameter before executing a stored procedure.
wasNull()	Was the last OUT parameter read a SQL NULL?
Advanced Features	
getObject()	Return the value of a parameter as a Java object.

ResultSet Class

The single most important class in the JDBC API is *ResultSet*. A resultset is a class used to analyze the results of a SQL select (Table 6-7 contains a list of all methods for the ResultSet class). If you've just executed a SQL Select and you get back a ResultSet object that describes the rows in the resultset, you can walk the resultset rows in sequence and extract each of the fields in a given row. A ResultSet maintains a cursor pointing to its current row of data. Initially, the cursor is positioned before the first row. The next() method moves the cursor to the next row. The following line of code demonstrates declaring the ResultSet object rs and assigning the results of a query to it:

```
ResultSet rs =
stmt.executeQuery("SELECT Inv_ID, Price
FROM Inventory");
```

When executing a query, how much of the resultset is sent back to the client as you iterate using the next() call depends entirely on the driver. Although this could have been part of the API, such things are better optimized at the driver level, and this portion of the resultset was consciously not part of the API. A given driver writer can determine the optimal quantity of data to fetch from a particular database, so if the driver believes that to prefetch 50 rows from the result-set is prudent, then the process would be done in the driver. Remember, however, that actually two levels of transfer take place: from the application program to the driver, where you access one record and one field at a time, and also the driver-to-database transfer, which as indicated above, could be many rows at once.

I recommend that ResultSet columns within each row be read in left-to-right order and each column be read only once. Adhering to this process will ensure maximum portability.

For each resultset field, you can issue one of the getXXX() methods (e.g., getString(), getInt(), etc.) to extract the field value. This scheme allows you to program consistently in terms of Java types. You may be surprised that since JDBC is a SQL interface, SQL type names are not used. This fact was another heated subject during the design of the API (the question was whether to use such methods as getVarChar(), getInteger(), getBigInt(), etc., instead of the Java type methods that were ultimately accepted). The SQL-type approach worked well for the database tool vendors, but was not the preferred method for the average developer who would rather program consistently in terms of Java types. So now JDBC resultsets can be referenced only with Java types.

In the get methods, you can refer to a specific resultset column either by *index* or by *name* (another design compromise for tool vendors, who wanted to use indexes, and for developers, who preferred names). Column names used as input to getXXX() methods are case-insensitive. For example, to retrieve the value of the second column of a table, you could say getString(2) or getString("partno"). This flexibility is necessary when writing complex SQL Selects with maybe a dozen fields. As part of ResultSet, the API provides data conversions for the case where you do a getString(), and the value that is returned from the database is an integer. The integer is converted into a string. A broad range of conversion functions exists. The exception is stored procedure execution, where basically no support for conversions exists. JDBC assumes that a stored procedure with OUT parameters will use database types and, if necessary, do manual conversions.

Let's take a look at how to use the ResultSet object. The following example illustrates how to establish a ResultSet object and traverse it in order to pull out required data:

```
String query =
  "SELECT Item_Name, Price, Cost FROM
     Inventory");
ResultSet rs = stmt.executeQuery(query);
While (rs.next()) {
    String n = rs.getString("Item_Name");
    Float p = rs.getFloat("Price");
    Float c = rs.getFloat("Cost");
    System.out.println(n + "     " +
      p + "     " + c);
}
```

In the above example, the getString() method is invoked on the Result-Set() object rs, so getString() will retrieve the value stored in the column Item_Name in the current row of rs. The value that getString() retrieves has been converted from an SQL VARCHAR to a Java String data type, and it is assigned to the String object s. The other two columns, Price and Cost, are retrieved with getFloat, which converts them from a SQL Float to Java float data types before assigning them to the variables p and c.

Although the emphasis of JDBC is to provide for a strongly typed metaphor, the API also meets the needs of the database tools community, which requires a more dynamic programming style. You may want to receive the field and determine its type at a later time. For this type of usage, JDBC has the getObject() interface. For example, you can say getObject(3) and receive a Java object that represents the value in that field. You can hold onto this object until needed and then determine its type. For example, you could hand a field value to a generic display routine that will display based on the type, instead of doing static typing along the way.

The above mechanism also allows for database-specific extensions. If your database has some abstract data types, then you can create new Java objects that reflect those database abstract types. So when an application calls getObject(), it may return your new FOO type. Furthermore, if the developer realizes that she's dealing with your new FOO types, she can coerce the result to FOO and program against your extra abstract types. This feature also shows up in the PreparedStatement and CallableStatement execution.

Consider the following example, where an Employee table contains two columns: name with SQL type CHAR and yearswithfirm with SQL type SMALLINT. The getObject() method returns a Java object whose type is the equivalent of the SQL type of the ResultSet column:

```
ResultSet rs =
stmt.executeQuery("SELECT name, yearswithfirm
    FROM employee");
while (rs.next()) {
    Object strName = rs.getObject("name");
    Object intYearsWithFirm =
      rs.getObject("yearswithfirm");
}
```

In certain cases, a column value may be retrieved as a stream of ASCII characters, Unicode characters, or uninterpreted bytes, and then read in groups from the stream. This method is particularly suitable for retrieving large LONGVARCHAR values in the case of ASCII and Unicode, or large LONGVARBINARY values in the case of uninterpreted bytes. The JDBC driver will do any necessary conversion from the database format into the required format, either ASCII or Unicode. All the data in the returned stream must be read prior to getting the values of any other column. The next call to a get method implicitly closes the stream.

A ResultSet is automatically closed by the Statement object that generated it when that Statement is closed, re-executed, or used to retrieve the next resultset from a series of multiple resultsets.

Table 6–7	ResultSet Class Methods
Method	**Description**
close()	Release ResultSet's database and JDBC resources.
getAsciiStream()	Retrieve a column's contents as a stream of ASCII characters and then read in chunks from the stream.
getBigDecimal()	Return the specified column value of the current row as a Java Numeric object.
getBinaryStream()	Retrieve a column's contents as a stream of uninterpreted bytes and then read in chunks from the stream.
getBoolean()	Return the specified column value of the current row as a Java boolean.
getByte()	Return the specified column value of the current row as a Java byte.
getBytes()	Return the specified column value of the current row as a Java byte array.
getDate()	Return the specified column value of the current row as a Java date object.
getDouble()	Return the specified column value of the current row as a Java double.
getFloat()	Return the specified column value of the current row as a Java float.
getInt()	Return the specified column value of the current row as a Java int.
getLong()	Return the specified column value of the current row as a Java long.
getShort()	Return the specified column value of the current row as a Java short.
getString()	Return the specified column value of the current row as a Java string.
getTime()	Return the specified column value of the current row as a Java time object.
getTimestamp()	Return the specified column value of the current row as a Java timestamp object.
getUnicodeStream()	Retrieve a column's contents as a stream of Unicode characters and then read in chunks from the stream.
next()	Advance to the next row in the resultset, if any.
wasNull()	Did the last column read contain the value SQL NULL?
Advanced Features	
clearWarnings()	Cause getWarnings() to return null until a new warning is reported for ResultSet.
findColumn()	Return column index integer values based on the specified columnName.
getCursorName()	Return the SQL cursor name used by ResultSet.
getMetaData()	Return the number, types, and properties of a ResultSet's column.
getObject()	Return the value of a column as a Java object. May be used to read database-specific abstract data types.
getWarnings()	Return the first SQL warning reported by calls on this ResultSet.

Using Database MetaData

From the outset, the JDBC API was designed to work well for human programmers as well as with automated database tools. Unlike humans, database tools place additional requirements on the API. For example, they need to make a connection with a database, determine the set of available tables, find out the list of columns, present forms back to the user, etc. These tasks require much more insight into the structure of the database and resultsets. JDBC therefore provides two additional classes, *ResultSetMetaData* and *DatabaseMetaData*, which provide the means for doing this kind of analysis. In the original JDBC specification, JavaSoft describes these classes as for expert use only; they are de-emphasized for introductory programming as developers learn the API. The classes are included here only for completeness.

ResultSetMetaData Class

The ResultSetMetaData class provides information describing a ResultSet object. Table 6-8 contains a complete list of ResultSetMetaData class methods. This information lets you do generic resultset handling. For example, you can find out the number of columns in the resultset with getColumnCount(), or a column's name with getColumnName(), or the SQL type of a column with getColumnType(), etc. With ResultSetMetaData, you could write a generic formatted HTML display routine, that will create tags for a formatted resultset, that uses the meta-data to determine the structure of the resultset.

You can obtain information about a ResultSet object by creating a ResultSetMetaData object and invoking ResultSetMetaData methods on it. Here is a short example that demonstrates this concept:

```
Statement stmt = con.createStatement();
ResultSet rs =
    stmt.executeQuery(
    "select * from INVENTORY");

ResultSetMetaData rsmd = rs.getMetaData();
int columnCount = rsmd.getColumnCount();

while (rs.next()) {
    for (int i = 1; i <= columnCount; i++) {
      String s = rs.getString(i);
      System.out.println("Column " + i +
        ": " + s);
      System.out.println("");
    }
}
```

The ResultSetMetaData object rsmd contains all the meta-data information about the ResultSet object rs. You can now use rsmd to invoke ResultSet-

MetaData methods to access this information. In the example, the method getColumnCount returns the number of columns in the resultset. All other ResultSetMetaData methods return information describing an individual column in rs. We use the column count value to control the for loop to iterate through the columns in a row of the resultset. Notice that the ResultSet method getString is used for all the columns in the resultset, regardless of their actual types. You can retrieve an SQL type with getString, because conversions are handled (with some limitations) automatically.

Table 6–8	ResultSetMetaData Class Methods
Method	**Description**
getCatalogName()	Return the catalog name of the specified column's table.
getColumnCount()	Return the number of columns in the resultset.
getColumnDisplaySize()	Return the maximum width in characters of the specified column.
getColumnLabel()	Return the title used for displays and printouts of the specified column.
getColumnName()	Return the name of the column.
getColumnType()	Return the column's SQL data type.
getColumnTypeName()	Return the type name of the specified column's data source.
getPrecision()	Return the number of decimal digits for the specified column.
getScale()	Return the number of digits to the right of the decimal for the specified column.
getSchemaName()	Return the schema name of the column's table.
getTableName()	Return the columns' table name.
isAutoIncrement()	Is the specified column automatically numbered (read-only)?
isCaseSensitive()	Does the specified column's case matter?
isCurrency()	Is the specified column a currency value?
isDefinitelyWritable()	Will a write on specified column definitely succeed?
isNullable()	Does the specified column accept NULL entries?
isReadOnly()	Is the specified column read-only (i.e., not writable)?
isSearchable()	Can the specified column be used in a SQL WHERE clause?
isSigned()	Is the data in the specified column signed?
isWritable()	Can a write on the specified column succeed?

DatabaseMetaData Class

You can use the DatabaseMetaData class to return information about the database as a whole. Table 6-9 contains a list of all methods for the DatabaseMetaData class. For example, isReadOnly() determines whether the database is in read-only mode, getDatabaseProductName() gives the name of the database product in use, and getStringFunctions() returns a comma-separated list of all string functions supported by the database. Most importantly, the DatabaseMetaData class lets you explore the underlying database schema. For example, you can find the set of tables and their structures, or the set of stored procedures and their parameters that are found in the database. Specifically, you could call the getTables() method of the DatabaseMetaData object, passing it the schema, and giving it a pattern that says to return a list of the tables. The resultset in this case contains rows, each having a single String column that is a schema name, which in turn can be used to ask the DatabaseMetaData object to return the foreign keys.

These abilities allow you to build generic tools to work on the database. DatabaseMetaData will also let you find out the exact features of the supported SQL. In general, a JDBC-compliant driver must support the SQL 92 entry-level standard, but the database may support features beyond that.

Some vendors are building JDBC-style drivers that are in essence the JDBC API, but not entirely, because the target database does not support all features. As part of DatabaseMetaData, JDBC has several methods to allow for those kinds of queries—for a non-JDBC-compliant driver to determine its limitations.

Once you have an open database connection, you can create a Database MetaData object that contains information about that database system. Using the Connection object con, the following line of code creates the DatabaseMetaData object dbmd:

```
DatabaseMetaData dbmd = con.getMetaData();
```

As a more involved example, the following is some JDBC code that utilizes the DatabaseMetaData class to show what types of tables are available in the sample pub database for Microsoft SQL Server (SYSTEM TABLE, TABLE, and VIEW will be displayed):

```java
import java.sql.*;

public class DBMSTableTypes  {

    public static void main(String args[]) {

        String url = "jdbc:odbc:pubsDSN";
        Connection con;
```

```
Try
{
  Class.forName("Driver.ClassName");

}
catch(
java.lang.ClassNotFoundException e)
{
  System.err.print(
    "ClassNotFoundException: ");
  System.err.println(
    e.getMessage());
}

try
{
  con =
  DriverManager.getConnection(url,
    "username", "password");

  DatabaseMetaData dbmd =
    con.getMetaData();
  String dbName =
  dbmd.getDatabaseProductName();
  ResultSet rs =
    dbmd.getTableTypes();
  System.out.print(
    "Table types for ");
  System.out.println(
    dbName + ":  ");

  while (rs.next()) {
    String tableType =
    rs.getString("TABLE_TYPE");
    System.out.println(
      "    " + tableType);
  }

  rs.close();
  con.close();

}
catch(SQLException ex) {
System.err.print("SQLException: ");
System.err.println(ex.getMessage());
}
}
}
```

Table 6–9	DatabaseMetaData Class Methods
Method	**Description**
allProceduresAreCallable()	Can procedures returned by getProcedures() be called by the current user?
allTablesAreSelectable()	Can tables returned by getTable() be SELECTed by the current user?
getCatalogSeparator()	Return a separator character between the catalog and table names.
getCatalogTerm()	Return the vendor's term for "catalog."
getDatabaseProductName()	Return the name of the database product.
getDatabaseProductVersion()	Return the version of the database product.
getDriverMajorVersion()	The JDBC driver's major version number.
getDriverMinorVersion()	The JDBC driver's minor version number.
getDriverName()	The name of the JDBC driver.
getDriverVersion()	The version of the JDBC driver.
getExtraNameCharacters()	Return characters allowed in unquoted identifier names (beyond a-z, 0-9, and _).
getIdentifierQuoteString()	The character to quote SQL identifiers.
getNumericFunctions()	A comma-separated list of all math functions supported by the database.
getProcedureTerm()	Return the vendor's term for "procedure."
getSchemaTerm()	Return the vendor's term for "schema."
getSearchStringEscape()	The string used for wildcard characters, e.g. "_" for a single character and "%" for zero or more characters.
getSQLKeywords()	A comma-separated list of non-SQL92 keywords supported by the database.
getStringFunctions()	A comma-separated list of all string functions supported by the database.
getSystemFunctions()	A comma-separated list of all system functions supported by the database.
getTimeDateFunctions()	A comma-separated list of all time and date functions supported by the database.
getURL()	Return the URL for this database.

Table 6–9	DatabaseMetaData Class Methods (Continued)
Method	**Description**
getUserName()	Return the user name as known to the database.
isCatalogAtStart()	Does a catalog appear at the start of a qualified table name?
isReadOnly()	Is the database in read-only mode?
nullPlusNonNullIsNull()	Are concatenations of NULL and non-NULL values equal to NULL?
nullsAreSortedAtEnd()	Are NULL values sorted at the end, regardless of order?
nullsAreSortedAtStart()	Are NULL values sorted at the start, regardless of order?
nullsAreSortedHigh()	Are NULL values sorted high?
nullsAreSortedLow()	Are NULL values sorted low?
storesLowerCaseIdentifiers()	Does the database store mixed-case unquoted SQL identifiers in lowercase?
storesLowerCaseQuoted Identifiers()	Does the database store mixed-case quoted SQL identifiers in lowercase?
storesMixedCaseIdentifiers()	Does the database store mixed-case unquoted SQL identifiers in mixed-case?
supportsMixedCaseQuoted Identifiers()	Does the database support mixed-case quoted SQL identifiers?
supportsAlterTableWithAdd Column()	Does the database support SQL ALTER TABLE with an add column?
supportsAlterTableWithDrop Column()	Does the database support SQL ALTER TABLE with a drop column?
supportsANSI92EntryLevelSQL()	Does the database support ANSI92 entry-level SQL grammar?
supportsANSI92FullSQL()	Does the database support ANSI92 full SQL grammar?
supportsANSI92IntermediateSQL()	Does the database support ANSI92 intermediate-level SQL grammar?
supportsCatalogsInData Manipulation()	Does the database support a catalog name in a data manipulation statement?
supportsCatalogsInIndex Definitions()	Does the database support a catalog name in an index definition statement?
supportsCatalogsInPrivilege Definitions()	Does the database support a catalog name in a privilege definition statement?

Table 6–9	DatabaseMetaData Class Methods (Continued)
Method	**Description**
supportsCatalogsInProcedure Calls()	Does the database support a catalog name in a procedure call statement?
supportsCatalogsInTable Definitions()	Does the database support a catalog name in a table definition statement?
supportsCatalogsInProcedure Calls()	Does the database support a catalog name in a procedure call statement?
supportsCatalogsInTable Definitions()	Does the database support a catalog name in a table definition statement?
supportsColumnAliasing()	Does the database support column aliasing?
supportsConvert()	Does the database support a CONVERT function between SQL data types?
supportsCoreSQLGrammar()	Does the database support ODBC core SQL grammar?
supportsCorrelatedSubqueries()	Does the database support correlated subqueries?
supportsDifferentTable CorrelationNames()	If table correlation names are supported by database, must they be different from the names of the tables?
supportsExpressionsInOrderBy()	Does the database support expressions in ORDER BY clause lists?
supportsExtendedSQLGrammar()	Does the database support Extended SQL grammar?
supportsExtendedSQLGrammar()	Does the database support Extended SQL grammar?
supportsFullOuterJoins()	Does the database support full nested outer joins?
supportsGroupBy()	Does the database support the GROUP BY clause?
supportsGroupByBeyondSelect()	In the GROUPBY clause, does the database support adding columns that were not in SELECT?
supportsGroupByUnrelated()	In the GROUP BY clause, does the database support the use of columns that were not in SELECT?
supportsIntegrityEnhancement Facility()	Does the database support the SQL Integrity Enhancement Facility?
supportsLikeEscapeClause()	Does the database support the scape character in LIKE clauses?
supportsLimitedOuterJoins()	Does the database support limited outer joins?
supportsMinimumSQLGrammar()	Does the database support ODBC minimum SQL grammar?
supportsMixedCaseIdentifiers()	Does the database support mixed-case unquoted SQL identifiers?

Table 6–9	DatabaseMetaData Class Methods (Continued)
Method	**Description**
storesMixedCaseQuoted Identifiers()	Does the database store mixed-case quoted SQL identifiers in mixed-case?
storesUpperCaseIdentifiers()	Does the database store mixed-case unquoted SQL identifiers in uppercase?
storesUpperCaseQuoted Identifiers()	Does the database store mixed-case quoted SQL identifiers in uppercase?
supportsMultipleResultSets()	Does the database support multiple ResultSets from a single execute?
supportsMultipleTransactions()	Does the database support multiple open transactions on different connections?
supportsNonNullableColumns()	Does the database support non-nullable defined columns?
supportsOpenCursorsAcross Commit()	Does the database allow for cursors to remain open across commits?
supportsOpenCursorsAcross Rollback()	Does the database allow for cursors to remain open across rollbacks?
supportsOpenStatementsAcross Commit()	Does the database allow for statements to remain open across commits?
supportsOpenStatementsAcross Rollback()	Does the database allow for statements to remain open across rollbacks?
supportsOrderByUnrelated()	In ORDER BY clause expressions, does the database support the use of columns that were not in SELECT?
supportsOuterJoins()	Does the database support outer joins?
supportsPositionedDelete()	Does the database support a positioned DELETE?
supportsPositionedUpdate()	Does the database support a positioned UPDATE?
supportsSchemasInData Manipulation()	Does the database support a schema name in a data manipulation statement?
supportsSchemasInIndex Definitions()	Does the database support a schema name in an index definition statement?
supportsSchemasInPrivilege Definitions()	Does the database support a schema name in a privilege definition statement?
supportsSchemasInProcedure Calls()	Does the database support a schema name in a procedure call statement?

Table 6-9	DatabaseMetaData Class Methods (Continued)
Method	**Description**
supportsSchemasInTable Definitions()	Does the database support a schema name in a table definition statement?
supportsSelectForUpdate()	Does the database support SELECT for UPDATE?
supportsStoredProcedures()	Does the database support stored procedure calls using the stored procedure escape syntax?
supportsSubqueriesIn Comparisons()	Does the database support subqueries in comparison expressions?
supportsSubqueriesInExists()	Does the database support subqueries in EXISTS expressions?
supportsSubqueriesInIns()	Does the database support subqueries in IN statements?
supportsSubqueriesInQuantifieds()	Does the database support subqueries in quantified expressions?
supportsTableCorrelationNames()	Does the database support table correlation names?
supportsUnion()	Does the database support SQL UNION?
supportsUnionAll()	Does the database support SQL UNION ALL?
usesLocalFilePerTable()	Does the database use a file for each table?
usesLocalFiles()	Does the database store tables in local file?
Current JDBC Driver Limitations on Target Database	Description
dataDefinitionCausesTransaction Commit()	Does a DDL statement within a transaction force a commit?
dataDefinitionIgnoredIn Transactions()	Does the database ignore a DDL statement within a transaction?
doesMaxRowSizeIncludeBlobs()	Does getMaxRowSize() include LONGVARCHAR and LONGVARBINARY blobs?
getMaxBinaryLiteralLength()	Return the maximum number of hex characters in an inline binary literal.
getMaxCatalogNameLength()	Return the maximum length of a catalog name.
getMaxCharLiteralLength()	Return the maximum length for a character literal.
getMaxColumnNameLength()	Return the limit on column name length.
getMaxColumnsInGroupBy()	Return the maximum number of columns in a GROUP BY clause.
getMaxColumnsInIndex()	Return the maximum number of columns allowed in an index.

Table 6–9	DatabaseMetaData Class Methods (Continued)
Method	**Description**
getMaxColumnsInOrderBy()	Return the maximum number of columns in an ORDER BY clause.
getMaxColumnsInSelect()	Return the maximum number of columns in a SELECT list.
getMaxColumnsInTable()	Return the maximum number of columns in a table.
getMaxConnections()	Return the maximum number of active concurrent connections to the database.
getMaxCursorNameLength()	Return the maximum length for a cursor name.
getMaxIndexLength()	Return the maximum length in bytes of an index.
getMaxProcedureNameLength()	Return the maximum length of a procedure name.
getMaxRowSize()	Return the maximum length of a row.
getMaxSchemaNameLength()	Return the maximum length of a schema name.
getMaxStatementLength()	Return the maximum length of a SQL statement.
getMaxStatements()	Return the maximum number of concurrently open active statements.
getMaxTableNameLength()	Return the maximum length of a table name.
getMaxTablesInSelect()	Return the maximum number of tables in SELECT.
getMaxUserNameLength()	Return the maximum length of a user name.
getDefaultTransactionIsolation()	Return the default transaction isolation level of the database.
supportsDataDefinitionAndDataManipulationTransactions()	Does the database support both DDL and DML statements within a transaction?
supportsDataManipulationTransactionsOnly()	Does the database support only DML statements within a transaction?
supportsTransactionIsolationLevel()	Does the database support the specified transaction isolation level?
supportsTransactions()	Does the database support transactions?
Get Descriptive MetaData	Description
getBestRowIdentifier()	Return a description of a table's optimal set of columns that uniquely identifies a row.
getCatalogs()	Return the catalog names available in this database.
getColumnPrivileges()	Return a description of the access rights for a table's columns.

Table 6–9	DatabaseMetaData Class Methods (Continued)
Method	**Description**
getColumns()	Return a description of table columns available in a catalog.
getCrossReference()	Return a description of the foreign key columns in the foreign key table that references the primary key columns of the primary key table; a single foreign key/primary key pair.
getExportedKeys()	Return a description of foreign key columns that reference a table's primary key column.
getImportedKeys()	Return a description of the primary key columns referenced by a table's foreign key columns.
getIndexInfo()	Return a description of a table's indices and statistics.
getPrimaryKeys()	Return a description of a table's primary key columns.
getProcedureColumns()	Return a description of a catalog's stored procedure parameters and result columns.
getProcedures()	Return a description of the stored procedures available in a catalog.
getSchemas()	Return the schema names available in this database.
getTablePrivileges()	Return a description of the access rights for each table available in a catalog.
getTables()	Return a description of tables available in a catalog.
getTableTypes()	Return the table types available in this database.
getTypeInfo()	Return a description of all standard SQL types supported by the database.
getVersionColumns()	Return a description of a table's columns automatically updated when any value in a row is updated.

Implementing a Driver

Although not a topic for the average Java developer, just how to go about building a JDBC driver is nevertheless an interesting subject. You can take a number of approaches to implementing a driver, but regardless of the approach, drivers must implement the standard JDBC abstract classes. Specifically, the classes to implement are java.sql.Connection, java.sql.Statement, java.sql.PreparedStatement, java.sql.CallableStatement, and java.sql.ResultSet. In addition, each driver needs to provide a class that implements the java.sql.Driver interface used by the generic DriverManager class when it needs to locate a driver for a particular database URL. The preferred way is to write some pure Java code running on the client that connects over the network to a target database. Thus, the driver can be downloaded as part of an applet and is not tied to a specific platform. JavaSoft expects that at this point is where the development community will be in two years' time, where only pure Java drivers are part of JDBC.

In the near term, however, the desire is to allow developers to bridge to existing native database libraries. For example, a lot of ODBC drivers are around, since ODBC is a widely deployed library. The idea is to allow vendors to write JDBC/ODBC bridges, where the JDBC driver uses native methods to call through to a platform library. These are an efficient path to initiate communication with particular databases. So the JDBC driver has to implement the standard classes in the JDBC API, and it has to register itself with the DriverManager when it starts up in class static initialization code.

Security Model

Another area of concern when adopting the JDBC API for attaching to corporate data is the *security model*. Basically, JDBC follows the standard applet security model. Specifically, if a JDBC driver is downloaded as part of an applet and registers itself with the DriverManager, that driver is limited in terms of what it is allowed to do. For example, it is not allowed to write on your local disk, it is not allowed to read your private files, it is not allowed to connect to random servers in your environment, etc. Moreover, JDBC will use that driver only to satisfy connection requests from code that has been loaded from the same source as the driver. In other words, an applet can connect back to its server only and cannot connect to random databases. These policies may appear to be overly restrictive, because in many environments to have an applet downloaded from a server would be nice, which connects back to some different database. Such abilities, however, can be quite costly when considering all the security penetration scenarios, and they are thus not supported.

One can dream up many potential damaging situations if this security model were not in place. One possible scenario is if a corporate user connects to an applet source outside the firewall and downloads some applet that does some simple animation, but behind the scenes, that applet was engineered to connect through to a corporate database and delete records. When pondering such scenarios, most would agree that the strict applet security model should not be loosened. However, you have a couple of important alternatives here. First, in the case of developing Java applications that are loaded from the local disk, they are trusted and can therefore connect to any desired database. Second, JDBC provides support for *signed* applets. Some applets are trusted because they have been signed with a cryptographic key, or because they come from a particular source, and consequently can connect to any desired server. Such applets are treated, in a security sense, in the same manner as applications. Inside large corporations, the IS department maintains a public key/private key pair used for signing all internal IS applets. The end-user workstations will then use the IS public key to validate the incoming applets, and then those applets will be allowed to connect to all the corporate databases.

In general, when downloading an applet, the applet security manager enforces all these security rules. For the JDBC driver vendors providing a driver that bridges through to native methods with the requirement that the driver must be usable from applets, JDBC requires those drivers to do some security checks (which are documented in the JDBC specification) to make sure that the applet is well behaved. In general, drivers must assume the worst case. The potential is great for unscrupulous applets out on the Internet. Drivers have to be designed under the assumption that someone may be trying to misuse them.

Coding Examples

Now turn your attention to some situations where JDBC can be used, as well as examples of Java code using the JDBC API. Consider a simple customer list application with add, edit, and delete record features. Let's say that the table is in Sybase SQL Server running on a Windows NT Server. The database connection is via JDBC through the JDBC/ODBC bridge using the Visigenic Sybase driver. This is a simple *three-tier* application. The Java applet handles only the GUI part of the application; the back-end logic is done by a *middle-tier* Customer List *server-let*, and the server-let is using JDBC to make calls to access the underlying database. These calls might be made through Remote Procedure Calls (RPC) or through an Object Request Broker (ORB). Here, Java is running on the client side, as well as JDBC on the server side. Corporations will embrace three-tiered deployment of Java and JDBC because they are able to explicitly define the legal operations on their corporate data rather than allowing direct and unrestricted updates to the database servers. See Figure 6-5 for how this arrangement plays out. Now let's look at some simple code.

A SELECT Example

The first example is a simple SQL SELECT statement and a traversal of the returned resultset. Most of the exception handling code has been omitted where this method throws the SQLException to a higher level. You see in the first line a call to the method DriverManager.getConnection(), to which we pass a database URL. In this case, the URL indicates that the connection will go through an ODBC bridge to a data source name called Customer. The connection object that represents a connection to this database is returned and

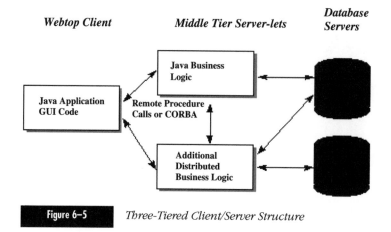

Webtop Client	**Middle Tier Server-lets**	**Database Servers**

Figure 6-5   *Three-Tiered Client/Server Structure*

stored in the reference con. Next, we create a statement object and use it to execute a query. The actual query is a simple SQL string—SELECT CustID, Phone, Balance FROM Customer—which when executed, returns the result-set. The focus of the while loop is the method ResultSet.next() used to traverse the rows of the resultset. Within each row, you can do things like get-Int(), getNumeric(), and getString() to extract the values of the different fields in that row and then print them out.

```
public void MySelect() throws SQLException {
    // Open a database connection
    Connection con =
      DriverManager.getConnection(
      "jdbc.odbc:Customer");

    // Create and execute a statement.
    Statement stmt = con.createStatement();

    // Execute the query.
    ResultSet rs =
      stmt.executeQuery(
        "SELECT a, b, key FROM Table1");

    // Step through the result set.
    While (rs.next()) {
      // Get the values from the current row:
      int a = rs.getInt(1);
      Numeric b = rs.getNumeric("b");
      String key = rs.getString("key");
      println("a=" + a + ", b=" + b + ",
        key=" + key);
    }
}
```

UPDATE Example

As a second example, this time I'll do an update query to modify existing data in the table. To do so, you need to use a prepared statement. Again, begin by connecting to the database. Then define an SQL string as a template containing question marks that act as place holders, which will be filled in later. At that point, the driver pre-compiles and pre-checks the statement and returns a prepared statement object. Then each time you want to execute that statement, you must call stmt.setInt() or stmt.setString() to provide parameter values that qualify the statement. Finally, issue stmt.executeUpdate(), since this statement will execute an update to the database and will return every row that's updated in the database.

```
public void MyUpdate() throws SQLException {
    // Open a database connection
    Connection con =
      DriverManager.getConnection(
        "jdbc.odbc:Customer");

    // Create a prepared statement.
    PreparedStatement stmt =
      con.preparedStatement(
        "UPDATE Customer SET Phone = ? WHERE
          CustID = ?");

    // Step through the result set.
    Stmt.setInt(1, "310-798-3414");
    Stmt.setString(2, "DDG001");
    int rows = stmt.executeUpdate();

    System.out.println("Updated " + rows +
      " rows.");
}
```

Summary

This chapter provides a general introduction to the JDBC API that supports a framework for accessing relational databases from Java applets and applications. In addition to discussing the JDBC class hierarchy, I also reviewed many of the underlying design decisions that went into JDBC, with hopes of giving some rational reasons for the ways things are done in the API. You are encouraged to experiment with JDBC and the reference ODBC driver made available by JavaSoft. Java and JDBC, working in tandem, seem to be well positioned to capture a large share of the active-content, database-enabled, Web site development industry.

Active Server and ADO

....

Since this book's focus is on the Wintel hardware/software platforms for publishing database content on the Web, we must consider utilizing the Active Server technology embedded in the IIS 3.0/4.0 Web server software. This chapter focuses on several related technologies. First I look at what's commonly known as the Active Server and the associated Active Server Pages. This discussion includes an overview of the objects exposed by this technology and their functionality. Next, I show how the new Object Linking and Embedding Database (OLE DB) concept of data providers and data consumers yields a very flexible interface for a vast array of data sources. Last, I examine the ActiveX Data Objects (ADO) API, which provides access to OLE DB data providers, including ODBC data sources.

ActiveX Scripting

All of this chapter's code examples use the scripting languages supported by the Microsoft IIS Web server and IE Web browser. Using the published ActiveX Scripting interface, various scripting languages can be incorporated into Web servers, browsers, or other application software. Through this interface, IIS 3.0/4.0 and IE 4.0 provide built-in support for Visual Basic Scripting Edition, *VBScript*, and Microsoft's JavaScript-compatible scripting engine, *JScript*, although other scripting engines are available. Typically, VBScript is used on the server side, specifically inside Active Server Pages that execute on the server, and JScript is used on the client side for Web browsers that support this scripting language (both Netscape and Microsoft browsers). The official syntax definitions for both VBScript and JScript can be found on the Microsoft Web site and in the Visual InterDev help system.

ActiveX scripting files have the extension ASP, instead of the usual HTM (or HTML) extension. ASP files can contain HTML, ActiveX scripting code, VBScript code, JScript code, or a combination of two or more formats. You can create an ASP file by simply renaming an existing HTM file with an ASP extension.

The default scripting language for ASP is VBScript. However, you can change the scripting language at three levels: the server level, the page level, and the function level. Changing the default at the server level affects all applications that run on the server and requires a modification to the Windows NT registry. To change the default to JScript, for example, use the Windows NT registry editor (REGEDIT) to open the following key:

```
HKEY_LOCAL_MACHINE\SYSTEM\CurrentControlSet\
Services\W3SVC\ASP\Parameters
```

Then change the DefaultScriptLanguage entry from VBScript to the new default, JScript. You must then stop and restart IIS for the change to take effect. When the process is complete, the JScript engine will process all scripts on the server unless otherwise specified at the page or function level.

When IIS reads an ASP file requested by a browser, it parses the file and executes any ActiveX script code in the file. The execution of this code occurs on the server. Since the server-side script code never leaves the server—unlike client-side script code, which is run on the client browser—an inherent level of security exists (note that CGI offers similar source code security). Users cannot simply use the View Source feature of the browser to see your server-side scripts. Server-side scripting allows a developer to program in a familiar programming language, using the scripting language's control constructs to dynamically build HTML pages that can then be viewed by most browsers. The scripts are run on the server, not the client, so many liberties can be taken, because you control the execution environment. An example of one such liberty is direct access to the Web server's file system. The resulting output from the page returns to the browser as pure HTML. The HTML stream may contain only pure HTML functions and options, or it may contain client-side script code and references to ActiveX components.

ASP pages that generate pure HTML work with any type of browser. This fact is a primary advantage of server-side scripting: you can create dynamic pages that work with any browser. However, ASP pages that use VBScript, JavaScript, and/or ActiveX controls will work only with browsers that support those features. The reason you wouldn't use VBScript client-side scripting is that only Internet Explorer supports it. Script code inside an ASP page can also determine what type of browser the viewer is using. This information can be used to tailor the output of the HTML stream to that type of browser.

The Active Server architecture uses VBScript as its scripting language, so anyone familiar with VB or VBA should quickly come up to speed on ActiveX scripting. The actual code resembles VB, except for being surrounded by the delimiter symbols <% and %> used to identify server-side script. As an alternative, you can enclose ActiveX script in a new variation of the <SCRIPT> tag, as in:

```
<SCRIPT FOR=Session EVENT=OnEnd
LANGUAGE=VBSCRIPT RUNAT=Server>
</SCRIPT>
```

The FOR and EVENT qualifiers give the server information about when this script is supposed to execute. The RUNAT=Server syntax tells the server that this code is intended for server-side execution. Any text not surrounded by one of these two types of ActiveX script delimiters is treated as HTML. I discuss this concept further in the next section, "Active Server Framework."

Active Server Framework

The *Active Server Framework* allows application developers to create interoperable extensions to Web servers and other server software. Part of the Active Server Framework is the Internet Services API (ISAPI), which allows high-performance multi-threaded extensions to be created for IIS and other products. Because they expose COM interfaces, all of Microsoft's Back Office™ family of business products can be easily integrated into custom solutions. The Active Server Framework also includes the Internet Database Connector, which allows developers to integrated existing client-server databases from various vendors into Web sites (see Chapter 4 for more information about IDC).

Active Server is designed to provide a comprehensive runtime environment that manages distributed components. By providing extensive system services to handle low-level tasks, Active Server enables developers to focus on business and/or application logic.

As shown in Figure 7-1, when the browser calls for an Active Server Page, the server first reads it. Any HTML goes straight to the browser with any browser-side scripting code in the ASP file. The server script generates output based on existing conditions. The output goes to the browser and then mingles with browser-side HTML. The browser simply sees HTML and displays it.

The primary goal of the Active Server Platform is to give developers an environment that supports multi-tier, distributed applications across different system platforms. Its three core technologies (ActiveX, Active Desktop, and Active Server) are designed to provide a high level of integration among the operating system, PC component technology, and HTML standards.

The Active Server Platform

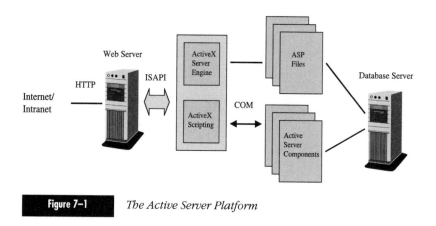

Figure 7–1 *The Active Server Platform*

ActiveX

Formerly known as OLE Automation Servers, ActiveX components (or controls) are objects that can be accessed from either a Web page or an application. They are designed to be language-independent and to operate in a networked environment. ActiveX controls can be created using languages such as Visual Basic, Java, and C++.

Active Desktop

Active Desktop supports ActiveX controls as well as Java applets, and it provides a language-independent scripting environment for developers, who can use VBScript or JScript to create client-side program logic for Web applications. Internet Explorer, the central component of Active Desktop, gives programmers a vehicle for delivering a wide range of applications that integrate HTML, scripting code, component software, and operating system service.

Active Server

Active Server, the server component of Active Platform, supports server-side, script-based programming. It is used to process Active Server Pages files, which provide the flexibility of CGI scripts and programs, which are now considered antiquated. Active Server is tightly coupled to the NT operating system; therefore, the Active Server Pages can take advantage of the multithreaded environment to yield significant performance gains over CGI-based Web applications. ASP files can be developed in any scripting language, and they support components developed in virtually all languages.

Active Server Pages

Active Server Pages work with IIS to provide a server-side scripting environment that uses VBScript and JScript (Microsoft's implementation of JavaScript). ASP allows you to embed scripts into your HTML files. ASP scripts are interpreted and executed when the page is accessed, making your Web pages truly dynamic. The VBScript applications embedded into an Active Server Page are executed on the server side, not the client side. When IIS reads an ASP file, it interprets the page and returns the appropriate HTML page to the requesting client browser. The process of ASP working together with VBScript is analogous to the discussion of CGI in Chapter 2. Figure 7-2 contains a conceptual view of how ASP interacts with the client browser and the Web server.

A standard Web page generally contains text and HTML formatting commands. Standard Web pages are usually found in files that have an .HTM or .HTML file extension and work with any Web server. An Active Server Page contains text, HTML formatting commands, and scripting commands. Active Server Pages have the .ASP file extension and work only with IIS (although the third-party vendor Chilisoft is now shipping an ASP platform for other Web server environments). The scripts contained with the ASP files are executed on the server side. So the directory in which ASP files reside on the server must have execute permissions. You should consider keeping your ASP files in a separate directory that has only read and execute permissions. When an Active Server Page is executed, only the resulting HTML page is returned to the client. The client cannot view the actual server-side scripting

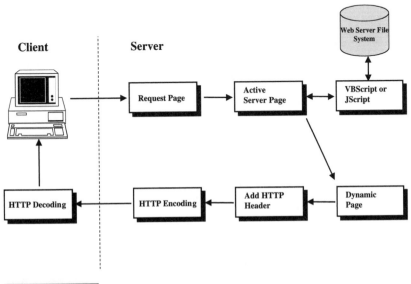

Figure 7-2 *Processing an Active Server Page*

(using the browser's View Source feature), which helps to ensure the security of your ASP files and scripting code.

Just as HTML pages use the <HTML></HTML> tags to enclose the body of the document, Active Server Pages use the <% %> delimiters to enclose the server-side scripts. These are not to be confused with the <SCRIPT></SCRIPT> tags, which define client-side scripts to be executed by the browser (the one exception is when the RUNAT=Server attribute is used). Remember, server-side scripts are executed on the Web server.

A slight problem occurs if we want to use a procedure in our ASP file. ASP doesn't allow us to place VBScript procedures inside the <% %> delimiters; they can be used only to enclose code that is executed as the page is being interpreted. To include a procedure, we have to enclose it in the normal <SCRIPT></SCRIPT> tags, like code destined for the browser. To solve this problem of confusing the two and to prevent the script from being sent to the browser, ASP introduces a new attribute, RUNAT. So to include a procedure that is executed on the server, we could use:

```
<SCRIPT LANGUAGE=VBScript RUNAT=Server>

Function ConcatStr()
    'Return the concatenated string
    ConcatStr = strText1 & strText2
End Sub
</SCRIPT>
```

Then elsewhere in the page, you could embed more scripting code to use this procedure:

```
<% strText1 = "Hello " %>
<% strText2 = "World" %>
<% strNew = ConcatStr() %>
```

Server-Side Includes

Server-side includes (SSI) allow you to reuse ASP code by including the same code in multiple files. The VBScript engine inserts the code into the ASP file before any other compiling or interpreting is done. For example, if you had an SSI called CybercashSubmit.asp, it would be included in an ASP file with the following statement:

```
<!-#includes virtual=
    "ASP_Cybercash/CybercashSubmit.asp"->
```

SSIs are useful for inserting commonly used procedures, global variables, or global constants. You can use SSIs to insert constants and procedures related to page attributes (e.g., font, color, etc.) that are common to all ASP files in your application. In this way, you can easily make changes to the client-side interface presented by your ASP files.

Active Server Objects

Although ActiveX scripting coupled with Active Server Pages yields a framework that exceeds the capabilities of generic HTML, the scripting languages, as a rule, have very limited functionality. Scripting code does have one intriguing ability, and that is to interact with objects that are part of the ASP environment, by calling methods and setting properties. Active Server Pages provide a complement of objects that we can manipulate using VBScript or JScript. Coupled with the ActiveX Data Objects technology, which I discuss in the latter half of this chapter, ASP presents a very dynamic framework from which you can build database-enabled Web sites.

Five built-in objects are provided by ASP, which we can use in the interactions between client browsers and the server. The hierarchy of these objects begins with the *Server Object*. The Server object represents the environment in which the Web pages run, and the remaining four objects fit together to make up an Active Server Application. These objects are: Application, Request, Response, and Session. Figure 7-3 shows this organization.

The implication from the diagram is that multiple applications can be running on a single server. An application is defined as all the ASP files, HTML files, graphic images, etc., that make up a Web site and that are stored in a single *virtual directory*. This virtual directory maps to a physical directory in the server's file system. The IIS documentation has information about establishing such a mapping.

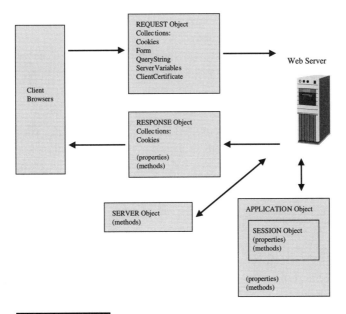

Figure 7–3   *ASP Object Model*

Each Application object can have many Session objects. A Session object is maintained for each user requesting a page from the application. Session objects are maintained for 20 minutes (you may change this time-out default) after the last request for a page by that user. The time-out mechanism is how the interaction between a client and the server is handled, because the HTTP protocol over which HTML pages are sent is asynchronous. Without sessions, the server would have no indication whether this page was the first, second, or 50th page that this particular client had requested.

This arrangement differs from client/server environments, where the client connects to the server and maintains the connection until all the necessary work is done. With HTTP-based applications, the Session object allows us to monitor whether a user has just entered our site or has been traversing our site for six hours. The concept of an application, and the sessions contained within it, is the crux of the Active Server Pages architecture.

Due to the manner in which HTTP functions, ASP has to maintain information from each request made by a client browser and store it so that it can be accessed in the application. This requirement means that the details of the browser, the request itself, and additional information are placed in a Request object. The scripting code can then use the methods and properties of this object to determine what action to take and what kind of page to return to the user.

In order to get information back to the browser, we use the Response object. This object stores all the information required for the server's response to the client. It provides methods and properties that can be used to create and modify what is returned to the client browser, and to perform other tasks such as redirecting a request to another page.

The above notes describe the ASP object model in general terms. Let's now spend some time examining each Active Server object.

APPLICATION OBJECT

Since a Web server can have multiple ASP applications running at once, you need a way to manage these applications. The Application object can store information for use by server-side scripting code, can process requests, and can even respond to events. You can store both simple data values in application variables as well as references to objects such as database connections. This data becomes global to the whole application and is available in any of its pages.

The Application object has two methods, *Lock* and *UnLock*. The need to lock the information stored in the Application object arises from instances where more than one user attempts to access the same data at the same time. To prevent the data from being corrupted, you can Lock and UnLock access to the object. When the Lock method is invoked, no other clients may modify application properties until the UnLock method is called.

The Application object also provides an event-driven interface to the application through use of two events, *onStart* and *onEnd*. The onStart event fires when a page in the application is first referenced, and the onEnd event fires when the application ends, i.e., when the last user leaves the application or is timed out. Also, two equivalent events are at the session level, tied to the Session object. I cover the session events in "Session Object," the next section. The scripting code associated with each event resides in a special file named global.asa. A global.asa file exists for each application. The file resides in the directory on the server that is the root of that application. When I speak of an application in ASP, I am actually referring to all the files included in the same directory as global.asa, and any of its subdirectories.

If you need to do some processing at the beginning or end of an application, you can put some code in the global.asa:

```
<SCRIPT LANGUAGE="VBScript" RUNAT="Server">
Sub Application_OnStart
    'Script code goes here
End Sub

Sub Application_OnEnd
    'Script code goes here
End Sub
</SCRIPT>
```

The script code you place in each of these procedures is called *event handler* code. When the first user accesses a file in the application, the Application_onStart event is triggered. The event handler code may be used to initialize any application-wide global variables. The code should not, however, be specific to any one particular user. For example, you may wish to store the date and time that the application started:

```
Sub Application_onStart
    Application.Value("dtmAppStart") = Now()
End Sub
```

Here, I'm using the one property of the Application object, *Value*, to create a new global application variable named dtmAppStart and then assign a value to it, namely the return value of the VBScript Now() function.

You might also use application variables to keep a hit count for your application:

```
Application.Lock
Application("NumHits") =
    Application("NumHits") + 1
Application.UnLock
```

The first time the above code executes, the NumHits application variable is created and stored in the application. Like all numeric variables in VBScript, it starts off with a value of zero. Every subsequent time the line executes, the same value will be updated, regardless of how many users are on the Web page simultaneously.

Your ability to share this number between different running instances of the application brings up an interesting question: what happens when two instances hit that statement at the same time? This scenario is very feasible. The Lock and UnLock methods take care of this issue. Lock puts a lock on the statement so that no other copy of the application can perform an operation on the Application object. UnLock reverses the process, giving the other copies access to the Application object again.

When this block of code executes, the Application object temporarily locks, the variable is modified, and the Application object unlocks. This way, no two instances can modify the Application object at the same time. If an ASP file tries to modify a locked Application object, it will be forced to wait until either the copy holding the lock unlocks it or the page times out.

This point brings up an important consideration when using the Application object and its Lock and UnLock methods. You must keep the Application object locked for as short an interval as possible, because other copies of the application may be waiting to lock it themselves. In this example, we lock it for only as long as necessary to update the hit counter, and then we release it.

SESSION OBJECT

In contrast to the Application object, which makes data available to different clients of an application, the Session object shares data only between different pages. Each client that requests a page from the application is assigned a Session object. A Session is created when the client first makes a document request, and only if a Session_OnStart event handler is in the global.asa file. The Session is destroyed twenty minutes (the default value for the Timeout property) after the last request is received.

The Session object has three properties, *SessionID, Timeout,* and *Value.* When we store information in the Session object, the client that owns that session is assigned a SessionID, which can be used in your pages to identify the client while it is browsing the site. The SessionID is assigned by the server, and is available only as a read-only property. The SessionID is implemented as a cookie with no expiration date, so that it expires when the client browser is closed. If the browser does not accept cookies, ASP cannot create a session for that user.

The Timeout property specifies the timeout period (measured in minutes with a default of 20) for sessions in this application. The Value property is used to access Session variables, which are analogous to the Application variables in "Application Object," earlier in this chapter. You can use the following syntax to retrieve the value of a session variable:

```
<%=Session("variable_name")%>
```

If you use this syntax to write information to the browser in multiple places in your code, consider "batching" those writes by replacing multiple, interspersed <%= %> writes with one Response.Write statement (I cover the Response object later in this chapter). While you are making that change, take a look at how you have your HTML code with regard to your script code. Try not to intersperse HTML and script code too much; instead, try to have blocks of script and blocks of HTML. Arranging your HTML and script code will save valuable server processing time.

The two Session object events, *onStart* and *onEnd*, are similar to those of the Application object. You can define event-handling code in the global.asa file, as in:

```
Sub Session_OnStart
    'Script code goes here
End Sub

Sub Session_OnEnd
    'Script code goes here
End Sub
```

The onStart event fires when a user first requests a page in the application. The onEnd event fires when the session ends, i.e., when no requests have been received for the timeout period (default of 20 minutes).

The Session object also has a single method, *Abandon*, which destroys a Session object and releases its resources.

As a simple example, say that you have the following line of code in your global.asa file to initialize a session variable intVisitCount:

```
Session.Value("intVisitCount") = 0
```

Let's say that you have an ASP file named SessionVariables.asp that contains the following code:

```
SessionID: <%=Session.SessionID%> <BR>

<P>You have visited this page
<%=Session("intVisitCount")%>
    times this Session</P>

<%Session("intVisitCount")=
    Session("intVisitCount")+1%>
```

You can see that the page first retrieves the current value of the Session variable and then increments it. The new value of the counter is displayed each time the user visits the page.

REQUEST OBJECT

The Request object provides information about a user's request to the site or application. The Request object consists of five collections of variables. You can view a collection as a data structure, which stores values and their associated unique keys. You can retrieve and set values in the collection by referencing the keys. The values stored in the collections can be used in scripting code in order to make decisions. The values in collections are read-only, because the information is just a copy of the request made by the browser. Table 7-1 summarizes the available collections.

Table 7–1	Request Object Collections
Object	**Description**
Cookies	Values of cookies sent from the browser.
ClientCertificate	Client certificate values sent from the browser.
Form	Values of form elements sent from the browser.
QueryString	Values of variables in the HTTP query string.
ServerVariables	Values of the HTTP and environment variables.

As a simple example of using one of the Request object's collections, the following line of VBScript code saves a value, if any, associated with the key "UserName" in the QueryString collection:

```
StrUserName = Request.QueryString("UserName")
```

Let's take a brief look at each Request object collection to see what type of information is maintained.

THE QUERYSTRING COLLECTION • When an HTML form is submitted (if the form uses the GET method), the data from the form comes back in the query string appended to the URL. Take, for example, the HTML code for a form below:

```
<HTML>
<TITLE>Request Object QueryString Collection
</TITLE>

<BODY>

<H2>New Employee Form</H2>

<FORM NAME="frmEmployee"
    ACTION="GetEmployee.asp" METHOD=GET>
    <TABLE>
```

```
   <TR>
     <TD>Employee Name <INPUT TYPE=TEXT
     NAME="txtName"></TD>
   </TR>
   <TR>
     <TD>Resume <TEXTAREA SIZE="30,10"
     NAME=txtResume></TEXTAREA>
     </TD>
   </TR>
   <TR>
     <TD><INPUT TYPE=RADIO NAME=optGender
       VALUE="Male">Male
     </TD>
   </TR>
   <TR>
     <TD><INPUT TYPE=RADIO NAME=optGender
       VALUE="Female">Female
     </TD>
   </TR>
   <TR>
     <TD><INPUT TYPE=CHECKBOX
       NAME="chkFullTime"
       VALUE="True"> Full time?</TD>
   </TR>
   <TR>
     <TD>
     <INPUT TYPE=SUBMIT VALUE="Add
       Employee">
     <INPUT TYPE=RESET VALUE="Clear">
     </TD>
   </TR>
   </TABLE>
</FORM>

</BODY>
</HTML>
```

Figure 7-4 shows the form inside a browser. The resulting query string from this form might look like the following (depending, of course, on the data entered by the user):

```
txtName=Dubaldie+Fritz&txtResume=
    BS+Computer+Science%0D%0A
UCLA%0D%0A&optGender=Male&chkFullTime=True
```

Here, we see that the form's values are included in the query string as ordered pairs of key name and value. Each pair is delimited with an ampersand character, "&", and all embedded spaces are replaced by the plus-sign, "+", character. Notice that each time the user used the Enter key inside the TextArea field, the ANSI codes in hexadecimal for carriage return and line

Figure 7–4   *HTML Form Passes a Query String*

feed are inserted, each code preceded by a "%" character. This technique is called *URL-encoding*.

From the appearance of the string, to parse out each value may seem like a difficult task. Fortunately, the Request object's QueryString collection facilitates retrieving values from the query string. For example, if you wanted simply to display all the data values sent from the form, the following code enumerates the QueryString collection:

```
<% For Each Item in Request.QueryString %>
    Form control name: '<% = Item %>'
    Value: '<% = Request.QueryString(Item) %>'
    <BR>
<% Next %>
```

For the above server-side code to function properly, you must be sure to actually name each form field, even though this step is optional in HTML. Figure 7-5 displays the output of this code.

THE FORMS COLLECTION • In "The QueryString Collection," earlier, you found that the data from a form is sent in a query string when the METHOD attribute of the form is GET, or when it's directly added to the URL in the HREF attribute of an <A> tag on the page. When the METHOD attribute of a form is POST, however, the data comes wrapped up in the HTTP headers

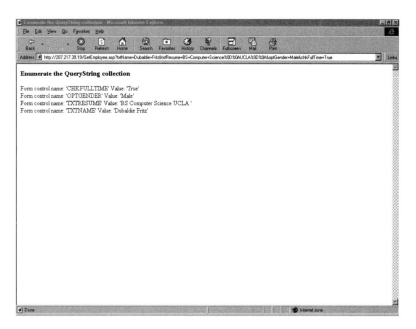

Figure 7–5   *Iterate through the QueryString Collections*

instead. In this case, the QueryString collection is empty, and the values from the controls are placed in the Request object's Form collection.

Here is an example of how you can retrieve values from a form by iterating through the Forms collection (assuming that all the form fields are named and unique):

```
<% For Each Item in Request.Form %>
    Form control name: '<% = Item %>'
    Value: '<% = Request.Form(Item) %>' <BR>
<% Next %>
```

THE SERVERVARIABLES COLLECTION • The ServerVariables collection is the primary collection with regards to client requests. Much of the information in the other Request object collections originates in the ServerVariables collection. Any HTTP header that is sent by a client browser is available in this collection. For instance, you could retrieve the original query string passed by an HTML form by coding:

```
strQueryString =
    Request.ServerVariables("QUERY_STRING")
```

The standard HTTP headers are automatically defined as members of this collection. Here is an ASP file that displays the values of all the server-side include variables using the members of the ServerVariables collection:

```
<HTML>
<TITLE>Display all items in the
     ServerVariables collection
</TITLE>
<BODY>

<H3>Values in the ServerVariables collection
</H3>

Authorization type:
<% = Request.ServerVariables("AUTH_TYPE") %>
<BR>
# bytes sent by client:
<% = Request.ServerVariables("CONTENT_LENGTH")
%> <BR>
POST content type:
<% = Request.ServerVariables("CONTENT_TYPE")
%> <BR>
Document file name:
<% = Request.ServerVariables("DOCUMENT") %>
<BR>
Document path:
<% = Request.ServerVariables("DOCUMENT_URI")
%> <BR>
Current date GMT:
<% = Request.ServerVariables("DATE_GMT") %>
<BR>
Current date local:
<% = Request.ServerVariables("DATE_LOCAL") %>
<BR>
CGI specs:
<% = Request.ServerVariables(
     "GATEWAY_INTERFACE") %> <BR>
Last edit date:
<% = Request.ServerVariables("LAST_MODIFIED")
%> <BR>
User's logon account:
<% = Request.ServerVariables("LOGON_USER") %>
<BR>
Path information:
<% = Request.ServerVariables("PATH_INFO") %>
<BR>
Physical path:
<% = Request.ServerVariables(
     "PATH_TRANSLATED") %> <BR>
Query string:
<% = Request.ServerVariables("QUERY_STRING")
%> <BR>
Unescaped query string:
<% = Request.ServerVariables(
```

```
        "QUERY_STRING_UNESCAPED") %> <BR>
User's IP address:
<% = Request.ServerVariables("REMOTE_ADDR") %>
<BR>
Remote host:
<% = Request.ServerVariables("REMOTE_HOST") %>
<BR>
Remote ID:
<% = Request.ServerVariables("REMOTE_IDENT")
%> <BR>
Remote user:
<% = Request.ServerVariables("REMOTE_USER") %>
<BR>
Script name:
<% = Request.ServerVariables("SCRIPT_NAME") %>
<BR>
Server name:
<% = Request.ServerVariables("SERVER_NAME") %>
<BR>
Server port:
<% = Request.ServerVariables("SERVER_PORT") %>
<BR>
Encrypted port:
<% = Request.ServerVariables(
        "SERVER_PORT_SECURE") %> <BR>
Protocol name:
<% = Request.ServerVariables(
        "SERVER_PROTOCOL") %> <BR>
Web server:
<% = Request.ServerVariables(
        "SERVER_SOFTWARE") %> <BR>
MIME data types:
<% = Request.ServerVariables("HTTP_ACCEPT") %>
<BR>
Client languages:
<% = Request.ServerVariables(
        "HTTP_ACCEPT_LANGUAGES") %> <BR>
Browser: <% = Request.ServerVariables(
        "HTTP_USER_AGENT") %> <BR>
URL: <% = Request.ServerVariables(
        "HTTP_REFERER") %> <BR>
Cookie sent:
<% = Request.ServerVariables("HTTP_COOKIE") %>
<BR>
Entire HTTP string:
<% = Request.ServerVariables("ALL_HTTP") %>
<BR>

</BODY>
</HTML>
```

The following code, which enumerates the ServerVariables collection with the VBScript For Each construct, could also be used to display each variable and its value:

```
<TABLE>
<% For Each strName In
      Request.ServerVariables %>
    <TR><TD> <% = strName %> </TD><TD>
    <% = Request.ServerVariables(strName) %>
    </TD></TR>
<% Next %>
</TABLE>
```

THE COOKIES COLLECTION • A *cookie* is a persistent type of data storage tied to a user request. This is in contrast to the QueryString and Forms collections, which are available only as an immediate result of a browser request. A cookie is a packet of information sent by a browser to the server with each request. Data items within each cookie are available in the Cookies collection. The cookie is often stored as a file on the client machine, an arrangement that yields the persistent nature of this mechanism. You can access information stored inside the cookie through use of the Request object, but the values are read-only, since the information resides on the client machine, not the server. You can change cookie information, but only with the Response object. Here is some code to iterate through the Cookies collection:

```
<% For Each Item in Request.Cookies %>
   <% = "Cookie name: " & Item & " Value: " &
      Request.Cookies(Item) %> <BR>
<% Next %>
```

THE CLIENTCERTIFICATE COLLECTION • Security is an important issue when building database-enabled Web sites, and ASP technology provides all the necessary ingredients to allow access to the *secure sockets layer* (SSL). A browser using the SSL protocol has the https:// prefix instead of the standard http:// prefix for all requested URLs. When SSL is in use, the browser sends the server *certificates* that identify the client. The ClientCertificate collection of the Request object can be used to ensure that the ASP application sends out information only to those users who are authorized to receive it. To access information in this collection, use predefined keys associated with the items required. Table 7-2 contains a list of available keys.

From the table, you can see that two keys, Subject and Issuer, have subfields. Take a closer look at the Subject key. If you need to verify a user's identity, you must first check for the presence of a certificate. The Subject key's length is greater than zero when a certificate is present. Here is the code to check for a certificate:

Table 7–2	ClientCertificate Collection Keys	

Key	Description
Certificate	The entire certificate content.
Flags	Flags: ceCertPresent and ceUnrecognizedIssuer.
Issuer	Sub-field values containing certificate issuer information.
ValidFrom	The date the certificate becomes valid.
ValidUntil	The date the certificate expires.
SerialNumber	The certificate serial number.
Subject	Sub-field values containing certificate owner information.

```
<% If Len(Request.ClientCertificate(
      "Subject")) > 0 %>
   Certificate was found
<% End If %>
```

Once you've confirmed the existence of a certificate, you can further scrutinize the aspects of the certificate before allowing client access to a database. To do so, you need to use the Subject and Issuer keys and their sub-fields. Table 7-3 has a list of sub-field identifiers.

Table 7–3	ClientCertificate Collection Sub-Field Identifiers	

Sub-Field	Description
C	Country of origin.
CN	Common name.
GN	Given name.
I	Set of initials.
L	Locality.
O	Company or organization name.
OU	Organizational unit.
S	State or province.
T	Title of the person or organization.

We may, for example, wish to check whether a user is from another country, in which case an overseas shipping charge must be added. For this, we use the SubjectC key. To access sub-field information, you concatenate the key name and the sub-field. Here is a sample of this code:

```
<% If Request.ClientCertificate("SubjectC") <>
     "USA" Then
   ExtendedPrice = ExtendedPrice +
     SHIP_ABROAD_FEE
End If %>
```

In this example, the constant SHIP_ABROAD_FEE must have previously been defined. You'll notice that two constants are referenced for the Flags key. These constants are found in the server-side include file named cervbs.inc, which can be found in the ASP samples directory supplied with Active Server Pages. Here are the definitions for the two constants:

```
Const ceCertPresent = 1
Const ceUnrecognizedIssuer = 2
```

You can use the value of the Flags key combined logically with the constants defined in the cervbs.inc file to make decisions about the requesting client.

RESPONSE OBJECT

Another main object in the ASP hierarchy is the Response object. This object's functionality is normally coupled with the Request object discussed above. The Request object is concerned with information coming into the server from the browser, whereas the Response object is concerned with information sent back to the browser. The Response object has a single collection, the Cookies collection. Table 7-4 shows all the properties for the Response object, and Table 7-5 shows the methods.

Table 7–4	Response Object Properties
Property	**Description**
Buffer	Indicates whether to buffer the page until complete.
ContentType	HTTP content type for the response.
Expires	Time duration before a cached page on a browser expires.
ExpiresAbsolute	Date/time when a cached page on a browser expires.
Status	HTTP status line returned by the server.

The Response object is frequently used to send back a page containing text, graphics, and other content that a user may wish to view. Here are some

Table 7–5	Response Object Methods
Method	**Description**
AddHeader	Add or update a value in the HTML header.
AppendToLog	Add text to the Web server log file for this request.
BinaryWrite	Send text to the browser without performing a character set conversion.
Clear	Purge the buffered HTML output.
End	Stop processing the page and return the current result.
Flush	Send the buffered output immediately.
Redirect	Tell the browser to connect to the specified URL.
Write	Write a variable to the current page as a string.

simple examples of what can be achieved. First, if you need to insert a string into the HTML output received by the browser, the Write method can be used:

```
Response.Write("<H2>Customer name is: " &
    strCust & "</H2>")
```

Notice how you can embed HTML tags directly in the output string. If you need to add a special identifying string to the Web server's log file, you can use the AppendToLog method:

```
Response.AppendToLog(
    "*** Access to secure intranet ***")
```

Here is an interesting way to combine the Request and Response objects to implement specialized security that prohibits users from a specific IP address from accessing the page, or the entire site if strategically placed:

```
<% If Request.ServerVariables("REMOTE_ADDR") =
    "207.217.39.06" Then
    Response.Buffer = TRUE
    Response.Status = ("401 Unauthorized")
    Response.End
End If %>
```

In this example, I check the user's IP address as retrieved from the Request object's ServerVariables collection against a specific address (if you wanted to enhance this idea, you could scan a database for authorized IP addresses). If it matches, I turn on buffering. Buffering allows an extra degree of control over when a client receives information, as well as what they receive. The Buffer property is set to True to indicate to the server that all of a page's script must be executed before any data is sent back to the requesting client. When it is False (the default setting), the server streams the page to the client as it is created. Only when Buffer is True are the methods Clear, End, and Flush available.

Buffering is useful in other situations, too. To make an ASP application appear faster, you can use buffering to send parts of the results early. You can also handle data access or other errors in pages using buffering, as in the following code:

```
<% 'An error occurred while reading a database

'Clear, but do not send buffered output
Response.Clear

Response.Write(
    "<H2>A database error has occurred.</H2>")

'Halt processing page and send buffer contents
Response.End
%>
```

You can also use the buffering to assist in the display of large quantities of information generated by a database report. You may use the Flush method to send the report contents to the browser at regular intervals. This way, the user may begin viewing the data before the report is complete.

Another use of the Response object is to refer users to alternate pages using the Redirect method. This method specifies a new page that the browser loads immediately. Suppose that you wish to add a security feature to your site whereby the user must enter his or her first name into a form on your default.asp page and submit it prior to moving to main.asp (your main menu page). You can prevent a user from bypassing the default.asp page with the Redirect method. First, you must write the user's first name to a session variable when you process the form data:

```
<% Session("FirstName") =
    Request.Form("fname") %>
```

Then you add the following lines of code prior to the <HTML> tag at the top of each page in your site (except default.asp). If the FirstName session variable is blank, indicating that the user did not yet enter his name, he'll be redirected back to the default.asp page.

```
<% If Session("FirstName") = "" Then
    Response.Redirect("default.asp")
End If %>
```

You can add or update a cookie by using the Response object's Cookies collection. The Response object provides an interface for setting or changing a cookie's value that is sent back to the client with the page. This approach is in contrast to the Request object, which allows you to access cookie values on the server when a request is received from the browser.

SERVER OBJECT

The Server object is the foundation for the ASP object hierarchy. It provides fundamental functionality used in nearly all Active Server Pages. The object has a single property, ScriptTimeout, and several methods, as shown in Table 7-6.

Table 7-6	Server Object Methods
Method	**Description**
CreateObject	Create an instance of an object or server component.
HTMLEncode	Apply HTML encoding to the specified string.
MapPath	Convert a virtual path into a physical path.
URLEncode	Apply URL encoding to a string.

ScriptTimeout is the length of time the server allows a piece of script to run before the script is terminated. The ScriptTimeout property protects against rogue scripting language code that has a bug causing it to enter into an infinite loop. The server eventually terminates the script to protect itself from being overloaded by running processes. The default timeout value is 90 seconds.

The *CreateObject* method is potentially the most useful object method, since it allows us to embed server components in our Active Server Pages. You'll see in the next section, "Active Server Components," that several standard server components that accompany the ASP environment can significantly extend your applications. The first step in using server components is to instantiate the objects, so that you can use their methods and access their properties. The job of the Server object's CreateObject method is to instantiate server components.

Every server component has a programmatic identifier with which to reference it. You pass this identifier to the CreateObject method, and it creates an object of the appropriate type. For example, to create an instance of the Ad Rotator server component, you would use the following line of code:

```
Set objAdRot =
    Server.CreateObject("MSWC.AdRotator")
```

In this example, the identifier is MSWC.AdRotator. You can actually leave off the Server object qualifier before the CreateObject method name, and the code would still work, because the Server object is the default object if you fail to specify one.

The *HTMLEncode* method takes a string of text and converts any illegal characters it contains into the appropriate HTML escape sequence. For example, to produce the text <TITLE> in a page without it being interpreted as an opening page title tag, you could use the following line of code:

```
<% = Server.HTMLEncode("<TITLE>") %>
```

In the HTML page, the result is <TABLE>—which produces what we wish to see in the page. The &lt character string is called an *escape* sequence that the browser understands.

The *MapPath* method provides file location information for use in server-side scripting. MapPath translates the logical path information, possibly used by the client browser, into a physical path on the Web server. Consider an example that obtains the physical path information for a virtual directory:

```
<% Dim strDirPhysical
    strDirPhysical =
      Server.MapPath("/Client1") %>
```

After this code runs, the variable could have a value of something like: C:\InetPub\Client1. This string could then be used by either the FileSystemObject or TextStream objects covered later in "Text Stream Component."

Finally, we have the *URLEncode* method. This method converts a string into URL-encoded form (unlike the HTMLEncode method, which converts to HTML). Space characters in the string are converted to plus signs (+), and various other characters are converted into their hexadecimal equivalent preceded by a percent sign (%).

Remember the discussion of the Request object's QueryString collection? This is the same kind of string you saw then. The need to construct such a string may arise with the need to pass a query string along to an ASP file, or to create links to old CGI programs. In the following example, a string of text and an HTML tag are passed to the URLEncode method:

```
<%= Server.URLEncode(
    "Employee Roster Report: <BR>") %>
```

The output produced is:

```
Employee+Roster+Report%3A+%3CBR%3E
```

Active Server Components

Active Server Components, formerly known as Automation Servers, are designed to run on your Web server as part of a Web application. These components allow you to extend the functionality of your script behind the scenes. No interface is involved in running them.

Server components are typically invoked from Active Server Pages. However, they can be invoked from other sources as well, such as an ISAPI application, another server component, and other OLE-compatible languages. Server components allow packaging and reuse of common dynamic features such as database access.

A single function call allows you to create a reference to an Active Server component. Once you have a reference to the component, you can call the methods of the component or set and read server component properties. As an example, the following ASP code creates a reference to the Browser-Type component:

```
<% Set bc =
Server.CreateObject("MSWC.BrowserType") %>
```

Another way to create an instance of an object is to use a special implementation of the HTML <OBJECT> tag supported by ASP. For instance, to declare an Ad Rotator object, you could use the code:

```
<OBJECT RUNAT=Server ID=objAdRot
PROGID="MSWC.Adrotator">
</OBJECT>
```

The special RUNAT attribute must be set to Server. The ID attribute defines the name by which you'll refer to the object in your code. The PROGID attribute is the name of the object or component in the Windows Registry and is of the form: [Vendor.]Component[.Version]. You can also use the CLASSID instead of the PROGID, as in:

```
<OBJECT RUNAT=Server ID=objAdRot
CLASSID=
"Clsid:00000293-0000-0010-8000-00AA006D2EA4">
</OBJECT>
```

The main reason for using server components in Active Server Pages is to benefit from the added functionality they provide. Once the object instance is available and you have a reference to it, you can call its methods and manipulate its properties to achieve the desired effects.

The main difference between using CreateObject and the <OBJECT> tag is the point at which the object is actually instantiated. The CreateObject method creates the instance of the object as soon as it is called. The <OBJECT> tag, however, doesn't actually create the object until it is first referenced. You can create instances of objects in the global.asa file, as opposed to an ASP file, which will have a scope that is defined by the Session or Application. The special SCOPE attribute can have the value of Application, Session, or Page. Page is the default when the definition occurs in an ASP file and may be omitted. The following example creates a Session scope object:

```
<OBJECT RUNAT=Server SCOPE=Session
    ID=objAdRot
    PROGID="MSWC.Adrotator">
</OBJECT>
```

You might wonder where server components come from. Some are provided as part of the ASP installation, and others are available free on the Web or as a for-sale product. In this section, I briefly discuss the various components available from Microsoft. I conclude the section by mentioning how you may build your own server components.

ADVERTISEMENT ROTATOR COMPONENT

In your application, you might want to display advertisements for other companies and provide links to their sites. The Ad Rotator component makes this option easy. You can keep a list of advertisements in a text file, and the Ad Rotator component displays them as appropriate. The following ASP code sets that stage for displaying an ad when a user requests a page:

```
<% Set objAdRot =
    Server.CreateObject("MSWC.Adrotator") %>
```

In addition to creating the object, the Ad Rotator component uses several additional files: the graphic images containing the ad, the rotator scheduler file, and the redirection file.

Every time the page containing the rotator component is opened or reloaded, ASP uses the information in the *Rotator Schedule File* (an ASCII text file) to select a graphic and insert it into the page. Furthermore, the component can define the ad to be a hypertext link rather than a static image, and even record the number of clicks on an ad.

```
objAdRot.Clickable(TRUE)'Ad is also a link
objAdRot.Border(0)'No border
objAdRot.TargetFrame("AdFrame")

strHTML =
objAdRot.GetAdvertisement("/ads/adlist.txt")
'Insert HTML into page
Response.Write(strHTML)
```

Once you've created an Ad Rotator object, you can work with its properties, *Border*, *Clickable*, and *TargetFrame*. Border specifies the size of the border around the ad. Clickable defines whether the ad is also a link. TargetFrame supplies the name of the frame in which to display the ad. Next, call the single method, GetAdvertisement, of this object in order to get the details of the next ad to display from the rotator schedule file. To place the HTML code that is returned in the string variable into the page, use the Response object's Write method.

Here is a sample rotator schedule file:

```
REDIRECT /ads/AdRedirect.asp
*
/ads/advertisement1.jpg
http://www.adcompany1.com
The best software on earth
25
/ads/advertisement2.jpg
http://www.adcompany2.com
The greatest software in the universe
25
```

The above file specifies the name of the redirect file, followed by a delimiter line containing only an asterisk. The redirect file will be loaded and executed on the server when the user clicks on the advertisement. The two groups of four lines that follow specify the ads. The first group has the graphic image file name containing the ad, the advertiser's URL (or a hyphen indicating that no line exists for the ad), text for display if the browser doesn't support graphics, and a number called impressions, indicating the relative display time for the advertisement (e.g., 25 causes the ad to display 25% of the time).

Unfortunately, the Ad Rotator component uses an ASCII file for scheduling the rotator, not a database. A database-driven approach could be conceived using a custom-built server component.

BROWSER CAPABILITIES COMPONENT

Because of the variety of browsers and browser capabilities on the Web, you will often want to determine what capabilities a user's browser has before sending content. You can use the *Browser Capability* component to do so. This component determines the capabilities, type, and version of each client browser that accesses your Web site. When a browser connects to the Web server, it automatically sends a User Agent HTTP header. This header is an ASCII string that identifies the browser and its version number. The Browser Capabilities component compares this header to entries in a Browscap.ini file. This text file must be in the same directory as Browscap.dll, the Browser Capability component.

If the component finds matches, it takes on the properties of the browser that matched the User Agent header. If the component does not find a match for the header in the text file, it takes on the default browser properties.

You will need to make sure that Browscap.ini is kept up-to-date with new browsers being released, or even old or special-purpose browsers of which you need to maintain an awareness. A reasonably comprehensive version of the file is included with ASP, and updated versions can be obtained from the Microsoft Web site. Readers are encouraged to examine their version.

Here is an example of the Browser Capabilities component in use. I wish to determine whether the browser supports tables:

```
Set objBrowsCap =
    Server.CreateObject("MSWC.BrowserType")
blnTableSupport = objBrowsCap.Tables
If blnTableSupport Then
    Response.Write "Tables supported"
Else
    Response.Write "Tables NOT supported"
End If
```

First, I create an instance of the component, and refer to one of its properties called Table. Table is actually an entry found in the Browscap.ini file with a value of either True or False. I store the retrieved value and save it in a variable, which makes the code more efficient, since it's read only once. The code simply displays the status of the Table property, but I could go further and custom-tailor the generated HTML code to make do without table support.

CONTENT LINKING COMPONENT

The Content Linking component manages a list of URLs so that you can treat the pages in your Web site like the pages in a book. You can use the functionality of the Content Linking component to automatically generate and update tables of contents and navigational links to previous and following Web pages. This is ideal for applications such as online newspapers and forum message listings. The reference for this component is stored in the Window's Registry as MSWC.NextLink.

The component automatically matches the URL of the currently displayed page to a list of pages stored in a text file on the server, and can allow users to browse through the list of pages in forward or reverse order.

The *Content Linking List* file contains a simple list of page URLs, in the order they are to be displayed. You can also include corresponding descriptions, which are displayed in the contents page, as well as some comments. Here is a sample file:

```
contact.htmWays to contact usrarely updated
guestbook.htmSign our guest bookwritten to database
chat.htmChat with other users
search.htmSearch our siteMS Index Server
links.htmRelated sites
```

Once you've created a content-linking file, you can add the component to a page. Once created, a Content Linking component has several methods, as shown in Table 7-7, that you can use to manipulate the list.

Table 7-7	Content Linking Component Methods
Method	**Description**
GetListCount	The number of items in the file.
GetListIndex	The index of the current page in the file.
GetNextURL	The URL of the next page in the file.
GetNextDescription	The description of the next page in the file.
GetPreviousURL	The URL of the previous page in the file.
GetPreviousDescription	The description of the previous page in the file.
GetNthURL	The URL of the nth page in the file.
GetNthDescription	The description of the nth page in the file.

Here is an example of using the Content Linking component:

```
<UL>
<% Set objNextLink =
    Server.CreateObject("MSWC.Nextlink")
intListCount =
    objNextLink.GetListCount("linklist.txt")
For intLoop = 1 To intListCount %>
    <LI>
    <A HREF=
    "<%= objNextLink.GetNthURL("linklist.txt",
      intLoop) %>">
    <%= objNextLink.GetNthDescription(
      "linklist.txt", intLoop) %>
    </A>
<% Next %>
</UL>
```

The above code creates a Content Linking object and then uses the GetListCount method to find out how many links are in the Content Linking List. It then loops through the list items and places each in an <LI> tag to build an HTML unordered list, followed by an <A> tag. The HREF is retrieved from the list file using the GetNthURL method, and the description is retrieved with GetNthDescription.

DATABASE ACCESS COMPONENT

I do not cover the Database Access Component, otherwise known as ActiveX Data Objects, in this section. One of the principal uses of dynamic Web site technologies is to publish information directly from some type of database system. This, and the need to collect data and store it in a database, led to the original development of server-side programming. To achieve these tasks using ASP, you can take advantage of a special, but general-purpose component, called ActiveX Data Objects. Since this subject is of prime concern to you readers of this book, I devote an entire section to ADO later in this chapter, in "ActiveX Data Objects."

FILE ACCESS COMPONENT

The FileSystemObject object provides access to the server's file system, allowing you to manipulate text files from within server-side scripting code. To create an instance of the FileSystemObject, you can use the following code:

```
Set objFileSystem =
    CreateObject("Scripting.FileSystemObject")
```

Once you have a reference to a FileSystemObject, you can use the two available methods, *CreateTextFile* and *OpenTextFile*. The CreateTextFile method creates a new text file or overwrites an existing one. It returns a Text-Stream object that you can use to read from or write to the file. The Open-TextFile method opens an existing text file. It returns a TextStream object that we can use to read from or append data to the file.

As an example using the FileSystemObject, you can determine whether your server folder contains a certain file:

```
<SCRIPT LANGUAGE=VBScript RUNAT=Server>
FUNCTION FileExists (ByVal strFileName)
    On Error Resume Next
    strFileName = Server.MapPath(strFileName)
    Set objFileObject =
      Server.CreateObject(
        "Scripting.FileSystemObject")
    Set InStream =
      FileObject.OpenTextFile(strFileName, 1,
      FALSE, FALSE)
    If err = 0 Then
      FileExists = TRUE
    Else
      FileExists = FALSE
    End If
End Function
</SCRIPT>
```

In the OpenTextFile method call above, the third argument is FALSE, indicating that if a file with the specified name does not already exist in the specified directory, an error condition is raised; thus the existence of an error determines the file's existence.

TEXT STREAM COMPONENT

The *TextStream* component allows you to read from and write to files on the server. The TextStream component uses the FileSystem object to retrieve and modify information stored in a text file. Once you have a reference to a TextStream object, you can use several different methods (shown in Table 7-8) and properties (shown in Table 7-9), all of which are read-only.

Table 7–8	TextStream Component Methods
Method	**Description**
Close	Close an open file.
Read	Read the specified number of characters from a file.
ReadAll	Read an entire file as a single string value.
ReadLine	Read a line from a file as a string.
Skip	Skip and discard the specified number of characters while reading a file.
SkipLine	Skip and discard the next line while reading a file.
Write	Write the specified string value to a file.
WriteLine	Write the optional string value and a new-line character to a file.
WriteBlankLines	Write the specified number of new-line characters to a file.

Table 7–9	TextStream Component Properties
Property	**Description**
AtEndOfLine	True if the file pointer is at the end of a line in a file.
AtEndOfStream	True if the file pointer is at the end of a file.
Column	The column number of the current character in a file, beginning with the value 1.
Line	The current line number in a file, beginning with the value 1.

Say that you've already used either the OpenTextFile or CreateTextFile methods of the FileSystemObject object to obtain a TextStream object reference. You can write to it and then close it using:

```
Set objFSO =
    CreateObject("Scripting.FileSystemObject")
Set objTS =
    objFSO.OpenTextFile(
```

```
    "C:\RepFiles\logrep.txt",8)
objTS.WriteLine("ASCII file output line")
objTS.Close
```

CREATING SERVER COMPONENTS WITH VB

Up until now in this section, the discussion of Active Server Components has centered around pre-existing components that come packaged with Active Server Pages (or even from third-party companies). You do have the ability, however, to create your own custom components that can be integrated with the built-in components.

Server components are really nothing more than ActiveX controls that have the ability to interact with ASP code. Therefore, any development environment that can create ActiveX controls can also be used to build custom server components. Until recently, that possibility meant using either the C++ or the Delphi programming language. Now, however, you have another choice, namely Visual Basic 5.0. VB 5.0 has the ability to create standalone ActiveX controls that will run on any ActiveX host, including VB, Internet Explorer, or as Server Components inside of IIS. A Wizard is even in VB 5.0 that assists in the creation of ActiveX controls.

Visual InterDev Data Form Wizard

From the discussions in the preceding sections, you can certainly tell that ASP technology maintains many features that contribute to the successful integration of database connectivity with Web sites. In the sections that follow, I discuss the nuts and bolts that make this integration possible using ActiveX Data Objects (ADO), but for now, I want to briefly mention a very useful tool that automatically generates ASP files that include database connections.

The Data Form wizard inside Visual InterDev is specifically suited to take advantage of all that ASP technology has to offer when interfacing to an ODBC data source. The Data Form wizard is actually an ASP code generator that builds fully functional server-side VBScript program modules, providing seamless access to database tables. The database access is provided via ADO, a data access object model that I cover shortly. For a particular table, the wizard constructs three distinct ASP files. These files, and brief descriptions, are listed below. You learn more about the capabilities of Visual InterDev and the Data Form wizard in Chapter 8.

TableNameAction.asp

The *TableName*Action.asp file is responsible for reacting to user interaction with the two other ASP files, *TableName*List.asp and *TableName*Form.asp. *TableName* is the name of the data form you provide to the Data Form wizard, and is automatically prefixed to the three ASP files. This file consists of several functions defined within the <SCRIPT> tags at the beginning of the .asp file. When the file is called, it looks to see what button was pressed and reacts accordingly. After performing some action, it redirects the browser to either the *TableName*Form.asp or the *TableName*List.asp file.

TableNameForm.asp

The *TableName*Form.asp file is called initially and displays a single record from the database table or recordset. This ASP file consists of four major sections. The first section contains various VBScript functions called by the form. The most important function is the ShowFields function, which is responsible for taking a field name and displaying it in the HTML document.

The second major section is an ActiveX design-time control, the Data Range Header. The data range header is followed by more VBScript code that calls the ShowFields function for each field in the recordset. Finally, another ActiveX design-time control is used, the Data Range Footer. This control serves the purpose of the end of a loop established by the Data Range Header.

TableNameList.asp

The *TableName*List.asp file is very similar to the *TableName*Form.asp file. It contains the same sections in the same order, with one exception. This file displays multiple records at a time in a list view format within an HTML table. Before the Data Range header design-time control are the <TABLE> tag and the column headings.

COM/DCOM

OLE DB is the central part of Microsoft database connectivity technology for the Web. Much of what OLE DB is all about, however, involves the *Component Object Model* (COM). Before I discuss OLE DB, I want to spend some time now defining what COM is and how it is important, as well as the model's key elements.

COM is an object-based specification for developing application components that can dynamically communicate with each other, even across networks, in a standard and uniform way. The COM architecture also provides the means to assemble components to support new capabilities, using object-oriented programming techniques to build encapsulated application components. These components provide an interface to an object, and that interface is used to manipulate the object's state and can be determined dynamically at runtime. *Componentizing* application development generally speeds up and simplifies the development process. The COM architecture helps modularize the development process by allowing components to work together even if they have been developed with different programming languages or by different developers. COM components can be used to facilitate inter-application communication. Unlike other component models, such as early Dynamic Link Libraries (DLLs), developers use the COM architecture to create a methodology for applications to communicate directly with one another. Once this communication is established, the COM architecture does not impose any overhead. Using an extension of COM called *Distributed Component Object Model* (DCOM), components are able to work together in a distributed computing environment.

Aside from the specification, COM also exists as a library, which provides a number of services that support the binary specification of COM.

Following are some of the key characteristics of COM:

1. The COM architecture provides a strict rule set that a component must follow. This is contrary to previous component models, such as Dynamic Data Exchange (DDE) and DLLs. COM technology enables developers to build robust components that can evolve over time. Developers can upgrade COM components without also having to upgrade the applications that use those components, a welcome situation due to the strict rules that define application components.

2. COM components are object-oriented, because they define an encapsulated object that presents a fixed set of interfaces, hiding the implementation details from the users of the components.

3. COM is lightweight, fast, and supports versioning.

4. ActiveX components are COM objects.

5. COM components are independent of programming language and do not require any specialized interface to bridge inter-application communications. By nature, all COM components are compatible.

6. COM components use 128-bit *Globally Unique Identifiers* (GUIDs) for the purpose of uniquely identifying COM objects.

7. Security is inherent in the COM architecture.

8. COM supports a distributed object model, allowing components to be used in a networked environment, as well as accessed and executed on remote systems. DCOM is a special case of COM. DCOM supports COM components over a networked environment without requiring you to write any specialized network code. DCOM enables ActiveX components to run anywhere. DCOM is an extension of the distributed computing environment (DCE) remote procedure call (RPC) specification. DCOM is an object-oriented representation of RPC. DCOM is fully supported on TCP/IP networks and provides all other COM benefits.

OLE DB combines a number of components, data providers, and data consumers that together provide access to distributed enterprise data. OLE DB is firmly based on the COM architecture and leverages COM to provide an interface between these application components and provide distributed data access.

Introduction to OLE DB

Microsoft introduced open database connectivity (ODBC) with the promise of creating a singular common access methodology for databases. The earliest versions of ODBC suffered from inconsistent support and performance. In fact, very few database products supported ODBC, and those that did support it also provided their own database drivers, which were often more reliable and faster.

ODBC has come a long way since those early days. Two versions of ODBC are currently available: version 2.0, which supports 16-bit applications, and version 3.0, which supports 32-bit applications (for Windows 95 and NT). Almost every major database in use today supports ODBC drivers, and third-party developers provide optimized driver versions. ODBC drivers have become as ubiquitous as video and other Windows device drivers. Also, many data processing applications (such as Excel, Access, etc.) support ODBC data access. ODBC has become the omnipresent methodology for providing access to database resources.

The beauty of ODBC is that it lets you access different database systems with the same code through the use of database-specific ODBC drivers. The drawback to ODBC is that it isn't designed to access the multitude of data types found in spreadsheets, text files, and message systems. If a non-SQL-based data provider wants to expose its data, it is forced to implement the equivalent of a SQL engine in the ODBC driver. Now that businesses are storing more information in documents, spreadsheets, project files, Lotus Notes, or Microsoft Exchange, a definite need to uniformly access these non-SQL data stores has arisen.

To solve this growing problem, Microsoft developed a new OLE DB specification for accessing any and all data. The name, however, is somewhat of a misnomer, since OLE DB has nothing at all to do with Object Linking and Embedding. OLE DB is not restricted to databases. It is a COM-based API, and through its 50+ interfaces, you can access all data, regardless of data type. OLE relies on an object model to represent data, thus exposing the underlying data through an object-oriented paradigm.

The primary goal behind ODBC was to provide a consistent interface to database data sources. OLE DB is designed with an even broader goal in mind: to provide a methodology to access data regardless of the data source. Figure 7-6 shows how OLE DB becomes the data access vehicle for documents, e-mail systems, file systems, spreadsheets, COM components, and other database sources using ODBC drivers.

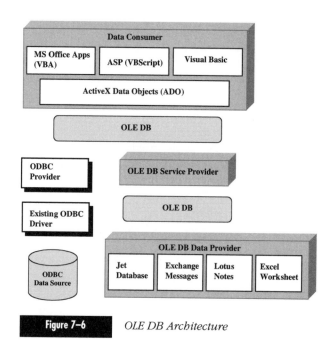

Figure 7–6   *OLE DB Architecture*

Components of an OLE DB Application

An OLE DB implementation has two basic components: a data provider and a data consumer. A *data provider* is an application that responds to queries and returns data in a usable form. An OLE DB data provider responds to various OLE DB calls to provide the information it contains in a usable tabular form. For example, a spreadsheet OLE DB provider may allow access to a selection of cells or properties of the sheet, such as the creator, description, and creation date.

A *data consumer* is an application or other COM component that uses the application program interface (API) of OLE DB to access a data source. A data consumer can be any application that requires access to data. OLE DB allows a data consumer to access the entire range of enterprise data, regardless of where it is stored.

The key feature of OLE DB is that it simplifies the requirements for implementing a data provider interface. With OLE DB, the only requirement for a data provider is to return data in a tabular form. The provider is not required to support a command interface. In conjunction with a query processor, OLE DB provides a unified way to access enterprise data.

Also available is an OLE DB component called a *service provider*, which plays the role of a go-between in the OLE DB architecture. Acting as a consumer of raw OLE DB data sources and as a provider to other OLE DB consumers, a service provider manipulates and processes the raw OLE DB data sources. OLE DB segments an application, providing diverse data source components, a query processing component, and an application. Because OLE DB provides a consistent data interface, any one of the components can be exchanged without affecting functionality.

OLE DB extends the capabilities of ODBC by enabling less sophisticated data applications to become data providers. OLE DB and ODBC coexist by providing for both non-database and database sources of data, respectively. ODBC will still be used to support database data sources, but instead of relying on the ODBC interface, applications will now use the OLE DB interface to access these data sources. The OLE DB Software Development Kit (SDK) contains an OLE DB provider for ODBC data, which allows you to access ODBC data sources from your OLE DB consumer applications.

ActiveX Data Objects (ADO)

ActiveX Data Objects (ADO) operate with OLE DB data providers to supply a methodology for manipulating the data they contain. In this light, ADO can be considered a specialized OLE DB consumer. You may notice that ADO is very similar to the traditional Data Access Objects (DAO) and Remote Data Objects (RDO) models. An understanding of Open Database Connectivity (ODBC) is useful here, too, because the relationship between RDO and ODBC is the same as that for ADO and OLE DB. Just as the RDO API accesses ODBC data sources, the ADO API accesses OLE DB data sources. In addition, when using the OLE DB ODBC data provider, ADO can access ODBC data sources as well.

As a primary goal, the Microsoft design team took the best of these two earlier models to build ADO as a new, more refined programming model. ADO is a very easy-to-use, language-independent, and extensible interface for programmatic access to all types of data. ADO can also be thought of as an object model exposing objects, properties, methods, and events. ADO was designed as a programming model, with a simple-to-use set of interfaces that would be common for any high-level data access library. ADO supplies a common programming model for a broad range of developers. ADO's ease of use is based on existing models built for a consumer of data. ADO is also language-independent, supporting a dual interface for IDispatch and the regular VTable interface as well. So languages such as VB, Java, and C++ can bind directly to the VTable interface and get fast performance. Scripting languages such as VBScript and JavaScript can use those same objects through IDispatch, and the object model works the same.

The DAO model was first designed for the Microsoft JET database. This was the model's sole purpose at the time. Certain things in DAO, however, were JET- and ISAM-specific. ADO was designed without anything that was too specific to any one kind of access method. As mentioned before, ADO is a programming model and an object model for accessing data. Microsoft left the design so that developers can have a general implementation of ADO that goes over OLE DB. However, the realization occurred that some developers need specialized access to specialized data sources. Many data sources can implement the standard OLE DB interfaces, but they have other interesting and necessary functionality that they need to expose through their provider. OLE DB interfaces are called custom interfaces and are accessible from languages like C++ that can deal with pointers and unsigned data types. So if a provider wants to expose some specialized functionality, the model gives the provider the ability to also get the functionality exposed in higher-level languages like VB, VBA, VBScript, and JavaScript but not to invent a totally new object model. So Microsoft made these interfaces such that they are just interfaces. As an OLE DB provider, you can implement these ADO interfaces in addition to the OLE DB interfaces, when you want to expose additional functionality that's not part of the general core OLE DB set.

ADO for OLE DB can be used in different ways. You have to factor your application into different tiers. You might have a single-tier application, two tiers, three tiers, or multiple tiers. You can use ADO in any of the tiers. You can also use several languages such as Visual C++, Visual Basic, Visual J++, Access (a desktop database with Visual Basic for Applications), VBScript, and JavaScript. Because ADO for OLE DB is an ActiveX automation server, it is totally language-neutral.

The ADO for OLE DB component is an implementation of this ADO programming model for any generic OLE DB provider. They talk to the generic OLE DB interfaces. ADO for OLE DB can access both OLE DB providers and ODBC data sources. The latter is made possible by the MSDASQL (Microsoft ODBC Provider for OLE DB) gateway. Also, a specialized implementation of ADO is available—*ADO for Fox Cursors* (ADOFX), a specialized implementation of ADO for the Fox cursor engine. This is an example of taking the same programming model and implementing it in two places. To a consumer of data, it's the same object model and the same code, but it can do some specialized work. When someone goes and makes a specialized version of the ADO model, he or she will implement the ADO interfaces, but is free to extend or add on to them. For object oriented aficionados, this action is subclassing, where standard ADO is the base class.

ADO Features

During the design of the ADO programming model, the design team took the existing DAO and RDO models and noted considerable overlap and commonality. The emphasis was to take the best of both of these API worlds, clean out what is no longer relevant, and establish a new programming interface. ADO's features now include:

1. Objects in the ADO model are independently instantiable instead of a hierarchy of objects. In the DAO model, you started with the Engine object, then the Workspace object, then the Database object, and then the recordset object. What resulted was basically a tree of instances. This model works, but it doesn't allow a tool to come in and design a specialized Recordset object. Imagine that the Recordset object in DAO (and also the one in ADO) is made to handle any sort of results returned from a data source. It can determine through metadata calls all the column information, build up a recordset, and hand it to you. But metadata calls take some time at runtime, so ADO allows for you to design a recordset object that is specialized for a certain query against a back-end database. So at design–time, you capture all the information about the metadata of all the columns, and at runtime, you're able to open the recordset and immediately bind and start fetching without doing metadata calls. The way this procedure can happen is when the objects are allowed to instantiate by themselves, i.e., the recordset instantiates by itself, separate from a connection. You then relate these objects together by setting a property. This action opens up the future of the model for things like customization, as well as temporary recordsets. You can create a new recordset, with certain fields, and start filling data. The object is not from a server, but rather just a temporary recordset, something like a temporary table.

2. ADO allows customization of objects by designers.

3. The ADO model includes all capabilities of DAO and RDO. In the first releases of the ADO object model, you have most of the Data Manipulation Language (DML) functionality exposed, but not all. Remember, the DAO and RDO libraries have been out for awhile. Future versions, ADO version 2.0 and beyond, will surpass what is in DAO and RDO, at which time we'll say that ADO replaces both DAO and RDO. In the short run, some features in DAO and RDO are not in ADO libraries, but they will soon come. The first version of ADO for OLE DB is included with ASP.

4. ADO is a specification for a set of object interfaces (a programming model), not a specific implementation. The core implementation is called ADO for OLE DB.

5. ADO has support for batch updating, where a number of record updates are cached and transmitted individually.

6. ADO contains support for active filtering of the records returned, limits on the number of records returned, and prepared statements.

7. ADO interfaces to server-side stored procedures.

8. ADO supports queries that return multiple resultsets.

9. ADO supports many cursor types: forward-only, key set, dynamic, and static cursors.

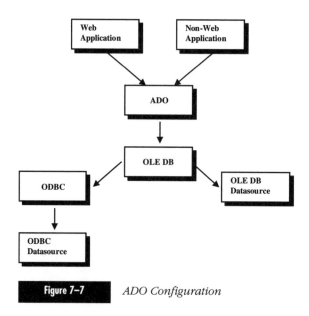

Figure 7–7   *ADO Configuration*

When I discuss ADO objects later in this chapter, much will be familiar to those of you who have programmed with DAO and RDO. Figure 7-7 shows a typical ADO configuration with respect to how both Web and non-Web applications use the ADO API.

When viewing ADO as a programming model, a common user model works for any implementation, no matter how specialized it becomes (specialized towards ISAM programming, specialized towards a certain type of data source). You will always see a base interface exposed out of any of these libraries. If an implementation extends the base interface, it does so by exposing another interface that is inherited from the base interface. A good example of this is the JET database. JET has certain features that are not in the OLE DB general set of interfaces, such as replication, user security management, etc. To make a specialized interface for the JET database engine, implement the base interface, and then extend it to have things like replication to a database and a users collection. In this way, to you as a programmer accessing data, the base interface is the same.

ADO Integration

Each ADO object provides a number of methods and properties with which you may customize their functionality. *Methods* perform some function with an object, and *properties* set special object attributes. In the sections that follow, I examine each ADO object, its methods and properties, and how each may be utilized in providing ways to communicate with a data source. The methods and properties presented for each ADO object are complete in a generic sense. Which methods and properties a specific ADO object supports depend on the data source in use. An OLE DB data source does not necessarily have to support the complete functionality supported by the OLE DB specification. As an example, not all OLE DB data sources support the concept of a transaction.

The ADO programming model can be used from any programming language that supports COM. This list includes ASP and VBScript, Visual Basic, Visual J++, and Visual C++. The discussions in this chapter center around the use of ADO with VBScript and Visual Basic.

ADO Objects

The ADO programming model consists of the following objects: Command, Connection, Error, Field, Parameter, and Recordset. Figure 7-8 shows the hierarchy of the ADO objects.

You can create the various ADO objects using the HTML <OBJECT> tag. The <OBJECT> tag declaration contains a number of attributes shown in Table 7-10. VBScript requires only two attributes, CLSID and ID, to create an ADO object. You must set the CLSID attribute to one of the ADO Globally Unique Identifiers (GUIDs), which are itemized in Table 7-11. The ID attribute is set to an identifier of your choosing that will identify the ADO object within

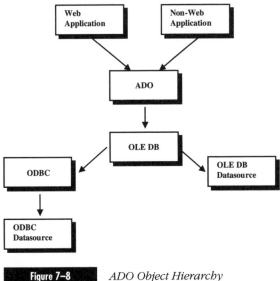

Figure 7-8   *ADO Object Hierarchy*

the current HTML document. Using the <OBJECT> tag, VBScript creates the ADO object and automatically releases it when it is no longer required.

Table 7–10	OBJECT Tag Attributes
Attribute	**Description**
ALIGN	Use one of the possible attribute values to specify how the object should be aligned in the page: BASELINE, CENTER, LEFT, MIDDLE, RIGHT, TEXTMIDDLE, TEXTBOTTOM, and TEXTTOP.
BORDER	Specify the width of the border around the object.
CLASSID	An ADO class identifier that creates the object (see Table 7-11).
CODEBASE	The URL where the object can be found if not available.
CODETYPE	The object's Internet Media Type; not necessary when creating an ActiveX object.
DATA	The URL specifying the location of the object's data.
DECLARE	Used only to declare, but not initialize, the object.
HEIGHT	Specify the height of the object.
HSPACE	Specify the horizontal space above and below the object.
ID	Used to identify the object in the current HTML document.
ISMAP	Associate an image map on the server to the image used by the object.
NAME	The name used when the object is submitted to the server as part of a form.
SHAPES	Shape associated links.
STANDBY	The text to display while the object is loading.
TYPE	The Internet Media Type of the data specified by the <DATA> tag.
USEMAP	The URL pointing to the client-side image map.
VSPACE	The vertical margin to the left and right of the object.
WIDTH	The width of the object.

When creating an ADO object in an Active Server Page and VBScript, you can use either the <OBJECT></OBJECT> tags or the VBScript CreateObject function. The CreateObject function has the following syntax:

```
CreateObject(class)
```

Table 7-11	ADO Globally Unique Identifiers

ADO Object	GUID
ADOCommand	0000022C-0000-0010-8000-00AA006D2EA4
ADORecordset	00000281-0000-0010-8000-00AA006D2EA4
ADORRecordset	00000301-0000-0010-8000-00AA006D2EA4
ADOConnection	00000293-0000-0010-8000-00AA006D2EA4
ADOParameter	00000231-0000-0010-8000-00AA006D2EA4

where class is a string value containing the name of the server and object. For ADO, the server name can be the lightweight ADO Recordset (ADOR) server or the complete ADO Database (ADODB) server. The ADOR server provides access only to the Recordset object. The object names for the ADODB server appear in Table 7-12.

Table 7-12	ADODB Server Objects

Object	Description
Connection	Encapsulates a connection to a data source and allows commands to be executed with the Execute method.
Command	Encapsulates a command that can be interpreted by the data source.
Error	Encapsulates errors returned from the data source.
Field	Encapsulates a column of a Recordset object.
Parameter	Encapsulates a command parameter.
Recordset	Accesses column data, specifies a cursor, navigates a collection of records, updates records in a batch mode, adds and deletes new records, and applies filters to records returned.

The following simple example shows an Active Server Page that creates an ADO Recordset object. Notice that VBScript will automatically destroy the object after it is no longer needed.

```
<%
    set rs =
      server.CreateObject("ADODB.Recordset")
    <!-- Use the rs Recordset object here -->
    rs.close()
%>
```

Connection Object

The Connection object represents a unique session with a data source much like the ODBCDirect Connection or RDO's rdoConnection object. As the pipeline to the data source, the Connection object handles all the communication between the application and data source. Unlike the ODBCDirect or RDO equivalents, you don't have to instantiate a Connection object before creating other objects like Command or Recordset.

The Connection object has an optional Errors Collection, which functions the same as the JET Engine's Errors Collection or RDO's rdoErrors collection of the rdoEngine object. The purpose of the Errors Collection is to let you iterate through errors returned by the data source.

With the Connection object, you're able to control and customize the connection to the data source. For example, you can customize a connection's isolation level option. Connection is the object you start with when working with any DBMS.

Transactions are an important part of a connection to a data source. You can use the transaction methods exposed by the Connection interface to start and end transactions. ADO for OLE DB also works with Microsoft Transaction Server, so you don't need to do your own transaction management when working inside the Transaction Server framework.

As a generic example of using the Connection object, consider the VB code below.

```
Dim con as New Connection
con.Open "DSN", "UserName", "Password"
con.Execute "sql-string"
```

You can see that the Connection object is instantiable, but the first line is something like what you'd see in VB. In a scripting language, you'd replace it with a CreateObject call. Actually, when creating an ADO object in an Active Server Page with VBScript, you can use either the <OBJECT></OBJECT> tags or the VBScript CreateObject function.

An Open method is on Connection, using an open/close metaphor for objects that have an open and closed state like a Connection object. You pass a data source name, user name, and password as separate arguments, or you can send an entire connection string as the first argument, and it will be automatically parsed into individual components.

You can use an Execute method for the Connection object. Unlike with DAO and RDO, whether a recordset is returned doesn't matter. If results are returned from the query, then the Execute method will return a Recordset object. If no results exist, nothing is returned. This new model is better than before, because the programmer doesn't have to worry about whether results are returned or not.

Here is a Web-specific example of how to open a connection:

```
<!-- Create an ADO Connection object -->
<object id=connect
classid=
"clsid:00000293-0000-0010-8000-00AA006D2EA4">
</object>

<script language="VBScript">
    Set NumRecs = 0
    'Open the connection object
    connect.Open "data source=pubs"

    'Now execute a query, NumRecs has # records
    'retrieved
    Set rs =
    connect.Execute "SELECT * FROM authors",
    NumRecs, 1

    'Close the connection and recordset objects
    connect.Close
    rs.Close
</script>
```

Methods

Table 7-13 shows the methods supported by the Connection object.

Table 7–13	Connection Object Methods
Method	**Description**
BeginTrans	Begins a new transaction with the data source.
Close	Closes a data source connection.
CommitTrans	Saves any changes to the data source and ends the current transaction.
Execute	Executes a query or command by the data source and returns a Recordset object.
Open	Opens a connection with the data source.
RollbackTrans	Cancels any changes made to the data source in the current transaction and ends the transaction.

Properties

Table 7-14 lists the properties supported by the Connection object.

Table 7–14	Connection Object Properties	
Property	**Read/Write**	**Description**
Attributes	R/W	The Connection object attributes.
CommandTimeout	R/W	The number of seconds (default is 30) to wait for a command to execute.
ConnectionString	R/W	The string used to connect to a data source when the ConnectString parameter is not passed to the Open method.
ConnectionTimeout	R/W	The number of seconds (default is 15) to wait for a connection to a data source.
DefaultDatabase	R/W	The default database name currently connected to or used by the Open method when a database name has not been specified.
IsolationLevel	R/W	Determines how the connection handles transactions.
Mode	R/W	Permissions for modifying data in a connection.
Provider	R/W	The name of the current data provider for a connection.
Version	R	The ADO version number.

Recordset Object

The Recordset object is the most used and flexible object in ADO. It is equivalent to ODBCDirect's Recordset object and RDO's rdoResultset object. The Recordset object exposes data, which is potentially scrollable and updateable. A Recordset contains a collection of Field objects. You can view a Recordset as a cursor of data. The main difference in ADO from the DAO or RDO model is that a recordset can be thought of as a *buffer* of data. Generically, a recordset is the entity that you iterate over in the results of a query. ADO, however, moves beyond this notion. ADO treats the recordset (query results) as a data buffer, separate from the connection to the database, with the ability to pass the recordset around to other objects.

A middle-tier business object might issue a query to the database, create a Recordset data buffer, and hand it back to the client By-Value so that it's separated from the database connection. The idea here is that you're working with business objects and not having your user interface talk directly to the database. You can use the concept of a data buffer (i.e., recordset) that can be passed around, and all changes made to it are buffered in the recordset.

The recordset tracks the changes: it knows which rows have changed, which have not, and which columns are dirty. It keeps the old value and new value. When you want to post all the changes back to the database, you're able to hand the recordset to another middle-tier object.

In ADO, you can take the recordset and re-associate it with a connection, and use an automatic method called UpdateBatch, which will take care of sending all the update, insert, and delete statements to the server for you.

As a generic example of using the Recordset object, consider the following VB code:

```
Dim rs As New Recordset

rs.MaxRows = 100
rs.Open "<sql>", "<connection string>",
    adOpenKeyset

While Not rs.EOF
    Ö
    rs.MoveNext
Wend
```

You can easily do an open operation on a Recordset object. In the preceding example, instead of using the Connection object to open a recordset, I'm creating the recordset by itself. Notice that the MaxRows property has to be set before the query is executed, because the data source has to know when to chop off the results.

This area is another where ADO is much more streamlined than its predecessors. In DAO and RDO, these kinds of properties had to be set at higher-level objects, even though they didn't really belong there. For example, MaxRows, or the cursor type, concurrency type, and cache size, had to be set after the cursor was open. They had to put them on the Database object in DAO, the Connection object in RDO, or on the QueryDef or PreparedStatement object. Now, all the properties are directly set on the Recordset object.

In the example, I instantiate the Recordset object in the Dim statement. The result is a recordset object in a pre-opened state. At this point, you can set various properties. Then you can just call the Open method to open the cursor (just like you can call the Open method of a connection). In the example, I'm specifying some parameters on the Open call, but you could also set each parameter by assigning a value to the equivalent property. For example, a property called Source typically has a SQL string. The reason you might specify various optional parameters in the Open call is that in a scripting language such as VBScript, more overhead results from doing each separately. You can use fewer lines of code by using the optional parameters on the Open call.

The source property can also be a Command object. For example, if you've created some Command objects, to prepare them or to work with stored procedures, you pass the Command object as the source argument.

The second argument has a connection string. This is the connection that the recordset is going to use when it executes a statement and opens the cursor. Here, you can pass a Connection object as well.

These two arguments are overloaded so that you can pass either strings or objects. If you decide to pass a string, an object is created for you automatically. This pre-establishes the connection as in this example, and relates the recordset to that connection. For scripting code, you don't have to take all the normal steps and make all the normal calls individually. So the scripting code is much more streamlined.

The third argument is the cursor type, which is also settable as a property, but usually it is set by passing a parameter.

The model for moving through the recordset is exactly the same as for DAO and RDO using the EOF property, which lets you detect the end of the recordset. Then you use the MoveNext method. You can use the familiar navigation methods: MovePrevious, MoveLast, AbsolutePage, BookMark, etc.

Adding and changing rows involves the AddNew and Update methods, which have been extended in the ADO model to make things easier. ADO allows you to pass new values along with the AddNew method call, instead of having to do an AddNew call to set each column's value and then issue the Update. This technique is good for scripting languages to minimize the amount of code, since you can now do in one operation what used to take several steps.

Here is a Web-specific example of how to use a Recordset object:

```
<!-- Create an ADO Recordset object -->
<object id=rsclassid=
"clsid:00000281-0000-0010-8000-00AA006D2EA4">
</object>
<script language="VBScript">
    connect = "data source=pubs"
    sql = "select * from authors"

    'Now execute the query
    rs.Open sql, connect
    'Move to the first record in the resultset
    rs.MoveFirst
    'Loop through the records
    Do While (NOT rs.EOF)
      rs.MoveNext
    Loop
    'Close the recordset object
    rs.Close
</script>
```

Methods

Table 7-15 describes the methods supported by the Recordset object.

Table 7–15	Recordset Object Methods
Method	**Description**
AddNew	Add a new record to a Recordset.
CancelBatch	Cancel a batch update before calling the UpdateBatch method.
CancelUpdate	Cancel changes made to a record before calling the Update method.
Clone	Create a new Recordset object containing a copy of the current Recordset object.
Close	Close the current Recordset object connection.
Delete	Delete the current record.
GetRows	Get a number of rows from a Recordset and place them in an array.
Move	Move to a specific record.
MoveFirst	Move to the first record in the Recordset.
MoveLast	Move to the last record in the Recordset.
MoveNext	Move to the next record in the Recordset.
MovePrevious	Move to the previous record in the Recordset.
NextRecordset	Get the next Recordset of a query or stored procedure that returns multiple Recordsets.
Open	Open a new Recordset object connection to a data source.
Requery	Execute the current query again.
Supports	Determine whether a Recordset object supports specific methods or properties.
Update	Post changes to the current record.
UpdateBatch	Post changes to the current batch of records.

Properties

Table 7-16 lists the properties supported by the Recordset object.

Table 7–16	Recordset Object Properties	
Property	**Read/Write**	**Description**
AbsolutePage	R/W	Gets/sets the current Recordset page.
AbsolutePosition	R/W	Gets/sets the current record position.
ActiveConnection	R/W	Gets/sets the current Connection object.
BOF	R	Has true value if the current record position is at the beginning of file of the Recordset.
Bookmark	R/W	Gets/sets a bookmark to the current record.
CacheSize	R/W	Gets/sets the number of records from a Recordset object that are cached locally in memory.
CursorType	R/W	Gets/sets the current cursor type.
EditMode	R	Returns the current edit mode.
EOF	R	Has true value if the current record position is at the end of file of the Recordset.
Filter	R/W	Gets/sets the filter applied when navigating the Recordset.
LockType	R/W	Gets/sets the current locking mode.
MaxRecords	R/W	Gets/sets the maximum number of records returned by a query. The default for this property is 0, indicating no limit.
PageCount	R	Returns the number of pages used by the Recordset.
PageSize	R/W	Get/sets a value indicating how many records constitute a page in the Recordset.
RecordCount	R	Returns the number of records in the Recordset.
Source	R	Returns the source of the records in the Recordset.
Status	R	Returns the status of the current record.

Command Object

The Command object represents a SQL statement, stored procedure, or other command that can be processed by the data source. The object contains command text and parameters to specify queries and stored procedure calls.

Server-side stored procedures can increase performance because they are processed entirely on the server. Command operates in conjunction with the Parameter object, allowing Command to accept parameters when it is executed. When defining a Command object, you can request a compiled version for the duration of the connection. This precompiled version of the command is called a *prepared statement*.

Command is analogous to the QueryDef object in DAO model and the prepared statement in the RDO model. It is called "Command" because Query-Def is really a very JET-specific name. Also, Command satisfies the notion in OLE DB for a generic command executing against a data source. Command is a way to encapsulate a certain command you're going to execute against a data source. Remember, you don't need to use a Command object if you simply need to execute a one-time command, since an Execute method is on the Connection object that you can use to execute such things. The Command object allows you to work with parameterized things, where the command contains parameter markers. For example, with stored procedure calls, this fact is very important. If your stored procedure has output arguments or return values, you use a Command object with Parameter objects that map to these parameters. Furthermore, they can be marked as input-only, input-output, or return values. So when you execute commands, you'll be able to get output values. This method is similar to RDO and the prepared statement object.

As a generic example of using the Command object, consider the following VB code:

```
Dim cmd As New Command

cmd.ActiveConnection = "<connection string>"
cmd.CommandText = "<sql>"

cmd.Parameters(0) = <value>
cmd.Execute

cmd.Parameters(0) = <value>
cmd.Execute
```

In the preceding example, you can see that a Command object can be associated with any Connection object. An important concept is in play here: Command objects live on their own so that you can associate a Command with one Connection object and execute it. Then you can associate it with another Connection object. The Command object is not tied to one Connection object for its lifetime. In the example, the ActiveConnection property is set to a connection string, but it can also be set to a Connection object as well. This possibility establishes the relationship between this Command and a connection. Then you can assign a SQL string to the CommandText property, but you can do more here with OLE DB. OLE DB allows you to work with data sources that are not necessarily SQL relational databases. CommandText is therefore any command text that the OLE DB provider is able to understand.

In the example, you can set parameters to different values at different times and then execute the Command based on those values. Parameter objects can also capture output values and can be marked with a direction of input or output. In the case of output, after a stored procedure call, the output value will be available in the Parameter object after the execution.

Methods

Table 7-17 shows the methods supported by the Command object.

Table 7–17	Command Object Methods
Method	**Description**
CreateParameter	Create a new command Parameter object.
Execute	Execute the specified command or stored procedure.

Properties

Table 7-18 describes the properties supported by the Command object.

Table 7–18	Command Object Properties	
Property	**Read/Write**	**Description**
ActiveConnection	R/W	Gets/sets the connection associated with this command.
CommandText	R/W	Gets/sets the command text string.
CommandTimeout	R/W	Gets/sets the number of seconds (default is 30) to wait for the command to execute.
CommandType	R/W	Gets/sets the type of the command as defined by the CommandTypeEnum constants.
Prepared	R/W	Gets/sets the Boolean value indicating whether a prepared statement is created before the command is executed.

You can set the CommandType property with values coming from the *CommandTypeEnum*: adCmdText (value is 1), where the command is an actual query or data definition statement; adCmdTable (value is 2), where the command is a table name; adCmdStoredProc (value is 4), where the command refers to a server-side stored procedure; and adCmdUnknown (value is 8), where the content of the command is unknown.

Following is a Web-specific example of how to use a Command and the Field collection object:

```
<!-- Create an ADO Connection object -->
<object id=connect classid=
"clsid:00000293-0000-0010-8000-00AA006D2EA4">
</object>

<!-- Create an ADO Command object -->
<object id=cmd classid=
"clsid:0000022C-0000-0010-8000-00AA006D2EA4">
</object>

<script language="VBScript">
    adCmdText = 1
    'Open the connection object
    connect.Open "data source=pubs"
    'Associate the Command with the Connection
    cmd.ActiveConnection = connect
    'Define the query
    cmd.CommandText = "select * from authors"
    cmd.CommandType = adCmdText
    set rs = cmd.Execute(NumRecs)

    'Start generating the HTML
    Document.Write "<TABLE BORDER>"
    'Display the table column names
    Document.Write "<TR>"
    For Cnt=0 To rs.Fields.Count - 1
      Document.Write "<TD>" &
        rs.Fields(Cnt).Name & "</TD>"
    Next
    Document.Write "</TR>"

    'Display the table column values
    Do While (NOT rs.EOF)
      Document.Write "<TR>"
      For cnt=0 To rs.Fields.Count - 1
        Document.Write "<TD>" &
          rs.Fields(cnt) & "</TD>"
      Next
      Document.Write "</TR>"
      rs.MoveNext
    Loop

    'Complete the HTML
    Document.Write "</TABLE>"

    'Close the recordset and connection objects
    rs.Close
    connect.Close
</script>
```

Field Object

A Field object represents a column of data in a recordset. A recordset object has a Fields collection, which is composed of Field objects. A Field object also contains all the metadata (schema information) describing a particular column in a recordset. Information that you can obtain about a particular field in a recordset includes: the field's name, data type, size, numeric precision, scale, etc. Depending on the functionality an OLE DB provider exposes, you may not be able to get all the field-level information normally provided by the Field object. The Field object's Value property is the mechanism you use to get the value of a column for the current record. A Properties collection contains all the Property objects for a specific instance of the Field object. A Field object also provides methods to access BLOB (Binary Large Object) type fields, one chunk at a time.

Methods

Table 7-19 lists the methods supported by the Field object. The Field object provides two methods that store and retrieve large text and binary type column data (BLOBs). When using the *AppendChunk* method, the first call on a Field object writes data to the field, overwriting any existing data. Subsequent AppendChunk calls to the same field add to existing data.

Getting field data operates in a parallel fashion using the *GetChunk* method. Here is an example of retrieving a portion of a recordset's Resume field:

```
Set strResumeData = Resume.GetChunk(64)
```

In this example, if the number of bytes of data in Resume is greater than 64, then subsequent calls to the GetChunk method return data starting from where the previous GetChunk left off.

Table 7–19	Field Object Methods
Method	**Description**
AppendChunk	Appends data to a large text or binary data field object.
GetChunk	Retrieves the contents of a large text or binary field object.

Properties

Table 7-20 lists the properties supported by the Field object. The Field object properties determine the column name, type, size, value, scale, original value, and current value.

Table 7–20	Field Object Properties	
Property	**Read/Write**	**Description**
ActualSize	R	Gets the actual length of the field.
Attributes	R	Gets the field properties. The Attribute property value must be one of the FieldAttributeEnum type constants.
DefinedSize	R	Gets the maximum length of the field.
Name	R	Gets the name of the field.
NumericScale	R	Gets the number of places to the right of the decimal point for numeric fields.
OriginalValue	R	Gets the original value of a field before any changes were made.
Precision	R	Gets the total number of digits used to represent a numeric value.
Type	R	Gets the type of the field.
UnderlyingValue	R	Gets the current value of the field at the data source.
Value	R/W	Gets/sets the value of the field.

Parameter Objects

The ADO Parameter object is used in a manner analogous to function and procedure parameters in traditional programming languages. An ADO parameter can be one of three types: *input* (passed By Value), *output* (passed By Reference, but used only upon return), and *input/output* (passed By Reference). Parameter describes parameters in a SQL command or arguments to a stored procedure. Parameter is used with the Command object to execute parameterized queries. It is intended as a parameter marker in a command. Command objects have a *Prepared* property. When this property is set to True, a prepared statement is created before the command is executed. A notion exists that if you're going to be executing a SQL statement a lot of times, even if you're not going to be changing part of the WHERE clause, you are better off to create a command object and then prepare it. The data source will optimize the command for successive invocations better than if you continually executed it directly from the Connection object. In SQL Server, a temporary stored procedure is actually created on the server, and the query plan is cached the first time it's run, so successive runs are very fast.

Methods

The Parameter object has one method, *AppendChunk*. Parameters can pass BLOB-type data to commands and queries. The AppendChunk method stores large text and binary information in a parameter. The Parameter object can use BLOB-type parameters only for input (you can't return BLOB-type output parameters with ADO). You must be sure to set the Parameter object's *Attribute* property to adFldLong before the AppendChunk method can be used. The first time a Parameter object calls the AppendChunk method, any existing data is overwritten. On subsequent calls, the data is appended to the parameter.

Properties

Table 7-21 has the properties supported by the Parameter object.

Table 7–21		Parameter Object Properties
Property	**Read/Write**	**Description**
Attribute	R/W	Properties of the parameter.
Direction	R/W	Input, output, or input/output.
Name	R/W	The name of the parameter.
NumericScale	R/W	The number of decimal places for floating-point values.
Precision	R/W	The number of digits used to represent a numeric value.
Size	R/W	The maximum size (bytes) of the parameter.
Type	R/W	The type of the parameter.
Value	R/W	Gets/sets the value of the non-BLOB parameter.

The following is an example of how to create a parameterized query using the Parameter object. After the parameter query is executed towards the end of the script, the resulting recordset will contain only authors from the state of Texas.

```
<!-- Create an ADO Connection object -->
<object id=connect classid=
"clsid:00000293-0000-0010-8000-00AA006D2EA4">
</object>

<!-- Create an ADO Command object -->
<object id=cmd classid=
"clsid:0000022C-0000-0010-8000-00AA006D2EA4">
</object>
```

```
<script language="VBScript">
    adCmdText = 1
    adParamInput = 1
    adParamOutput = 2
    adParamInputOutput = 3
    adParamReturnValue = 4
    adBSTR = 8

    'Open the connection object
    connect.Open "data source=pubs"

    'Associate the Command with the Connection
    cmd.ActiveConnection = connect

    'Define the query
    cmd.CommandText =
        "select * from authors where state = ?"

    'Create a prepared version of the query
    cmd.Prepared = True
    cmd.CommandType = adCmdText

    'Create the command parameters
    Set param  =
        cmd.CreateParameter("State", adBSTR,
        adParamInput)

    'Now give parameter a value, and add to
    'collection
    param.Value = "TX"
    cmd.Parameters.Append param

    rs = cmd.Execute(NumRecs)

    rs.Close
    connect.Close
</script>
```

ADO Error Handling

ADO error handling is managed through use of the *Errors collection* and the *Error object*. ADO objects (i.e., a single ADO call) can generate multiple errors, a process that yields an Errors collection containing multiple Error objects. The Errors collection is associated with the Connection object. Each Error object contains information generated by the data source to describe the error condition. You may get, for example, the native error number, a description, etc. Just as in the DAO and RDO models, the most descriptive error that comes back from the data source will be raised as a runtime error in VB or as an OLE exception. Every time an ADO object generates an error, the Errors collection is automatically cleared.

Errors Collection

The Errors collection has one method, *Clear.* This method manually empties the Errors collection. Even though the Errors collection is automatically cleared when an ADO object generates its first error, some Recordset methods and properties can also generate warnings. A warning will also generate an Error object, even though it won't cause an application to stop. So before calling methods such as CancelBatch, Delete, Resync, and UpdateBatch, you should clear the Errors collection by calling the Clear method. Since the Errors collection is associated with a Connection object, you can use the ActiveConnection property to access the Connection object, as in the following code:

```
rs.ActiveConnection.Errors.Clear
```

The reference rs is to a valid Recordset object (a Command object is also possible).

Table 7-22 displays the properties supported by the Errors collection. The *Count* property contains the number of Error objects found in the Errors collection. This value is often useful when looping through the Errors collection to find all errors encountered by the data source. The *Item* property provides a means to access an Error object in the Errors collection, as in:

```
Connect.Errors.Item(3)
```

Remembering that index values for collections begin at 0, you can use the value of the Count property minus 1 to loop through all items.

Table 7-22	Errors Collection Properties	
Property	**Read/Write**	**Description**
Count	R	The number of Error objects in the Errors collection.
Item	R	Used to access an Error object in the Errors collection.

Error Object

The Error object results from an ADO error or warning. The Error object provides a means for you to access information describing the error and to take necessary actions. The Error object has no methods. Table 7-23 describes the properties supported by the Error object.

Table 7–23		Errors Object Properties
Property	**Read/Write**	**Description**
Description	R	An error or warning message.
HelpContext	R	The help file context used to retrieve more information about the error.
HelpFile	R	The name of the help file for the data source provider.
NativeError	R	The error number known to the data source provider.
Number	R	The ADO error constant value.
Source	R	The name of the ADO object that caused the error.
SQLState	R	The ANSI SQL error code value.

Here is an example of ADO error handling.

```
<!-- Create an ADO Connection object -->
<object id=connect classid=
"clsid:00000293-0000-0010-8000-00AA006D2EA4">
</object>

<script language="VBScript">
    'Just resume when an error occurs
    On Error Resume Next

    'Open the connection object
    connect.Open "data source=pubs"

    'Check for a connect error
    If(connect.Errors.Count > 0) Then
      MsgBox "Error during connect: " &
        Connect.Errors(0).Description
    End If
    connect.Close
</script>
```

Connection Pooling with ADO

Although ADO is a generic data access API, you should consider how best to use ADO with ASP. We often need to access a single instance of ADO several times in a page and across an application. For example, you can use the ADODB Connection object to create a database connection. Instead of establishing a connection, you may consider opening a single database connection once in the Session_onStart or Application_onStart event handlers of the global.asa file, and then use that connection throughout the entire session or application.

Database applications designed for a multi-user environment will generally use a back-end database such as Microsoft SQL Server, Oracle, or other enterprise-level relational database. Reusing a connection stored in the Session or Application object method loses its attractiveness as the number of users of the application grows.

Fortunately, ODBC 3.0 includes a feature called *connection pooling*, which manages connections across multiple users. The process works by opening a pool of connections, and then using those existing connections from the pool rather than opening a new connection for each request as it comes in from the application. Connection pooling is necessary for scaling database-enabled Web sites. When using connection pooling, the best approach is to open and close the database connection on each page that uses it. This technique allows ODBC to manage the connections in the most efficient manner. Without connection pooling working, 20 users could be logged onto the application but not actually doing anything. This situation could cause 20 idle connections that decrease performance and consume server and database resources.

With Microsoft Access, consider a Session_onStart instantiation of connection, whereas for other databases, to use local connections in each page may work out better.

ADO Examples

In this section, I present a number of examples illustrating general techniques discussed in this chapter. The examples will be generic in the sense that I use Visual Basic as the base language (I did the same thing in prior sections discussing each ADO object). You can translate these concepts into Web-based applications.

Using Connection, Command, and Recordset Objects

In this example, I use all the objects, Connection, Command, and Recordset.

```
Dim connect As New Connection
Dim cmd As New Command
Dim rs As New Recordset

connect.Open "dsn", "usr", "pwd"

Set cmd.ActiveConnection = connect
cmd.CommandText = "<sql>"
rs.Open cmd
```

```
While Not rs.EOF
    'Do something here
    rs.MoveNext
Wend
```

Here I instantiate all three required objects from scratch. First I call the Open method of Connection to establish the connection. Then I associate the Command object with the connection I just created using the Connection object (instead of a connection string). Then I set the CommandText to some random SQL statement. Then I call the Open method of the Recordset object and pass the Command object as the source of the recordset. Effectively, the recordset is associated with the command, but it doesn't need to know the connection, because the command is associated with the connection. The recordset executes that command, and any results returned are loaded into the cursor. You're able to traverse the cursor to get to the data.

Open a Recordset

In this example, see how to open a recordset object, iterate through the recordset, and use the Fields collection.

```
Dim rs As New Recordset
Dim fld As Field

rs.ActiveConnection = "dsn=pubs;uid=sa;pwd=;"
rs.Open "select * from authors"

While Not rs.EOF
    For each fld In rs.Fields
      Debug.Print fld.Value
    Next
    rs.MoveNext
Wend
```

Here, I'm using a Field object to iterate over the Fields collection. The ActiveConnection is set to a connection string, which will create a connection object, establish a connection, and then in the next statement associate the recordset with the connection. Then I call the Open method of the Recordset object and pass a SQL string as the recordset source. Then I execute the statement against the connection, and any results that come back are loaded into the recordset object. The while loop steps through the resultset. The For/Each construct enumerates the Fields collection (a collection of Field objects). For/Each is easier to use than a For/Next, since you don't have to maintain a loop variable. The MoveNext method is used to iterate through the cursor.

By default, I've opened a forward-only, read-only cursor, which is the best-performing type of cursor. The other cursor types are: forward-only, static, keyset, and dynamic. The lock types supported are: optimistic, pessimistic, and the new batch-optimistic.

Invoke a Stored Procedure

When working with an enterprise-level relational database, to invoke a stored procedure while coding ADO is quite useful. Here is an example of how to do this:

```
Dim connect As New Connection
Dim rs As Recordset
Dim cmd As New Command
Dim prm As Parameter

connect.Open "pubs", "sa", ""

Set cmd.ActiveConnection = connect
cmd.CommandText = "sp_tables"
cmd.CommandType = adCmdStoredProc
Set prm =
    cmd.CreateParameter("name", adChar,
    adParamInput, 30, "authors")
cmd.Parameters.Append prm

Set rs = cmd.Execute
'Recordset is now populated
```

Here I open a Recordset based on a stored procedure, where the stored procedure takes an input argument. I manually build the parameters collection using the CreateParameter method. Some data sources are not capable of describing the parameters of a stored procedure (e.g., the data type, length, or precision of a parameter). Furthermore, getting this information from data sources that do provide it can be expensive. Therefore, ADO lets you build the parameters collection manually. You tell ADO the parameter's data type, and it will be bound and executed.

In the above example, I give the Command object the stored procedure's name using the CommandText property. You can also set the CommandType property, here set to stored procedure, so that ADO won't have to first try it as a generic SQL statement and if not, then it can try it as something more complex. If you tell ADO up front that it's a stored procedure, the process is much faster.

In the next statement, I create a Parameters object and append it to the Parameters collection. The CreateParameter method of the Command object lets you specify the parameter name, data type, whether it's an input or output parameter, length, etc. Next, the Append method of the Parameters collection takes your new Parameter object and places it in the collection. The Execute method of the Command object then returns a recordset object.

Now that you've seen the general case, consider three Web-specific examples that illustrate different ways to invoke a stored procedure. The examples use the Command object to call a sample stored procedure sp_test. This stored procedure accepts an integer and has a return value of an integer as well. The first method queries the data source about the parameters of the stored procedure. This is the least efficient method of calling a stored procedure due to the overhead involved.

```
<%
Set connect =
    Server.CreateObject("ADODB.Connection")
Set cmd = Server.CreateObject("ADODB.Command")

connect.Open "dsn", "userid", "password"
Set cmd.ActiveConnection = connect
cmd.CommandText = "sp_test"
cmd.CommandType = adCmdStoredProc

'Ask the server about the parameters for
'the stored proc
cmd.Parameters.Refresh

'Assign a value to the 2nd parameter.
'Index of 0 represents 1st parameter.
cmd.Parameters(1) = 25
cmd.Execute

'Write out the return value.
Response.Write cmd.Parameters(0)
%>
```

The next example demonstrates a technique that first declares the stored procedure, and then explicitly declares the parameters:

```
<%
Set connect =
    Server.CreateObject("ADODB.Connection")
connect.Open "dsn", "userid", "password"
Set cmd = Server.CreateObject("ADODB.Command")

Set cmd.ActiveConnection = connect
cmd.CommandText = "sp_test"
cmd.CommandType = adCmdStoredProc

cmd.Parameters.Append cmd.CreateParameter("RetVal",
    adInteger, adParamReturnValue)
cmd.Parameters.Append cmd.CreateParameter("Parm",
    adInteger, adParamInput)

'Set value of Parm of the Parameters
```

```
'collection to 25
cmd("Parm") = 25
cmd.Execute
'Write out the return value
Response.Write cmd(0)
%>
```

The technique in the following, third example is the most formal way of calling a stored procedure:

```
<%
Set connect =
    Server.CreateObject("ADODB.Connection")
connect.Open "dsn", "userid", "password"
Set cmd = Server.CreateObject("ADODB.Command")

Set cmd.ActiveConnection = connect
'Define the stored procedure's inputs and
'outputs. Question marks act as placeholders
'for each parameter for the stored procedure
cmd.CommandText = "{?=call sp_test(?)}"

cmd.Parameters.Append cmd.CreateParameter("RetVal",
    adInteger, adParamReturnValue)
cmd.Parameters.Append cmd.CreateParameter("Parm",
    adInteger, adParamInput)
cmd.Parameters("Parm") = 25
cmd.Execute

'Write out the return value.
Response.Write cmd("RetVal")
%>
```

Perform a Batch Update

Batch updating involves the notion of a recordset as a data buffer that can track its changes, cache the changes in the recordset, and then post them all back to the database at one time. Batch updating works with slow links like the Internet, and it has the ability to pass the data buffer around to other objects that can change the data. To do this, you use a lock type called *batch-optimistic*. In the example below, the recordset opens, and you can make changes (without the old Edit method found in DAO and RDO, which is no longer needed in the ADO model) and then call the *Update* method, which puts the changes in the data buffer; but the changes are not immediately written to the database. It waits until you request a batch update using the *UpdateBatch* method. It tracks the state of the data when you first open the cursor, as well as your change. The UpdateBatch method results in posting all the changes (add, edit, and delete) with one trip to the server, which is very efficient.

```
Dim con As New Connection
Dim rs As New Recordset
con.Open "pubs", "sa", ""

rs.Open "select * from test", con,
    adOpenStatic, adLockBatchOptimistic

rs!CharColumn = "newstring"
rs.Update

rs.AddNew
rs!intColumn = 99
rs!CharColumn = "NewRow"
rs.Update

rs.UpdateBatch
```

Batch update uses *optimistic concurrency*, so no locks are held on the server. When working with an optimistic batch cursor, all data is unlocked, but when the batch update is posted, ADO constructs a WHERE clause using the old values, so that if the data has changed on the server, it gets a conflict or collision and lets you know which rows got a collision and which ones didn't. You can deal with a collision because you have the value now on the server, namely the old value, as well as the new value.

Summary

This chapter has brought forth two sizable technological areas, namely Active Server Pages and ActiveX Data Objects, which together comprise the Microsoft offering for building active-content Web pages with database connections. You can appreciate how firmly tied this technology is to the Windows NT and IIS software platforms, and how well it competes with other popular technologies, specifically the dated CGI technology and the new Java solutions. ASP and ADO are also integral parts of the Microsoft Site Server and Commerce Server solutions, so Microsoft is quite evidently very serious about bringing both ASP and ADO to the leading edge of Web development. If you're running an all-Microsoft shop, then both ASP and ADO should be the technology base from which you construct your database-enabled Web site.

Visual InterDev

As a WebTop application developer wanting to remain within the realm of Microsoft tool solutions, an excellent choice is the Visual Inter-Dev integrated Web application development environment. InterDev meets the needs of developers who want to build dynamic, database-enabled WebTop applications for corporate intranets, extranets, and the Internet. Visual InterDev combines all the tools developers require to create, publish, and manage Web applications that can be accessed by any Web browser running on any platform. The tool offers a Rapid Application Development (RAD) platform for building Active Server Pages, a feature of Microsoft Internet Information Server (IIS) version 3.0 and 4.0.

Visual InterDev also includes extensive database tools for connecting a Web site to any database using ODBC (with special consideration for Microsoft SQL Server and Oracle). With visual database tools such as an integrated *Data View, Query Designer, Database Designer*, database wizards, and programmable data access components, Visual InterDev allows you to easily create sophisticated database-enabled Web applications. Lastly, Visual Inter-Dev also offers advanced publishing and site management features, as well as support for team-based projects through interoperability with the Microsoft FrontPage 98 Web authoring tool and integration with Visual SourceSafe.

The product is available separately or as a member of the *Visual Studio* suite of software development tools. The Visual InterDev integrated development environment (IDE) shown in Figure 8-1 is virtually identical to the Developer Studio first introduced with Visual C++ 4.0 and is now the common

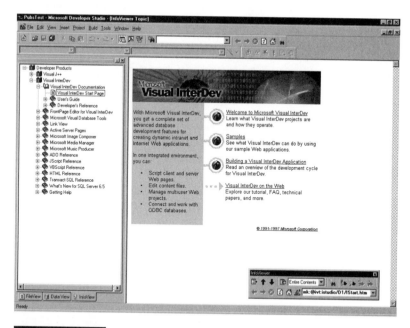

Figure 8–1   *Visual InterDev IDE*

interface for all members of the suite, including Visual Basic, Visual FoxPro, Visual C++, and Visual J++. Visual InterDev contains an abbreviated version of the FrontPage 98 editor that can be used to construct ASP pages using ADO for providing connections to databases. The requirements for this tool are Windows NT 4.0 Server, Microsoft SQL Server 6.5 or 7.0, and IIS 3.0 or 4.0. If you manage an NT-based Web site with IIS as the Web server software and require data connections, then Visual InterDev is the logical choice for a robust development environment.

One of the design goals behind Visual InterDev was to include the tools required for building a database-enabled Web site in the same IDE (shell, menus, UI metaphor) as the other development tools normally used for building Web sites. Rather than learning the interfaces for various tools for constructing different pieces of the Web application, users can utilize Visual InterDev features for nearly all components of the site.

Visual InterDev has several wizards, including an integrated *Web Project Wizard,* which leads you through naming your project and connecting to the appropriate Web server where the completed application ultimately resides. You can create Web pages in either source code or visual mode. The source code editor uses a color-coded syntax representation. The visual mode is handled by the Visual InterDev edition of Microsoft FrontPage 98. Also, the Active Server Pages wizard generates code.

Probably the most useful wizard for your consideration is the Database Project Wizard. It provides a relatively simple path where WebTop application developers may step through a series stages, culminating in a complete prototype application with a data connection.

In this chapter, I examine the Visual InterDev development tool, focusing on its data connection capabilities.

Basic Architecture

In order to fully appreciate how Visual InterDev provides an environment whereby you may efficiently organize your work when building a WebTop application, in this section I discuss the overall architecture of the IDE.

A WebTop application designed with Visual InterDev may consist of several parts. The application may be comprised of projects and/or workspaces. In terms of a hierarchy, the workspace is at a higher level than a project; in fact, one or more projects are normally contained inside a workspace. I want to more fully develop these concepts.

Web Projects

When you create an application in Visual InterDev, the files that make up your application are stored together on a Web server, in what is called a *Web*. A Web is a collection of components, Active Server Pages, HTML files, graphics, etc., that together constitute a Web application. In order to access the files in the Web using Visual InterDev, you need a local file that points to the server and to the specific Web with which you wish to work. This local file is called a *project* file and has an extension of .dsp. To work with the files in a Web, you must open the project file for that Web from within the Visual Inter-Dev client software. The Web files on the server, together with the project file on the local client, make up a Web project.

Multiple developers can work on files in the same application concurrently, because the files in an application are stored in a Web on a Web server. To participate in this team development approach, each developer must create a local project file on his or her individual client workstation that points to the same Web on the server. Microsoft Visual SourceSafe can assist with this process if it is installed on the server machine and if your Web is enabled for source control. With this utility, you can ensure that only one person can edit a file at a time, because Visual InterDev automatically checks out the file before allowing modifications.

Creating and Editing a Web Project

You begin by using the *Web Project Wizard* to create a local project file that points to an existing Web on a Web server, or to create a new Web on a Web server and a corresponding local project file that points to it. To access the Web Project Wizard, from the File menu, click on New, and then click on the Projects tab. You should see the wizard listed as one of the new options.

The Web Project Wizard allows you to specify the directory on your local machine for the project file. This directory becomes your working directory for this project. When you open a source file in your project, for example, an .asp file or an .htm file, this file is copied from the server to the working directory on your local machine. The location of the file in your working directory exactly matches the location of the file on the server relative to the server's virtual root. For example, if you have a file named SuppliersRep.asp in the location indicated by the URL //MyServer/NWIND and your working directory is C:\Program Files\DevStudio\MyProjects\NWIND, the file is copied to C:\Program Files\DevStudio\MyProjects\NWIND\SuppliersRep.asp. Note that the subdirectory is automatically created on your local machine, because it exists on the server.

Once a file has been copied to your working directory, you can edit it using the Visual InterDev editors. When you save the file, Visual InterDev automatically updates the server copy of the file with your changes. You can then view your changes using any Web browser, by right-clicking on the file in the FileView tab of the Project window and choosing Preview in Browser.

Several actual files comprise your Web project. The most typical files include:

- Global file
- Image and multimedia files
- Active Server Pages
- ActiveX Layout files

HTML FILES

HTML files contain your HTML code and have an .htm file name extension. These files may also contain references to ActiveX Controls, Java applets, Netscape plug-ins, ActiveX Layout files, graphic images, and multimedia files. HTML files can also have client-side scripting code using languages such as VBScript and JScript (Microsoft's implementation of JavaScript).

GLOBAL FILE

The Global file is automatically generated when you create a new project and is named global.asa. This file enables you to use server-side scripting for initializing your application at startup, handling your database connections, and cleaning up the application when the application is finished.

GRAPHIC IMAGE AND MULTIMEDIA FILES

Most contemporary Web sites contain a number of graphic images to place on the various pages that comprise the site. Visual InterDev helps you keep track of these files for use in the Web project. In addition, multimedia files such as sound and video files may be incorporated into the site.

ACTIVE SERVER PAGES

Active Server Pages are probably the most important file type used with Visual InterDev. These files, having an .asp file extension, may contain HTML, images, client-side script code, but one major difference exists between an ASP file and an HTML file, namely that the ASP file may also contain server-side scripting code. This scripting code is actually executed on the server instead of the client workstation. The language of choice for server-side code in ASP files is VBScript.

ACTIVEX LAYOUT FILES

Through use of the ActiveX Layout Editor, you can create layout files, having an .alx file extension, that assist in the process of designing and building an effective interface for your WebTop application. Inside the editor, you can use a familiar toolbox containing simple controls such as: textbox, label, check box, option button, command button, combo box, etc. Once you have a form completed, you can then save the layout for integration into the site.

Workspaces

A *workspace* is a container for one or more projects. Projects in a workspace can be of the same type or of different types. For instance, a workspace can include both a Web project and a database project, or two Web projects, each pointing to different Webs.

When you create a new Web project, you can either add the new Web project to your open workspace or create a new workspace for it. Adding the Web project to your open workspace allows you to have multiple Web projects open at the same time.

You can have only one workspace open at a time in Visual InterDev. When you open a new workspace, any currently open workspace and the projects it contains are closed. Therefore, if you want to work on more than one project at a time, you should add the additional projects to your current workspace.

Establishing Database Connectivity

Visual InterDev delivers a comprehensive set of tightly integrated database tools for developers who program applications for the World Wide Web. Powerful database connectivity options and visual database tools are an integral component of building most solutions for the Web. The database connectivity features are based on the industry-standard ODBC, and the Visual Tools work with any database supporting ODBC, including Oracle, Microsoft SQL Server, Microsoft Access, Microsoft Visual FoxPro, Informix, Sybase, IBM DB/2, and many others

In addition, using Visual InterDev, a developer can create scalable database solutions using Active Server Pages. The core database components of Visual InterDev include ActiveX Data Objects (ADO), Integrated Data View, Design-time ActiveX Controls, Database Wizards, Query Designer, and the Database Designer.

In this section, I provide an overview of a number of ways you can include database connections for your Web pages.

Database Project

The first step in incorporating database connectivity with Visual InterDev is to use the File menu's New option. From here, you may create a new database project. Figure 8-2 shows the New Project dialog box. Here you must select the type of project required (in this case, Database Project), supply the name of the new project, and specify the directory in which to place the resulting control files built by Visual InterDev. A typical scenario would be to create a project directory on the NT server while using the Visual InterDev client software from a workstation on the network.

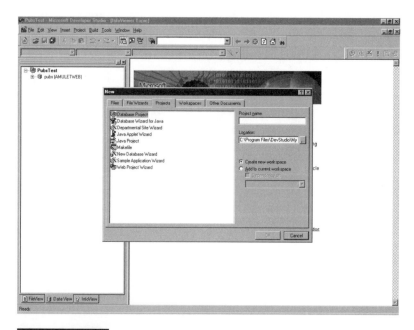

Figure 8–2   *Creating a New Database Project*

You must also determine what the data source shall be for the database project and make sure that an ODBC data source name is available. You would create the DSN on the client workstation for design work and then another on the server where the database resides, for times when the Web database goes live. For our purposes in this chapter, I focus on using a Microsoft SQL Server database as a data source for the project. Specifically, I use the sample Pubs database installed with SQL Server.

After the new database project has been created, you need to log into the Pubs database by specifying the user name and password. So that security issues won't become an issue, you may use the "sa" user (system administrator) with the default null password. You may have to check with your server administrator to see whether this is allowed.

After successfully connecting to the database, you see a Data View window similar to the one shown in Figure 8-3. Here, the tree view shows the new database project, PubsTest, as the highest level in the hierarchy. Next you see the database name, pubs (and the server on which it resides). Finally, you see the components that comprise the database: database diagrams, tables, views, and stored procedures. I discuss each of these components in later sections of this chapter.

Upon creating a new database project, you can also select the File View tab, which shows the components of the project as files in a disk directory

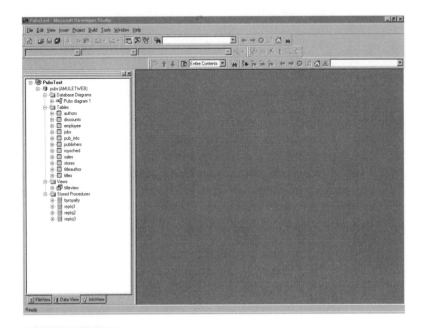

Figure 8-3   *Data View Window with Project Hierarchy*

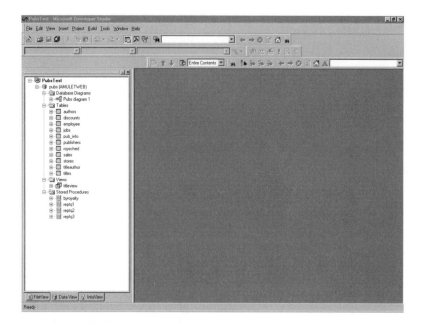

Figure 8–4 *Data Connection Properties*

hierarchy instead of a tree view. You see various file types and file name extensions for the files created by Visual InterDev. For example, workspace definitions are kept in file with a .dsw extension.

Notice that the properties dialog box for the database connection appears in Figure 8-4. It is accessed by right-clicking on the pubs database branch in the tree view hierarchy or by selecting the Properties option from the View menu. Here you see various descriptive properties of the connection, including the ODBC data source, PubsDSN, which is a system DSN created earlier.

At this point, you can now begin using the Visual InterDev visual tools to manipulate the data source. If your data source is a SQL Server database, you'll find an unparalleled approach to database maintenance.

Database Wizards

In addition to Design-time ActiveX Controls, which I cover shortly, Visual InterDev also offers a number of wizard-like services that lead a developer through the process of creating custom data-bound HTML forms. In this section, I review the different wizards that assist you in building data connections.

DATABASE CONNECTION WIZARD

In order to add a new data connection to a Visual InterDev project, you can select the *Add to Project* item from the Project menu, and then choose *Data*

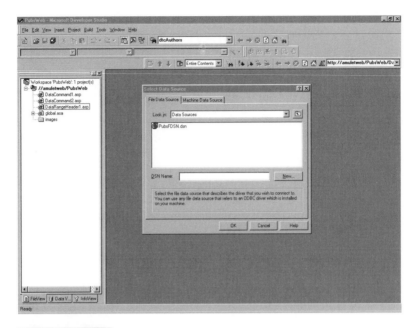

Figure 8-5   *Database Connection Wizard Dialog Box*

Connection. The dialog box sequence that follows is called the Database Connection Wizard. Starting up this wizard results in the familiar data source dialog box shown in Figure 8-5 that asks you to select a pre-existing data source name associated with the desired database or, alternately, to create a new DSN. A project can have more than one data connection. You can also right-click on the project name while in File View and select *Add Data Connection* from the shortcut menu to achieve the same goal. The global.asa file now contains additional VBScript ADO code required to establish the connection to the new database. You'll also notice a change in the tree structure shown in the project's File View and Data View, in that the new data connection is now included.

From the initial dialog box, you can select an existing data source from either the *File Data Source* tab or the *Machine Data Source* tab. You can also type in the data source name or click on the New button to create a new DSN.

A File Data Source enables you to set up a file-based connection that is local to a specific computer. Multiple users can share this connection. A file-based connection means that the information to connect to the database is stored in a .dsn file. You must install an ODBC driver on this computer to communicate with the database. After the database connection is created for your project, the information in the .dsn file is inserted into the connect string within your global.asa file.

The Look In combo box (shown only for File DSNs) lets you browse the file system for a data source. The default directory is \ODBC\Data Sources\ on the development workstation.

The New button is for creating a new File Data Source name. Selecting this option starts another Wizard prompting sequence.

Two types of Machine Data Sources exist, a User DSN and a System DSN. The User DSN can be used only by the designated user and is specific to a particular machine. A System DSN is specific to a machine but can be shared by multiple users. This information is stored in the Windows Registry and must migrate with the application, if the application is moved to another machine.

The New button is for creating a new User DSN or System DSN. Selecting this option starts another Wizard prompting sequence.

NEW DATABASE WIZARD

The Visual Database Tools include a wizard to help you create new SQL Server databases. To run the wizard, select New from the File menu, click on the Projects tab, and select the *New Database Wizard*. Provide a new database project name and location, and then click OK. The wizard proceeds to lead you through four dialog boxes, collecting information required to create the new database. Figure 8-6 shows the first dialog box asking for the name of a SQL Server, Login ID, and Password. The next two dialog boxes prompt for the name of the database and log devices on which to store the new database, the name of the database itself, and the storage allocation for the database and log. When you finish the wizard, a new project will be created with a connection to your new database already included in it. You may also choose to place the new database project in a new workspace or add to the current workspace.

DATA FORM WIZARD

The Data Form Wizard assists you in building a data bound HTML form. The wizard creates one or more Active Server Pages containing forms that let users search, update, delete, or insert data into an existing database on a server. The wizard creates an Active Server Page .asp file to execute the database calls. The .asp files must reside on an IIS server that supports the ActiveX Server framework. To use the wizard, select New from the File menu, click on the File Wizards tab, and select *Data Form Wizard*. This file definition dialog box appears in Figure 8-7. Next, you must provide a file name and location for the new data form, and then click OK. I use the File name of Authors-DataForm, and the location is the default project directory we've been working with up to now.

After prompting a developer for information, the Data Form Wizard automatically generates the HTML and ActiveX server scripting information required to create complex HTML forms that are bound to databases. The

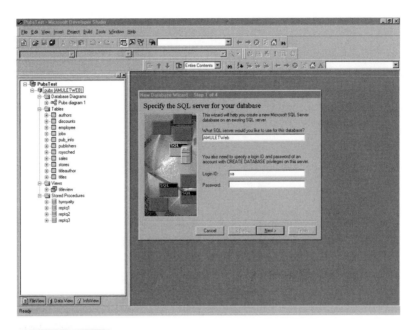

Figure 8–6   *Creating a New SQL Server Database*

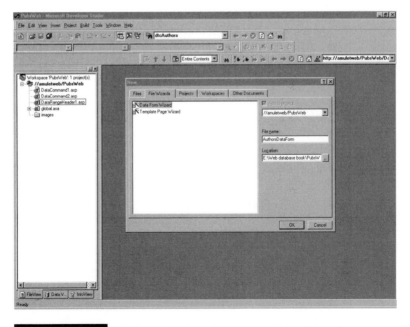

Figure 8–7   *Defining the Files for the Data Form Wizard*

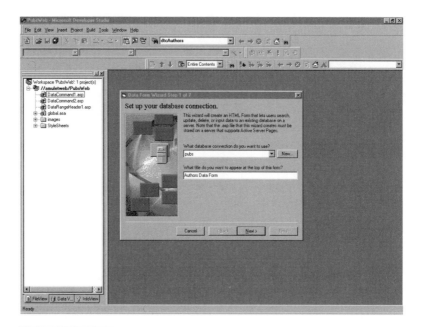

Figure 8-8 *Defining the Connection for the Data Form Wizard*

Data Form Wizard works with ODBC-based databases, and generates HTML forms with professional layouts and advanced functionality such as viewing and updating data in multiple tables on a single form. The output of the Data Form Wizard is standard HTML and script that a developer can modify further, if desired.

I want to go through the Data Form Wizard's dialog box sequence now. The first dialog box requests the name of the database connection to use for the new form, as well as the text string name to appear on the top of the form. I use the pubs database and the name *Authors Data Form,* respectively. This dialog box is in Figure 8-8.

The second dialog box asks for you to supply the record source of the data form. The list box in Figure 8-9 displays four types of record sources: table, stored procedure, view, or SQL statement. Depending on which record source you choose, the next dialog box is tailored accordingly. For example, if you choose SQL statement, the next dialog box is a mini-editor for you to type in a SQL statement. In this example, I choose table as my source.

The third dialog box in the sequence appears in Figure 8-10. It is customized for table record sources and asks for you to select the fields needed on the data form. You can use the up and down arrow buttons to rearrange the order of the fields. Also, a subsidiary dialog box is accessible by clicking on the *Advanced* button. This subsidiary dialog box provides a means to asso-

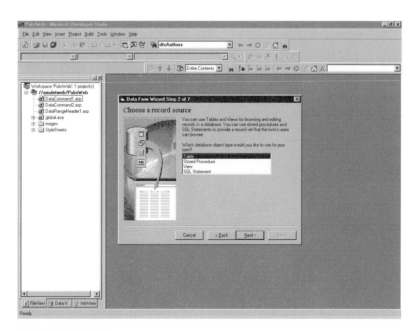

Figure 8–9   *Choosing a Record Source for the Data Form Wizard*

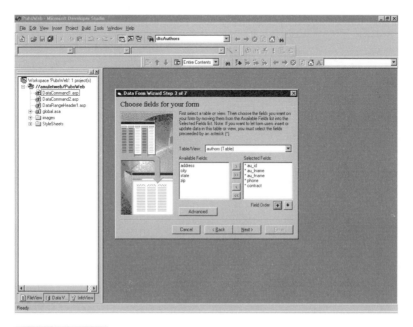

Figure 8–10   *Selecting Fields from the Record Source*

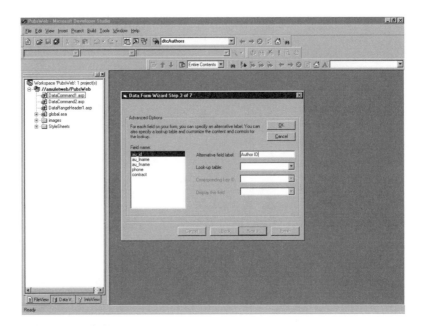

Defining Alternate Labels for Table Fields

ciate custom label strings with each of the selected fields. These labels would normally be more readable to the user than obscure database field names. For example, instead of using "au_id" as the form label for the author ID field, you could use "Author ID." This dialog box is in Figure 8-11.

The fourth dialog box, shown in Figure 8-12, specifies whether you wish to allow the user to edit information in the form. If you click on Yes, then you have the ability to specify modify, insert, and delete functionality. The edit features are appropriate for table maintenance forms, but not query-style forms. Also, a check box is available for requesting a feedback page to appear after an update.

The fifth dialog box, shown in Figure 8-13, lets you define the type of form view to use, either *Form View* or *List View*. Form View displays the data in a single record, whereas List View displays multiple records in a table format. For List View, you can also specify whether you want a link to Form View for each item in the list, as well as how many items to display in the list (10 is the default).

The sixth dialog box, shown in Figure 8-14, lets you choose the graphic theme to use for the form. Visual InterDev comes with a number of themes as choices. You can get a preview of each theme by clicking on each name. I choose the Redside theme. Note that once you build a form using the Data

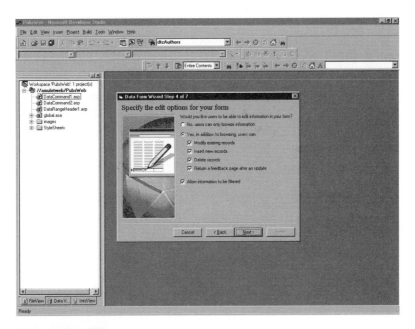

Figure 8–12   *Specifying Edit Capabilities*

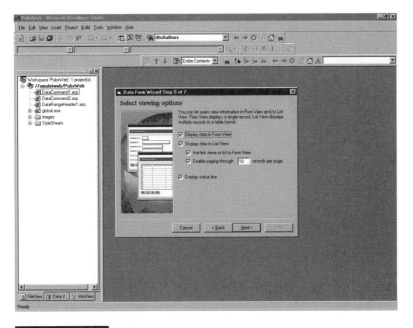

Figure 8–13   *Choosing File View or List View*

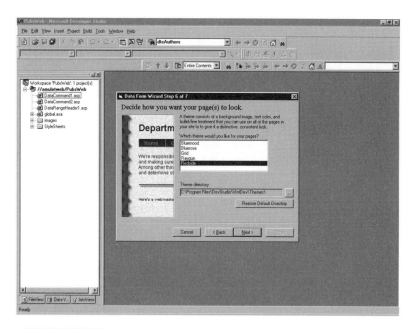

Figure 8-14   *Choosing a Style Sheet for the Form*

Form Wizard, a folder named StyleSheets is added to your project. In this folder, you find a cascading style sheet file (.css file) for each theme you use.

The seventh and last dialog box of the Data Form Wizard simply contains a Finish button that causes the HTML and ADO code to be generated. You'll actually find that the wizard generated three distinct forms: AuthorsDataFormAction.asp, AuthorsDataFormForm.asp, and AuthorsDataFormList.asp, each providing a different style of viewing the underlying data. Examining the code in each ASP page will provide an excellent learning tool to develop more custom data entry platforms using Active Server Pages. Figure 8-15 shows the form view of the data, complete with navigation buttons and command buttons for Update, Delete, and New operations. Clicking on the List View button produces a tabular view, as shown in Figure 8-16.

DATA RANGE BUILDER WIZARD

Although I cover the topic of Data Range Design-time controls at length later in this chapter, since I'm discussing all the available wizards inside Visual InterDev for building database connections, let me provide the following discussion now. The Data Range Builder is a special type of wizard that builds HTML. You can use the wizard by opening up a new ASP file and right-click the mouse to display the shortcut menu. Select *Insert HTML Using Wizard*, as

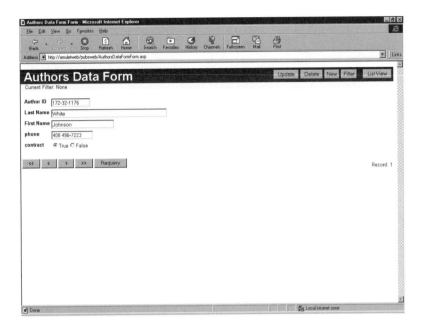

Figure 8–15   *Form View*

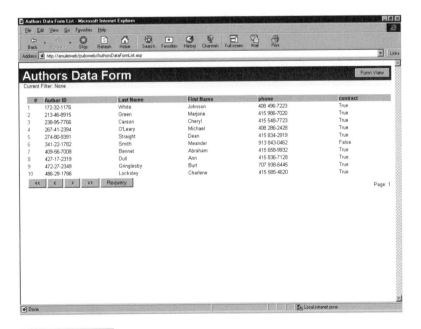

Figure 8–16   *List View*

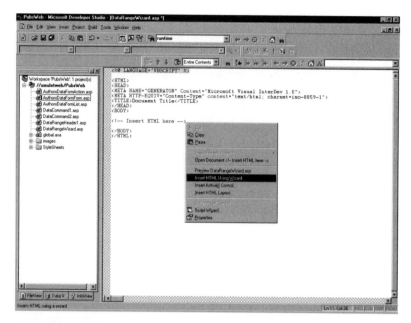

Figure 8–17 *Invoking the Data Range Wizard*

shown in Figure 8-17. Then proceed to select *Data Range Wizard* from the Choose Builder dialog box.

Two dialog forms exist for the Data Range Wizard, the first of which appears in Figure 8-18. This form asks whether all records are to be displayed in the form or only a specified number at a time. If you choose the latter option, then the wizard also generates a navigation bar. The second and last dialog box simply prompts you to name the Data Range, as in Figure 8-19.

After you click on the Finish button to complete the wizard's operation, the Object Editor activates, enabling you to further customize the properties of the Data Range header control. You can choose the data connection and use the Query Designer to construct your SQL statement. Once you complete this process and close the Object Editor, the Data Range Header and Footer controls are displayed in your ASP file. The concepts surrounding design-time controls are explained in depth later in this chapter, in "Design-Time ActiveX Controls."

Inserting a New Database Item

Although you have other means to add database-related objects to a Visual InterDev project, the Insert menu has the *New Database Item* option that provides a central place to add the following into the selected database: table, database diagram, stored procedure, and trigger. Figure 8-20 shows the dialog box. After selecting one of the objects, the appropriate designer opens.

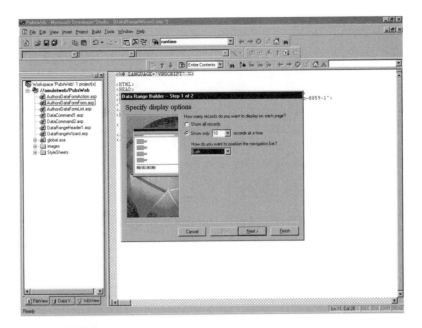

Figure 8-18   *Displaying Options for the Data Range Wizard*

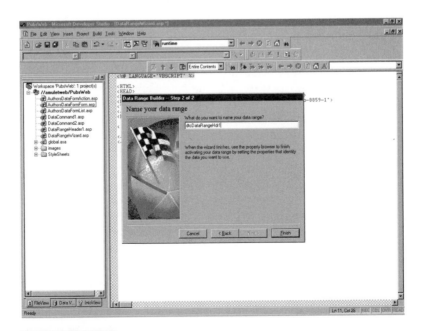

Figure 8-19   *Naming the Design-Time Control*

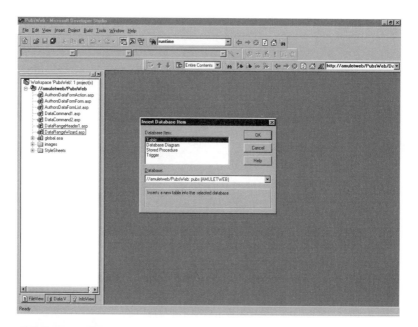

Figure 8–20   *Inserting a New Database Item*

Design-Time ActiveX Controls

Design-Time ActiveX Controls (DTC) are an important new feature introduced with Visual InterDev for building database-enabled Web sites. A DTC is an ActiveX control, complete with .ocx extension. These controls provide all the benefits of component software offered by standard ActiveX Controls, such as plug-and-play functionality and visual editing at design time. Two big differences exist between standard ActiveX controls and DTC. First is that design-time ActiveX controls contain no binary runtime component. They are never active when the page is being viewed and are never run on a client system. The DTCs included with Visual InterDev run in the Visual InterDev environment on a developer's workstation. Another distinguishing characteristic of a DTC is that is has a special interface, called IActiveDesigner, that lets it generate text that is saved into a file by the editor and processed at runtime. The structure and content of the text that is generated is entirely up to the control. Any text that can be inserted into the file by a standard text editor can be generated by a design-time control. The content can be any HTML, script code, or even Java code, viewable on any platform by any browser. A DTC will typically generate HTML and Active Server Pages code that is inserted into an ASP page by the control.

Design-time ActiveX controls are analogous in operation to wizards, and they provide a visual interface for developers while automatically generating the HTML and scripting necessary to provide sophisticated functionality in a WebTop application. In essence, they are visual helper components that allow developers to build dynamic Web applications more easily. Because they generate text into a Web page, design-time controls can target any downstream processor that consumes text, such as HTML browsers and template processors like Cold Fusion.

I can hardly overstate the importance of design-time ActiveX controls for Visual InterDev. The environment derives maximum extensibility using design-time ActiveX controls, since third-party software vendors and corporations can seamlessly extend the tool with specialized functionality using custom design-time ActiveX controls. These controls are based on the Component Object Model (COM) and hence can be created with any tool that can create a standard ActiveX control, including Visual Basic 6.0. In fact, the DTCs that are part of Visual InterDev were created with VB 6.0. They make use of the DTC SDK and the tools it provides.

Visual InterDev provides several integrated design-time ActiveX controls, such as the Data Command control and the Data Range controls. As you interact with a design-time control, selecting options and specifying properties, it generates the relevant HTML and scripting code and inserts it into your page. The client-side HTML and scripting code forms the basis of all that is necessary for the runtime processing of the application that any standard Web browser can access. For example, Visual InterDev builds on the ADO foundation by providing special design-time ActiveX Controls that automatically generate the server-side scripting, including the ADO calls necessary to establish database connections within a Web site, perform queries, and display results. In many cases, a developer can use the design-time ActiveX Controls to create database-enabled Web sites with little additional programming.

Microsoft plans to deliver a growing set of design-time ActiveX controls on the Visual InterDev Web site, in effect dynamically upgrading the tool with new functionality. In addition, Microsoft expects that over time, independent software vendors will offer design-time ActiveX controls compatible with Visual InterDev, the same way that thousands of ActiveX controls are available today.

Data Command Design-Time Control

The *Data Command* design-time control uses a database connection to perform a basic query against a database. The Data Command control creates a Recordset object that you can use to perform your queries. The Data Command control may be used to retrieve or modify a single row within a table. You can see two more controls in the next section, "Inserting a Data Command Control," that may be used to handle multiple rows. You can specify command text properties for the Data Command control that indicate the type of command to execute against the database. This information is used with the Recordset object to perform the specified type of database action against the desired row within a table.

INSERTING A DATA COMMAND CONTROL

In order to insert a Data Command DTC into a Web application, you must first create a new Active Server Page that will contain the control. In File View, pull down the File menu and select New. Click on the Files tab and highlight Active Server Page. Next, type in the name of the new ASP page and accept all the defaults for Project name and Location. Figure 8-21 shows the completed dialog box form. Once you click on OK, a skeleton page is automatically generated with a comment instructing you where new HTML can be inserted. Right-click on the desired position within the page to place the Data Command control, and select Insert ActiveX Control from the menu. Finally, click on the *Design-time* tab and choose Data Command Control from the list. Note that a *Controls* tab is also in this dialog box. The only difference in these two tabs is that the Design-time tab picks up the registry entry that identifies a DTC and shows only those controls. The Controls tab displays all controls on your system, which usually comprise quite a list. Figure 8-22 illustrates the status of the screen at this point.

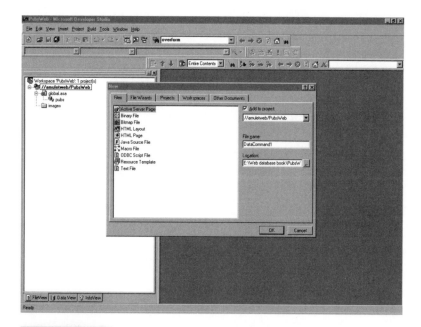

Figure 8-21   *Creating a New ASP for the Data Command*

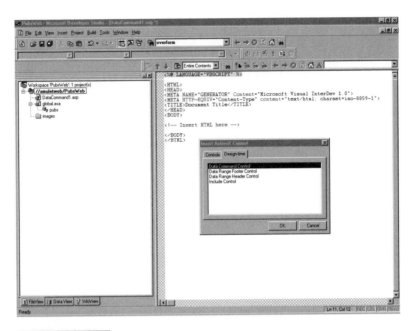

Figure 8–22   *Beginnings of an ASP with a Data Command*

CONFIGURING A DATA COMMAND CONTROL

Now I need to fill in the dialog box form with various properties to configure the Data Command DTC according to my requirements. The dialog box is organized by tab: Control, Advanced, Parameters, and All.

In the Control tab, I begin by setting the ID of the control. The *ID* field for the DTC is used as the name for the control in your code. Although a default exists, you can change the ID to the name you wish to use. Using the Visual Basic naming standards with a prefix to indicate the object's type is preferable. I use the dtc prefix, so the name of the control will be dtcAuthors to indicate that the recordset return by the query will contain author names from the authors table in the pubs database. The ID becomes meaningful in your code because it is the name not only for the control but also for the recordset returned from the database.

Next, select the pubs entry in the *Data Connection* combo box. You should see any data connections you previously created for this Web project. If you don't see any data connections, then you most likely used the Database Project Wizard instead of the Web Project Wizard. The latter creates a global.asa file that you'll need when using design-time controls.

In the *Command to Submit* group, I need to select the *Command Type*. For our purposes here, I choose 0-SQL, which means that I need to create a

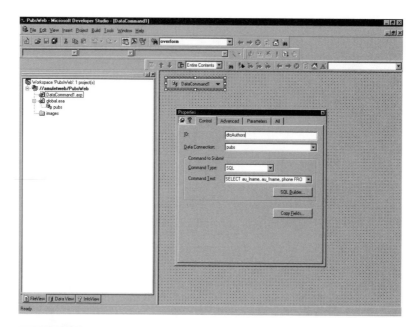

Figure 8–23   *Fully Defined Data Command Control*

SQL statement to attach to the control. Other options are stored procedure, table, and view. Instead of typing in a SQL statement in the *Command Text* field (which I could have done), I use the Query Designer to do all the work. Click on the SQL Builder command button to launch the Query Designer. Once in the designer, create a query that includes the fields au_lname, au_fname, and phone with the criteria state='CA', close the query, and save it. The SQL string from the query is now placed in the Command Text field for the Data Command control. See Figure 8-23 for the completed dialog box form.

The next step is to take the fields in the recordset for the design-time control and place them on the clipboard. The *Copy Field* button enables you to copy the fields from the database table for insertion into your Web page document. Click on this button and see the dialog box shown in Figure 8-24. In our case, select all the fields, but if you only choose a subset, make sure that the fields are in the order you wish to use them. The fields that you choose are copied to the clipboard. You can then insert them into your Web page document using the text editor. This feature provides an easy way to access the values of the columns within a row in your table. Here are the contents deposited in the clipboard by the Copy Fields button:

```
<%= DataCommand1("au_fname") %><br>
<%= DataCommand1("au_lname") %><br>
<%= DataCommand1("phone") %><br>
```

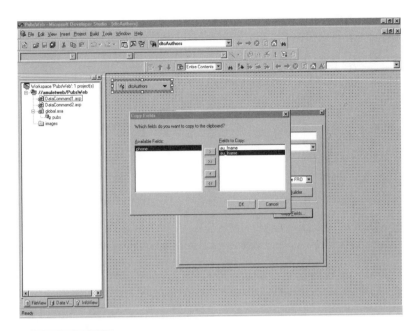

Figure 8–24   *Copy Fields Dialog Box*

The Advanced tab enables you to customize your database commands. In many cases, you can accept the defaults for this tab. Advanced database developers typically use the dialog box to fine-tune the performance of the application. For example, you can specify the type of cursor to use with a query. You can also choose the type of locking scheme that you want to use for database requests among different users. You can also set the number of records to cache into local memory. The Advanced tab enables you to prepare, or compile, an SQL statement when it's initially executed.

The Parameters tab is used with stored procedures. If you choose Stored Procedure for your Command Type on the Control property tab, you can then enter values for any parameters required for the stored procedure.

Use the All tab to view all the properties for the Data Command DTC.

After the Data Command control has been configured, you find the following server-side VBScript code using ADO in your ASP page:

```
<!--METADATA TYPE="DesignerControl" startspan
<OBJECT ID="DataCommand1" WIDTH=151 HEIGHT=24
CLASSID=
"CLSID:7FAEED80-9D58-11CF-8F68-00AA006D27C2">
<PARAM NAME="_Version" VALUE="65536">
<PARAM NAME="_Version" VALUE="65536">
<PARAM NAME="_ExtentX" VALUE="3986">
<PARAM NAME="_ExtentY" VALUE="635">
```

```
<PARAM NAME="_StockProps" VALUE="0">
<PARAM NAME="DataConnection" VALUE="pubs">
<PARAM NAME="CommandText"
VALUE="SELECT au_lname, au_fname, phone FROM
authors WHERE (state = 'CA')">
</OBJECT>
-->


<%
Set pubs =
    Server.CreateObject("ADODB.Connection")
pubs.ConnectionTimeout =
    Session("pubs_ConnectionTimeout")
pubs.CommandTimeout =
    Session("pubs_CommandTimeout")
pubs.Open Session("pubs_ConnectionString"),
    Session("pubs_RuntimeUserName"),
    Session("pubs_RuntimePassword")
Set cmdTemp =
    Server.CreateObject("ADODB.Command")
Set dtcAuthors =
    Server.CreateObject("ADODB.Recordset")
cmdTemp.CommandText =
    "SELECT au_lname, au_fname, phone
    FROM authors WHERE (state = 'CA')"
cmdTemp.CommandType = 1
Set cmdTemp.ActiveConnection = pubs
dtcAuthors.Open cmdTemp, , 0, 1
%>

<!--METADATA TYPE="DesignerControl" endspan-->
```

In this code, you can see both the object declaration and the ADO code. The object declaration is enclosed in comments and will not be interpreted by the browser. The ADO code is the only item that persists after the application is executed.

The first line of the ADO code creates a database connection object and stores the instance of this object in a variable named pubs. The next line illustrates how the global.asa file and the ASP file that contains the database control work together to connect to the database. Using the pubs connection object that was created in the first line of the ADO code, the ConnectionTimeout and CommandTimeout properties are set, based on the database connection that was created for the project. The connection information can be found in the Session_OnStart procedure within the global.asa file. The information in the global.asa file stores general property information about the database connection. This information is used to assist the ASP in creating the connection dynamically when it's required. The ConnectionTimeout property defines the maximum length of time for the connection, whereas the CommandTimeout property specifies the maximum duration for execution of the SQL command.

A session is then opened for the pubs object, based on information contained in the Session_OnStart procedure in the global.asa file. The user name and password are used to connect to the database. The cmdTemp variable is used to create a Command object. This object is used later in the code to capture the SQL command to execute against the database. The dtcAuthors variable is used to create the Recordset object. After this object is created, the Recordset object is opened, using the SQL statement as a parameter. In this case, the value of the CommandText object contained in the cmdTemp variable is a SQL SELECT statement that selects all the columns au_lname, au_fname, and phone columns from the Authors table where the state column is equal to "CA."

What the above code now provides is a database connection ready for additional code to iterate through the resultset based on your query.

CREATING A DATA COMMAND CONTROL USING DRAG AND DROP

One other method exists for creating a Data Command control on an ASP page. Here, you begin by creating a new ASP page and then switching to Data View. Choose a table for which you wish to create a Data Command control and then drag it onto the ASP page to the location appropriate for the object declaration. Drop the table and then notice that the object declaration code is automatically deposited on the page. You can then right-click on the code and select Edit Design-time Control to find the property list already configured.

Data Range Header and Footer Design-Time Controls

Two other particularly useful design-time ActiveX controls are the *Data Range Header* and the *Data Range Footer* controls. These controls allow you to retrieve records from a database. First, the Data Range Header control is used to create the Recordset object and begin retrieving rows from the table. Next, the Data Range Footer control operates in conjunction with the Data Range Header control, allowing you to page through the records in the table.

The process of inserting a Data Range Header control into an ASP page is very similar to how I inserted a Data Command control in "Inserting a Data Command Control," earlier in this chapter. In this section, however, I go further by using these two DTCs to create a page that pulls data from a SQL Server database and places the results in an HTML table.

To begin, I create a new ASP file in preparation for using it with the Data Range controls. To display the data in a tabular form, I need to set up a table. The following HTML serves as the basis for this display. Previewing this page in the browser yields Figure 8-25.

```
<%@ LANGUAGE="VBSCRIPT" %>

<HTML>
<HEAD>
<META NAME="GENERATOR"
    Content="Microsoft Visual InterDev 1.0">
<META HTTP-EQUIV="Content-Type"
    content="text/html; charset=iso-8858-1">
<TITLE>Document Title</TITLE>
</HEAD>
<BODY>

<p align="center">
<font size="5">
<strong>
ONLINE BOOKSTORES, INC.
</strong></font>
</p>

<p align="center">
<font size="5">
<strong></strong></font> </p>

<hr>

<table border="1" cellpadding="3"
cellspacing="3" width="100%">
    <tr>
      <th align="left" width="10%">
      Book ID</th>
      <th align="left" width="40%">Title</th>
      <th align="left" width="20%">
      Category</th>
      <th align="left" width="20%">
      Publisher</th>
      <th align="left" width="10%">Price</th>
    </tr>

    <tr>
      <td width="10%"> </td>
      <th align="left" width="40%">
       </th>
      <td width="20%"> </td>
      <td width="20%"> </td>
      <td width="10%"> </td>
    </tr>
</table>

<hr>
```

```
<p><font color="#000000" size="1">
(c) Copyright 1999 by AMULET Development
</font></p>

</BODY>
</HTML>
```

Now I need to add a Data Range Header Design-Time control to this page. The appropriate place to insert the control is between the two rows in the sample table. Just open up a blank line or two in the Visual InterDev FrontPage editor. Right-click on the blank line and choose Insert ActiveX Control. You should now see the Insert ActiveX Control dialog box. Select the Design-time tab on this dialog box, and select *Data Range Header Control.*

The Properties dialog box for the Data Range Header control is the same as for the Data Command control. I need to configure the control for our purposes. Choose the Data Connection as pubs. Choose Range Type as Table. Make sure that the Command Type is set to 0-SQL. Enter the name dtcDataRangeHdr1 for the control's ID field.

Now, as before, I use the SQL Builder button to invoke the Query Designer in order to construct the SQL for the Command Text field on this dialog box. The desired query is an inner join between the publishers and titles tables with various fields in the field list. Here is the generated SQL:

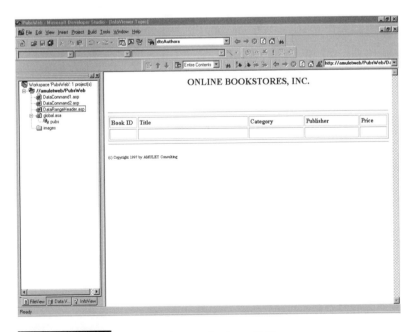

Figure 8–25   *Rendered HTML for Data Table*

```
SELECT titles.title_id, titles.title,
    publishers.pub_name, publishers.city,
    publishers.state, publishers.country
FROM publishers INNER JOIN titles ON
    publishers.pub_id = titles.pub_id
```

After closing the Query Designer and answering Yes to the prompt to update the design-time control, you now see the generated SQL statement in the control's properties dialog box. Next, click on the Copy Fields button. Make sure that you select the fields in the right order—title_id, title, type, pub_name, and price—using the single arrow button to move the field to the right-hand pane. The order is important because I need it to match the way I set up the HTML table previously. Click on the OK button to copy the fields to the clipboard and then proceed to close the design-time control. You'll immediately notice one big difference between my Data Range Header control and the Data Command control used in the previous section—a lot more code is generated this time, because the Data Range Header control does a lot more work. Here is the resulting code:

```
<%@ LANGUAGE="VBSCRIPT" %>
<HTML>
<HEAD>
<META NAME="GENERATOR"
Content="Microsoft Visual InterDev 1.0">
<META HTTP-EQUIV="Content-Type"
content="text/html; charset=iso-8858-1">
<TITLE>Document Title</TITLE>
</HEAD>
<BODY>

<p align="center">
<font size="5"><strong>
ONLINE BOOKSTORES, INC.
</strong></font>
</p><p align="center"><font size="5"><strong>
</strong></font> </p><hr><table border="1"
cellpadding="3"
cellspacing="3" width="100%">
    <tr>
      <th align="left" width="10%">
      Book ID</th><th align="left" width="40%">Title</th>
      <th align="left" width="20%">
      Category</th><th align="left" width="20%">
      Publisher</th><th align="left" width="10%">Price</
th>
    </tr>

    <!--METADATA TYPE="DesignerControl"
    startspan<OBJECT ID="dtcDataRangeHdr1" WIDTH=151
HEIGHT=24CLASSID="CLSID:F602E721-A281-11CF-A5B7-
```

```
0080C73AAC7E">
<PARAM NAME="_Version" VALUE="65536">
<PARAM NAME="_Version" VALUE="65536">
<PARAM NAME="_ExtentX" VALUE="3969">
<PARAM NAME="_ExtentY" VALUE="635">
<PARAM NAME="_StockProps" VALUE="0">
<PARAM NAME="DataConnection" VALUE="pubs">
<PARAM NAME="CommandText"
    VALUE="SELECT titles.title_id,
    titles.title, titles.type,
    publishers.pub_name, titles.price FROM
    publishers INNER JOIN titles ON
    publishers.pub_id = titles.pub_id"><PARAM
NAME="RangeType" VALUE="2">
</OBJECT>
-->

<%
fHideNavBar = False
fHideNumber = False
fHideRequery = False
fHideRule = False
stQueryString = ""
fEmptyRecordset = False
fFirstPass = True
fNeedRecordset = False
fNoRecordset = False
tBarAlignment = "Left"
tHeaderName = "dtcDataRangeHdr1"
tPageSize = 0
tPagingMove = ""
tRangeType = "Table"
tRecordsProcessed = 0
tPrevAbsolutePage = 0
intCurPos = 0
intNewPos = 0
fSupportsBookmarks = True
fMoveAbsolute = False

If IsEmpty(Session(
    "dtcDataRangeHdr1_Recordset")) Then
    fNeedRecordset = True
Else
    If Session("dtcDataRangeHdr1_Recordset")
      Is Nothing ThenfNeedRecordset
 = True
    Else
      Set dtcDataRangeHdr1 =
      Session("dtcDataRangeHdr1_Recordset")End If
End If
```

```
If fNeedRecordset Then
    Set pubs =
      Server.CreateObject("ADODB.Connection")
    pubs.ConnectionTimeout =
      Session("pubs_ConnectionTimeout")
    pubs.CommandTimeout =
      Session("pubs_CommandTimeout")
    pubs.Open Session("pubs_ConnectionString"),
      Session("pubs_RuntimeUserName"),
Session("pubs_RuntimePassword")Set cmdTemp =
      Server.CreateObject("ADODB.Command")Set
dtcDataRangeHdr1 =
      Server.CreateObject("ADODB.Recordset")
cmdTemp.CommandText =
      "SELECT titles.title_id, titles.title,
      titles.type, publishers.pub_name,
      titles.price FROM publishers INNER JOIN
      titles ON publishers.pub_id =
      titles.pub_id"cmdTemp.CommandType = 1Set
cmdTemp.ActiveConnection = pubs
    dtcDataRangeHdr1.Open cmdTemp, , 0, 1
End If

On Error Resume Next

If dtcDataRangeHdr1.BOF AnddtcDataRangeHdr1.EOF Then
fEmptyRecordset = True

On Error Goto 0
If Err Then fEmptyRecordset = True
If Not IsEmpty(Session(
    "dtcDataRangeHdr1_Filter")) And
    Not fEmptyRecordset Then
      dtcDataRangeHdr1.Filter =
      Session("dtcDataRangeHdr1_Filter")If
dtcDataRangeHdr1.BOF And
      dtcDataRangeHdr1.EOF ThenfEmptyRecordset = True
End If
If fEmptyRecordset Then
      fHideNavBar = True
      fHideRule = True
    End If

    Do
      If fEmptyRecordset Then Exit Do
      If Not fFirstPass Then
        dtcDataRangeHdr1.MoveNext
      Else
        fFirstPass = False
```

```
     End If

 If dtcDataRangeHdr1.EOF Then Exit Do%>
 <!--METADATA TYPE="DesignerControl" endspan
 -->
 <tr>
   <td width="10%"> </td>
   <th align="left" width="40%">
    </th><td width="20%"> </td><td
width="20%"> </td>
   <td width="10%"> </td>
   </tr>
</table>

<hr>

<p><font color="#000000" size="1">
(c) Copyright 1999 by AMULET Development
</font></p></BODY></HTML>
```

The DTC code is placed between the HTML <METADATA> tags ending with *startspan* and *endspan*. You should never directly edit the code for a DTC in any way. If you do and then you edit the control in design view, your changes will be overwritten. This result is not necessarily a flaw, because DTC design is not a two-way tool. You should be able to use DTC design view to make any required changes to the operation of the control without resorting to modifying code.

Next, I need to modify the HTML table to incorporate the fields from the recordset. This task can be accomplished by using the contents of the clipboard. Place the mouse cursor after the <TR> tag just after the endspan statement and add a blank line. Now paste the contents of the clipboard here. Now use the lines from the clipboard and insert them into the correct position in the HTML table definition. Here is the result I need:

```
<tr>
    <td width="10%">
    <%= dtcDataRangeHdr1("title_id") %>
     
    </td>
    <th align="left" width="40%">
    <%= dtcDataRangeHdr1("title")%> 
    </th>
      <td width="20%">
      <%= dtcDataRangeHdr1("type") %> 
      </td>
    <td width="20%">
    <%= dtcDataRangeHdr1("pub_name") %> 
    </td>
    <td width="10%">
```

```
<%= dtcDataRangeHdr1("price") %> 
</td>
</tr>
```

The last thing to do is to add a Data Range Footer control to the page. This DTC is simple to insert and does not require you to set any properties. To insert the control, highlight the </TABLE> tag at the end of the ASP file (I explain why you need to highlight the tag later). Now right-click and choose Insert ActiveX Control. Select the Data Range Footer control, and then close the ActiveX Control Designer. The code added to the ASP file is as follows:

```
<tr>
    <td width="10%">
    <%= dtcDataRangeHdr1("title_id") %>
     </td>
    <th align="left" width="40%">
    <%= dtcDataRangeHdr1("title") %>
     </th>
    <td width="20%">
    <%= dtcDataRangeHdr1("type") %>
     </td>
    <td width="20%">
    <%= dtcDataRangeHdr1("pub_name") %>
     </td>
    <td width="10%">
    <%= dtcDataRangeHdr1("price") %>
     </td>
</tr>

<!--METADATA TYPE="DesignerControl" startspan
<OBJECT ID="DataRangeFtr1" WIDTH=151
 HEIGHT=24
 CLASSID=
"CLSID:F602E722-A281-11CF-A5B7-0080C73AAC7E">
<PARAM NAME="_Version" VALUE="65536">
<PARAM NAME="_ExtentX" VALUE="3969">
<PARAM NAME="_ExtentY" VALUE="635">
<PARAM NAME="_StockProps" VALUE="0">
</OBJECT>
-->

<%
Loop
    If tRangeType = "Table" Then
      Response.Write "</TABLE>"
      If tPageSize > 0 Then
        If Not fHideRule Then
           Response.Write "<HR>"
        If Not fHideNavBar Then
        %>
```

```
<TABLE WIDTH=100% >
<TR>
<TD WIDTH=100% >
<P ALIGN=<%= tBarAlignment %> >
<FORM <%= "ACTION=""" &
Request.ServerVariables(
  "PATH_INFO") &
  stQueryString & """" %>
  METHOD="POST">

  <INPUT TYPE="Submit"
  NAME="<%= tHeaderName &
  "_PagingMove" %>
  " VALUE="    &lt;&lt;    ">

  <INPUT TYPE="Submit"
  NAME="<%= tHeaderName &
  "_PagingMove" %>
  " VALUE="    &lt;    ">

  <INPUT TYPE="Submit"
  NAME="<%= tHeaderName &
  "_PagingMove" %>
  " VALUE="    &gt;    ">

<% If fSupportsBookmarks Then %>
  <INPUT TYPE="Submit"
  NAME="<%= tHeaderName &
  "_PagingMove" %>
  " VALUE="    &gt;&gt;    ">
<% End If %>

<% If Not fHideRequery Then %>
  <INPUT TYPE="Submit"
  NAME="<% =tHeaderName &
  "_PagingMove" %>
  " VALUE=" Requery ">
<% End If %>
</FORM>
</P>
</TD>
<TD VALIGN=MIDDLE ALIGN=RIGHT>
<FONT SIZE=2>

<%
If Not fHideNumber Then
  If tPageSize > 1 Then
    Response.Write
```

```
                    "<NOBR>Page: " &
                    Session(tHeaderName &
                    "_AbsolutePage") &
                    "</NOBR>"
                Else
                    Response.Write
                    "<NOBR>Record: " &
                    Session(tHeaderName &
                    "_AbsolutePage") &
                    "</NOBR>"
                End If
            End If
            %>
            </FONT>
            </TD>
            </TR>
            </TABLE>
            <%
        End If
    End If
%>


<!--METADATA TYPE="DesignerControl" endspan-->
```

Before ending this section, I need to provide a bit of explanation about what we've accomplished. You might ask yourself, "What do the DTC controls really do?" At a high level, the Data Range Header and Data Range Footer controls insert all the server-side VBScript and ADO code you need to manage the output of a recordset. This process includes creating special variables and setting their values, determining whether the code needs to generate a recordset, handling the empty recordset case, handling the error status of the query, and displaying the proper controls for the user to navigate through the recordset. The amount of code generated and its overall structure will change, depending on which options you choose when you set the properties for the control. A useful experiment is to select different property values to see what effect they have on the generated code.

The purpose of the special variables created by the design-time control is generally easy to determine by reviewing the ASP and HTML code. For instance, when you chose the Range Type option on the properties tab for the Data Range Header, this caused the following line of code to be generated by the Data Range Header control:

```
tRangeType = "Table"
```

The Data Range Footer control uses the tRangeType variable to output the correct HTML syntax. You can see this by examining the If statement that checks this variable and outputs a </TABLE> tag to terminate the table if the range type is Table:

```
If tRangeType = "Table" Then
Response.Write "</TABLE>"
```

For this reason, you needed to highlight the </TABLE> tag before inserting the Data Range Footer control. If you did not highlight the </TABLE> tag, then you would end up with two of the same tags and the page would not work properly. You should not be concerned about any DTC code, except for the implications it has on how you should write your own page. The rRange-Type variable is a good example.

Figure 8-26 shows the resulting ASP page after the Data Range controls populate it with data.

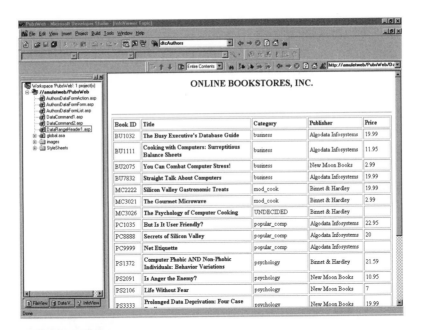

Figure 8-26 *ASP with Data from Data Range DTC Control*

Visual Data Tools

The Visual InterDev *Visual Data Tools* provide effective methods for creating and maintaining Web-to-database connections. The Web application developer may use the integrated *Database Designer* and the *Query Designer* to make dynamic connections to a wide range of databases, although the focus in the Data Tools is towards back-end server databases such as SQL Server.

The tools will work fine against the JET database engine; however, the database designer functionality supports only SQL Server. This focus recognizes the widely held belief that high-end WebTop applications of the future will most likely be built around database servers.

The Data Tools contain a high-end database design and schema definition environment that works against SQL Server, which lets you manipulate the database and various objects; e.g., you can change the tables, fields, etc. The query tool allows you to design complex SQL that you'll need to extract data from the database and insert information into the database. Furthermore, since the most efficient interactions with server databases involve the use of stored procedures, the Data Tools include a stored procedure editor for SQL Server and Oracle databases. Microsoft's goal for the Data Tools is to bring the ease-of-use lessons learned from building Microsoft Access to the server and integrate those tools inside the same environment used by the rest of the IS department.

The following is a feature summary for the Data Tools. The Data View project workspace window lets you drill down inside your database so that can visualize the objects inside the database just as easily as you can see objects inside your Web or database project. Second, a database designer is available for organizing, creating, and modifying database objects, as well as a facility for editing and debugging SQL Server stored procedures. Finally, a query designer can help with building and maintaining ODBC queries. The SQL builder can generate ODBC SQL, which you can attach to different objects in your Web code as the SQL property for databound Web objects such as ADO objects. The query designer also provides an updateable data browser for ODBC. This last feature is useful to enter or cut and paste test data in a browser window. Not many server products provide this feature today.

Data View

Data View provides a visual interface for database components included in a project. Data View becomes accessible when you add a database connection to an Active Server Page within your project. Within each database for which a connection is established, objects are organized into a folder hierarchy. The number of folders displayed depends on the type of data source upon which the connection is based. For a SQL Server database, the folders and corresponding objects are Database Diagrams, Tables, Views, and Stored procedures. For a Microsoft Access database, on the other hand, you see only Tables and Views.

The Data View tab appears on the Project Workspace window along with File View and Info View. See Figure 8-4 again to help understand the visual metaphor used in this environment.

To use Data View, you begin by creating a Web or database project, and then add a data connection to it. To do so, use the Project menu, then Add To

Project, and the Data Connection option. You can connect your projects to any ODBC-compliant database, provided that you have the necessary ODBC driver and networking software on your development workstation.

When you add a data connection based on a SQL Server database to a project, you will be prompted to log into the database, at which point the Data View tab becomes visible. You can navigate through the Data View hierarchy to see objects inside the database down to the field level, and inspect the properties of those objects. You can also launch editors for many of the objects by right-clicking on them and selecting Design or Open. If you are using SQL Server for the data source, entering design view for a table allows full editing of the table's structure, including data types. For other data sources, such as Access, structure changes are not allowed from within Visual InterDev.

In order to insert, update, or delete data in a table directly, you may right-click on a table object in Data View and select Open. This action allows you to open a table directly and get a datasheet view just like in the Access environment (Visual InterDev actually got source code from the Access product). The only difference between this process and Access is that you're going native against the server through ODBC.

In Data View, you define sources for data connections in a project via ODBC 3.0 (which ships with Microsoft Office 97 and Visual InterDev) driver manager dialog boxes. One big difference in ODBC 3.0 is *File Data Sources*, which are similar to the usual data source names as in prior versions of ODBC, but instead of being stored in the registry, they are stored in the file system so that you can include them in Web projects. I found that File Data Sources are easier to manage when using a non-SQL Server database, because you can develop the project on the workstation and then simply copy the File Data Source file to the Web server when it is time.

You can click on Pubs database and log into the server. The philosophy of the Data Tools is to not impose any additional security beyond that provided by the server. Upon logging in, you get a new data connection to Pubs in the project. You can have as many database connections in a project as you want.

Table Structure Maintenance

The Web application developer can modify existing SQL Server table structures using the Data View. Although you can also use SQL Server Enterprise Manager for this purpose, Visual InterDev contains many more database administration functions and is generally much more flexible. To begin, open the Tables tree view hierarchy, select a table name, click the right mouse button, and select Design. Figure 8-27 shows the table structure design window for the authors table of the pubs database.

Notice the table design tool box positioned just above the design window. It contains icons for specifying the primary key of the table, saving the SQL change script, specifying the magnification factor of the structure window, and the table property list.

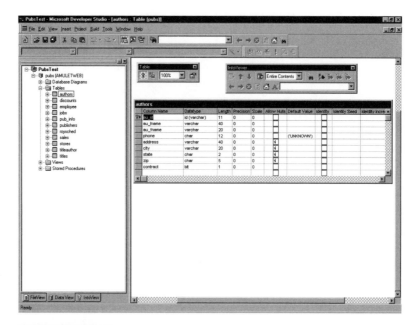

Figure 8–27   *Table Design View for the Pubs Database Authors*

The table structure design window has the following columns: column name, data type, length, precision, scale, allow nulls, default value, identity, identity seed, and identity increment. Each of these attributes may be changed at any time. This ability is contrary to the standard interaction with SQL Server databases using Enterprise Manager, which does not allow changing fundamental attributes of a field such as data type, allow nulls, and identity. Using Visual InterDev for this purpose makes it a valuable database administration tool in its own right.

Once you've finished modifying the table's structure, you can immediately save the table's new structure by using the File menu and the Save option. This action results in a *SQL script* being generated and automatically applied against the table, resulting in the new table structure. Alternately, you can choose the Script output option, as shown in Figure 8-28. The SQL script can either be saved to an ASCII text file by clicking on the Yes button or discarded by clicking on the No button in the Save Change Script dialog box. In the Database Designer section of this chapter, you see a full SQL script used to change the data type of the author table's zip field from CHAR to VARCHAR.

You can also create a trigger to be associated with the table design, by right-clicking on a table name in the Data View tab window and selecting the New Trigger option. A trigger is a special kind of stored procedure, comprised of Transact/SQL code, that goes into effect when you modify data in a speci-

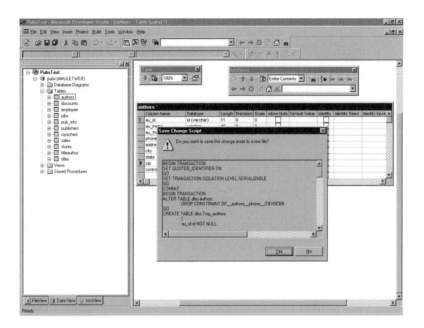

Figure 8–28   *Save Change Script Dialog Box*

fied table using one or more data modification operations: UPDATE, INSERT, or DELETE. Triggers can query other tables and can include complex SQL statements. They are primarily useful for enforcing complex business rules or requirements. If the data source is not a SQL Server database, then this option is not available. Figure 8-29 shows the program editor used for entering or maintaining trigger code. The statements shown in the figure were automatically generated by Visual InterDev. All the developer must do is replace the prototype values with actual values, such as the trigger name, table name on which the trigger will operate, query type (Insert, Update, or Delete), and the trigger code itself.

Table Properties Dialog

When you are in table design view, you can right-click and select the Properties option to access the various table level properties. The table properties are organized in a tabbed dialog box with the tabs: Table, Relationship, and Index/Keys. Take a look at each tab and the properties it contains.

TABLE PROPERTIES

Figure 8-30 depicts the Table tab of the properties dialog box. The *Selected table* combo box enables you to choose another table from the list and view

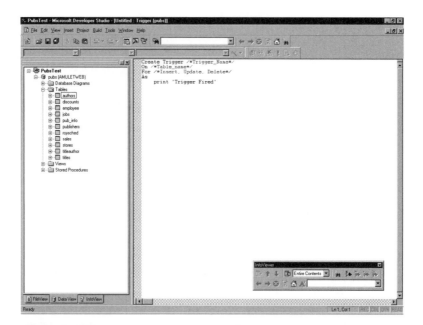

Figure 8–29 *Creating a New Trigger*

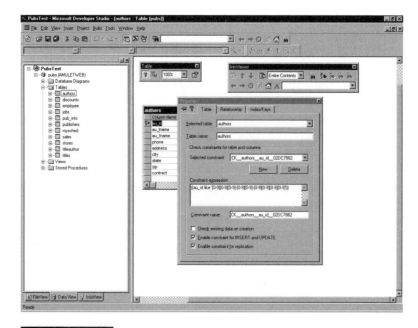

Figure 8–30 *Table Properties Tab*

its properties. This combo box displays only tables that are included in the current database diagram in which you are working. The *Table name* text box enables you to view and change the name of the selected table. The bottom portion of the dialog box enables you to see the selected constraints for the table and its columns. The *Selected constraints* combo box enables you to choose a column that contains a constraint. You can also create new and delete existing constraints for tables and columns by using the *New* and *Delete* command buttons. Also, you have text boxes for the *Constraint expression* (where you enter a Transact SQL expression representing the constraint) and *Constraint name*. In addition, three check boxes allow you to specify how and when the constraint is to be applied. The first is used so that you can check existing data by immediately applying the constraint upon its creation. The second enables you to apply the constraint to all insertions and updates into the database. The third enables you to use the constraint for replicating the database to a different database.

RELATIONSHIP PROPERTIES

Figure 8-31 shows the Relationships tab of the Properties dialog box. This tab enables you to change the properties of the relationships of the tables contained in your database diagrams. The *Selected relationship* combo box shows the currently selected relationship and allows you to select another. The *Relationship name* text box enables you to change the name of the currently selected relationship. The *Primary key table* shows the name of the primary key table in the relationship and the columns that make up the primary key. The *Foreign key table* displays the name of the foreign key table in the relationship and the columns that make up the foreign key. The next three check boxes are similar in meaning to the check boxes contained on the Table tab. These check boxes apply to the foreign key in the table relationship. If the *Check existing data on creation* check box is enabled, the constraint is applied to existing data in the database when the relationship is added to the Foreign key table. You can select the *Enable constraint for INSERT and UPDATE* check box to apply the constraint to all insertions and updates to the Foreign key table. Doing so also prevents a deletion of a row in the Primary table if a related row in the Foreign key table exists. The *Enable relationship for replication* check box allows you to use the constraint for replicating the Foreign key table to a different database.

INDEX/KEYS PROPERTIES

You can use the Index/Keys tab shown in Figure 8-32 of the Properties dialog box to view and change the keys and indexes for the tables within your database diagrams. The *Selected index* combo box shows the indexes and keys for the selected table. The *Type* display field indicates whether you're viewing a primary key, unique key, or index for the selected table. The *Column name*

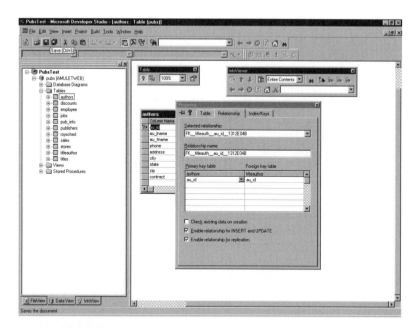

Figure 8–31   *Relationship Tab*

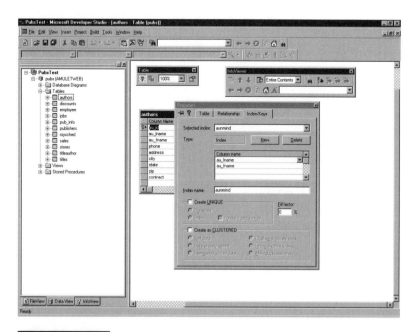

Figure 8–32   *Index/Keys Properties Tab*

subform displays the column names that are included in the index or key. You may use the *New* and *Delete* command buttons to add, change, or delete columns from the list. The *Index name* text box enables you to establish a name for the index. The *Create UNIQUE* check box lets you create a unique constraint or index for the table by selecting the appropriate radio button. If you create a unique index (not constraint), you can choose to ignore duplicate keys. You can also use the *Fill Factor* text box to specify how full to make the index page within the database. The *Create as CLUSTERED* check box lets you create a clustered index. You may further define the clustered index by selecting the various radio buttons.

Views

To think of a *view* in Visual InterDev as a virtual table may be helpful. You may, for example, create a view on a table that selects only three out of ten columns in a table. Views are often used in SQL Server databases to assign permissions so that certain users are able to access the view but not the underlying tables. Table updates are possible with views as well. The *Views* folder in Data View contains references to view objects that are stored in the database. Figure 8-33 shows the titleview sample view found in the SQL Server Pubs database with the Diagram, SQL, and Results panes open

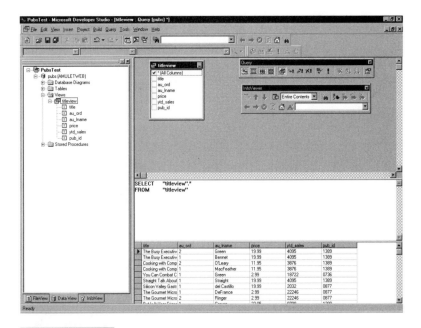

Figure 8–33   *Sample View from the Pubs Database*

When using a Microsoft Access data source, a query (also known as a QueryDef object) is equivalent to a view in SQL Server terminology. Consequently, the Views folder for an Access data source contains the queries found in the Access .MDB database file. This fact points to an important distinction between queries and views. Queries in Visual InterDev terminology are actually the SQL SELECT statements associated with design-time controls, whereas views are actual objects stored in the database.

The Views folder simply lists all the views in the database, but does not contain a facility for creating or editing a view. To create a view, you must first use the Query Designer to create and test a query. Once the query is working properly, you must then edit the SQL statement in the SQL pane of the Query Designer. The following syntax must be added before the SELECT statement:

```
CREATE  VIEW <viewname> AS
```

The CREATE VIEW statement will construct a new view using the included SELECT statement as a model. Next, save the query. Finally, you must run the query to create the view. Now to see your new view displayed in the Views folder, you must refresh the data connection by right-clicking on the connection item in the Data View hierarchy. From this point, opening the new view yields the resultset of the original SQL SELECT.

Stored Procedures

Although formally part of Data View, the Stored Procedure folder is discussed in depth in its own section later in this chapter. The topic of stored procedures is sufficiently important to the construction of Web database applications, such that this special focus is warranted.

Database Designer

The Visual InterDev *Database Designer* is a graphical tool used to create or modify entire Microsoft SQL Server (version 6.5 or later) database structures while directly connected to the database. Currently, no other back-end server databases are supported; however, the database designer is based on an extensible architecture so that support for other database systems will most likely follow in the future. Note that if you are using version 6.5 of SQL Server, you must have applied Service Pack 2 or later in order to use the database designer (this requirement is not present for other components of InterDev). Since many Windows-NT-based WebTop applications use SQL Server as the back-end database, a tool such as the Database Designer becomes instrumental during both the initial implementation and maintenance phase of the application. InterDev also provides generic database administration functionality beyond what is found in *SQL Server Enterprise Manager*, the standard user interface component for SQL Server, making the product an invaluable tool for database administrators (DBA) aside from its Web uses.

The Database Designer provides a graphical environment in which you can visualize the structure of your database tables and their relationships and manipulate database objects, such as tables, relationships, indexes, and constraints, without having to write Transact-SQL code. You can provide different views of complex databases and experiment with database changes without actually modifying the underlying database. The Database Designer also lets you view and save change scripts of Transact-SQL code for changes you may have made in a database diagram or changes you may have made by creating new objects and relationships. After you've completed your design work, you can print your database diagrams.

With the Database Designer, you can create and modify database objects, including:

- Tables
- Table columns and their properties
- Indexes
- Constraints
- Table relationships

Whereas you modify tables and their columns directly in a database diagram, for other changes, you modify indexes, constraints, and relationships through the Properties window for a table in your diagram.

Database Diagrams

The Database Designer allows you to interact with the server database using database diagrams called *schemas*. The schemas graphically represent tables, the columns they contain, and the relationships between them. These features are not currently available in the SQL Server Enterprise Manager. Traditionally, SQL Server developers have had to enlist the help of other third-party database design tools, or do without these features altogether and manually script files. If you are familiar with the Microsoft Access product's relationship window, the same visual metaphor is used in the Database Designer—but with significant enhancements to handle large complex databases and the ability to track changes, so you don't have to immediately commit the changes to the database.

Many developers working in large MIS shops rarely want to commit changes to the database before they make sure that the changes are correct, since with mission-critical applications, intense review procedures are often in place concerning changes in the database schema. Visual InterDev's deferred commit model is therefore a desirable feature for enterprise-level database design efforts.

You can use database diagrams to view the tables in your database and their relationships, in order to perform potentially complex operations that alter the physical structure of the database. When you modify a database object through a database diagram, the modifications you make are not saved in the database until you save the table or the database diagram. Thus, you can experiment with "what if" scenarios on a database's design without permanently affecting its existing design or data.

After you've made some structural changes to the schema, you have several options for the new design. You can either save the changes to selected tables or to the database diagram and have the changes modify the server database, or you can discard your changes. You can also save the Transact-SQL code generated by your changes to the diagram in a *SQL script*. If you save a SQL script instead of saving your changes to the database, either you can apply the script to the database at another time via an interactive tool such as SQL Server's ISQL command-line utility, or you can edit the SQL script in a text editor and then apply the modified script to the database. The bottom line is that you control the timing, type, and extent of the changes to your database by choosing how changes to the database diagram affect the server database. In the next section, I explore how to manipulate database diagrams by looking at a specific example.

You can use database diagrams to:

- Create new objects and relationships.
- Alter the structure of your database.
- Manipulate database objects without having to write Transact-SQL code.
- Visualize the structure of your database tables and their relationships.
- Provide different views of large, complex databases.
- Experiment with database changes without committing the changes to the underlying database.

Creating a Database Diagram

To create a new database diagram, you must first add a data connection to a SQL Server database to your Web or database project and log into the database (the standard SQL Server login dialog box appears after you open the connection). Then in Data View, right-click on the Database Diagrams folder and select New Diagram. Next, drag a table from the Tables folder onto your diagram. At this point, you can modify tables and their columns directly in a database diagram. In addition, you can modify indexes, constraints, and relationships through the Properties window for a table in your diagram.

Figure 8-34 shows a database diagram called *Pubs diagram*. With the diagram open, you see a simple graphical representation of a relationship among three tables—authors, titleauthor, and titles—in the SQL Server sample database called Pubs. If you hover the mouse over a relationship line, you get information about the relationship. This meta-data is acquired from the server when you first make the connection to the database to create the diagram. You

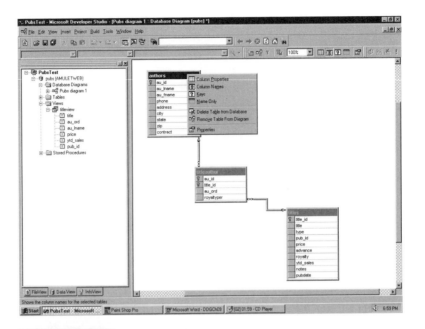

Figure 8-34   *Database Diagram with Table Option List*

can right-click on any table to customize how the table is represented in the diagram. In Figure 8-34, the design items are shown for the authors table. Seven items are in the list: *Column Properties, Column Names, Keys, Name Only, Delete Table from Database, Remove Table from Diagram*, and *Properties*. You can also get to these options through the Database Designer floating toolbar. The first four items specify how you wish the table to appear in the diagram. All the tables in the diagram are shown with the Column Names option.

Another useful feature available only from the toolbar (not available from the right-click table option list) is the ability to zoom. You can zoom in or out of the diagram presentation (a great enhancement over Access) to get an effective amount of information on the screen—100%, 200%, 75%, etc. This feature is especially useful when maintaining large, complex databases found in contemporary WebTop applications.

Table Structure Changes

The Database Designer can also facilitate changing the name, data type, and other properties of a field in a SQL Server table. Normally, this is a difficult task, because Enterprise Manager does not allow for such fundamental changes. This limitation may seem strange for those accustomed to the ease with which these kinds of table structure changes are accommodated in desktop databases such as Access. Now, with Visual InterDev, to make these kinds of changes is simple. For example, you can change the data type of a primary key field, say from CHAR(4) to CHAR(6). Since this is a primary key of a table, it is most likely bound via constraints to other fields in the database. So if we change the data type here, we also have to change the data types of fields in related tables. InterDev also handles this situation.

Take another simple example of changing the data type of a field in the authors table. Right-clicking on the table and selecting Column Properties, we can go in and specify the VARCHAR data type for the zip field instead of its current CHAR type. Notice that now an asterisk is next to the table name, indicating that you've made a change to the table's structure without committing the change. At this point, you have a choice as to how to proceed. You can select the File menu option Save Change Script and see a dialog box appear (the same dialog shown in Figure 8-28), asking whether you wish to save the script to a text file. At this point, you have not yet committed this change. You've been working on an in-memory model of the database and can experiment with different scenarios so that you can get the schema precisely how you would like it before committing the changes. If you choose to save the change script to a file, you can run the script at a later time of your choosing in order to commit the change. Another alternative is to select the Save option from the File menu, which will commit the change immediately and not save the change script to a file.

Since SQL Server does not directly support altering a data type, in order to make these changes, the script first creates a new table with the new data type, transfers all the data from the old table to the new table, reads in the permissions from the old table, copies those permissions to the new table, and drops the old table. If you'd like to see exactly how, just study the following SQL Script generated by the Database Designer for the data type change suggested above:

```
/* Friday, June 06, 1997 19:27:28 PM */
  BEGIN TRANSACTION
SET QUOTED_IDENTIFIER ON
GO
SET TRANSACTION ISOLATION LEVEL SERIALIZABLE
GO
COMMIT
BEGIN TRANSACTION
ALTER TABLE dbo.authors
DROP CONSTRAINT DF__authors__phone__03D09CBB
GO
CREATE TABLE dbo.Tmp_authors
(
    au_id id NOT NULL,
    au_lname varchar(40) NOT NULL,
    au_fname varchar(20) NOT NULL,
    phone char(12) NOT NULL CONSTRAINT
      DF__authors__phone__03D09CBB DEFAULT
```

```
        ('UNKNOWN'),
     address varchar(40) NULL,
     city varchar(20) NULL,
     state char(2) NULL,
     zip varchar(5) NULL,
     contract bit NOT NULL
) ON "default"
GO
IF EXISTS(SELECT * FROM dbo.authors)
     EXEC('INSERT INTO dbo.Tmp_authors(au_id,
     au_lname, au_fname,phone, address, city,
     state, zip, contract)
     SELECT au_id, au_lname, au_fname, phone,
     address, city,state, CONVERT(varchar(5),
     zip), contract FROM dbo.authors
     TABLOCKX')
GO
ALTER TABLE dbo.titleauthor
DROP CONSTRAINT
     FK__titleauth__au_id__1312E04B
GO
DROP TABLE dbo.authors
GO
EXECUTE sp_rename 'dbo.Tmp_authors', 'authors'
GO
CREATE NONCLUSTERED INDEX aunmind ON
     dbo.authors
     (
     au_lname,
     au_fname
     ) ON "default"
     GO
     ALTER TABLE dbo.authors ADD CONSTRAINT
     UPKCL_auidind PRIMARY KEY CLUSTERED
     (
     au_id
     ) ON "default"
     GO
ALTER TABLE dbo.authors WITH NOCHECK ADD
CONSTRAINT
CK__authors__au_id__02DC7882
CHECK (((au_id like
'[0-9][0-9][0-9]-[0-9][0-9]-[0-9][0-9][0-9][0-
9]')))
GOALTER TABLE dbo.authors WITH NOCHECK ADD
CONSTRAINT
CK__authors__zip__04C4C0F4
CHECK (((zip like
'[0-9][0-9][0-9][0-9][0-9]')))
GOGRANT REFERENCES ON dbo.authors TO guest
```

```
GRANT SELECT ON dbo.authors TO guest
GRANT INSERT ON dbo.authors TO guest
GRANT DELETE ON dbo.authors TO guest
GRANT UPDATE ON dbo.authors TO guest
COMMIT
BEGIN TRANSACTION
ALTER TABLE dbo.titleauthor WITH NOCHECK ADD
     CONSTRAINT
     FK__titleauth__au_id__1312E04B FOREIGN KEY
     (
     au_id
     ) REFERENCES dbo.authors
     (
     au_id
     )
GO
COMMIT
```

Another use of the Database Designer is to create multiple data diagrams to subset a database. Many times, with large databases, you need to logically subset the schema to divide up the structure into logical groups and work on the application in separate development teams. For example, you can select groups of tables of an existing database and drag them over to another diagram. You can save the new subset diagram and see it in your data view. Later, when building queries, you can use these subset diagrams as a basis for the queries.

Query Designer

The Visual Database Tools *Query Designer* uses visual design tools to create SQL statements that query or update databases. Using the Query Designer, you can create queries to retrieve data from any ODBC-compliant database, preview the query results, and join tables to create multi-table queries. You can easily specify elements, such as which tables, views, and columns to display, how to order the query results, and what values to locate. Data in databases can be edited by updating, inserting, or deleting rows. You can also create special-purpose queries, such as parameter queries, in which search values are provided when the query is executed. For those of you familiar with desktop database environments such as Access, the Query Designer is similar to what's commonly known as Query-by-Example.

If you are familiar with SQL, you can also enter SQL statements directly or edit the statements created by the Query Designer. You can create back-end specific SQL statements to take advantage of the features of a particular relational database, and execute stored procedures.

You can launch the Query Designer in two ways. The first is to modify the SQL property of Visual InterDev Data Range Header design-time control or Data Command design-time control. See "Database Designer," earlier in this chapter, to see how to insert these controls into your Active Server Pages. When viewing the properties of the controls, select the Control tab, and then click the command button labeled *SQL Builder* to launch the Query Designer and build the SQL statement for the control.

The second way to launch the Query Designer is to create a database project. To do this, select New from the File menu, click the Projects tab, select Database Project, and click OK. You will be prompted to add a data connection to your database project. Once you've added a data connection to your database project and logged into your database, select the data connection in the File View tab of your Project Workspace window. Right-click on it and select New Query. This action launches the Query Designer on the database to which you are connected. After you've finished building your query, you are prompted to save it as a Database Tools Query file (with a .DTQ file extension) on your local computer. Once a query file has been saved, you can drag and drop it onto any text editor, including the Visual Studio source code editor, to insert your saved SQL statement into your application code.

The Query Designer consists of four panes: the Diagram pane, the Grid pane, the SQL pane, and the Results pane. See Figure 8-35 for an overall view of the Query Designer. You can work in a graphical mode or a SQL mode, depending on your preference. For example, you can enter SQL and execute it against an ODBC data source, thus using the Query Designer as an interactive query tool. The Diagram pane displays the input sources (tables or views) that you are querying. You add input sources to the diagram pane by dragging them from the Data View window. Each input source appears in its own window, showing the available data columns as well as icons that indicate how each column is used in the query. Joins are indicated by lines between the input source windows. The Grid pane contains a spreadsheet-like grid in which you specify query options, such as which data columns to display, how to order the results, what rows to select, how to group rows, and so on. The SQL pane displays the SQL statement for the current query. You can either edit the SQL statement created by the Query Designer or enter your own. The Results pane shows a grid with the results of the most recently executed query. You can modify the database by editing values in the cells of the grid, and you can add or delete rows.

Although the database designer is SQL-Server-specific, the Query Designer is ODBC-generic, meaning that all the SQL generated by the Query Designer can run against any database that supports ODBC, such as SQL Server, Microsoft Jet, FoxPro, Oracle, Sybase, Informix, DB2, etc. As you can see in File View, once you've created and saved some queries, queries are local objects that are usually local to your project and not known to the database, unlike database diagrams, which are shared among all users of your database.

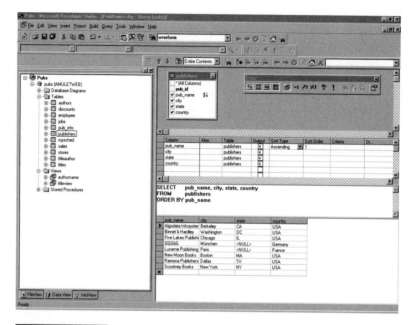

Figure 8-35   *The Query Designer*

You can create a query by working in all the panes together. For example, you can specify a column to display in the query results by choosing it in the Diagram pane, entering it into the Grid pane, or making it part of the SQL statement in the SQL pane. The Diagram, Grid, and SQL panes are synchronized; when you make a change in one pane, the Query Designer updates the other panes to reflect the change. This way, the Query Designer can represent your query using both graphics (in the Diagram and Grid panes) and text (in the SQL pane).

Diagram Pane

The Diagram pane is the primary component of the Query Designer for creating new queries. It is visually similar to the Database Diagram tool described earlier in this chapter. Now take a look at using the Diagram pane to build a specific query against the SQL Server Pubs sample database. Begin by going to File view, right-click on the pubs database connection, and then select New Query. You need some tables to populate the query, so choose authors, titles, titleauthor, and sales. To do so, you can drag and drop the tables on the Diagram pane. Notice that the Query Designer inspects the meta-data from the database and automatically determines all the relationships between the tables. You can even see the chosen join type (e.g., inner join) and join expression by hovering the mouse over the join type icon that appears in the

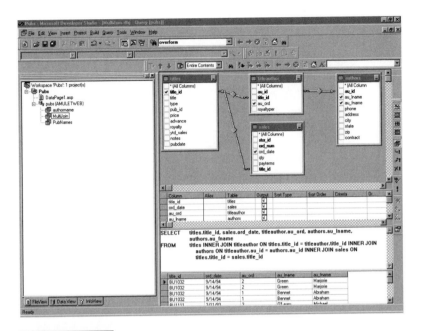

Figure 8–36   *Joined Tables in the Design Pane*

middle of the line joining the two tables. Meanwhile, in the SQL pane, the actual SQL statements for the joins appear. Figure 8-36 illustrates the screen at this point.

The Diagram pane supports multiple undo/redo requests so that you can experiment with ad-hoc queries, test their results, and easily return to previous states. The Diagram and the SQL panes are also two-way tools, where changes in one always affect the other. For example, you may manually type in SQL statements in the SQL pane, and immediately see the graphical representation in the Diagram pane.

The next step is to run the query. The query is sent back to the server, which in turn processes the query and returns the results back to the Output pane. If you then change the SQL or graphical display, the results pane turns gray, indicating that the results are stale. In other words, the results no longer match the SQL. Queries are not automatically run again after a change, since running queries against the server can be expensive. You can also check whether you've entered valid SQL syntax without running the query, by selecting the *Verify SQL Syntax* option from the Query menu. It takes the SQL and sends a prepare back to the server. If you have server-specific SQL that the query tool does not necessarily understand or parse, it can verify it against the back-end database. If, for example, you're using an Oracle-specific construct, the server will verify the SQL syntax for you. Visual InterDev queries are stored in text format and saved to a project workspace window. You can create views of queries, which are maintained on the server.

QUERY DESIGNER TOOLBAR

The Query Designer has a special toolbar containing icons providing special functionality for the creation of queries. The toolbar appears in Figure 8-36 in the Diagram pane next to the publishers table. You have the ability to customize the Query Designer elements shown on the screen using these icons: *Show Diagram Pane*, *Show Grid Pane*, *Show SQL Pane*, and *Show Results Pane*. You can also use the toolbar to create different types of new queries by selecting these icons: *Create Select Query* (SQL SELECT statement), *Create Insert Query* (SQL INSERT statement), *Create Update Query* (SQL UPDATE statement), and *Create Delete Query* (SQL DELETE statement). Other available icons are: *Verify SQL Syntax*, *Run*, *Remove Filter*, *Sort Ascending*, *Sort Descending*, and *Properties*.

The Remove Filter button is activated once you specify an expression in the Criteria column in the Grid Pane. For example, you might enter >0 in the cell on the ytd_sales row. Note: this button is active only when you click on the field in the Diagram Pane that has a criteria. Clicking on the button erases the criteria expression from the Grid Pane and removes the appropriate part of the SQL WHERE clause in the SQL Pane.

The Sort Ascending and Sort Descending icons are used in conjunction with the Diagram pane. To sort the query results by a particular field, click on the desired field in the Diagram pane, and then click on one of these buttons in the toolbar. You'll see a special symbol next to the field, and the SQL is automatically modified to include an ORDER BY clause to match the new sort.

The Properties icon displays a small property list for the query, consisting of a two-tabbed dialog box. The first tab is *Query*, with two check box properties, *Output all columns* and *Distinct values*. Checking the first property adds an * to the field list of the SELECT statement, indicating that all columns should be included in the resultset. Checking the second property adds the DISTINCT keyword to the SELECT statement. The second tab is *Parameters*, which lets you specify special prefix, suffix, and escape characters recognized by the database you're using.

JOINS • Five types of joins are supported by the Query Designer (each having its own icon that appears on the line used to join the two tables together): Inner Join, Inner Join using the greater than sign, Left Outer Join, Right Outer Join, and Full Outer Join. You also have four possible types of relationships between two tables: one-to-one, one-to-many, many-to-one, and undefined. To change a specific join's type, right-click on the join line in the Diagram Pane to bring up a shortcut menu and then click on Properties. You now see the *Join Line* dialog box, which has the two fields participating in the join, a list of relational operators — =, >, >=, <, <=, and <>—and two check boxes used to indicate which side of the join should accept all the records. Specifying different combinations of these items yields different graphical representations of the join in the Diagram Pane and different SQL keywords in the SQL Pane. For example, say that you want to change the join type between the titles and sales tables from an inner join using the fields titles.title_id and sales.title_id to a left outer join. By default, the Query Designer creates inner joins, so you must use this dialog box to change the type of join. In the dialog box, check the box labeled *All rows from titles*. The SQL join terminology is not used in this dialog box; it uses English instead in an attempt to reinforce the meaning of the different join types. Notice that the keywords change from INNER JOIN to LEFT OUTER JOIN in the SQL Pane. Now select the less than operator, <, instead of the equal sign, =, in order to specify how the key fields are to be related.

Grid Pane

The Grid Pane provides a tabular representation of all the elements of the query. Each row in the grid represents a column in the resultset, and each column in the grid describes each column in a specific way. The following is a list of each column in the grid: *Column, Alias, Table, Output, Sort Type, Sort Order, Criteria*, and multiple *Or* columns.

The Column grid pane column holds the field name to be referenced on this line of the Grid Pane. The Table column holds the name of the table from which the field comes. The Alias column contains the alternate name by which you wish to refer to the field. Specifying an alias generates an AS keyword in the resulting SQL statement as in: titles.ytd_sales AS YearlySales. Checking the Output box specifies that the field should be included in the resultset. The Sort Type has two options: Ascending or Descending. Sort Order specifies the sort priority for data columns used to sort the resultset. When you change the sort order for a data column, the sort order for all other columns is updated accordingly. The Criteria column allows you to specify an expression to use in determining whether a record should be included in the resultset. For example, specifying the expression <=20000 for the titles.ytd_sales field would limit the resultset to records having year-to-date sales less than or equal to $20,000. The Grid Pane also has a number of additional columns to the right of the Criteria column. Each column is labeled with the word Or. You can simply add additional expressions in each column to define more complex selection criteria. As you specify additional expressions, notice how the resulting SQL is affected.

You can also change the query to a "group by" query by selecting the *Group By* option in the query menu. This adds another column in the Grid Pane called Group By, which has a combo box containing the following items: Group By, Min, Max, Count, Expression, and Where. The GROUP BY clause is added to the generated SQL statement.

SQL Pane

In addition to creating queries in the Diagram and Grid panes, you can enter SQL statements directly into the SQL pane. When you move to another pane, the Query Designer parses the SQL statement and synchronizes the other panes to reflect the new statement. The SQL pane is particularly useful for entering code that cannot be created through the Diagram and Grid panes. For example, you can create a SQL statement in the SQL pane to create a Union query, which is not supported in the graphical panes.

To help you create queries, the SQL pane automatically formats your SQL statement. In addition, after you have finished entering the statement, you can send it to the database to verify that its syntax is correct. If you create a SQL statement that cannot be represented in the diagram and Grid panes, the Query Designer grays those panes to indicate that they no longer reflect the state of the current query.

Executing the Query

When you have finished designing your query, you can run it by clicking on the Run icon from the Query Designer toolbar. Another way to run a query is by right-clicking in the Results Pane. This action displays the shortcut menu for the Results Pane, enabling you to choose Run from the menu item list. If you're creating a Select query, you can view the results in the Results pane. The Query Designer runs a Select query in small batches incrementally, so that you can begin viewing rows immediately and so that you can perform other tasks while the query is underway. If you're creating an action query such as an Insert, Update, or Delete query, running the query will affect rows in the underlying tables. The Query Designer displays a message box indicating how many rows were affected by the action query.

If you change the current query using either the Grid Pane or SQL Pane, the Query Designer grays out the contents of the Results Pane to indicate that the results no longer reflect the current query. You can, however, still navigate in the Results Pane to view the results of the previous query. In addition, you can still use the Results pane to edit data in the resultset of the most recently executed query.

Stored Procedures

One very important component of a growing number of WebTop applications that use a back-end relational database is the *stored procedure*. Stored procedures are pre-compiled program modules that are stored in the database. Stored procedures can be entered and maintained through the project's Data View. They can contain multiple SQL statements, as well as logical programming constructs such as looping, variables, conditional logic, and recursion. Since stored procedures are compiled, they execute more quickly than individual SQL statements. Stored procedures can also be used to precisely control access to your database. Row-returning stored procedures can be used as a row source or record source for a Web application. You can use the database's security to prevent users from issuing updates directly to a table, and then grant them execute permissions on a stored procedure that updates the table only after logical validations have been passed.

A stored procedure is written in a special-purpose language that includes standard SQL statements, for the purpose of automating commonly needed database processing. For Microsoft SQL Server, the stored procedure language is called *Transact-SQL*. I have found this language to be seriously lacking in many respects; specifically, it does not have commonly accepted language constructs such as arrays, flexible expressions, and operators, and several quirky characteristics detract from the actual programming task. For these reasons, the next version of SQL Server will provide stored procedure programming in Visual Basic, Java, or both. This change would be welcome.

Stored Procedure Editor

Visual InterDev gives the developer an integrated means for creating and maintaining stored procedures called from WebTop applications. The *stored procedure editor* included in Visual InterDev is the same source code editor for all members of the Developers Studio family. Although SQL Server Enterprise Manager also has a stored procedure editor, the one found in Visual InterDev is superior. You can use the stored procedure editor to create, edit, and run stored procedures, functions, triggers, and ODBC script files and view their results.

When you create a stored procedure in Visual InterDev, it appears in the Stored Procedures folder in Data View. You can extend a stored procedure in Data View to see a list of the parameters it contains, and if it is a row-returning stored procedure, you can see the names of columns that it returns. If you have a row-returning stored procedure that is parameterized, make sure that you include default values for the parameters; this measure will allow you to see the names of the return columns in Data view without running the stored procedure.

Look at an example of using the stored procedure editor. First, I want you to create a new stored procedure. Begin by clicking on the data tab and finding the Stored Procedure folder. Right-clicking displays the shortcut menu. Choose New Stored Procedure from the list of menu items. The stored procedure editor opens and presents a template for creating your new stored procedure. Instead of entering the T-SQL code for the procedure yourself, take an easy way out, by using an existing query.

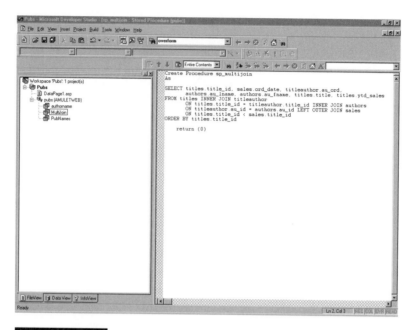

A New Stored Procedure Borrowing SQL from a Query

You want to define a row-returning stored procedure such as a simple SELECT statement. The query will be used frequently from the WebTop application, so you want it pre-compiled by the database so that performance is good. One way to do so is to extract the SQL property from a query object by copying and pasting the contents of the SQL Grid to the stored procedure editor. Use the multi-table join example I used in the previous section. Figure 8-37 shows the new stored procedure, sp_multijoin, that contains the SQL from this query. Now save the procedure and then run it. I discuss executing a stored procedure in the next section. In this example, you started with the Query Designer and extracted an SQL statement that is reusable in different places. Once created, a stored procedure can be called from a data command object in ADO code on an ASP Web page.

Executing Stored Procedures

Once you have created and saved your stored procedure, you should test the procedure to ensure that it produces the desired results. You can execute the procedure from within the stored procedure editor by right-clicking the mouse anywhere within the stored procedure. Choose Run from the list of menu items, or you can select the Run item from the Tools menu. If an error is in your procedure, the stored procedure debugger displays an error message indicating the problem. If no errors are found, the result is displayed in the

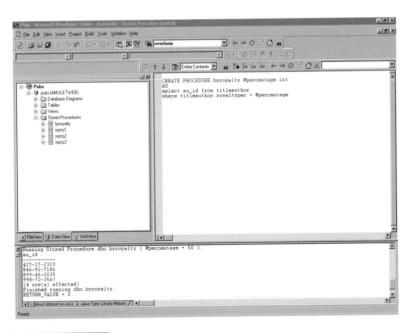

Figure 8-38   *Executing a Sample Stored Procedure*

Output window at the bottom of the Visual InterDev project workspace. Figure 8-38 shows the execution of a sample stored procedure, byroyalty, which is included with the pubs database.

Even if the stored procedure executes without an error, you still need to make sure that the stored procedure returned the expected results. A runtime error-free procedure does not mean that the results are accurate. You need to test the procedure to make sure that it meets your application requirements both now and in the future. A stored procedure is normally shared among the Web application developers. Develop these procedures with reuse in mind, so that they can be universally applied across the application. Do not make the functionality of a stored procedure so specialized that it benefits only one developer or one application.

ODBC Script Files

You can also use the Visual InterDev source code editor to create, modify, and run *ODBC script files*. Unlike stored procedures, ODBC script files are stored in the file system, in a file with a .SQL extension, not in the database. They are not pre-compiled and therefore don't execute as quickly as stored procedures. The advantage of ODBC script files is that they can be easily executed against many different databases. To create an ODBC script file, select New from the File menu, click on the Files tab, and select ODBC script file.

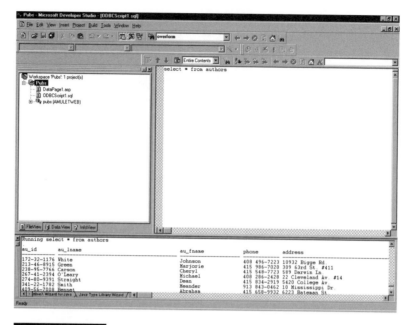

Figure 8–39   *Running an ODBC Script File*

The Visual InterDev source code editor now opens. You can enter any valid script that your database can understand.

As an example of creating and executing an ODBC script file against a database, create a new ODBC script file or open an existing script file using the Open command on the File menu. Any existing ODBC script files also appear in File View underneath the project name. In Data View, select the data connection against which you want to run your script file. Right-click in the text of the script file and select Run from the menu. If your Data View is connected to multiple databases, you can execute your script file in another database by simply selecting it in Data View and selecting Run again. The results from your script file are displayed in the Output window. You can use this method to execute a script file generated by the Database Designer to mirror changes made in one database to another. Figure 8-39 depicts a simple ODBC script run against the authors table in the pubs database.

Scalability

Visual InterDev delivers the scalability required for mission-critical, database-enabled Web sites through ease of use and extensive visual tools. For example, global database connections can be established for an entire site, and IIS will automatically pool these database connections across users. Pooling, connection caching, and time-out values are all established automatically based on default properties, but they can also easily be customized by a developer. Visual InterDev also makes connecting to multiple heterogeneous databases within a Web site easy, returning or updating data that has been visually integrated within a single HTML page for a Web site visitor.

For example, Visual InterDev can be used to return data from an Oracle database running on a UNIX server, as well as data from a SQL Server database running on Windows NT, all integrated within a single HTML page to satisfy a user request. In addition, based on ODBC support, a workgroup version of an intranet application can easily be designed on desktop databases, such as Microsoft Access or Visual FoxPro, and then easily be scaled up to a server-based database such as Microsoft SQL Server, without requiring complex code changes.

Summary

Microsoft Visual InterDev is a very valuable tool for anyone developing a Web database on the Wintel platform. Its complement of component design tools such as the Database Designer and the Query Designer makes the process of including data connections on a Web page a relatively simple task. Furthermore, the concept of design-time ActiveX controls is a compelling technology that seems to be open-ended in its ability to provide automated means for generating ADO and HTML code. The fact that these controls can be developed using Visual Basic is very encouraging and opens the door for new useful design-time controls. Finally, Visual InterDev is simply an excellent tool for maintaining SQL Server relational databases.

Publishing Desktop Databases

In prior chapters, I've used a variety of technologies such as ASP, ADO, Visual InterDev, HTML, client-side scripts, Java, and CGI to develop interactive WebTop applications containing database-querying and updating capabilities against SQL data sources. These techniques dealt with using ODBC as the conduit to these data sources, which live in back-end SQL databases. Much corporate data, however, is not found in SQL databases. Some information, especially for the smaller organization or department in a large enterprise, is found in desktop databases maintained by a single user or small workgroup of users. Many times, benefit is derived from publishing this kind of data on the Web.

You can follow two general approaches towards basing WebTop applications around this kind of data. First, you can use the ODBC desktop drivers by setting up a data source name to have your Web application directly connect to a desktop database in order to process query requests. In this chapter, you see the steps required for this approach. Second, I discuss how you may publish information found in corporate databases using far simpler techniques that do not involve any interactivity. Instead of dynamically generating data pages as the result of an online query, the site's pages are manually produced and updated on the server on a periodic basis by IS department staff, reflecting the current state of the data. Although this sort of implementation is not as easy to use as the interactive methods discussed in this book thus far, it does offer a vastly more cost-effective alternative that is attractive to the smaller organization having only a simple Web site hosted by an ISP, a dial-up connection to the Internet, and no on-site Web server. This technique addresses the needs of companies with considerably smaller budgets for publishing frequently updated information on the Net. Besides, with well thought-out structuring of the HTML pages, simple point-and-click queries could be devised (e.g., drill-down structure where users click on small groups of hypertext options fashioned in a tree hierarchy to find information).

Although my discussions here will center around using Microsoft JET Engine databases, you can easily extrapolate the concepts to include data existing in many other desktop databases, such as .DBF files, or the database file structure used in Xbase languages, most notably Microsoft Visual FoxPro.

Microsoft Access as an ODBC Data Source

One of the first thoughts a desktop or LAN database developer has with regard to the Web is how to publish his or her Microsoft Access (or other desktop database) for online users to query and browse. You see later how you can use the integrated components in Access 97 to publish static result-sets in HTML; but what if you wish to provide active content features on your Web site where users can pose queries against the actual Access database? In the construction of a site like this, the database development tool, such as those discussed in prior chapters in this book, would need to attach to an ODBC data source. Luckily, you can define an ODBC data source that points to an Access database file (.MDB file). In this section, I go through the steps required to establish this data source and connect it up with a typical Web development tool for the purpose of defining queries.

To begin, move the .MDB database file containing your data (i.e., assuming that you've already used the Database Splitter Add-in included with Access 97 to produce separate code and data .MDB files) to a directory on your Web server. For example, if your database application code (query, form, report, macro, and module) and data (table objects) both exist in a database file named Project.MDB, after running the *Database Splitter* tool, you will have two .MDB files named Project.MDB and Project_be.MDB (the be_ suffix stands for "back end"). For the latter file, an ODBC data source must be defined.

Next, go into your NT server's Control Panel and open the *32-bit ODBC* icon. Clicking on the Drivers button in the Data Sources dialog box shows you all the installed ODBC desktop drivers. You should see an entry in the drivers list labeled *Microsoft Access Driver (*.mdb)*. This is the driver I'll be using for the balance of the chapter. You should also see a number of other drivers you could use for publishing desktop databases, including: dBASE, Excel™, FoxPro, Paradox and Text drivers. All of these drivers are located in the ODBCJT32.DLL, the Microsoft ODBC Desktop Driver Pack 3.5. Two other drivers you may see in the list are for Oracle™ and SQL Server, which are for defining data sources in these back-end relational databases. Figure 9-1 shows the ODBC driver list dialog box. Although I don't consider examples of using

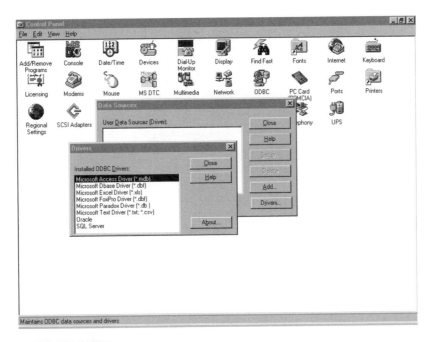

Figure 9-1   *ODBC Desktop Driver List Dialog Box*

these other drivers, they do provide you with the ability to publish data stored in the most popular desktop database environments today.

Since I am publishing data on the Web and not for a specific set of users, I need to define a *System Data Source* (a feature available with ODBC 2.5 and 3.0). Clicking on the System DSN button in the Data Sources dialog box yields the System Data Source dialog box. Initially, the list should contain no data sources. You must click on the Add button in order to begin the definition process. The Add Data Source dialog box that appears next contains a list of all installed ODBC drivers. You should locate the Microsoft Access Driver and select it. You should now see the ODBC Microsoft Access 97 Setup dialog box (see Figure 9-2), which lets you provide a data source name and description. With the Select button, you can then browse your disks to locate the .MDB file to provide data as an ODBC resource.

A data source can be set up with a system data source name (DSN) that can be used by more than one user on the same machine. The system DSN can also be used by a system-wide service, which can then gain access to the data source even if no user is logged onto the machine.

Table 9-1 contains all the various controls (e.g., text boxes, check boxes, etc.) found in the ODBC Setup dialog box upon clicking on the Options button, and is provided here to serve as a reference for defining new desktop

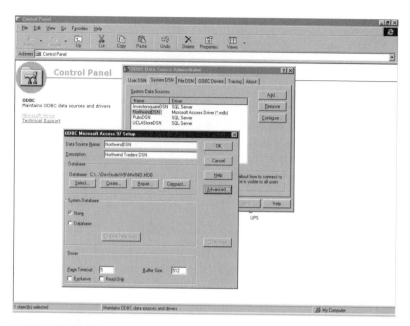

Figure 9-2   *ODBC Microsoft Access 97 Setup Dialog Box*

database data sources. Many controls are specific to the driver being used and appear in the dialog box only when referencing certain drivers. The driver(s) pertaining to each control are also noted in the table. Although I primarily focus on Access and SQL Server in this chapter, you may use a variety of data sources. The information in Table 9-1 will prove useful in such cases.

Table 9-1   ODBC Setup Dialog Controls

Control	Description
Approximate Row Count	This control is displayed only for the dBASE and FoxPro drivers. The control determines whether table size statistics are approximated.
Buffer Size	The size of the internal buffer, in kilobytes, that is used by Microsoft Access to transfer data to and from the disk. The default buffer size is 512K (displayed as 512).
Collating Sequence	This control is displayed only for the dBASE, Microsoft FoxPro, and Paradox drivers. The control contains the sequence in which the fields are sorted. When the dBASE or Microsoft FoxPro driver is used, the sequence can be ASCII or International. When the Paradox driver is used, the sequence can be ASCII, International, Swedish-Finnish, or Norwegian-Danish.

....

Table 9–1	ODBC Setup Dialog Controls (Continued)
Control	**Description**
Data Source Name	A name that identifies the data source, such as "Inventory" or "Human Resources Records."
Database	This control is displayed only for the Microsoft Access driver. The control contains the full path of the Microsoft Access database you want to access. Use the *Select* button to select an existing database. Use the *Create* button to create and select a new Access database. A Microsoft Access data source can be set up without selecting or creating a database. If no database is provided upon setup, the user is prompted to choose a database file when connecting to the data source. Use the *Repair* button to repair a damaged database. Use the *Compact* button to compact a database.
Define Format	This control is displayed only for the Text driver. The control displays the Define Text Format dialog box and enables you to specify the schema for individual tables in the data source directory.
Description	An optional description of what the data source contains; for example, "Accounting Data," "Western Region Sales History," or "Alumni Association Member Information."
Directory	Displays the currently selected directory. Before you add the data source, you must either use the Select Directory button to select a directory, or select the Use Current Directory check box to use the application's current working directory. This control does not apply to the Microsoft Access driver. Note: for Microsoft Excel 3.0/4.0 files, the path display is labeled "Directory," whereas for Microsoft Excel 5.0 files, the path display is labeled "Workbook."
Exclusive	This control is displayed only for the Access, dBASE, FoxPro, and Paradox drivers. If the Exclusive box is selected, the database will be opened in *Exclusive* mode and can be accessed by only one user at a time. If the Exclusive box is empty, the database will be opened in *Shared* mode and can be accessed by more than one user at a time. Performance is enhanced when running in Exclusive mode.
Extensions List	This control is displayed only for the Text driver. The control lists the file name extensions of the text files on the data source. To use all files in the directory, select the Default (*.*) check box. To use only those files with certain extensions, clear the Default (*.*) check box and add each extension you want to use. To add an extension, type the extension in the Extension box and click the Add button. The extension must be of the correct form, for example, .dat or .txt. You may also remove extensions from the Extension List with the Remove button. Removing all extensions is equivalent to checking the Default (*.*) check box: all files will be displayed.

Table 9–1	ODBC Setup Dialog Controls (Continued)
Control	**Description**
Network Directory	This control is displayed only for the Paradox driver. The control has the path of the directory containing the PDOXUSRS.net file. If the directory does not contain a PDOXUSRS.net file, the Paradox driver creates one. Before you can select a network directory, you must enter your Paradox user name in the User Name text box. Use the Select Network Directory button to select a network directory.
Page Time Out	This control is displayed only for the dBASE, Microsoft Access, Microsoft FoxPro, and Paradox drivers. It specifies the period of time, in tenths of a second, that a page (if not used) remains in the buffer before being removed. The default is 600 tenths of a second (60 seconds).
Read Only	This control specifies the database as read-only.
Rows to Scan	This control applies only to the Microsoft Excel and Text drivers. The control contains the number of rows to scan to determine the data type of each column. The data type is determined, given the maximum number of kinds of data found. If data is encountered that does not match the data type guessed for the column, the data type will be returned as a NULL value. For the Microsoft Excel driver, allowable values are from 1 to 16 for the rows to scan. For the Text driver, you may enter values from 1 to 32767. The default value for both drivers is 1.
Select Directory	This control is displayed only for the dBASE, Excel, FoxPro, Paradox, and Text drivers. The control displays a dialog box where you can select a directory containing the files you want to access. When defining a data source directory (for all drivers except Microsoft Access), specify the directory where your most commonly used files are located. The ODBC driver uses this directory as the default directory. Copy other files into this directory if they are used frequently. Alternatively, you can qualify file names in a SELECT statement with the directory name: SELECT * FROM C:\ACCT\CLIENTS.
Select Indexes	This control is displayed only for the dBASE and FoxPro drivers. The control displays the Select Indexes dialog box, with which you can associate dBASE or FoxPro files with index files. The Select Indexes dialog box contains the following fields: tables, indexes, and list files of type, enabling you to associate an index with a table. Note: the ODBC dBASE and FoxPro drivers do not support Clipper™ .NTX index files.
Show Deleted Rows	This control is displayed only for the dBASE and FoxPro drivers. The control specifies whether or not rows that have been marked as deleted should be displayed.
Sort Order	This control is displayed only for the Microsoft Access drivers. The control sets a default sort order for the database.

Table 9–1	ODBC Setup Dialog Controls (Continued)
Control	**Description**
System Database	This control is displayed only for the Microsoft Access drivers. It contains the full path of the Microsoft Access system database to be used with the Microsoft Access database you want to access. Click on the System Database option button to select the system database to be used. The ODBC Microsoft Access driver prompts the user for a name and password. The default name is Admin, and the default password in Microsoft Access for the Admin user is an empty string. To increase the security of your Microsoft Access database, create a new user to replace the Admin user and delete the Admin user, or change the objects to which the Admin user has access. Select the None option button if no system database will be used. Select the None option button to log into the Microsoft Access database as the Admin user; no system database will be used.
Use Control Directory	This control is displayed only for the dBASE, Excel, Microsoft FoxPro, Paradox, and Text drivers. When selected, the control makes the application's current working directory the data source directory and disables the Select Directory option.
User Name	This control is displayed only for the Paradox driver. The control contains the Paradox user name.
Version	This control enables you to select the version of the files used.
Workbook	This control is displayed only for the Microsoft Excel 5.0 driver; it displays the currently selected workbook. Before you add the data source, you must click on the Select Workbook button to select a directory. Worksheets within workbooks are treated as System Tables. Defined or named ranges within a worksheet are treated as Tables.

Using an ODBC Data Source

Now take a look at how you can use an ODBC data source to publish an Access desktop database on the Web. For this illustration, I continue to use the familiar Microsoft Access sample database, Northwind Traders. I plan to attach it to a Web application structured around the Microsoft dbWeb tool. dbWeb is a freeware database publishing tool available for no charge from the Microsoft Web site. The tool comes complete with an administrative tool, an NT ISAPI component, a tutorial, and sample files. Figure 9-3 shows the dbWeb Administrator, which provides a means for building and maintaining Web database schemas. I've actually created a new schema named NWIND, which is listed in the Data Sources dialog. If you select this name and then click on Modify datasource, you see the dialog box in the foreground dialog box entitled *Data Source [NWIND]*. This is where you specify the ODBC DSN,

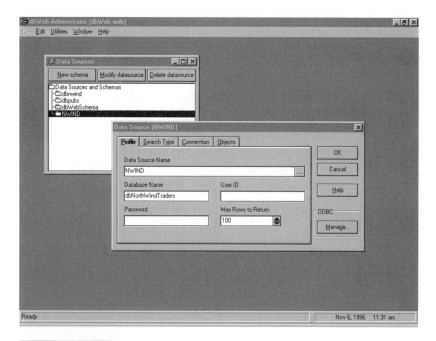

Figure 9–3   *dbWeb Administrator*

as well as the database name dbNorthWindTraders. Once attached, the set of tables found in the database can be used as the basis of live Web query forms such as the one shown in Figure 9-4.

Inefficiencies Using Desktop ODBC Data Sources

The above section demonstrates that you certainly can base a WebTop application around a desktop database such as Access. But you should consider the penalties and limitations of doing so. When a Web server hits a database to process a query request, from the perspective of the database, the Web server is just another client. The database doesn't know that a special kind of client is asking for information. The purpose of a database, regardless of the environment, is to receive query requests and send out results. In a normal file server environment found on a LAN, if you want to share an Access database, you simply put the data component (.MDB file) on the file server and the users each run a copy of Access and the code component (another .MDB file) on their local PCs. The tables are linked and open across the network. In this architecture, Access launches on the client's computer, and the application reaches across the file system and locks individual pages in the file system to provide multi-user concurrency. This scenario works great and is reasonably scaleable; you could have 15–25 concurrent users hitting the data-

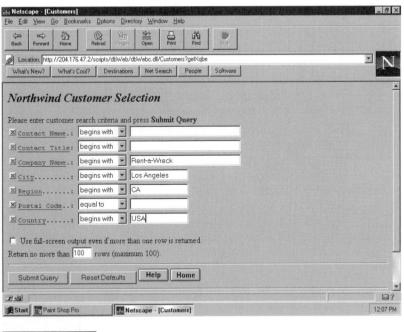

Figure 9-4   *Web Query Form with ODBC Data Source*

base. If you're using FoxPro, you could get upwards of 80–100 users and still have reasonably good performance, because this product pushes the limits of scalability of the file server database model. The bottom line is that the computing power for managing the database is distributed among the users on their desktop PCs.

Now I want to switch focus to the Web. What's happening at runtime is that all the database users have client browsers that fire query requests to the Web server. For each of those users, the Web server creates a separate session into the database. The issue here is that the size of those sessions, the size of the in-memory component that the Web server needs to track each user, becomes important. What this means is for a WebTop database application using a desktop database normally well suited for a file server architecture, the Web server needs to launch a separate instance of the engine itself for every user that comes in. From the point of view of the database, it may be receiving 10 concurrent client requests. The only thing that's changed is that the Web server now has 10 copies of that application running in its memory. So it's not as scaleable as one would like in the case of a large Web site with, say, 100–150 concurrent users hitting the database. The desire is for the client-side piece (in this case, the piece that is running on the Web server) to be very small. A server database such as SQL Server will supply this small footprint and provide increased performance.

Microsoft Access 97 Upsizing Tools

As evidenced in "Microsoft Access as an ODBC Data Source," earlier, publishing an Access database on the Web is a reality and a logical choice if simplicity of design warrants it. As you saw, an Access database itself can be set up as an ODBC data source and be the target of online Web transactions. Here, the Access file server system is being extended to accommodate the client-server architecture, however, without all the high-performance features normally associated with client-server database software (more on these features in a moment). A point does come when moving to a more robust relational database environment, such as SQL Server, becomes justified. Aside from the limitations mentioned in the previous section, some possible reasons for this transition might be the need to handle a larger number of concurrent users; the need for advanced features like fault tolerance, live backups, and transaction logging; or the need to embed business logic at the database level through use of stored procedures and triggers. Whatever the reason, upsizing from the file-server model to the client-server model of computing requires a special tool for porting the data, indexes, and other facets of database design into a SQL database.

Fortunately, such a vehicle exists for making this transition. It is called the *Microsoft Access Upsizing Tools* and is an Access add-in composed of two separate components: a *SQL Server Browser* that lets you view objects in a SQL Server database and an *Upsizing Wizard* that walks you through the steps to move your data from Access to SQL Server. You can obtain the tools free of charge, by downloading them from the Microsoft Web site, www.microsoft.com/accessdev. Look in the "Free Stuff" link for this and other free tools. The tools are compatible only with Access 8.0 for Windows 95/98 and SQL Server versions 4.21, 6.0, 6.5, and 7.0, although old versions of the tools may still be available for Access 95 and Access 2.0.

Once you have run the setup program and the tools are installed, you see two new components listed in your *Add-ins* list. With a database opened, select Add-ins from the Tools menu and you now see: *SQL Server Browser* and *Upsize to SQL Server*. First turn your attention to the upsizing process, since it is the crucial step towards publishing desktop databases on the Web; however, I return to a brief discussion of the browser later, because reviewing table contents is useful for an Access developer, once the contents reside in SQL Server.

Upsizing Wizard

The Upsizing Wizard offers a step-by-step approach for creating a SQL Server database based on the structure and data in an Access .MDB file. The wizard's primary job is as a conduit to the client-server environment; however, for our purposes, it is also for populating a Web database based on SQL Server. If moving an Access application from a file-server approach to client-server, the main idea is to keep an Access application intact (i.e., the code objects function unaltered) after moving the data to SQL Server. With respect to the Web, however, although keeping the original application intact is important, the real goal is to move the data to SQL Server so that another application, a WebTop application, can more efficiently access it.

The Wizard can upsize any tables in your database, along with the relationships between them. It supports several new SQL Server 6.x features, including *Declarative Referential Integrity* (DRI) and the identity data type, SQL Server's equivalent to the Access Auto-number type. You can choose to upsize to an existing SQL Server database or create a new one. The Upsizing Wizard also creates a report showing what happened during the process, including any errors that may have occurred meanwhile (in certain cases, however, these error messages leave much to be desired).

To start the upsizing process, select *Upsize to SQL Server* from the Add-ins list. See Figure 9-5 for the wizard's opening dialog box, which asks whether you want to use an existing SQL Server database or create a new one. If you choose to use an existing database, the Upsizing Wizard prompts you to select and log into an ODBC data source. The login required is standard for ODBC data sources, where you must enter the user name and password that were defined when you first created the data source (see the previous section of this chapter). The wizard proceeds to create all new objects in the database specified in this data source. If you want to create a new database, you're required to provide answers to several more questions, as you see in the following discussion.

CREATE NEW SQL SERVER DATABASE

If you decide to build a new SQL Server database, you must first log in and then select the SQL Server device in which the new database will be created. In SQL Server terms, a *database device* is an object on the server similar to the database container object (.MDB file) in Access, except that devices can store multiple databases, not only multiple tables. I recommend that you create separate devices for only related databases possessing roughly related functionality. Figure 9-6 shows the device selection dialog box, which also displays the space available on each device on the selected server. You'll find two combo boxes here, one for the *database device* and the other for the *transaction log device*. At this point, you can select which device to use for the database and which device to use for the log, along with their sizes. With large databases, generally you want to place the log on a separate device, preferably on a separate physical drive. This separation helps protect against critical hardware failures.

If you do not have enough space on any available device, you can create a new device on the server by selecting the *<New Device>* option from

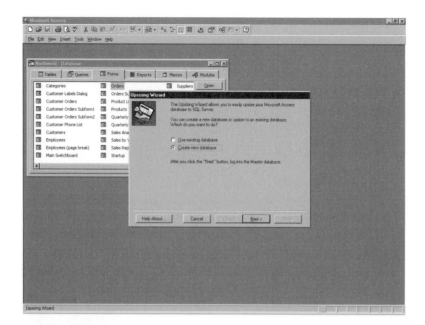

Figure 9–5 *Upsizing Wizard Opening Dialog Box*

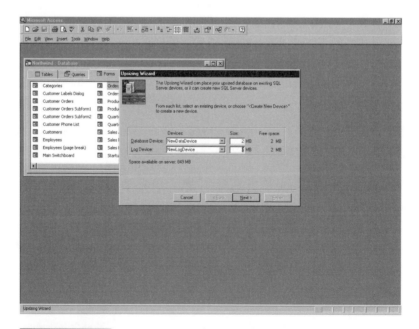

Figure 9–6 *Database Device Selection Dialog Box*

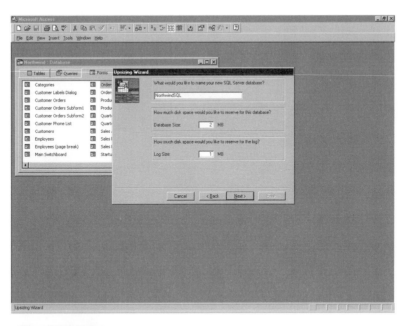

Figure 9–7 *Database Selection Dialog Box*

the combo box. The Upsizing Wizard then prompts for a new device name and the desired size. The new device is placed in the same directory as the master device.

After selecting the device, you're prompted for a name and size for the database (see Figure 9-7). The Upsizing Wizard suggests a name, but you can enter a name of your own. Keep in mind that when choosing a name for your database, SQL Server has more restrictions on names than Access does. When specifying the size of the database and its associated log, the general rule is to make the log about 20 percent of the size of the database.

SELECTING TABLES AND UPSIZING OPTIONS

Now that a database has been chosen, you need to tell the Upsizing Wizard which tables in the current Access database you wish to upsize. Figure 9-8 shows the multiple selection dialog box used for this purpose. From here, you can select one or more tables from the list to upsize at once. After selecting the tables, you're presented with other options that control how the wizard handles your data. See Figure 9-9 for this dialog box and associated options. You'll find that the wizard assigns default values for options in this dialog box that make the most sense for your configuration. The wizard handles the upsizing of all table and field-level attributes such as indexes, validation rules and associated validation text, default values, and table relationships.

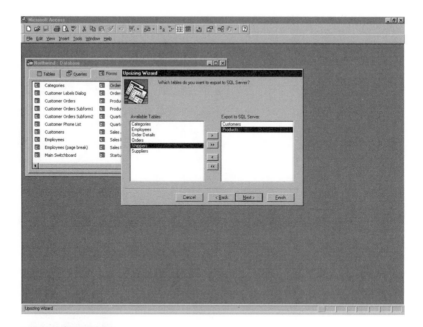

Figure 9–8   *Table Selection Dialog Box*

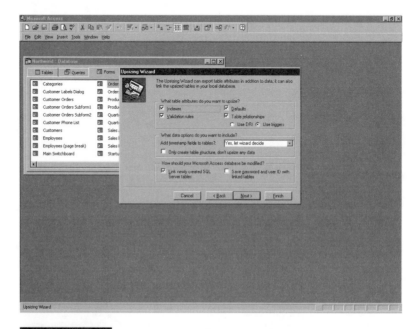

Figure 9–9   *Upsizing Wizard Option Dialog Box*

Although you normally want the wizard to upsize as many characteristics of your Access database as possible so that it more closely emulates the original behavior, you may select all, some, or none of these attributes by checking the appropriate boxes. If you choose to preserve the table relationships in the new SQL Server database, the wizard gives you two options, DRI or triggers, to enforce the relationships. DRI specifies relationships as part of the table design, appearing as clauses in the SQL CREATE TABLE statement. SQL Server's database engine can then enforce referential integrity between related tables. Triggers, although not as strong as DRI, also serve to enforce referential integrity. Triggers are SQL statements that run only when data is changed. You can also use triggers if you want cascading update and delete functionality, since DRI does not support these features.

Also included in this dialog box is a table design option that controls the creation of SQL Server time stamp fields. You can select one of three ways to handle time stamps: "No, never," "Yes, let wizard decide," and "Yes, always." The second option uses time stamps only if the table contains OLE, memo, or floating-point fields. When a time stamp field is added to a table, SQL Server automatically updates its value when a record is changed. In the case where the upsized tables are still part of a local application running on a LAN centered around a Web server, time stamp fields allow the Microsoft JET database engine to tell easily whether a record has been updated by another user before it is committed. This problem is common in multi-user applications. Without time stamp fields, JET must compare data field by field, which could result in poor performance. With time stamp fields, performance is better in an update-intensive application.

You also have the option to upsize only the structure of your database, without any data, and create links to the newly created SQL Server tables. The latter option provides the most seamless transition to SQL Server, because any existing queries, forms, and reports that depend on the old tables can instantly use the new tables. This becomes important when preserving local functionality of an Access application once the data is upsized for publication on the Web.

COMPLETING THE UPSIZING PROCESS

After completing the upsizing process, you will notice some changes to your Access database. If you opted to link to the newly created SQL Server tables, the Upsizing Wizard renames the original Access tables, using the "_local" suffix for all table names, and uses the original table names for the SQL Server tables. For example, if you upsize a table named "Products," the result after the upsize is both a local table named "Products_local" and a link to the upsized table having the name "Products" with a *world* icon next to it. If your Access tables have table names and/or field names not supported by SQL Server—i.e., those with embedded spaces, special characters, and reserved words—the Upsizing Wizard creates mapping queries that translate the SQL Server names (modified to remove spaces and special characters) to the names that your desktop application's queries, forms, and reports expect. In these cases, the Upsizing Wizard gives the linked tables names that end in "_remote," and names the mapping queries after the original tables.

Depending on the size of the table, the upsizing process can take awhile to complete. This is unfortunate but necessary due to the way the server tables are created. If you encounter this problem, you may consider upsizing only the table's structure and using a tool like SQL Server's bulk copy program (BCP) to transfer the data. Regardless of which method you use, after the data has been transferred, you should spend some time testing and tuning your database according to the recommendations in Chapter 3. The Upsizing Wizard is a useful but simple tool to assist you in the process of migrating your data from Access to SQL Server. At the same time, you are responsible for taking over after it has finished its job to tune the data for the SQL Server environment.

SPECIAL CONSIDERATIONS FOR UPSIZED DATA

As I mentioned earlier, accessing a live Web database is common from an Access desktop or multi-user LAN application running on a LAN attached to the Web server hardware. After upsizing your tables and testing them with your Access application, notice that a number of behavioral differences exist between the two platforms. Care should be taken here, because Access VBA program code that depends on Access's behavior can potentially not work properly after the upsizing process.

If you use the Access AutoNumber field type, a common choice for primary keys, the Upsizing Wizard creates the appropriate SQL Server equivalent, an Identity column or a trigger. When you use this on a form, however, realize that unlike Access, SQL Server determines new values only after the new records are saved. Access pre-allocates AutoNumber values when you make the first entry in a new record, and displays the new values on the form. VBA code that depends on reading the field value before the new record is saved no longer works correctly.

Also, differences exist in error handling between Access and SQL Server. When a data error is generated by SQL Server, for example, if a required field is left empty, Access displays two error dialog boxes. The first dialog box shows a generic "ODBC call failed" message, while the second message contains the specific error, plus additional information such as the source of the error and the SQL Server error number. If you don't want users confronted with these error dialog boxes, use the OnError event to trap, parse, and redirect any SQL Server errors.

Another area that may cause problems involves updateability of your tables. By default, JET tables are always updateable. To update ODBC tables, however, the tables must have at least one unique index. JET uses unique index values to re-query the database during update operations. If all the tables you upsize have a primary key, you have nothing to fear. If, however, a table does not have a primary key or other No Duplicates index, you will not be able to update it after upsizing it to SQL Server.

Performance issues may also be somewhat surprising after you upsize to SQL Server. Your native Access application may not perform as well when accessing data in SQL Server. One common difficulty is an application that uses too many queries or returns large resultsets. One primary goal of a client-server database design is to limit the amount of data moving across the network. For example, user interface designs that feature multiple combo boxes and list boxes can generate considerable network traffic. Remember to use these controls only where they add the most value to the application. When the Web is not involved, you could address this problem by storing unchanging data on local tables rather than on remote SQL Server tables. Combo and list boxes row source properties would then be based on the local tables to speed the user interface. A Web-based application, however, does not have the convenience of handling such components in this manner. For example, a Web-based picklist could be very slow if the page must issue a SQL query to populate itself with a large resultset. Drill-down techniques can be used to circumvent this situation.

SQL Server Browser

Now you can turn your attention to another useful component of the Microsoft Access Upsizing tools, the *SQL Server Browser*. This tool presents a view of objects in a SQL Server database similar to the Access database container window. You can view data, as well as create new objects and revise the definitions of existing objects. The SQL Server Browser provides a means within the Access environment to maintain an upsized database that is now the basis of a WebTop application. This tool may be easier to use for an Access or Visual Basic developer than the ISQL/w utility found in SQL Server.

To launch the utility, select *SQL Server Browser* from the Add-ins menu. You are prompted to select an ODBC data source followed by a SQL Server login requesting your user name and password. Access then displays the main SQL Server Browser window, as shown in Figure 9-10.

The browser has tabs for each SQL Server object type: tables, views, defaults, rules, and stored procedures. You can click on any tab to view the objects of that type in the selected SQL Server database. For table objects, you can view, but not modify, data in datasheet view. Data is read-only, because the browser issues the request for data as a *SQL pass-through query*. SQL pass-through queries permit an application to bypass the Microsoft JET database engine query processor and route foreign-dialect SQL statements (in this case, Transact-SQL, the SQL dialect understood by SQL Server) to an external database server such as SQL Server. If the SQL pass-through query returns a

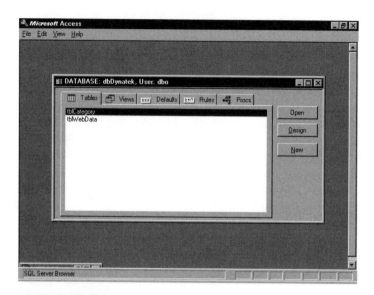

Figure 9-10 *SQL Server Browser Main Window*

resultset, the JET database engine creates a *snapshot-type* recordset object for the set. Snapshot recordsets are read-only; therefore, SQL pass-through queries are read-only as well.

You can modify table definitions by selecting a table from the list and clicking on the *Design* button. The browser displays an Access-like design view, as shown in Figure 9-11. If you decide to use the table design facilities of the SQL Server Browser, keep in mind that SQL Server is much more restrictive when it comes to modifying the design of existing tables. For example, you can add, but not remove, fields to a SQL Server table. Remember from the discussion of this topic in Chapter 8 that Visual InterDev can in fact provide a platform for making these kinds of table structure changes.

Viewing other SQL Server objects requires a much more rudimentary interface. For example, views, rules, defaults, and stored procedures are displayed in a text box showing their Transact-SQL definitions. You must be familiar with Transact-SQL to use these functions.

Static Database Content Web Page Generation

Many times, a business enterprise wishes to publish its corporate data on the Web but does not have an actual Internet connection with a Windows NT Web server to process database query requests. Maybe the company has only a Web site hosted by an Internet Service Provider that makes Web site space

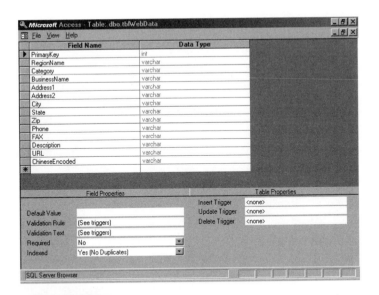

Figure 9-11   *Table Design from SQL Server Browser*

available to its dial-up customers. The company would typically use FTP to maintain its static Web pages. Few ISPs make database technology available to this level of customer. Smaller firms who can benefit from the Web are often shut out of this lucrative method of advertising their product inventories because of the startup and maintenance costs associated with operating a live Web server. Fortunately, a couple of low-cost alternatives are available, both involving static database content generation. The first method I consider is the built-in Internet capabilities of Microsoft Access 97, and the other method involves custom VBA for Access code that generates HTML pages. Both methods require the company's Webmaster to periodically transfer the generated pages over to the Web server, replacing previous, outdated pages. No real query capabilities are available using these methods, other than structuring the generated database content pages in a hierarchical way such that a user can drill down, and in effect pose queries, through the pages to locate the desired data.

Microsoft Access 97

Microsoft Access 97 (version 8.0) includes a number of new Internet-specific features that provide a platform for publishing database objects on the Web. Prior to Access 97, publishing desktop database information on the Web required the use of a free add-in developed and distributed by Microsoft called the *Microsoft Internet Assistant for Access*. This module was one of several available from Microsoft to add Internet functionality to the standard

Microsoft Office suite components. The last version of the Internet Assistant was for Access 95 (version 7.0). You can also find Internet Assistants for Excel, Word, PowerPoint™, and Schedule+ suite members. A short time after Microsoft became "serious" about the Internet (November 1995), the mandate was to include some kind of Internet functionality in all Microsoft products. The Internet Assistant series was the immediate result of this new product emphasis. As for Access 97, it is the first version of Access to have integrated Internet capabilities and will thus be the focus of this part of the chapter. In the sections that follow, I identify several areas of Internet functionality.

GENERAL WEB FACILITIES

Access 97 allows you to specify configuration items related to the Internet. To access these properties, select the Tools menu, Options, and click on the *Hyperlinks/HTML* tab, shown in Figure 9-12.

This dialog box has four general groups of configuration options. First, you can define the *Hyperlink Appearance* by specifying the color of the hyperlink text, the color of the hyperlink text after the link was followed, whether a hyperlink is underlined, and whether to show the hyperlink addresses in the status bar. Next, you can define the look and feel of the *HTML Output* by specifying the name of an HTML template file. A template file provides a common look for Web applications, such as a company logo or standard headers and footers. Next, you can define the *Data Source Infor-*

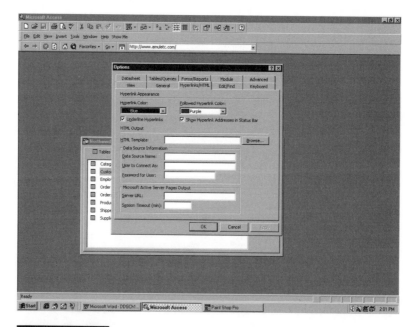

Figure 9–12   *Internet Configuration Options in Access 97*

mation used to define the data source name, user name, and password for the ODBC connection you will use to query your Access database when using dynamic Web pages created for use with IIS. Last, you can define the *Microsoft Active Server Pages Output* parameters. Here, you provide the URL of the location where the ASP file will be stored on the Web server. For example, if you are storing the ASP files in the \NewProject folder on the \\AMULETWeb server, then use the URL http://AMULETWeb/NewProject. You can also specify the session time-out interval, the number of minutes an inactive Web server session can be left open before it is timed out.

Another Web-related addition found in Access 97 is the introduction of the Web toolbar. To open up the Web toolbar, select the View menu, Toolbars item, and then select Web. Figure 9-13 shows the toolbar's default position in the Access user interface.

As you can see from the pulled-down combo box in Figure 9-13, Access keeps track of the last group of URLs that you referenced from Access. If you click on one of these URLs or type in a new one, the default browser on your PC will be invoked and the requested page loaded. The toolbar also has the typical Back, Forward, Stop, and Refresh buttons found in leading Web browsers. You can also use the navigation buttons, Start Page, Search the Web, and Favorites to quickly find your way around the Web. The Favorites selections come from your Internet Explorer browser favorites collection. Finally, the Go pull-down menu provides menu-based selections equivalent

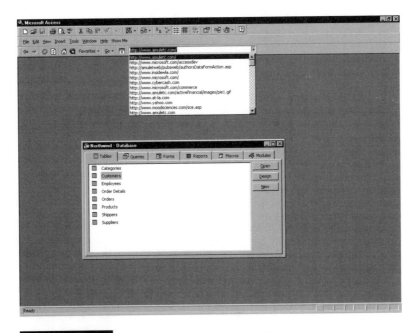

Figure 9–13   *The Web Toolbar in Access 97*

to the buttons in the Web toolbar. The Web toolbar seamlessly integrates the Access database environment with a common Web browser interface.

HYPERLINK DATA TYPE

Access 97 contains a new date type called *Hyperlink* that you choose to include in your tables. You'll see this data type in table design as you pull down the list of available types, as shown in Figure 9-14. The idea behind the Hyperlink data type is to provide a means to easily connect an application to the Internet or an intranet. A field having the data type Hyperlink contains a hyperlink address. Hyperlink fields can be placed on a form or report object. Three types of Access controls can contain hyperlinks: command button, label, and image controls.

Hyperlink fields can contain text of combinations of text and numbers stored as text that are used as a hyperlink address. A hyperlink address is the path to an object, document, Web page, or other destination. A hyperlink address can be a URL address to an Internet or intranet site, or a UNC (Universal Naming Convention, of the form \\server\share\path\filename) network path. When you click on a hyperlink, your Web browser or Access uses the hyperlink address to go to the destination. A hyperlink address can have up to three parts (each part can be up to 2048 characters) in the following syntax:

```
displaytext#address#subaddress
```

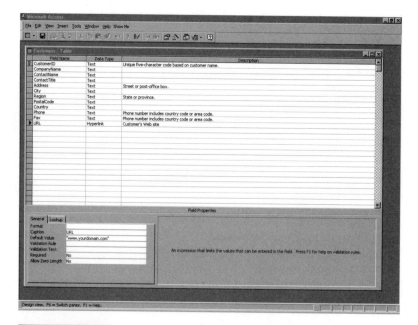

Figure 9–14   *Hyperlink Data Type in Access Table Design*

Displaytext is the text that appears in a field or control. Address is the path to a page (URL) or file (UNC). Subaddress is the location within the page or file. The following example establishes a hyperlink field for the author's company Web site displayed as "Web Database Development":

```
Web Database Development#www.amuletc.com#
```

When in Access form design view, you can use the Hyperlink item from the Insert menu to build a special type of label control for the link. Figure 9-15 shows the dialog box that prompts you for the URL on which the control is to be based. The control has its Caption and Hyperlink Address properties filled in with the URL specified in the dialog box. If you then run the form in form view, you can click on the label control to launch your default browser and load the page. Clicking on the control also fires the control's Click event, and any embedded event procedure is executed.

PUBLISH TO THE WEB WIZARD

In Access 97, you can save table, query, and form datasheets to a Web server in several ways. Using the File menu, select Save As/Export, Save As HTML, or Send HTML (*.html). These facilities also publish entire Web-based forms in addition to datasheets. For the greatest ease of generating Web pages from Access objects, you should limit your attention to the *Save As HTML* selection,

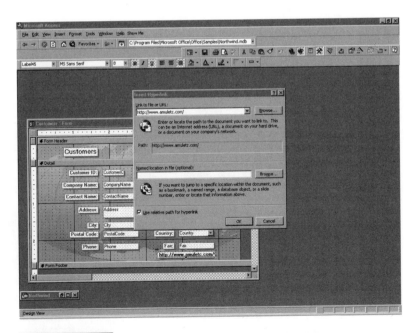

Figure 9–15 *Form Design Insert Hyperlink Dialog Box*

because it uses the *Publish to the Web Wizard* to assist you in the process. The wizard allows you to create a static page and/or a dynamic page that queries a Web server database, to post the Web publication to a Web server, to create a home page that ties together all the Web pages you create, and to specify an HTML template to create a common look for all your Web pages. Access comes with several ready-made templates, or you can design your own. The Publish to the Web Wizard has multiple dialog boxes, depending on what type of output you wish to generate: static HTML, HTX/IDC, or ASP format.

Now step through the process of using this wizard. From the database container window, open the File menu and select Save As HTML. You do not have to have an object open or in design view previous to selecting this menu item. The opening dialog box for the wizard appears in Figure 9-16.

The next dialog box, shown in Figure 9-17, presents a database container-like form having tabs for each object you might wish to publish on the Web, namely tables, queries, forms, and reports. You have the ability to select the objects you wish to create. You can select multiple objects for Web publication, if you desire. For an example, I click on the Tables tab and select the Customers table. This means I want to generate a Web page in datasheet view. Figure 9-18 shows the next dialog box in sequence, which lets you specify the HTML template file to use in generating the look and feel of the resulting Web page. The wizard prompts you with the default template direc-

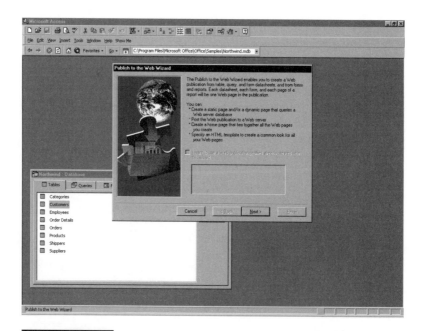

Figure 9–16   *Opening Publish to the Web Wizard Dialog Box*

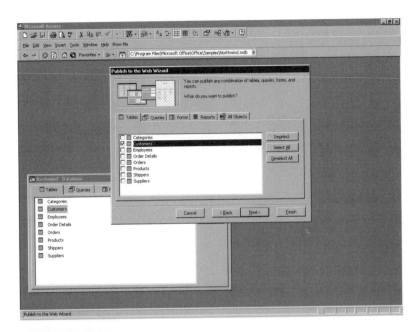

Figure 9-17   *Selecting Database Objects for Publication*

tory, although you can use the Browse button to point the wizard at your own directory containing custom templates. In the default directory, you find a number of sample templates that you can choose from in order to determine which one suits your needs.

The next dialog box is very important, because it asks for you to choose the type of Web page required. The choices shown in Figure 9-19 are static HTML, dynamic HTX/IDC for use with the Microsoft IIS Web server, and ASP. The wizard's prompting diverges slightly at this point, depending on the selection made here. Both the ASP and HTX/IDC formats support dynamic updating of published datasheets based on changes to their underlying database objects, but the HTX/IDC format does not offer as many options as ASP. Before trying to run a dynamic page, be sure to assign Execute Scripts permission to the Web server folder that stores the .asp, .idc, or .htx files that the wizard generates.

For static HTML Web pages, Figure 9-20 shows the next dialog box, which prompts for the folder in which the new Web publication will be placed. You may accept the default location or select a directory of your choosing. If you choose to build a dynamic HTX/IDC or ASP Web page, you see an additional dialog box, in Figure 9-21, where you are asked to supply data source information and ASP output options.

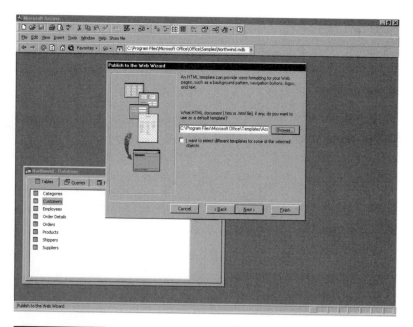

Figure 9–18   *Selecting an HTML Template*

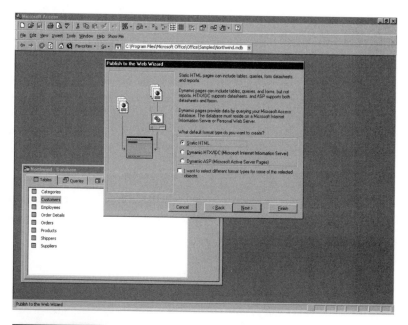

Figure 9–19   *Selecting the Web Page Format Type*

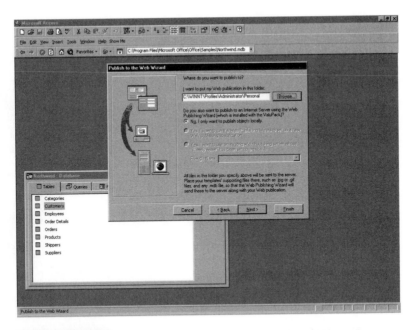

Figure 9–20   *Selecting the Web Publication Destination*

The Publish to the Web Wizard also constructs a home page used to bind together all the pages you create for each Access database object. In reality, the style of this so-called home page will most likely not satisfy most general requirements and will have to be modified, but at least it is a starting point. In the dialog box shown in Figure 9-22, you can enter the name of the home page. The default home page name is default.html.

The final dialog box for the Publish to the Web Wizard appears in Figure 9-23. This dialog box asks whether you wish to save the profile you've specified in the preceding dialog boxes for later use. When developing a profile, you should make the settings as simple as possible. For instance, selecting a single table to use instead of a group of table datasheets easily allows you to unselect it and go about selecting the new tables, queries, reports, and forms that you want to publish. The resulting Customer table datasheet Web page appears in the browser in Figure 9-24.

The above result was a purely static approach, which is satisfactory for some applications, but now consider a quite different result that occurs if you request the Publish to the Web Wizard to build an ASP page based on an Access form object. Access does not simply implement the Access form as an HTML form, but rather with an ActiveX control called the HTML Layout Control (known as an ALX file). The code that is generated is surprisingly long and complex, and it is listed below in its entirety so that you can peruse the

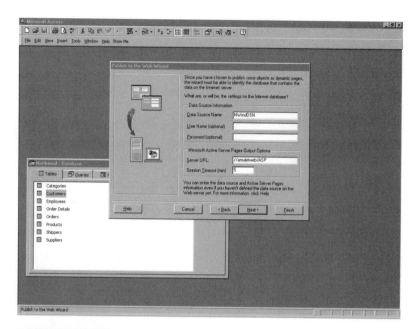

Figure 9–21   *Supplying Information for Dynamic Pages*

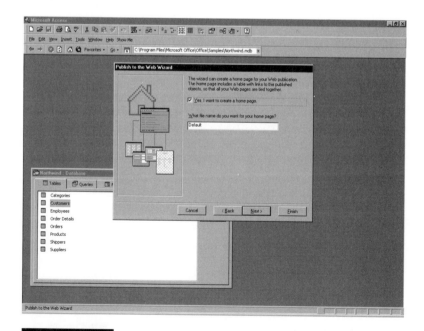

Figure 9–22   *Creating a Home Page*

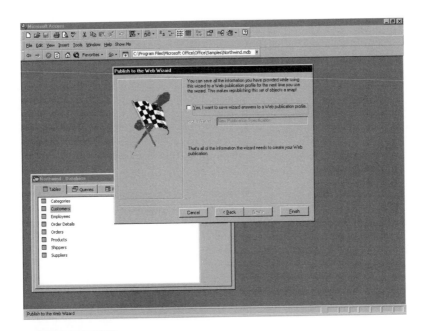

Figure 9–23   *Optionally Saving the Web Profile*

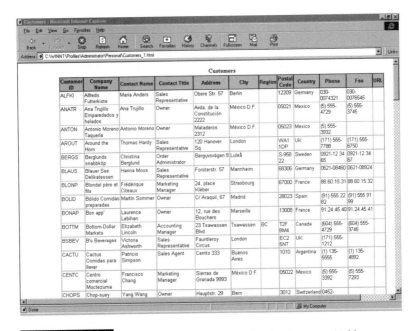

Figure 9–24   *The Resulting Web Page for the Customer Table*

various procedures. The code includes HTML, server-side VBScript, and ADO method calls. The primary ASP page is named Customers_1.asp (which is listed first), and the secondary page is Customers_1alx.asp file.

```
<HTML>

<TITLE>Customers</TITLE>

<BODY background = zigzag.jpg>

<%
If IsObject(Session("dbnwind_conn")) Then
    Set conn = Session("dbnwind_conn")
Else
    Set conn =
      Server.CreateObject("ADODB.Connection")
    conn.open "dbnwind","",""
    Set Session("dbnwind_conn") = conn
End If
%>


<%
If IsObject(Session("Form_Customers_rs")) Then
    Set rs = Session("Form_Customers_rs")
Else
    sql = "SELECT * FROM [Customers]"
    Set rs =
      Server.CreateObject("ADODB.Recordset")
    rs.Open sql, conn, 3, 3
    If rs.eof Then
      rs.AddNew
    End If
    Set Session("Form_Customers_rs") = rs
End If
%>


<%
If cstr(Request.QueryString("Country")) <> ""
Then
    rs.Fields("Country").Value =
      Request.QueryString("Country")
End If
If cstr(Request.QueryString("Fax")) <> "" Then
    rs.Fields("Fax").Value =
      Request.QueryString("Fax")
End If
If cstr(Request.QueryString("Phone")) <> ""
Then
    rs.Fields("Phone").Value =
      Request.QueryString("Phone")
```

```
End If
If cstr(Request.QueryString("PostalCode")) <>
"" Then
    rs.Fields("PostalCode").Value =
        Request.QueryString("PostalCode")
End If
If cstr(Request.QueryString("Region")) <> ""
Then
    rs.Fields("Region").Value =
        Request.QueryString("Region")
End If
If cstr(Request.QueryString("City")) <> ""
Then
    rs.Fields("City").Value =
        Request.QueryString("City")
End If
If cstr(Request.QueryString("Address")) <> ""
Then
    rs.Fields("Address").Value =
        Request.QueryString("Address")
End If
If cstr(Request.QueryString("ContactTitle"))
<> "" Then
    rs.Fields("ContactTitle").Value =
        Request.QueryString("ContactTitle")
End If
If cstr(Request.QueryString("ContactName")) <>
"" Then
    rs.Fields("ContactName").Value =
        Request.QueryString("ContactName")
End If
If cstr(Request.QueryString("CompanyName")) <>
"" Then
    rs.Fields("CompanyName").Value =
        Request.QueryString("CompanyName")
End If
If cstr(Request.QueryString("CustomerID")) <>
"" Then
    rs.Fields("CustomerID").Value =
        Request.QueryString("CustomerID")
End If


tempVar = Request.QueryString("nav_btn")
On Error Resume Next
If cstr(tempVar)="nav_btn_MoveFirstRecord"
Then
    rs.MoveFirst
End If
If cstr(tempVar)="nav_btn_MovePrevRecord" Then
```

```
        rs.MovePrevious
          If rs.bof Then
             rs.MoveNext
          End If
    End If
    If cstr(tempVar)="nav_btn_MoveNextRecord" Then
        rs.MoveNext
        If rs.eof Then
          rs.MovePrevious
        End If
    End If
    If cstr(tempVar)="nav_btn_MoveLastRecord" Then
        rs.MoveLast
    End If
    If cstr(tempVar)="nav_btn_MoveAddRecord" Then
        rs.AddNew
    End If
    If cstr(tempVar)="nav_btn_MoveCommitRecord"
    Then
        rs.Update
        rs.Requery
    End If
    If cstr(tempVar)="nav_btn_MoveCancelUpdate"
    Then
        rs.CancelUpdate
        rs.Resync
    End If
    If cstr(tempVar)="nav_btn_MoveDeleteRecord"
    Then
        rs.Delete
        rs.MoveNext
        If rs.eof Then
          rs.MovePrevious
          If rs.bof Then
             rs.AddNew
          End If
        End If
    End If

    On Error Goto 0
    %>

    <OBJECT ID="Customers_1alx"
    CLASSID=
    "CLSID:812AE312-8B8E-11CF-93C8-00AA00C08FDF"
    STYLE="TOP:0;LEFT:0;">
    <PARAM NAME="ALXPATH"
    VALUE="www.amuletc.com/Customers_1alx.asp">
    </OBJECT>
```

```
</BODY>
<BR><BR>

<IMG SRC = "msaccess.jpg">
</HTML>
```

The above primary ASP file makes an object reference in the OBJECT tag to the ALX file which is listed below:

```
<%
If IsObject(Session("dbnwind_conn")) Then
    Set conn = Session("dbnwind_conn")
Else
    Set conn =
    Server.CreateObject("ADODB.Connection")
    conn.open "dbnwind","",""
    Set Session("dbnwind_conn") = conn
End If
%>


<%
If IsObject(Session("Form_Customers_rs")) Then
    Set rs = Session("Form_Customers_rs")
Else
    sql = "SELECT * FROM [Customers]"
    Set rs =
    Server.CreateObject("ADODB.Recordset")
    rs.Open sql, conn, 3, 3
    If rs.eof Then
      rs.AddNew
    End If
    Set Session("Form_Customers_rs") = rs
End If
%>

<SCRIPT LANGUAGE=VBScript>
<!--
Dim rgszCtrls(20, 2)
Dim cMaxCtrls
cMaxCtrls = 20

Sub AddCtrlToList(szCtrl, szCtrlSrc)
Dim i
for i = 1 to cMaxCtrls
    if rgszCtrls(i, 1) = szCtrl Then Exit Sub
    if rgszCtrls(i, 1) = "" Then
      rgszCtrls(i, 1) = szCtrl
      rgszCtrls(i, 2) = szCtrlSrc
      Exit Sub
    End If
```

```
next
End Sub

Sub UpdateRefreshBtn()
    nav_btn_MoveCancelUpdate.Caption = "Cancel"
End Sub

Function MakeHTMLValue(szVal)
Dim i
Dim szRet
for i = 1 to Len(szVal)
    ch = Mid(szVal, i, 1)
    if ch = " " Then
      szRet = szRet & "%20"
    elseif ch = "&" Then
      szRet = szRet & "%26"
    elseif ch = "#" Then
      szRet = szRet & "%23"
    elseif ch = """" Then
      szRet = szRet & "%22"
    elseif ch = ";" Then
      szRet = szRet & "%3B"
    elseif ch = ":" Then
      szRet = szRet & "%3A"
    elseif ch = "'" Then
      szRet = szRet & "%27"
    else
      szRet = szRet & Mid(szVal, i, 1)
    end if
next

MakeHTMLValue = szRet

End Function

Function GetCtrlQueryString()
Dim szRet
Dim i
for i = 1 to cMaxCtrls
    if rgszCtrls(i, 1) = "" Then Exit For
    szRet = szRet & rgszCtrls(i, 2) & "=" &
    MakeHTMLValue(Customers_1alx.Controls(
    rgszCtrls(i, 1)).Value) & "&"
next

GetCtrlQueryString = szRet

End Function

<%
```

```
If IsObject(Session("RS_Customers_Country"))
Then
    Set tempRS = Session("RS_Customers_Country")
Else
    sql ="SELECT DISTINCT Customers.Country FROM
      Customers "
    Set tempRS =
    Server.CreateObject("ADODB.Recordset")
    tempRS.Open sql, conn, 3, 3
    Set Session("RS_Customers_Country") = tempRS
    tempRS.MoveFirst
End If
tempRS.MoveLast
%>

Dim Country_
    tempList(<% =tempRS.RecordCount %>, 1)

<%
tempRS.MoveFirst
I = 0
do while Not tempRS.eof
    If tempRS.Fields(0).value =
      rs.Fields("Country").Value Then

      selectedVarCountry =
        cstr(tempRS.Fields(0).value)

    End If
%>

    Country_tempList(<% =I %>,0)=
      "<% =tempRS.Fields(0).value %>"

<%
    tempRS.MoveNext
    I = I+1
loop
%>

Sub Customers_1alx_OnLoad()
    Country.list = Country_tempList
End Sub

Sub Country_AfterUpdate()
    call AddCtrlToList("Country", "Country")
    call UpdateRefreshBtn()
End Sub

Sub Fax_AfterUpdate()
```

```
        call AddCtrlToList("Fax", "Fax")
        call UpdateRefreshBtn()
    End Sub

    Sub Phone_AfterUpdate()
        call AddCtrlToList("Phone", "Phone")
        call UpdateRefreshBtn()
    End Sub

    Sub PostalCode_AfterUpdate()
        call AddCtrlToList("PostalCode",
          "PostalCode")
        call UpdateRefreshBtn()
    End Sub

    Sub Region_AfterUpdate()
        call AddCtrlToList("Region", "Region")
        call UpdateRefreshBtn()
    End Sub

    Sub City_AfterUpdate()
        call AddCtrlToList("City", "City")
        call UpdateRefreshBtn()
    End Sub

    Sub Address_AfterUpdate()
        call AddCtrlToList("Address", "Address")
        call UpdateRefreshBtn()
    End Sub

    Sub ContactTitle_AfterUpdate()
        call AddCtrlToList("ContactTitle",
          "ContactTitle")
        call UpdateRefreshBtn()
    End Sub

    Sub ContactName_AfterUpdate()
        call AddCtrlToList("ContactName",
          "ContactName")
        call UpdateRefreshBtn()
    End Sub

    Sub CompanyName_AfterUpdate()
        call AddCtrlToList("CompanyName",
          "CompanyName")
        call UpdateRefreshBtn()
    End Sub

    Sub CustomerID_AfterUpdate()
        call AddCtrlToList("CustomerID",
```

```
        "CustomerID")
    call UpdateRefreshBtn()
End Sub

Sub nav_btn_MoveFirstRecord_Click()
    Window.Location.Href =
      "www.amuletc.com/Customers_1.asp?
      nav_btn=nav_btn_MoveFirstRecord&" &
      GetCtrlQueryString()
End Sub

Sub nav_btn_MovePrevRecord_Click()
    Window.Location.Href =
      "www.amuletc.com/Customers_1.asp?
      nav_btn=nav_btn_MovePrevRecord&" &
      GetCtrlQueryString()
End Sub

Sub nav_btn_MoveNextRecord_Click()
    Window.Location.Href =
      "www.amuletc.com/Customers_1.asp?
      nav_btn=nav_btn_MoveNextRecord&" &
      GetCtrlQueryString()
End Sub

Sub nav_btn_MoveLastRecord_Click()
    Window.Location.Href =
      "www.amuletc.com/Customers_1.asp?
      nav_btn=nav_btn_MoveLastRecord&" &
      GetCtrlQueryString()
End Sub

Sub nav_btn_MoveAddRecord_Click()
    Window.Location.Href =
      "www.amuletc.com/Customers_1.asp?
      nav_btn=nav_btn_MoveAddRecord&" &
      GetCtrlQueryString()
End Sub

Sub nav_btn_MoveCommitRecord_Click()
    Window.Location.Href =
      "www.amuletc.com/Customers_1.asp?
      nav_btn=nav_btn_MoveCommitRecord&" &
      GetCtrlQueryString()
End Sub

Sub nav_btn_MoveCancelUpdate_Click()
    Window.Location.Href =
      "www.amuletc.com/Customers_1.asp?
      nav_btn=nav_btn_MoveCancelUpdate&"
```

```
End Sub

Sub nav_btn_MoveDeleteRecord_Click()
    If MsgBox("Press OK to delete current
       record", 1, "Customers_1") =1 Then
       Window.Location.Href =
          "www.amuletc.com/Customers_1.asp?
          nav_btn=nav_btn_MoveDeleteRecord&"
    End If
End Sub

-->
</SCRIPT>
<DIV ID="Customers_1alx"
STYLE="LAYOUT:FIXED;HEIGHT:462;WIDTH:807;">

<OBJECT ID="CustomersLabel"
CLASSID=
"CLSID:978C9E23-D4B0-11CE-BF2D-00AA003F40D0"
STYLE="TOP:12;LEFT:102;WIDTH:142;HEIGHT:39;
ZINDEX:0;">
<PARAM NAME="BackStyle" VALUE="1">
<PARAM NAME="BackColor" VALUE="13434879">
<PARAM NAME="BorderStyle" VALUE="1">
<PARAM NAME="BorderColor" VALUE="8421504">
<PARAM NAME="Caption" VALUE="Customers">
<PARAM NAME="ParagraphAlign" VALUE="3">
<PARAM NAME="ForeColor" VALUE="128">
<PARAM NAME="FontHeight" VALUE="240">
<PARAM NAME="FontWeight" VALUE="700">
<PARAM NAME="Font" VALUE="MS Sans Serif">
<PARAM NAME="FontName" VALUE="MS Sans Serif">
<PARAM NAME="Size" VALUE="3692;1014">
<PARAM NAME="VariousPropertyBits"
    VALUE="8388635">
<PARAM NAME="FontEffects" VALUE="1">
</OBJECT>

<OBJECT ID="Country"
CLASSID=
"CLSID:8BD21D30-EC42-11CE-9E0D-00AA006002F3"
STYLE="TOP:313;LEFT:561;WIDTH:144;HEIGHT:28;
TABINDEX:8;ZINDEX:0;">
<PARAM NAME="Value"
    VALUE="<%=selectedVarCountry%>">
<PARAM NAME="BackStyle" VALUE="1">
<PARAM NAME="BackColor" VALUE="13434879">
<PARAM NAME="BorderStyle" VALUE="1">
<PARAM NAME="BorderColor" VALUE="8421504">
<PARAM NAME="DisplayStyle" VALUE="3">
```

```
<PARAM NAME="ForeColor" VALUE="128">
<PARAM NAME="FontHeight" VALUE="160">
<PARAM NAME="Font" VALUE="MS Sans Serif">
<PARAM NAME="ShowDropButtonWhen" VALUE="2">
<PARAM NAME="FontName" VALUE="MS Sans Serif">
<PARAM NAME="Size" VALUE="3744;728">
<PARAM NAME="ListRows" VALUE="8">
<PARAM NAME="BoundColumn" VALUE="1">
<PARAM NAME="Width" VALUE="144;">
<PARAM NAME="cColumnInfo" VALUE="1">
<PARAM NAME="TextColumn" VALUE="1">
<PARAM NAME="VariousPropertyBits"
    VALUE="746604571">
</OBJECT>

<OBJECT ID="CountryLabel"
CLASSID=
"CLSID:978C9E23-D4B0-11CE-BF2D-00AA003F40D0"
STYLE="TOP:313;LEFT:462;WIDTH:84;HEIGHT:28;
ZINDEX:1;">
<PARAM NAME="BackStyle" VALUE="1">
<PARAM NAME="BackColor" VALUE="13434879">
<PARAM NAME="BorderStyle" VALUE="1">
<PARAM NAME="BorderColor" VALUE="8421504">
<PARAM NAME="Caption" VALUE="Country:">
<PARAM NAME="ParagraphAlign" VALUE="2">
<PARAM NAME="ForeColor" VALUE="8421376">
<PARAM NAME="FontHeight" VALUE="160">
<PARAM NAME="FontWeight" VALUE="700">
<PARAM NAME="Font" VALUE="MS Sans Serif">
<PARAM NAME="FontName" VALUE="MS Sans Serif">
<PARAM NAME="Size" VALUE="2184;728">
<PARAM NAME="VariousPropertyBits"
    VALUE="8388635">
<PARAM NAME="FontEffects" VALUE="1">
</OBJECT>

<OBJECT ID="Fax"
CLASSID=
"CLSID:8BD21D10-EC42-11CE-9E0D-00AA006002F3"
STYLE="TOP:362;LEFT:561;WIDTH:144;HEIGHT:28;
TABINDEX:10;ZINDEX:2;">

<%If Not IsNull(rs.Fields("Fax").Value) Then%>
    <PARAM NAME="Value"
    VALUE="<%=Server.HTMLEncode(rs.
      Fields("Fax").Value)%>">
<%End If%>

<PARAM NAME="BackStyle" VALUE="1">
```

```
<PARAM NAME="BackColor" VALUE="13434879">
<PARAM NAME="BorderStyle" VALUE="1">
<PARAM NAME="BorderColor" VALUE="8421504">
<PARAM NAME="ForeColor" VALUE="128">
<PARAM NAME="FontHeight" VALUE="160">
<PARAM NAME="Font" VALUE="MS Sans Serif">
<PARAM NAME="FontName" VALUE="MS Sans Serif">
<PARAM NAME="Size" VALUE="3744;728">
<PARAM NAME="VariousPropertyBits"
    VALUE="2894088219">
</OBJECT>

<OBJECT ID="FaxLabel"
CLASSID=
"CLSID:978C9E23-D4B0-11CE-BF2D-00AA003F40D0"
STYLE="TOP:362;LEFT:496;WIDTH:49;HEIGHT:28;
ZINDEX:3;">
<PARAM NAME="BackStyle" VALUE="1">
<PARAM NAME="BackColor" VALUE="13434879">
<PARAM NAME="BorderStyle" VALUE="1">
<PARAM NAME="BorderColor" VALUE="8421504">
<PARAM NAME="Caption" VALUE="Fax:">
<PARAM NAME="ParagraphAlign" VALUE="2">
<PARAM NAME="ForeColor" VALUE="8421376">
<PARAM NAME="FontHeight" VALUE="160">
<PARAM NAME="FontWeight" VALUE="700">
<PARAM NAME="Font" VALUE="MS Sans Serif">
<PARAM NAME="FontName" VALUE="MS Sans Serif">
<PARAM NAME="Size" VALUE="1274;728">
<PARAM NAME="VariousPropertyBits"
    VALUE="8388635">
<PARAM NAME="FontEffects" VALUE="1">
</OBJECT>

<OBJECT ID="Phone"
CLASSID=
"CLSID:8BD21D10-EC42-11CE-9E0D-00AA006002F3"
STYLE="TOP:362;LEFT:259;WIDTH:144;HEIGHT:28;
TABINDEX:9;ZINDEX:4;">

<%If Not IsNull(rs.Fields("Phone").Value)
    Then%>
    <PARAM NAME="Value"
    VALUE="<%=Server.HTMLEncode(rs.
      Fields("Phone").Value)%>">
<%End If%>

<PARAM NAME="BackStyle" VALUE="1">
<PARAM NAME="BackColor" VALUE="13434879">
<PARAM NAME="BorderStyle" VALUE="1">
```

```
<PARAM NAME="BorderColor" VALUE="8421504">
<PARAM NAME="ForeColor" VALUE="128">
<PARAM NAME="FontHeight" VALUE="160">
<PARAM NAME="Font" VALUE="MS Sans Serif">
<PARAM NAME="FontName" VALUE="MS Sans Serif">
<PARAM NAME="Size" VALUE="3744;728">
<PARAM NAME="VariousPropertyBits"
    VALUE="2894088219">
</OBJECT>

<OBJECT ID="PhoneLabel"
CLASSID=
"CLSID:978C9E23-D4B0-11CE-BF2D-00AA003F40D0"
STYLE="TOP:362;LEFT:171;WIDTH:73;HEIGHT:28;
ZINDEX:5;">
<PARAM NAME="BackStyle" VALUE="1">
<PARAM NAME="BackColor" VALUE="13434879">
<PARAM NAME="BorderStyle" VALUE="1">
<PARAM NAME="BorderColor" VALUE="8421504">
<PARAM NAME="Caption" VALUE="Phone:">
<PARAM NAME="ParagraphAlign" VALUE="2">
<PARAM NAME="ForeColor" VALUE="8421376">
<PARAM NAME="FontHeight" VALUE="160">
<PARAM NAME="FontWeight" VALUE="700">
<PARAM NAME="Font" VALUE="MS Sans Serif">
<PARAM NAME="FontName" VALUE="MS Sans Serif">
<PARAM NAME="Size" VALUE="1898;728">
<PARAM NAME="VariousPropertyBits"
    VALUE="8388635">
<PARAM NAME="FontEffects" VALUE="1">
</OBJECT>

<OBJECT ID="PostalCode"
CLASSID=
"CLSID:8BD21D10-EC42-11CE-9E0D-00AA006002F3"
STYLE="TOP:313;LEFT:259;WIDTH:144;HEIGHT:28;
TABINDEX:7;ZINDEX:6;">

<%If Not IsNull(rs.Fields("PostalCode").Value)
    Then%>
    <PARAM NAME="Value"
    VALUE="<%=Server.HTMLEncode(rs.
      Fields("PostalCode").Value)%>">
<%End If%>

<PARAM NAME="BackStyle" VALUE="1">
<PARAM NAME="BackColor" VALUE="13434879">
<PARAM NAME="BorderStyle" VALUE="1">
<PARAM NAME="BorderColor" VALUE="8421504">
<PARAM NAME="ForeColor" VALUE="128">
```

```
<PARAM NAME="FontHeight" VALUE="160">
<PARAM NAME="Font" VALUE="MS Sans Serif">
<PARAM NAME="FontName" VALUE="MS Sans Serif">
<PARAM NAME="Size" VALUE="3744;728">
<PARAM NAME="VariousPropertyBits"
    VALUE="2894088219">
</OBJECT>

<OBJECT ID="PostalCodeLabel"
CLASSID=
"CLSID:978C9E23-D4B0-11CE-BF2D-00AA003F40D0"
STYLE="TOP:313;LEFT:123;WIDTH:121;HEIGHT:28;
ZINDEX:7;">
<PARAM NAME="BackStyle" VALUE="1">
<PARAM NAME="BackColor" VALUE="13434879">
<PARAM NAME="BorderStyle" VALUE="1">
<PARAM NAME="BorderColor" VALUE="8421504">
<PARAM NAME="Caption" VALUE="Postal Code:">
<PARAM NAME="ParagraphAlign" VALUE="2">
<PARAM NAME="ForeColor" VALUE="8421376">
<PARAM NAME="FontHeight" VALUE="160">
<PARAM NAME="FontWeight" VALUE="700">
<PARAM NAME="Font" VALUE="MS Sans Serif">
<PARAM NAME="FontName" VALUE="MS Sans Serif">
<PARAM NAME="Size" VALUE="3146;728">
<PARAM NAME="VariousPropertyBits"
    VALUE="8388635">
<PARAM NAME="FontEffects" VALUE="1">
</OBJECT>

<OBJECT ID="Region"
CLASSID=
"CLSID:8BD21D10-EC42-11CE-9E0D-00AA006002F3"
STYLE="TOP:278;LEFT:561;WIDTH:144;HEIGHT:28;
TABINDEX:6;ZINDEX:8;">

<%If Not IsNull(rs.Fields("Region").Value)
    Then%>
    <PARAM NAME="Value"
    VALUE="<%=Server.HTMLEncode(rs.
      Fields("Region").Value)%>">
<%End If%>

<PARAM NAME="BackStyle" VALUE="1">
<PARAM NAME="BackColor" VALUE="13434879">
<PARAM NAME="BorderStyle" VALUE="1">
<PARAM NAME="BorderColor" VALUE="8421504">
<PARAM NAME="ForeColor" VALUE="128">
<PARAM NAME="FontHeight" VALUE="160">
<PARAM NAME="Font" VALUE="MS Sans Serif">
```

```
<PARAM NAME="FontName" VALUE="MS Sans Serif">
<PARAM NAME="Size" VALUE="3744;728">
<PARAM NAME="VariousPropertyBits"
    VALUE="2894088219">
</OBJECT>

<OBJECT ID="RegionLabel"
CLASSID=
"CLSID:978C9E23-D4B0-11CE-BF2D-00AA003F40D0"
STYLE="TOP:278;LEFT:466;WIDTH:79;HEIGHT:28;
ZINDEX:9;">
<PARAM NAME="BackStyle" VALUE="1">
<PARAM NAME="BackColor" VALUE="13434879">
<PARAM NAME="BorderStyle" VALUE="1">
<PARAM NAME="BorderColor" VALUE="8421504">
<PARAM NAME="Caption" VALUE="Region:">
<PARAM NAME="ParagraphAlign" VALUE="2">
<PARAM NAME="ForeColor" VALUE="8421376">
<PARAM NAME="FontHeight" VALUE="160">
<PARAM NAME="FontWeight" VALUE="700">
<PARAM NAME="Font" VALUE="MS Sans Serif">
<PARAM NAME="FontName" VALUE="MS Sans Serif">
<PARAM NAME="Size" VALUE="2054;728">
<PARAM NAME="VariousPropertyBits"
    VALUE="8388635">
<PARAM NAME="FontEffects" VALUE="1">
</OBJECT>

<OBJECT ID="City"
CLASSID=
"CLSID:8BD21D10-EC42-11CE-9E0D-00AA006002F3"
STYLE="TOP:278;LEFT:259;WIDTH:144;HEIGHT:28;
TABINDEX:5;ZINDEX:10;">

<%If Not IsNull(rs.Fields("City").Value)
    Then%>
    <PARAM NAME="Value"
    VALUE="<%=Server.HTMLEncode(rs.
      Fields("City").Value)%>">
<%End If%>

<PARAM NAME="BackStyle" VALUE="1">
<PARAM NAME="BackColor" VALUE="13434879">
<PARAM NAME="BorderStyle" VALUE="1">
<PARAM NAME="BorderColor" VALUE="8421504">
<PARAM NAME="ForeColor" VALUE="128">
<PARAM NAME="FontHeight" VALUE="160">
<PARAM NAME="Font" VALUE="MS Sans Serif">
<PARAM NAME="FontName" VALUE="MS Sans Serif">
<PARAM NAME="Size" VALUE="3744;728">
```

```
<PARAM NAME="VariousPropertyBits"
    VALUE="2894088219">
</OBJECT>

<OBJECT ID="CityLabel"
CLASSID=
"CLSID:978C9E23-D4B0-11CE-BF2D-00AA003F40D0"
STYLE="TOP:278;LEFT:193;WIDTH:51;HEIGHT:28;
ZINDEX:11;">
<PARAM NAME="BackStyle" VALUE="1">
<PARAM NAME="BackColor" VALUE="13434879">
<PARAM NAME="BorderStyle" VALUE="1">
<PARAM NAME="BorderColor" VALUE="8421504">
<PARAM NAME="Caption" VALUE="City:">
<PARAM NAME="ParagraphAlign" VALUE="2">
<PARAM NAME="ForeColor" VALUE="8421376">
<PARAM NAME="FontHeight" VALUE="160">
<PARAM NAME="FontWeight" VALUE="700">
<PARAM NAME="Font" VALUE="MS Sans Serif">
<PARAM NAME="FontName" VALUE="MS Sans Serif">
<PARAM NAME="Size" VALUE="1326;728">
<PARAM NAME="VariousPropertyBits"
    VALUE="8388635">
<PARAM NAME="FontEffects" VALUE="1">
</OBJECT>

<OBJECT ID="Address"
CLASSID=
"CLSID:8BD21D10-EC42-11CE-9E0D-00AA006002F3"
STYLE="TOP:218;LEFT:259;WIDTH:285;HEIGHT:48;
TABINDEX:4;ZINDEX:12;">

<%If Not IsNull(rs.Fields("Address").Value)
    Then%>
    <PARAM NAME="Value"
    VALUE="<%=Server.HTMLEncode(rs.
      Fields("Address").Value)%>">
<%End If%>

<PARAM NAME="BackStyle" VALUE="1">
<PARAM NAME="BackColor" VALUE="13434879">
<PARAM NAME="BorderStyle" VALUE="1">
<PARAM NAME="BorderColor" VALUE="8421504">
<PARAM NAME="ForeColor" VALUE="128">
<PARAM NAME="FontHeight" VALUE="160">
<PARAM NAME="Font" VALUE="MS Sans Serif">
<PARAM NAME="FontName" VALUE="MS Sans Serif">
<PARAM NAME="Size" VALUE="7410;1248">
<PARAM NAME="VariousPropertyBits"
    VALUE="2894088219">
```

```
</OBJECT>

<OBJECT ID="AddressLabel"
CLASSID=
"CLSID:978C9E23-D4B0-11CE-BF2D-00AA003F40D0"
STYLE="TOP:218;LEFT:157;WIDTH:87;HEIGHT:28;
ZINDEX:13;">
<PARAM NAME="BackStyle" VALUE="1">
<PARAM NAME="BackColor" VALUE="13434879">
<PARAM NAME="BorderStyle" VALUE="1">
<PARAM NAME="BorderColor" VALUE="8421504">
<PARAM NAME="Caption" VALUE="Address:">
<PARAM NAME="ParagraphAlign" VALUE="2">
<PARAM NAME="ForeColor" VALUE="8421376">
<PARAM NAME="FontHeight" VALUE="160">
<PARAM NAME="FontWeight" VALUE="700">
<PARAM NAME="Font" VALUE="MS Sans Serif">
<PARAM NAME="FontName" VALUE="MS Sans Serif">
<PARAM NAME="Size" VALUE="2262;728">
<PARAM NAME="VariousPropertyBits"
    VALUE="8388635">
<PARAM NAME="FontEffects" VALUE="1">
</OBJECT>

<OBJECT ID="ContactTitle"
CLASSID=
"CLSID:8BD21D10-EC42-11CE-9E0D-00AA006002F3"
STYLE="TOP:167;LEFT:561;WIDTH:193;HEIGHT:28;
TABINDEX:3;ZINDEX:14;">

<%If Not IsNull(rs.
    Fields("ContactTitle").Value) Then%>
    <PARAM NAME="Value"
    VALUE="<%=Server.HTMLEncode(rs.
      Fields("ContactTitle").Value)%>">
<%End If%>

<PARAM NAME="BackStyle" VALUE="1">
<PARAM NAME="BackColor" VALUE="13434879">
<PARAM NAME="BorderStyle" VALUE="1">
<PARAM NAME="BorderColor" VALUE="8421504">
<PARAM NAME="ForeColor" VALUE="128">
<PARAM NAME="FontHeight" VALUE="160">
<PARAM NAME="Font" VALUE="MS Sans Serif">
<PARAM NAME="FontName" VALUE="MS Sans Serif">
<PARAM NAME="Size" VALUE="5018;728">
<PARAM NAME="VariousPropertyBits"
    VALUE="2894088219">
</OBJECT>
```

```
<OBJECT ID="TitleLabel"
CLASSID=
"CLSID:978C9E23-D4B0-11CE-BF2D-00AA003F40D0"
STYLE="TOP:167;LEFT:489;WIDTH:57;HEIGHT:28;
ZINDEX:15;">
<PARAM NAME="BackStyle" VALUE="1">
<PARAM NAME="BackColor" VALUE="13434879">
<PARAM NAME="BorderStyle" VALUE="1">
<PARAM NAME="BorderColor" VALUE="8421504">
<PARAM NAME="Caption" VALUE="Title:">
<PARAM NAME="ParagraphAlign" VALUE="2">
<PARAM NAME="ForeColor" VALUE="8421376">
<PARAM NAME="FontHeight" VALUE="160">
<PARAM NAME="FontWeight" VALUE="700">
<PARAM NAME="Font" VALUE="MS Sans Serif">
<PARAM NAME="FontName" VALUE="MS Sans Serif">
<PARAM NAME="Size" VALUE="1482;728">
<PARAM NAME="VariousPropertyBits"
    VALUE="8388635">
<PARAM NAME="FontEffects" VALUE="1">
</OBJECT>

<OBJECT ID="ContactName"
CLASSID=
"CLSID:8BD21D10-EC42-11CE-9E0D-00AA006002F3"
STYLE="TOP:167;LEFT:259;WIDTH:187;HEIGHT:28;
TABINDEX:2;ZINDEX:16;">

<%If Not IsNull(rs.
    Fields("ContactName").Value) Then%>
    <PARAM NAME="Value"
    VALUE="<%=Server.HTMLEncode(rs.
      Fields("ContactName").Value)%>">
<%End If%>

<PARAM NAME="BackStyle" VALUE="1">
<PARAM NAME="BackColor" VALUE="13434879">
<PARAM NAME="BorderStyle" VALUE="1">
<PARAM NAME="BorderColor" VALUE="8421504">
<PARAM NAME="ForeColor" VALUE="128">
<PARAM NAME="FontHeight" VALUE="160">
<PARAM NAME="Font" VALUE="MS Sans Serif">
<PARAM NAME="FontName" VALUE="MS Sans Serif">
<PARAM NAME="Size" VALUE="4862;728">
<PARAM NAME="VariousPropertyBits"
    VALUE="2894088219">
</OBJECT>

<OBJECT ID="ContactNameLabel"
CLASSID=
```

```
"CLSID:978C9E23-D4B0-11CE-BF2D-00AA003F40D0"
STYLE="TOP:167;LEFT:105;WIDTH:139;HEIGHT:28;
ZINDEX:17;">
<PARAM NAME="BackStyle" VALUE="1">
<PARAM NAME="BackColor" VALUE="13434879">
<PARAM NAME="BorderStyle" VALUE="1">
<PARAM NAME="BorderColor" VALUE="8421504">
<PARAM NAME="Caption" VALUE="Contact Name:">
<PARAM NAME="ParagraphAlign" VALUE="2">
<PARAM NAME="ForeColor" VALUE="8421376">
<PARAM NAME="FontHeight" VALUE="160">
<PARAM NAME="FontWeight" VALUE="700">
<PARAM NAME="Font" VALUE="MS Sans Serif">
<PARAM NAME="FontName" VALUE="MS Sans Serif">
<PARAM NAME="Size" VALUE="3614;728">
<PARAM NAME="VariousPropertyBits"
    VALUE="8388635">
<PARAM NAME="FontEffects" VALUE="1">
</OBJECT>

<OBJECT ID="CompanyName"
CLASSID=
"CLSID:8BD21D10-EC42-11CE-9E0D-00AA006002F3"
STYLE="TOP:122;LEFT:259;WIDTH:354;HEIGHT:28;
TABINDEX:1;ZINDEX:18;">

<%If Not IsNull(rs.
    Fields("CompanyName").Value) Then%>
    <PARAM NAME="Value"
    VALUE="<%=Server.HTMLEncode(rs.
      Fields("CompanyName").Value)%>">
<%End If%>

<PARAM NAME="BackStyle" VALUE="1">
<PARAM NAME="BackColor" VALUE="13434879">
<PARAM NAME="BorderStyle" VALUE="1">
<PARAM NAME="BorderColor" VALUE="8421504">
<PARAM NAME="ForeColor" VALUE="128">
<PARAM NAME="FontHeight" VALUE="160">
<PARAM NAME="Font" VALUE="MS Sans Serif">
<PARAM NAME="FontName" VALUE="MS Sans Serif">
<PARAM NAME="Size" VALUE="9204;728">
<PARAM NAME="VariousPropertyBits"
    VALUE="2894088219">
</OBJECT>

<OBJECT ID="CompanyNameLabel"
CLASSID=
"CLSID:978C9E23-D4B0-11CE-BF2D-00AA003F40D0"
STYLE="TOP:122;LEFT:94;WIDTH:150;HEIGHT:28;
```

```
ZINDEX:19;">
<PARAM NAME="BackStyle" VALUE="1">
<PARAM NAME="BackColor" VALUE="13434879">
<PARAM NAME="BorderStyle" VALUE="1">
<PARAM NAME="BorderColor" VALUE="8421504">
<PARAM NAME="Caption" VALUE="Company Name:">
<PARAM NAME="ParagraphAlign" VALUE="2">
<PARAM NAME="ForeColor" VALUE="8421376">
<PARAM NAME="FontHeight" VALUE="160">
<PARAM NAME="FontWeight" VALUE="700">
<PARAM NAME="Font" VALUE="MS Sans Serif">
<PARAM NAME="FontName" VALUE="MS Sans Serif">
<PARAM NAME="Size" VALUE="3900;728">
<PARAM NAME="VariousPropertyBits"
    VALUE="8388635">
<PARAM NAME="FontEffects" VALUE="1">
</OBJECT>

<OBJECT ID="CustomerID"
CLASSID=
"CLSID:8BD21D10-EC42-11CE-9E0D-00AA006002F3"
STYLE="TOP:74;LEFT:259;WIDTH:88;HEIGHT:28;
TABINDEX:0;ZINDEX:20;">

<%If Not IsNull(rs.Fields("CustomerID").Value)
    Then%>
    <PARAM NAME="Value"
    VALUE="<%=Server.HTMLEncode(rs.
      Fields("CustomerID").Value)%>">
<%End If%>

<PARAM NAME="BackStyle" VALUE="1">
<PARAM NAME="BackColor" VALUE="13434879">
<PARAM NAME="BorderStyle" VALUE="1">
<PARAM NAME="BorderColor" VALUE="8421504">
<PARAM NAME="ForeColor" VALUE="128">
<PARAM NAME="FontHeight" VALUE="160">
<PARAM NAME="Font" VALUE="MS Sans Serif">
<PARAM NAME="FontName" VALUE="MS Sans Serif">
<PARAM NAME="Size" VALUE="2288;728">
<PARAM NAME="VariousPropertyBits"
    VALUE="2894088219">
</OBJECT>

<OBJECT ID="CustomerIDLabel"
CLASSID=
"CLSID:978C9E23-D4B0-11CE-BF2D-00AA003F40D0"
STYLE="TOP:74;LEFT:121;WIDTH:123;HEIGHT:28;
ZINDEX:21;">
<PARAM NAME="BackStyle" VALUE="1">
```

```
<PARAM NAME="BackColor" VALUE="13434879">
<PARAM NAME="BorderStyle" VALUE="1">
<PARAM NAME="BorderColor" VALUE="8421504">
<PARAM NAME="Caption" VALUE="Customer ID:">
<PARAM NAME="ParagraphAlign" VALUE="2">
<PARAM NAME="ForeColor" VALUE="8421376">
<PARAM NAME="FontHeight" VALUE="160">
<PARAM NAME="FontWeight" VALUE="700">
<PARAM NAME="Font" VALUE="MS Sans Serif">
<PARAM NAME="FontName" VALUE="MS Sans Serif">
<PARAM NAME="Size" VALUE="3198;728">
<PARAM NAME="VariousPropertyBits"
     VALUE="8388635">
<PARAM NAME="FontEffects" VALUE="1">
</OBJECT>

<OBJECT ID="nav_btn_MoveCancelUpdate"
CLASSID=
"CLSID:D7053240-CE69-11CD-A777-00DD01143C57"
STYLE="TOP:434;LEFT:336;WIDTH:84;HEIGHT:28;
ZINDEX:0;">
<PARAM NAME="BackStyle" VALUE="0">
<PARAM NAME="Caption" VALUE="Refresh">
<PARAM NAME="ParagraphAlign" VALUE="3">
<PARAM NAME="ForeColor" VALUE="0">
<PARAM NAME="Size" VALUE="2184;728">
<PARAM NAME="SpecialEffect" VALUE="0">
<PARAM NAME="VariousPropertyBits" VALUE="2">
</OBJECT>

<OBJECT ID="nav_btn_MoveDeleteRecord"
CLASSID=
"CLSID:D7053240-CE69-11CD-A777-00DD01143C57"
STYLE="TOP:434;LEFT:252;WIDTH:84;HEIGHT:28;
ZINDEX:1;">
<PARAM NAME="BackStyle" VALUE="0">
<PARAM NAME="Caption" VALUE="Delete">
<PARAM NAME="ParagraphAlign" VALUE="3">
<PARAM NAME="ForeColor" VALUE="0">
<PARAM NAME="Size" VALUE="2184;728">
<PARAM NAME="SpecialEffect" VALUE="0">
<PARAM NAME="VariousPropertyBits" VALUE="2">
</OBJECT>

<OBJECT ID="nav_btn_MoveCommitRecord"
CLASSID=
"CLSID:D7053240-CE69-11CD-A777-00DD01143C57"
STYLE="TOP:434;LEFT:168;WIDTH:84;HEIGHT:28;
ZINDEX:2;">
<PARAM NAME="BackStyle" VALUE="0">
```

```
<PARAM NAME="Caption" VALUE="Commit">
<PARAM NAME="ParagraphAlign" VALUE="3">
<PARAM NAME="ForeColor" VALUE="0">
<PARAM NAME="Size" VALUE="2184;728">
<PARAM NAME="SpecialEffect" VALUE="0">
<PARAM NAME="VariousPropertyBits" VALUE="2">
</OBJECT>

<OBJECT ID="nav_btn_MoveAddRecord"
CLASSID=
"CLSID:D7053240-CE69-11CD-A777-00DD01143C57"
STYLE="TOP:434;LEFT:112;WIDTH:28;HEIGHT:28;
ZINDEX:3;">
<PARAM NAME="BackStyle" VALUE="0">
<PARAM NAME="Caption" VALUE="&gt;*">
<PARAM NAME="ParagraphAlign" VALUE="3">
<PARAM NAME="ForeColor" VALUE="0">
<PARAM NAME="Size" VALUE="728;728">
<PARAM NAME="SpecialEffect" VALUE="0">
<PARAM NAME="VariousPropertyBits" VALUE="2">
</OBJECT>

<OBJECT ID="nav_btn_MoveLastRecord"
CLASSID=
"CLSID:D7053240-CE69-11CD-A777-00DD01143C57"
STYLE="TOP:434;LEFT:84;WIDTH:28;HEIGHT:28;
ZINDEX:4;">
<PARAM NAME="BackStyle" VALUE="0">
<PARAM NAME="Caption" VALUE="&gt;|">
<PARAM NAME="ParagraphAlign" VALUE="3">
<PARAM NAME="ForeColor" VALUE="0">
<PARAM NAME="Size" VALUE="728;728">
<PARAM NAME="SpecialEffect" VALUE="0">
<PARAM NAME="VariousPropertyBits" VALUE="2">
</OBJECT>

<OBJECT ID="nav_btn_MoveNextRecord"
CLASSID=
"CLSID:D7053240-CE69-11CD-A777-00DD01143C57"
STYLE="TOP:434;LEFT:56;WIDTH:28;HEIGHT:28;
ZINDEX:5;">
<PARAM NAME="BackStyle" VALUE="0">
<PARAM NAME="Caption" VALUE="&gt;">
<PARAM NAME="ParagraphAlign" VALUE="3">
<PARAM NAME="ForeColor" VALUE="0">
<PARAM NAME="Size" VALUE="728;728">
<PARAM NAME="SpecialEffect" VALUE="0">
<PARAM NAME="VariousPropertyBits" VALUE="2">
</OBJECT>
```

```
<OBJECT ID="nav_btn_MovePrevRecord"
CLASSID=
"CLSID:D7053240-CE69-11CD-A777-00DD01143C57"
STYLE="TOP:434;LEFT:28;WIDTH:28;HEIGHT:28;
ZINDEX:6;">
<PARAM NAME="BackStyle" VALUE="0">
<PARAM NAME="Caption" VALUE="&lt;">
<PARAM NAME="ParagraphAlign" VALUE="3">
<PARAM NAME="ForeColor" VALUE="0">
<PARAM NAME="Size" VALUE="728;728">
<PARAM NAME="SpecialEffect" VALUE="0">
<PARAM NAME="VariousPropertyBits" VALUE="2">
</OBJECT>

<OBJECT ID="nav_btn_MoveFirstRecord"
CLASSID=
"CLSID:D7053240-CE69-11CD-A777-00DD01143C57"
STYLE="TOP:434;LEFT:0;WIDTH:28;HEIGHT:28;
ZINDEX:7;">
<PARAM NAME="BackStyle" VALUE="0">
<PARAM NAME="Caption" VALUE="|&lt;">
<PARAM NAME="ParagraphAlign" VALUE="3">
<PARAM NAME="ForeColor" VALUE="0">
<PARAM NAME="Size" VALUE="728;728">
<PARAM NAME="SpecialEffect" VALUE="0">
<PARAM NAME="VariousPropertyBits" VALUE="2">
</OBJECT>
</DIV>
```

DESIGNING YOUR OWN PUBLISH TO THE WEB WIZARD TEMPLATES

Access 97 comes installed with several templates that supply you with a variety of background colors and styles and navigation buttons to go from page to page in a multi-page publication. These templates as well as the graphic files (JPEG files with a .jpg extension) reside in the Access template directory (normally the directory is \Program Files\Microsoft Office\Templates\Access). Not just any HTML page can serve as a template file. The reason the HTML template requires special tags in which to place items such as the body information or navigation references. For example, here's a sample HTML template. You can open any of the templates inside your HTML editor, the Windows Notepad utility, or even Visual InterDev.

```
<HTML>
<TITLE><!ACCESSTEMPLATE_TITLE></TITLE>
<BODY>
<!ACCESSTEMPLATE_BODY>
<A HREF="<!AccessTemplate_FirstPage>">
First</A>
<A HREF="<!AccessTemplate_PreviousPage>">
```

```
Previous</A>
<A HREF="<!AccessTemplate_NextPage>">Next</A>
<A HREF="<!AccessTemplate_LastPage>">Last</A>
</BODY>
<BR><BR>
<IMG SRC = "msaccess.jpg">
</HTML>
```

Notice the new tags embedded in the HTML comment lines that all begin with the ACCESSTEMPLATE attribute. Table 9-2 displays a complete list of all the Internet Assistant special tags recognized by the DLL.

Table 9–2	Internet Assistant Special HTML Tags
Tag	**Description**
<!ACCESSTEMPLATE_TITLE>	HTML page title
<!ACCESSTEMPLATE_BODY>	Detail data
<!ACCESSTEMPLATE_FirstPage>	First page navigation button
<!ACCESSTEMPLATE_PreviousPage>	Previous page navigation button
<!ACCESSTEMPLATE_NextPage>	Next page navigation button
<!ACCESSTEMPLATE_LastPage>	Last page navigation button

These special tags tell the wizard where to place the title, the body (your Access data), and the four navigation buttons. If the Publish to the Web Wizard can't find the navigation button tags, the resulting page doesn't contain them. If the Wizard cannot find the title or body tags, it replaces any existing text with the title and body information. The supplied templates contain many different styles and custom logos. For instance, you can specify the position of a logo with the <IMG SRC="ImageFileName"> tag.

THE WEBBROWSER CONTROL

The Microsoft WebBrowser control is an ActiveX control that enables you to view Web pages and other documents on the Internet or an intranet from a Microsoft Access form. The WebBrowser control is provided by Internet Explorer 3.0/4.0, which is included with Microsoft Office 97. The control is automatically registered with the operating system when you install Internet Explorer, so you can use it from Access without first registering it. To add the WebBrowser control to a form, bring up a new form in form design view, select the *ActiveX Control* item from the Insert menu, and then click on *Microsoft WebBrowser Control* in the list of ActiveX controls.

Once you have added the WebBrowser control to a form, you can use the control's Navigate method to open a Web page within the WebBrowser window. For example, if you've added a WebBrowser control named BrowserCtl0 to a form, you could create the following Load event procedure for the form:

```
Private Sub Form_Load
    Me!ActiveXCtl0.Navigate
        "http://www.amuletc.com"
End Sub
```

You can also access the WebBrowser control's property list by right-clicking on the control and selecting Properties.

VBA PROGRAMMING WITH WEB-ENABLED MACRO ACTIONS

Microsoft Access 97 widens the scope of the OutputTo method of the DoCmd object. The result of this added capability is that you can use this method in your VBA for Access code to customize or automate the process of outputting Access database objects to static HTML documents, dynamic HTX/IDC pages, or ASP pages. The syntax of the OutputTo method is:

```
DoCmd.OutputTo ObjectType [,ObjectName]
    [,OutputFormat] [,OutputFile] [,AutoStart]
    [,TemplateFile]
```

The method's parameters are defined in Table 9-3. As a simple example of how to use OutputTo for Web publishing, consider the following VBA procedure that outputs the contents of the Northwind Traders Employees table in HTML format and then opens the default browser to view it:

```
Public Sub OutputToHTML()

Dim strTableObj As String
Dim strHTMLOut As String

'Auto-start browser
Dim blnAutoStart As Boolean

strTableObj = "Employees"
strHTMLOut = "Employees.html"
blnAutoStart = True

DoCmd.OutputTo acOutputTable, strTableObj,
    acFormatHTML, strHTMLOut, blnAutoStart

End Sub
```

In the above example, I simply reference a database table object, specify the output format as HTML, and give an output file name having the correct file extension. With the AutoStart parameter, the default browser, say Internet Explorer, is automatically launched with the new page loaded.

Table 9–3	OutputTo Method Parameters
ObjectType	**Description**
ObjectType	One of the following intrinsic constants—acOutputTable, acOutputQuery, acOutputForm, acOutputReport, or acOutputModule—indicating the type of the object being passed to the OutputTo method.
ObjectName	The name of the object in the current database to be output.
OutputFormat	One of the following intrinsic constants—acFormatActiveXServer, acFormatHTML, acFormatIIS, acFormatXLS, acFormatTXT, or acFormatRTF—indicating the format of the output.
OutputFile	The full name, including the path, of the file to which you want to output the object.
AutoStart	Use True (-1) to start the appropriate Windows application immediately, with the file specified by OutputFile loaded. Use False (0) if you don't want to start the application. The application started depends on the output file type (such as Internet Explorer, Excel, Notepad, or Word).
TemplateFile	The full name, including the path, of the template file for an HTML, HTX/IDC, or ASP file.

Next you can invoke the OutputTo method in the same manner as before, this time using one of the dynamic output methods. Choose the IIS Internet Database Connector (.HTX and .IDC files) format using the acFormatIIS intrinsic constant. Note that both dynamic formats, HTX/IDC and ASP, are available only for tables, queries, and forms. This time do not request the default Web browser software to open the document once the page has been generated, since the fifth parameter is omitted.

```
DoCmd.OutputTo acOutputForm, "Customers", _
    acFormatIIS, "Customers"
```

Two files, customers.htx and customers.idc, were generated by the above VBA code.

Access 97 also expands the SendObject and TransferText methods, allowing for HTML as a valid target format.

Custom HTML Generation Using VBA for Access

You can now examine the more customized approach of generating static database content Web pages using the VBA for Access programming language. The technique involves using the Visual Basic language construct that allows for the creation and manipulation of simple ASCII text files. Instead of writing information to a table or the Windows screen, you direct output to a disk file.

The output will contain familiar HTML tags and table data in the form of tables for easy viewing with a standard Web browser. As a basis of our discussion, I use the products table out of the Northwind Traders sample application. My desire is to generate Web pages that contain specific fields from the table and present them in a custom manner, using HTML tables. Using this approach, you are not constrained by the HTML style or tags used by tools like Internet Assistant that automatically generate HTML. You're also free to experiment with browser-specific tags such as Cascading Style Sheets adopted by Internet Explorer. The VBA procedure that follows typifies this process.

```
Public Sub ExportToHTML()

Dim db As DATABASE
Dim rs As Recordset
Dim strSQL As String
Dim strCompany As String
Dim intFileNo As Integer

Set db = _
    DBEngine.Workspaces(0).Databases(0)

strSQL = _
"SELECT DISTINCTROW ProductName, "& _
"QuantityPerUnit, UnitPrice, UnitsInStock " &
"tblProducts WHERE Not Discontinued"

Set rs = db.OpenRecordset(strSQL, _
    dbOpenDynaset)

' Call FreeFile function to return the next
' file number available for use by the Open
' statement.
intFileNo = FreeFile
Open "htmlout.htm" For Output As intFileNo

'Generate HTML for page header
Print #intFileNo, "<HTML>"
Print #intFileNo, "<HEAD>"
Print #intFileNo, "</HEAD>"
Print #intFileNo, "<BODY>"
Print #intFileNo, "<H1>Export to HTML</H1>"
Print #intFileNo, _
    "<H2>Product Inventory List</H2>"
Print #intFileNo, "<P>"
Print #intFileNo, "<HR>"

'Traverse the result set and output HTML table
'tags
rs.MoveFirst
```

```
Do While Not rs.EOF
    Print #intFileNo, "</DL>"
    Print #intFileNo, "<P>"
    Print #intFileNo, "<H3>" & _
        rs![ProductName] & "</H3>"
    Print #intFileNo, "<DL>"
    Print #intFileNo, "<LI>" & "Qty/Unit: " & _
        rs![QuantityPerUnit] & _
        " Unit Price:" & _
        rs![UnitPrice] & _
        " Units In Stock:" & _
        rs![UnitsInStock] & "</LI>"
    Print #intFileNo, "<P>"
    Print #intFileNo, "<HR>"
    rs.MoveNext
Loop

Print #intFileNo, "</OL>"
Print #intFileNo, "<HR>"
Print #intFileNo, "</BODY>"
Print #intFileNo, "</HTML>"

Close intFileNo        'Close before leaving
End Sub
```

Notice in the code above that I use DAO (Data Access Objects) to obtain a resultset. I then get a file handle in order to open a disk file using the OPEN statement. This allows us to write HTML text strings to the file with simple PRINT statements. The resulting Web page created by the program appears in Figure 9-25.

A Static Database Content Desktop Implementation Case Study

In support of the ideas presented in this section, I conclude with a brief examination of a Web site that my firm developed for a music collectibles and memorabilia distributor. Rockaway Records is in the business of selling rare editions of various music items such as vinyl LPs, CDs, posters, concert tickets, tour programs, backstage passes, T-shirts, etc. Their customers are individual collectors and memorabilia dealers around the world. This type of business is a natural one to benefit from an Internet presence, because to reach potential customers in remote parts of the world is otherwise difficult by traditional print ad or direct mail methods.

In the early going, the company put together a simple text/graphics-only home page. The problem was that although the site immediately attracted the intended audience, the most important facet was missing, namely an organized list of inventory items from which the users could select. The users still

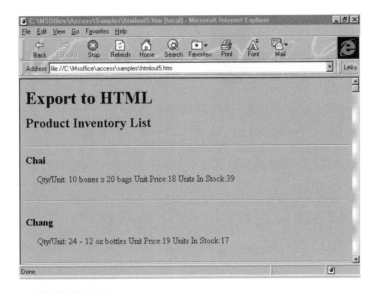

Figure 9–25   *Custom Web Page Generated from VBA Code*

had to dial up a phone number or FAX in an information request. The immediate goal was to eliminate the human-resource-intensive information hotline and replace it with a Web database resource. Since Rockaway specializes in specific types of collectible items of interest to collectors and dealers, only a certain subset of the entire inventory needed to be published (their database also held items for their retail outlets, not of interest to collectors). The plan became to use the Web site to display selected groups of items coming directly from the company's internal accounting system, which contained the most up-to-date picture of the inventory. You can browse the Rockaway site by pointing your browser to www.rockaway.com and bring up the mail order pages (see Figure 9-26 for a sample of the Beatles LP page).

From early on in the project, the decision was made that a full-blown Web server-based database implementation was not an option. The alternative was to take portions of the company's inventory database from its internal accounting system and format selected fields into HTML format. This process was facilitated by a custom front-end application that provides sophisticated querying capabilities centered around the inventory database of their FoxPro for DOS (using .DBF files) accounting software. The application allows the Rockaway IS department staff to extract qualified groups of records, automatically format the data for the Web using standard HTML table tags, and write the information to an ASCII text file with an .HTM extension. This process was achieved through application code much like that of the prior section of this chapter, using Access VBA.

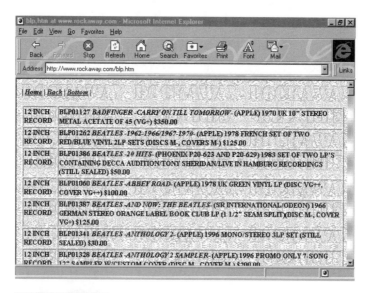

Static HTML for FoxPro-Based Accounting Inventory Data

The unique perspective of this Web implementation is the way the data pages, generated by the account system front-end, are organized. From the home page, the user may view various inventory items by clicking on the Mail Order graphic. From here, the user may select from a number of categories: new arrivals, showcase, Beatles, compact discs, posters, vinyl, and miscellaneous. From the perspective of the user, clicking on one of these graphics constitutes a query of sorts. He or she is requesting to drill down into the data, qualifying the request by the selected category. All but one of the pages below this initial level contain HTML pages consisting of pure formatted inventory data, generated offline by the accounting system front end. The Beatles page provides additional "querying," however, as it enables further qualification of the desired information. This page has links to additional data pages: compact discs, 7-inch vinyl, 12-inch vinyl, memorabilia, posters, tour programs, concert tickets, laser discs, videotapes, audiotapes, and books. Each of these second-tier pages contains inventory items that have something to do with the Beatles; for example, Beatles compact discs. Although the data is static and no back-end database is involved, to the user a query has taken place and the desired information is now available using point-and-click methods.

What is clear from the above description is that pseudo querying capabilities can be devised through a hierarchical organization of the data pages, which are periodically generated offline and placed on the Web site using FTP.

Summary

Much corporate data is stored in desktop databases, most notably Microsoft Access, and to a lesser degree Xbase .DBF format, including Microsoft Visual FoxPro. Publishing this data on the Web becomes a natural and contemporary requirement for organizations embracing the Internet, as well as local intranets. This chapter reviewed two primary methods of publishing desktop database data. Using the Microsoft desktop database ODBC driver allows any Web development tool able to connect to ODBC-compliant databases to directly access the desktop data. Other methods include non-interactive means towards WebTop database application development. For companies looking for an alternative to the relatively higher cost and effort associated with setting up and maintaining an in-house Web server, these approaches may be attractive.

Web Database
Case Study

·····················

In order to make the concepts of the preceding chapters hold more sig-
nificance for real-life business applications, I now examine how a spe-
cific real-life active-content, database-enabled Web site was developed.
In doing so, I consider the various stages of design and implementation,
along with the technologies involved during the process. The implemen-
tation described in this chapter could be the basis of many other target
WebTop applications, because it was developed in a generic manner.
One goal in presenting this case study in a rather detailed form is that
you can reuse this work for your own purposes.

Included with the case study is the following descriptive information
about the actual Web site on which the software is running: hardware platform and components used, system software chosen, back-end relational
database deployed, development tools utilized, application organization
(database design, queries, processes), and other details including some special items of interest.

A CGI Scripting Solution with ODBC

The case study I want you to consider is an integral component of a Chinese
community-based Web site sponsored by a Los Angeles company, Dynatek
Infoworld, Inc. The database connectivity components were developed by my
firm, AMULET Development Corp. This site caters to the special needs of
regional ethnic Chinese communities around the United States and Canada.

Although this site is rather comprehensive, with many components, the specific area of interest to us is the Yellow Pages feature. Here, users may interact with the online directory of businesses and services in much the same way one would use a physical Yellow Pages phone book. The primary difference, of course, is that the searching mechanism is automated through the Web.

One unique characteristic of the site is that it incorporates both English and Chinese character equivalents of several encoded database fields, allowing easy access for users whose primary language is Chinese. The way this important feature was implemented was by encoding Chinese characters during data entry into standard text fields in the database table. For the encoded data to be displayed properly by the browser, the client PC must be running special software for rendering foreign character sets. One such package is the NJWIN Multilingual Support System developed by Hongbo Data Systems, Inc., in Australia.

You can experiment with this Web site by browsing over to the URL http://www.info168.com and choosing the Search feature. Figure 10-1 contains the browser image of the community site's home page. For the full multilingual effect (even if you don't read Chinese), be sure to download the shareware version of NJWIN at www.njstar.com.au.

The database connectivity for the site was constructed using the Cold Fusion CGI environment from Allaire Corp.

Figure 10-1   *Dynatek InfoWorld Chinese Community Web Site*

Using the Chinese Yellow Pages

The database query implementation of the community site was done with ease of use in mind, due the relative lack of sophistication, in terms of database usage, of the target user base. We wanted to allow quick and easy "point-and-click" browsing capabilities, as well as the more customary "query-by-form" style of searching. Therefore, the topmost page of the Yellow Pages database portion of the site, dynatek.htm, has two user options, *Browse Mode* and *Search Mode,* which address the above stated requirements, respectively. This page appears in Figure 10-2. We were able to accommodate the two diverse searching styles with Cold Fusion by structuring the SQL queries differently in the case of Browse Mode, using multiple cumulative queries instead of a single SQL SELECT statement with a long WHERE clause. Now take a closer look at the usage specifics for each query style.

Browse Mode

The Browse Mode searching method was designed for users who prefer a more structured, point-and-click way to search through the community Yellow Pages database. No typing is actually required; you just find items that match your requirements and then click on the hypertext links. At each stage, as you'll see during the technical discussion that follows, a separate SQL

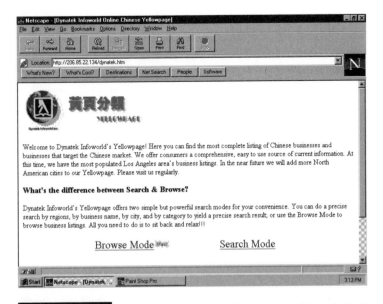

Figure 10-2   *Yellow Pages Page with Browse and Search Mode*

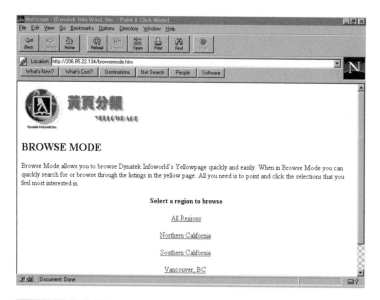

Browse Mode Select Region

query is issued and the results are carried forward to the next stage. The selection criteria accumulate as you continue down the selection path. The term "drill-down" is often applied to this method of narrowing the query down in stages.

Figure 10-3 shows the beginning page for Browse Mode. This page contains links for the currently supported regions. Because only three unique regions exist, the region selections are not stored in a table but are instead embedded in the HTML. Upon selecting a region, the user goes to the next page, where she or he may choose a group of categories based on the first letter of the category name. Figure 10-4 shows how each letter of the alphabet has its own hypertext link that sets up the first SQL query against the table tbl-Category to obtain the group of categories. Next, the user sees the list of selected categories, each with its own hypertext link leading to the next level. Figure 10-5 shows the category resultset after choosing the letter "A." At last, the final query is submitted to the database and a Yellow Pages resultset is retrieved. See Figure 10-6 for the business entries that qualify, according to the specified selection criteria, region and category.

The drill-down approach can generally be applied to most well defined search scenarios. Although the height of the search tree (i.e., the number of drill-down levels) can continue indefinitely, in reality, most topical searches should be limited to a relatively few number of steps. Less structured searches are best done with the more flexible Query-by-Form queries.

Figure 10–4   *Browse Mode Select Category First Letter*

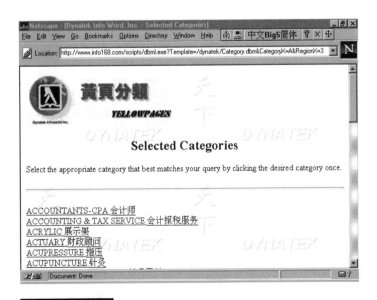

Figure 10–5   *Browse Mode Select Category*

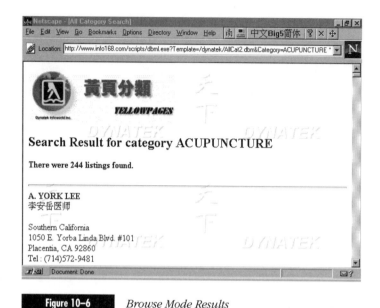

Figure 10-6
Browse Mode Results

Search Mode

The Search Mode style of searching for this site ascribes to the more conventional searching mechanisms that one normally encounters on the Web. This style uses the Query-by-Form metaphor made popular by GUI desktop database environments such as Access and Visual Basic, whereas a dialog box solicits selection criteria from the user by filling text boxes and using combo boxes for picklist selections. Figure 10-7 illustrates the Yellow Pages query form, complete with two picklists, one for Region and the other for Category. The latter is dynamically populated by a SQL query (see Figure 10-8) using the tblCategory table as a data source. The other fields, for business name, city, and zip code, accept either full or partial strings for a match. An implied logical "AND" is between these fields. For example, entering "ACME" for Business Name and "Santa Monica" for City requires both fields to match for a record to be selected. Also par for the course are two command buttons, *Submit Search* and *Clear Entries*. The first serves to execute the query using the entered criteria and return the results, and the latter allows the user to change his/her mind with the values entered and enter new values.

After submitting the query, the results are displayed as shown in Figure 10-9. Notice that we're able to advise the user how many records were selected based on the current criteria. Also notice that the category field has a hypertext link. This feature allows the user to click on the category, invoking a secondary query to obtain a complete category match list regardless of other previously selected criteria. You might think of this feature as a "drill-up" query.

Figure 10–7   *Search Mode Query-By-Form*

Figure 10–8   *Search Mode Category Pull-Down Menu*

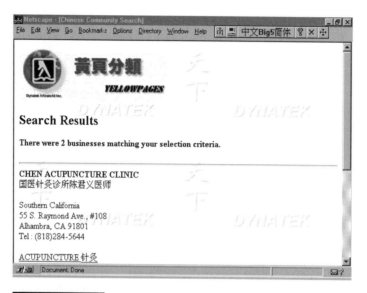

Figure 10–9 *Search Mode Results*

Hardware Implementation

The hardware selected for the Yellow Pages server was a custom-built, desktop PC put together by a local hardware vendor. The machine could not be considered a server-class PC due to the single processor, amount of available RAM, and lack of redundancy, etc. As is often the case, many sponsors of new Web sites choose to take the wait-and-see attitude before investing in heavy-duty enterprise server hardware from well known vendors such as Hewlett Packard, Compaq, Gateway, or Dell Computer. If the traffic warrants it, successful sites quickly upgrade to server-class machines to handle high-level bandwidth requirements for increased hit counts and higher volume database queries.

The specific characteristics for the Yellow Pages Web server are as follows:

- Pentium Pro 200MHz processor
- 32 MB of RAM
- 2.5GB SCSI hard drive
- 3COM EtherLink III NIC card
- 8X CD-ROM drive, 28.8K baud internal fax modem, 3.5-inch floppy drive, 17-inch monitor (1280x1024 resolution)
- American Power Conversion Backup UPS Pro 650

No back-up device was selected, in favor of doing regular backups from a LAN workstation onto an Iomega ZIP drive.

The local environment surrounding the Web server (which doubles as a file server) also included a small LAN with 6 workstations. Two workstations were configured with U.S. English Windows 98, and the rest had the Chinese language version of Windows running (along with a Chinese language keyboard). On a humorous note, I met with much challenge when using these workstations for the purpose of configuring ODBC and attaching the local installations of Access to the SQL back end. Very few English characters can be found on Chinese Windows menus and in dialog boxes. In most cases, I had to resort to my memory of the offset locations of needed menu items (for example, New is usually the first item on a File menu and Exit is the last).

The Yellow Pages site sponsors use the LAN workstations for running an Access 8.0 application that includes data entry forms for entering and editing records while attached to the live Web SQL Server database. The forms have record source properties set to the tblWebData and tblCategory tables. The tables are in turn attached to SQL Server via ODBC.

The Internet connection used for the site's bandwidth requirements is a fractional T1 line (128K Frame Relay).

System Software Implementation

The Yellow Pages site runs on a Windows NT 4.0 Web server using the Microsoft Internet Information Server (IIS) 4.0 Web server platform. The back-end relational database is Microsoft SQL Server 6.5 with the unlimited license extension required by Microsoft for any version of SQL Server that processes database queries on a Web server. The site is maintained using Microsoft FrontPage 98. All DSNs are through the standard 32-bit ODBC driver. For completeness, the ODBC dialog box for one of the Windows 98 workstations appears in Figure 10-10.

Application Software Implementation

The database connectivity was implemented using the Cold Fusion CGI-based database application development tool by Allaire Corp. For more information about this product, browse to www.allaire.com. The primary target browser used during the development of the Yellow Pages site was Netscape Communicator 4.0; however, all features function properly through Microsoft's Internet Explorer 4.0.

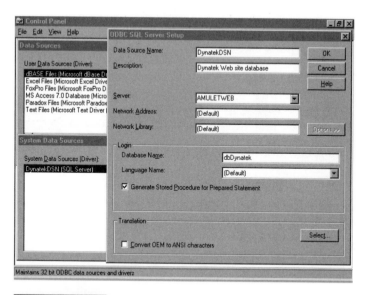

Figure 10–10   *Windows 98 Workstation ODBC Dialog Box*

Database Design

The database design, as shown in Figure 10-11, consists of only two tables. The primary table is tblWebData, which contains general information about the business, including its region, category, and even its URL, if one exists. The second table is tblCategory, containing over 1000 different classifications of businesses in the database. The implied relationship between these two tables is a Many-to-One (M:1), a category table lookup, or a One-to-Many (1:M)—a unique category with many potential businesses, depending on the perspective of the query. Region information is not kept in a separate table but rather is found in static HTML. This detail was an early design decision to simplify the implementation, because only three regions existed at the outset. As more regions are added, a new tblRegion will most likely be necessary.

The tables were created using the Microsoft Access 97 environment and then transferred to SQL Server using the Upsizing Wizard, available for free from the Microsoft Web site. The Access form shown in Figure 10-12 is used by local Windows 98 workstations connected on the LAN to maintain the live Web data via an ODBC connection to the SQL Server tables on the NT Web server. You can see the back-end organization in Figure 10-13, using the graphical facility in the SQL Server Enterprise Manager. We set up two database devices for the application, DynatekData and DynatekLog, because

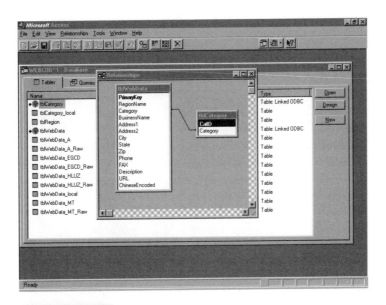

Figure 10–11   *Database Design*

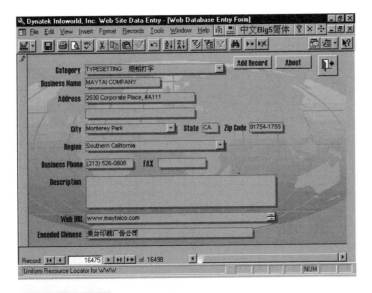

Figure 10–12   *Microsoft Access 97 Data Entry Form*

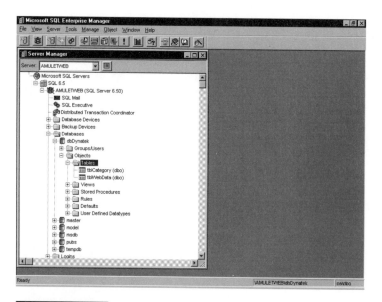

Figure 10-13 *SQL Server Enterprise Manager*

building separate devices is recommended (preferably on different drive partitions) for data and log information. The SQL database dbDynatek contains the two up-sized Access tables, which are listed under the Table object group.

Cold Fusion Implementation

Now direct your attention to the implementation of this site. The following standard HTML and Cold Fusion template files were necessary to implement the database functionality required for this site. The pages depend on several graphic images stored in the IIS \Graphics directory located off the standard IIS \WWWROOT directory. The Cold Fusion template files (those with a .DBM file name extension) are stored in the \Cfusion\Template\Dynatek directory. During a standard installation, the Cold Fusion setup program creates the \Cfusion\Template directory structure. For each Web database application you develop, a new directory is needed underneath the template directory. Table 10-1 contains a complete list of these files along with their purpose. I further describe some interesting ingredients of these files.

Users may enter into the database-enabled Web pages of the site with the Dynatek.htm page shown below. Most of this file contains very generic HTML; however, the hypertext links to move to either Browse Mode or Search Mode differ significantly. To get Browse Mode, we simply link to another HTML page, BrowseMode.htm. For Search Mode, however, we must invoke

Table 10-1	Yellow Pages Site Files
File Name	**Description**
Dynatek.htm	(Standard HTML) Primary Yellow Pages database component page. Includes two query options: Browse Mode and Search Mode.
BrowseMode.htm	(Standard HTML) Entry into Browse Mode to select region. Currently, three regions are available, or all regions.
Region.dbm	(Cold Fusion template) Select category by first letter. Each letter of the alphabet is presented and has a hypertext link.
Category.dbm	(Cold Fusion template) Select one category from list generated by first-letter criteria. SQL query result set of all category names beginning with chosen letter.
AllCat2.dbm	(Cold Fusion template) Display resultset for category query. Complete business information.
SrchMode.dbm	(Cold Fusion template) Query-by-Form dialog box for user selection criteria. Has static list for regions and dynamic list for categories. Clicking on Submit button runs the query.
Dynatek.dbm	(Cold Fusion template) Display resultset for Search Mode query. Includes hypertext link to display all businesses with category, regardless of region.
AllCat.dbm	(Cold Fusion template) Display all categories, regardless of region. "Drill-up" query, in effect, broadens the query, as compared to "drill-down" effect in Browse Mode.

the Cold Fusion CGI script DBML.EXE to load the SrchMode.dbm template file. A template file is necessary here because we require Cold Fusion functionality at this stage (you'll see why during the discussion of SrchMode.dbm a bit later).

```
<!-- DYNATEK.HTM -->
<HTML>
<HEAD>
<TITLE>
Dynatek InfoWorld, Inc. Online Chinese Yellow
Pages
</TITLE>
</HEAD>

<BODY BGCOLOR="#FFFFFF"
  BACKGROUND="graphics/watermark4.gif">
<IMG SRC="graphics/yellowpageheader.gif">
```

```
<P>Welcome to Dynatek Infoworld&#146;s Chinese
Yellow Pages! Here you can find the most
complete listing of Chinese businesses and
businesses that target the Chinese market.
We offer consumers a comprehensive, easy to
use source of current information. At this
time, we have the most populated Los Angeles
area&#146;s business listings. In the near
future we will add more North American cities
to our Yellow Pages. Please visit us
regularly.<BR> </P>

<P><B><FONT SIZE="+1">
What's the difference between Search &amp;
Browse?
</FONT></B><BR><BR>
Dynatek Infoworld&#146;s Yellow Pages
offers two simple but powerful search modes
for your convenience. You can do a precise
search by regions, by business name, by city,
and by category to yield a precise search
result; or use the Browse Mode to browse
business listings. All you need to do is to
sit back and relax!!!
<BR>
</P>

<CENTER>
<TABLE WIDTH="70%" BORDER="0">
<TR>
<TD ALIGN="CENTER" VALIGN="TOP" WIDTH="50%">
    <A HREF="browsemode.htm"><FONT SIZE="+2">
    Browse Mode</FONT></A>
    <IMG SRC="graphics/fast-burst.gif"
    WIDTH="35"
    HEIGHT="17">
</TD>

<TD ALIGN="CENTER" VALIGN="TOP" WIDTH="50%">
    <A HREF="/scripts/dbml.exe?Template=
    /dynatek/srchmode.dbm"><FONT SIZE="+2">
    Search Mode</FONT></A>
</TD>
</TR>
</TABLE>
</CENTER>

<P>
<IMG SRC="graphics/nt_web.gif" WIDTH="313"
```

```
          HEIGHT="40" ALIGN="absmiddle" HSPACE="80">
</P>

</BODY>
</HTML>
```

Browse Mode Implementation

Users begin in Browse Mode by selecting a region with BrowseMode.htm, shown below. Depending on which region the user selects, it must be retained, so we must pass the value as a parameter to the next page. Cold Fusion allows for passing parameters between pages by letting you define one or more parameters and values in *parameter=value* format, as in the sample <A HREF> from the template file:

```
<A HREF="/scripts/dbml.exe?Template=
     /dynatek/  Region.dbm&RegionX=3">
     Southern California</A>
```

All parameters passed to the CGI script must follow the question mark (?) and be separated by an ampersand (&). The first parameter in this case is Template=/dynatek/Region.dbm and the second parameter is RegionX=3. The RegionX parameter's value will be referenced later to determine which region was selected.

```
<!-- BROWSEMODE.HTM -->

<HTML>
<HEAD>
<TITLE>
Dynatek InfoWorld, Inc. - Point &amp;
Click Mode
</TITLE>
</HEAD>

<BODY BACKGROUND="graphics/watermark4.gif">
<IMG SRC="graphics/yellowpageheader.gif"
     BORDER="0">

<H2>BROWSE MODE</H2>
<P>Browse Mode allows you to browse Dynatek
Infoworld&#146;s Yellowpage quickly and
easily. When in Browse Mode you can quickly
search for or browse through the listings in
the yellow page.  All you need is to point
and click the selections that you feel most
interested in.
</P>

<CENTER><H4>Select a region to browse<BR></H4>
```

```
</CENTER>

<CENTER>
<A HREF="/scripts/dbml.exe?Template=/dynatek/
    Region.dbm&RegionX=1">All Regions</A>
<BR><BR>
<A HREF="/scripts/dbml.exe?Template=/dynatek/
    Region.dbm&RegionX=2">
    Northern California</A><BR><BR>
<A HREF="/scripts/dbml.exe?Template=/dynatek/
    Region.dbm&RegionX=3">
    Southern California</A><BR><BR>
<A HREF="/scripts/dbml.exe?Template=/dynatek/
    Region.dbm&RegionX=4">Vancouver, BC</A>
</CENTER>
</BODY>
</HTML>
```

The next file we must consider is Region.dbm, which was referenced by BrowseMode.htm above. The Region.dbm template appears next. Its purpose is to present all the letters of the alphabet for the user to match with the first letter of the category name she or he desires. As before, we need to pass along an indicator, in the form of a Cold Fusion parameter, for which letter was selected. The parameter in this case is called CategoryX. Notice that when the user selects the letter "A," CategoryX is given the value "A" and so on for the rest of the alphabet.

One trick we must play here is to also pass along the region selection from the previous page. To do this, we create another parameter with the same name, RegionX, and assign it a value equal to the RegionX value from the previous page. We refer to the previous parameter's value by using the URL parameter reference notation as in: #URL.RegionX#. We must repeat the <A HREF> for each letter, and they each must be enclosed inside a pair of <DBOUTPUT> </DBOUTPUT> tags for Cold Fusion to take notice.

```
<!-- REGION.DBM Cold Fusion Template -->

<HTML>
<HEAD>
<TITLE>
Dynatek InfoWorld, Inc. - Category Search
</TITLE>
</HEAD>

<BODY BACKGROUND="graphics/watermark4.gif">
<IMG SRC="graphics/yellowpageheader.gif">
<CENTER>
<H2>Select a Category by Letter</H2>
</CENTER>
<P>To begin, please select the alphabet that
```

matches your desired yellow page category. For
example: A for Architects, or D for Doctors.
You can only select one alphabet at a time.
</P>
<HR>

<CENTER>
<P>
<DBOUTPUT>
<A HREF="/scripts/dbml.exe?Template=
/dynatek/Category.dbm&
CategoryX=A&RegionX=#URL.RegionX#">A
</A>|

<A HREF="/scripts/dbml.exe?Template=
/dynatek/Category.dbm&
CategoryX=B&RegionX=#URL.RegionX#">B
</A>|

<A HREF="/scripts/dbml.exe?Template=
/dynatek/Category.dbm&
CategoryX=C&RegionX=#URL.RegionX#">C
</A>|

<A HREF="/scripts/dbml.exe?Template=
/dynatek/Category.dbm&
CategoryX=D&RegionX=#URL.RegionX#">D
</A>|

<A HREF="/scripts/dbml.exe?Template=
/dynatek/Category.dbm&
CategoryX=E&RegionX=#URL.RegionX#">E
</A>|

<A HREF="/scripts/dbml.exe?Template=
/dynatek/Category.dbm&
CategoryX=F&RegionX=#URL.RegionX#">F
</A>|

<A HREF="/scripts/dbml.exe?Template=
/dynatek/Category.dbm&
CategoryX=G&RegionX=#URL.RegionX#">G
</A>|

<A HREF="/scripts/dbml.exe?Template=
/dynatek/Category.dbm&
CategoryX=H&RegionX=#URL.RegionX#">H
</A>|

```
<A HREF="/scripts/dbml.exe?Template=
/dynatek/Category.dbm&
CategoryX=I&RegionX=#URL.RegionX#">I
</A>|

<A HREF="/scripts/dbml.exe?Template=
/dynatek/Category.dbm&
CategoryX=J&RegionX=#URL.RegionX#">J
</A>|

<A HREF="/scripts/dbml.exe?Template=
/dynatek/Category.dbm&
CategoryX=K&RegionX=#URL.RegionX#">K
</A>|

<A HREF="/scripts/dbml.exe?Template=
/dynatek/Category.dbm&
CategoryX=L&RegionX=#URL.RegionX#">L
</A>|

<A HREF="/scripts/dbml.exe?Template=
/dynatek/Category.dbm&
CategoryX=M&RegionX=#URL.RegionX#">M
</A>|

<A HREF="/scripts/dbml.exe?Template=
/dynatek/Category.dbm&
CategoryX=N&RegionX=#URL.RegionX#">N
</A>|

<A HREF="/scripts/dbml.exe?Template=
/dynatek/Category.dbm&
CategoryX=O&RegionX=#URL.RegionX#">O
</A>|

<A HREF="/scripts/dbml.exe?Template=
/dynatek/Category.dbm&
CategoryX=P&RegionX=#URL.RegionX#">P
</A>|

<A HREF="/scripts/dbml.exe?Template=
/dynatek/Category.dbm&
CategoryX=Q&RegionX=#URL.RegionX#">Q
</A>|

<A HREF="/scripts/dbml.exe?Template=
/dynatek/Category.dbm&
CategoryX=R&RegionX=#URL.RegionX#">R
</A>|
```

```
<A HREF="/scripts/dbml.exe?Template=
/dynatek/Category.dbm&
CategoryX=S&RegionX=#URL.RegionX#">S
</A>|

<A HREF="/scripts/dbml.exe?Template=
/dynatek/Category.dbm&
CategoryX=T&RegionX=#URL.RegionX#">T
</A>|

<A HREF="/scripts/dbml.exe?Template=
/dynatek/Category.dbm&
CategoryX=U&RegionX=#URL.RegionX#">U
</A>|

<A HREF="/scripts/dbml.exe?Template=
/dynatek/Category.dbm&
CategoryX=V&RegionX=#URL.RegionX#">V
</A>|

<A HREF="/scripts/dbml.exe?Template=
/dynatek/Category.dbm&
CategoryX=W&RegionX=#URL.RegionX#">W
</A>|

<A HREF="/scripts/dbml.exe?Template=
/dynatek/Category.dbm&
CategoryX=X&RegionX=#URL.RegionX#">X
</A>|

<A HREF="/scripts/dbml.exe?Template=
/dynatek/Category.dbm&
CategoryX=Y&RegionX=#URL.RegionX#">Y
</A>|

<A HREF="/scripts/dbml.exe?Template=
/dynatek/Category.dbm&
CategoryX=Z&RegionX=#URL.RegionX#">Z
</A>
</DBOUTPUT>
</CENTER>

</BODY>
</HTML>
```

Now that the user has selected both the region and category first letter, the database can present a list of categories from which the user can select one. The Cold Fusion template that performs this task is called Category.dbm and is shown next. We find a new pair of tags in this template, <DBQUERY> and </DBQUERY>. The purpose of these tags is to define a SQL query for a database associated with an ODBC DSN. The NAME attribute specifies what local name we'll use later to refer to this query. The name we use here is SelCategory. Next, we specify the ODBC DSN for the database in the DATASOURCE attribute. Finally, we include the SQL attribute with the actual SQL string that will be submitted to the database. The SELECT statement's WHERE clause pulls out only those records with category names beginning with the letter specified in the URL parameter CategoryX from Region.dbm.

The corresponding <DBOUTPUT>/</DBOUTPUT> tag pair effectively works as a looping structure, in this case applying the <A HREF> to all rows in the resultset. Remember, the resultset consists of only category names from the table tblCategory beginning with a selected letter, and these names appear as hypertext links on this HTML page. Notice that we refer to the Cold Fusion named query SelCategory in the QUERY attribute of the <DBOUTPUT> tag. Once the user clicks on a category, another template is invoked, AllCat2.dbm. Because this template must find all qualifying Yellow Pages records, it needs the two pieces of selection criteria chosen so far, the region and category. We must therefore pass two URL parameters, Category and RegionX, to AllCate2.dbm. All this coding is done as before in the <A HREF> tag reference to the CGI script DBML.EXE.

```
<!-- CATEGORY.DBM Cold Fusion Template -->
<DBQUERY NAME="SelCategory"
    DATASOURCE="DynatekDSN"
    SQL=" SELECT Category FROM tblCategory
    WHERE Category LIKE '#URL.CategoryX#%'
    ORDER BY Category">
</DBQUERY>

<HTML>
<HEAD>
<TITLE>Dynatek InfoWorld, Inc. - Selected
Categories</TITLE>
</HEAD>
<BODY>

<BODY BACKGROUND="graphics/watermark4.gif">
<IMG SRC="graphics/yellowpageheader.gif">

<CENTER>
<H2>Selected Categories</H2>
</CENTER>
<P>Select the appropriate category that best
matches your query by clicking the desired
category once.</P>
<HR>
```

```
<BR>

<!--- Display query result set --->

<DBOUTPUT QUERY="SelCategory">
    <A HREF="/scripts/dbml.exe?Template=
    /dynatek/AllCat2.dbm
    &Category=#Category#&RegionX
    =#URL.RegionX#"> #Category#
    </A>
    <BR>
</DBOUTPUT>

<BR>
<HR>
</BODY>

</HTML>
```

The structure of AllCat2.dbm shown next should be somewhat familiar by now. The <DBQUERY> tag sets up the SQL query against the specified ODBC DSN. Since the phone number data is stored in the table without punctuation, we have to do the formatting in the SQL Select statement with Microsoft SQL Server's Transact SQL string function SUBSTRING. Many other formatting possibilities can use this series of functions.

The query also has the propensity of delivering a large resultset, depending on the criteria selected. To combat this situation, which could result in poor performance, we include the MAXROWS Cold Fusion attribute that limits the resultset to the specified number of rows. Informing the user how many rows would have resulted based on the current criteria may be useful, as well as telling him or her that a restructure of the query to further limit the resultset may help. You'll see later that resultset size is even more an issue with Search Mode's freer use of selection criteria.

Both <DBOUTPUT> tag groups refer back to the AllCategory query name defined in the <DBQUERY> tag. The job of the first <DBOUTPUT> tag is to report how many records were found for the category selected using the #AllCategory.RecordCount# parameter. The second <DBOUTPUT> tag does all the final work, displaying each field from the resultset. Actually, some fields are checked for null values using Cold Fusion's <DBIF> </DBIF> tags. If the field has no value, this technique eliminates blank lines in the displayed resultset.

In analyzing the Yellow Pages site's Browse Mode, you have seen how the user is stepped through a series of point-and-click selections that in effect pose SQL queries against the back-end database to deliver the desired results to the client browser. This series of steps leading to the final desired resultset is a good example of the *drill-down* approach to database searching.

```
<!-- ALLCAT2.DBM Cold Fusion Template -->

<HTML>
<HEAD>
<TITLE>
All Category Search
</TITLE>
</HEAD>

<DBQUERY NAME="AllCategory"
    DATASOURCE="DynatekDSN"
    SQL=" SELECT BusinessName, City, State, Zip,
      Category, RegionName, Address1,
      Address2,
      PhoneFmt=
        ('('+SUBSTRING(phone,1,3)+')'+
    SUBSTRING(phone,4,3)+'-
    '+SUBSTRING(phone,7,4)),
      FAX, Description, URL, ChineseEncoded
      FROM tblWebData
      WHERE Category LIKE '#URL.Category#%'
      ORDER BY BusinessName" MAXROWS=50>

<BODY BACKGROUND="graphics/watermark4.gif">
<IMG SRC="graphics/yellowpageheader.gif">

<P>
<DBOUTPUT>
    <H2>Search Result for category
    #URL.Category#</H2>
    <P>
    <H4>There were #AllCategory.RecordCount#
      listings found.</H4>
</DBOUTPUT>

<!--- Display query result set --->

<HR>
<DBOUTPUT QUERY="AllCategory">
    <DBIF #URL# is not "">
      <B><A HREF="#URL#">#BusinessName#</A>
      </B><BR>
    <DBELSE>
      <B>#BusinessName#</B><BR>
    </DBIF>
    #ChineseEncoded# <BR><BR>

    #RegionName# <BR>
    #Address1# <BR>
```

```
<DBIF #Address2# IS NOT "">
  #Address2# <BR>
</DBIF>

#City#, #State#  #Zip# <BR>
Tel : #PhoneFmt# <BR>

<DBIF #FAX# IS NOT "">
  Fax : #FAX# <BR>
</DBIF>

#Description# <BR>

<HR>
</DBOUTPUT>


<!---> page footer --->
<P>
Thank you for using Dynatek Infoworld Yellow
ages!

</BODY>
</HTML>
```

Search Mode Implementation

Now turn your attention to the more flexible Yellow Pages Search Mode, which uses the query-by-form metaphor, familiar to those of us who use contemporary GUI desktop software interfaces. As seen in the usage discussion earlier in this case study, the user is presented with an HTML form in which selection criteria values may be entered. The form is achieved with the standard HTML <FORM> tag and associated attributes.

Notice how the two pull-down menus are populated. The first, with <SELECT NAME="region">, has manually coded options for three different regions plus one for all regions. The second pull-down menu, defined in <SELECT NAME="category">, is dynamically populated using a SQL Select query.

The query is defined towards the beginning of the template in a <DBQUERY> tag that creates the query name CategoryList. We then embed an <OPTION VALUE> tag inside the <DBOUTPUT> so that a new option is created for each record in the CategoryList resultset. Since no value exists for specifying all categories, it is coded in a separate <OPTION VALUE> tag. We'll have to check for this all-region "value" explicitly later, when determining which region to use.

Once the user clicks on the Submit Search button, all the user selection criteria are saved, and the next template, Dynatek.dbm, is invoked.

```
<!-- SRCHMODE.DBM Cold Fusion Template -->

<HTML>
<HEAD>
<TITLE>
Dynatek Info World, Inc. - Search Mode
</TITLE>
</HEAD>

<BODY BACKGROUND="graphics/watermark4.gif">
<IMG SRC="graphics/yellowpageheader.gif">
<HR>

<!--- Get information for the Category
picklist --->
<DBQUERY NAME="CategoryList"
    DATASOURCE="DynatekDSN"
    SQL=" SELECT Category
      FROM tblCategory
      ORDER BY Category">
<BODY>

<FORM ACTION="/scripts/dbml.exe?Template=
    /dynatek/Dynatek.dbm" METHOD="POST">

<PRE>
Region: <SELECT NAME="region">
    <OPTION>All Regions
    <OPTION>Northern California
    <OPTION>Southern California
    <OPTION>Vancouver
</SELECT>

Category: <SELECT NAME="category">
OPTION VALUE="All Categories" SELECTED>
    All Categories
<DBOUTPUT QUERY="CategoryList">
    <OPTION VALUE="#Category#">#Category#
</DBOUTPUT>

</SELECT>

Business Name: <INPUT TYPE="text" NAME="BName"
SIZE=40>

City: <INPUT TYPE="text" NAME="city" SIZE=40>

Zip Code: <INPUT TYPE="text" NAME="zip"
SIZE=10>
```

```
<INPUT TYPE="submit" VALUE="Submit Search">
<INPUT TYPE="reset"  VALUE="Clear Entries">

</PRE>
</FORM>

</BODY>
</HTML>
```

Once the Dynatek.dbm template file shown next gets control, its job is to construct a SQL SELECT statement that uses the selection criteria for determining a resultset. The more difficult part of this process is putting together the WHERE clause that must consider only criteria that were actually specified by the user. Normally, the rule, not the exception, is that the user enters only one or two pieces of criteria, say a category and a city. To properly build the WHERE clause, we must incrementally concatenate portions of the expression as we determine whether the criteria were specified.

The Cold Fusion <DBSET> tag and the <DBSQL> sub-tag (named because it must be contained entirely within a <DBQUERY>/</DBQUERY> block) serve this need well, because they allow us to create the clause after we check each criteria for null values with a <DBIF>.

Once the dynamically generated SQL has been submitted and the resultset found, the <DBOUTPUT> for the DynatekSearch query renders the results for the client browser. Note that the category field from each resultset record is enclosed inside an <A HREF> tag, indicating that it is a hypertext link. When clicked, the AllCat.dbm template is invoked. This template re-queries the Yellow Pages table for all records matching the category selected, regardless of any other criteria.

```
<!-- DYNATEK.DBM Cold Fusion Template -->

<DBQUERY NAME="DynatekSearch"
    DATASOURCE="DynatekDSN"
    SQL=" SELECT BusinessName, City, State, Zip,
    Category, RegionName, Address1, Address2,
    phonefmt=('('+substring(phone,1,3)+')'+
    substring(phone,4,3)+'-'+
    substring(phone,7,4)), FAX, Description,
    URL, ChineseEncoded
    FROM tblWebData"
    MAXROWS=50>

<DBSET #Prefix#="WHERE">

<DBIF #BName# is not "">
    <DBSQL SQL="#Prefix# BusinessName LIKE
      '#BName#%' ">
    <DBSET #Prefix#="AND">
```

```
    </DBIF>

    <DBIF #City# is not "">
        <DBSQL SQL="#Prefix# City LIKE
          '#City#%' ">
        <DBSET #Prefix#="AND">
    </DBIF>

    <DBIF #Zip# is not "">
        <DBSQL SQL="#Prefix# Zip LIKE
          '#Zip#%'">
        <DBSET #Prefix#="AND">
    </DBIF>

    <DBIF #Category# is not "All Categories">
        <DBSQL SQL="#Prefix# Category LIKE
          '#Category#%' ">
        <DBSET #Prefix#="AND">
    </DBIF>

    <DBIF #Region# is not "All Regions">
        <DBSQL SQL="#Prefix# RegionName =
          '#Region#' ">
    </DBIF>

    </DBQUERY>

    <HTML>
    <HEAD>
    <TITLE>
    Chinese Community Search
    </TITLE>
    </HEAD>

    <BODY BACKGROUND="graphics/watermark4.gif">
    <IMG SRC="graphics/yellowpageheader.gif">
    <H2> Search Results </H2>
    <DBOUTPUT>
        <H4>
        There were #DynatekSearch.RecordCount#
        businesses matching your selection
        criteria.
        </H4>
    </DBOUTPUT>

    <!--- Display query result set --->

    <HR>
```

```
<DBOUTPUT QUERY="DynatekSearch">
<DBIF #URL# IS not "">
    <B>
    <A HREF="#URL#">#BusinessName#</A></B><BR>
<DBELSE>
    <B>#BusinessName#</B><BR>
</DBIF>

#ChineseEncoded# <BR><BR>
#RegionName# <BR>
#Address1# <BR>

<DBIF #Address2# IS NOT "">
    #Address2# <BR>
</DBIF>

#City#, #State#  #Zip# <BR>
Tel : #Phonefmt# <BR>

<DBIF #FAX# IS NOT "">
    Fax : #FAX# <BR>
</DBIF>

#Description# <BR>

<A HREF="/scripts/dbml.exe?Template=
/dynatek/AllCat.dbm&Category=#Category#">
#Category#</A><BR>

<HR>
</DBOUTPUT>

<!---> page footer --->
<P>
Thank you for using Dynatek Infoworld Yellow
Pages!
<HR>

</BODY>
</HTML>
```

With the Yellow Pages Search Mode functionality, the user has a flexible means for posing queries against the business directory database. The Cold Fusion CGI tool provides a simple mechanism whereby the user has all the familiar capabilities of a desktop GUI environment, but with the far-reaching effects of a WebTop application.

Summary

This chapter has presented a case for using what has become mainstream methodology for publishing corporate data on the Web. I have demonstrated all the important ingredients in building a real-life WebTop application. The CGI/ODBC methods used in the development of this database-enabled site, however, represent just one possible direction, given the various technologies discussed in this book. Depending on many factors, such as software development expertise, hardware/software resources, desired performance, just to name a few, one method might be preferred over the others. Some techniques are simply more contemporary; for example, Java and ActiveX technologies have become quite popular as of late (but are also less evolved), whereas CGI, once the only tool of choice, is still an able choice for publishing data on the Web.

INDEX